THE AGE OF ROBERT GUISCARD:
SOUTHERN ITALY AND THE NORMAN CONQUEST

THE MEDIEVAL WORLD

Editor: David Bates

THE AGE OF ROBERT GUISCARD: SOUTHERN ITALY AND THE NORMAN CONQUEST

G.A. LOUD

An imprint of **Pearson Education**

Harlow, England · London · New York · Reading, Massachusetts · San Francisco
Toronto · Don Mills, Ontario · Sydney · Tokyo · Singapore · Hong Kong · Seoul
Taipei · Cape Town · Madrid · Mexico City · Amsterdam · Munich · Paris · Milan

Pearson Education Limited
Edinburgh Gate
Harlow
Essex CM20 2JE
England

and Associated Companies throughout the World.

Visit us on the World Wide Web at:
www.pearsoned.co.uk

First published 2000

ISBN 0 582 04529 0 LIMP
     0 582 04528 2 CASED

British Library Cataloguing-in-Publication Data
A catalogue record for this book can be obtained from the British Library

Library of Congress Cataloging-in-Publication Data
Loud, G.A.
     The age of Robert Guiscard: southern Italy and the Norman conquest / G.A. Loud.
        p. cm. — (The medieval world)
     Includes bibliographical references and index.
     ISBN 0-582-04528-2 (cased: alk. paper) — ISBN 0-582-04529-0 (softcover: alk.
paper)
     1. Robert Guiscard, Duke of Apulia, Calabria, and Sicily, ca. 1015-1085.   2.
Sicily—History—1016-1194.   3. Naples (Kingdom)—History—1016-1268.   4.
Nobility—Italy—Sicily—Biography.   5. Nobility—Italy—Naples (Kingdom)—
Biography.   I. Series.

     DG867.215.R64.L68   2000
     945'.8—dc21

                                                                      00–042126

10 9 8 7 6 5 4 3 2
05 04

Typeset by 35 in 11/13pt Baskerville MT
Produced by Pearson Education Asia Pte Ltd.
Printed in Malaysia, CLP

CONTENTS

EDITOR'S PREFACE

The Norman expansion in eleventh-century Europe is a movement of enormous historical importance which took men and women from the duchy of Normandy to settle in England and Wales, the southern parts of the Italian peninsula, Sicily and the principality of Antioch. These conquests were the springboard for further expansion in the twelfth century into Scotland, Ireland and, for a short time, north Africa, as well as for the transformation of the societies which the Normans took over or infiltrated. The Norman conquest of southern Italy and Sicily is a particularly interesting element in this history, since here the newcomers subdued local princes, drove out the Byzantine and Moslem rulers who claimed authority, and began to unify the territories which, in the twelfth century, became the kingdom of Sicily. They also consolidated their control by a series of complex alliances with the papacy which illuminate how secular and religious powers worked together in the process whereby western Europe and Christianity began the advance to hegemony which characterises the succeeding centuries. Ambition even extended to campaigns across the Adriatic against the Byzantine empire.

Graham Loud's splendid new book in the Medieval World series places the careers of Robert Guiscard and the Hauteville family in a wider framework in order to construct a new history of the expansion of Norman power in southern Europe. Beginning with a survey of southern Italy and Sicily before the arrival of the Normans, it shows how these conditions influenced future events. It deals effectively with long-standing controversies about the date of the Normans' arrival in the south and the precise extent of their participation relative to other peoples from neighbouring regions of northern France. Above all, the book sets out the twists and turns of a conquest which continued throughout most of the eleventh century, and which was still far from complete by the time of Guiscard's death. Almost every aspect of the politics and warfare of the time should be seen as a struggle to achieve limited objectives. The relationship between Guiscard and the papacy was usually ambivalent; Gregory VII's support for the attack on the Byzantine empire in 1081–2 cooled rapidly and Robert's efforts to save Gregory in 1084 were both flawed and subordinate to his wider military concerns. Although the island of Sicily was more thoroughly subdued than the mainland, here, as elsewhere, the regime which emerged was one which was largely founded on existing structures. Not only were the Normans a small minority in comparison with the peoples they subjected, relations between their leaders were fractious and competitive, and Robert Guiscard's career, while spectacular, was only relatively successful. By the time of his death, the turbulent politics of southern Italy were still dominated by the rivalries of major aristocratic families.

The book draws magnificently on its author's remarkable knowledge both of southern Italian sources and of the region itself. Having published extensively on a great range of aspects of the history of southern Italy and Sicily during the Norman period, Graham Loud's effective use of his own and others' researches to construct an up-to-date and thought-provoking account is exceptionally welcome. As Dr Loud makes clear in his Conclusion, the book's significance extends far beyond the eleventh century since it brings out extremely well the importance of changes which were to have an impact on the whole of western Europe. In analysing so effectively what Robert Guiscard and his contemporaries did – and did not – achieve, this book supplies an indispensable contribution to historical understanding of the Mediterranean regions and the later history of the kingdom of Sicily.

David Bates

ACKNOWLEDGEMENTS

I realise with something of a shock that *The Age of Robert Guiscard* is the result of some twenty-five years' work on Norman Italy, from the time in 1974 when I took my first faltering (and very nervous) steps to commence research on my doctorate. Inevitably, all the debts that have accrued during that long period of gestation are far too numerous to record individually, even if I could remember them with the accuracy that they deserve. None the less, some should be acknowledged here.

First and foremost, the actual preparation and writing of this book have taken much longer than I had originally intended, and I am indebted to the forbearance of the series editor, David Bates, and of Andrew MacLennan, formerly history editor at what was then Longmans, with an author whose prevarications must have been a sore trial to them. I am also grateful to David for contenting himself with the mildest of remonstrance at the eventual size of the manuscript. That this grew from the slim welterweight that was first envisaged into a somewhat portly heavyweight is entirely my fault. Chapter one was written while I was on study leave in the autumn of 1995, and chapters two to four during another period of leave in 1998 which was funded by a fellowship from the Leverhulme Trust. It is not just a duty but a pleasure to thank that organisation for its generosity. I must also thank Jenny Hooper and Alan Murray, to whom I was able to abandon my students with a clear conscience during these leaves, confident that they were in safe and capable hands.

I have over the years made many visits to southern Italy. This book has drawn upon the fruits of my archival research, even if perhaps not as much as it should have done, but especially from my work at the Badia di S. Trinità di Cava, where I was warmly welcomed as far back as 1980 by the late don Simeone Leone, and latterly by Sign. Enzo Cioffe. The British School at Rome generously granted me a research fellowship in 1990, for which I am very grateful. A number of people, but above all Errico Cuozzo, Edoardo and Daniela D'Angelo and Hubert and Marcella Houben, have welcomed me as a friend in what but for them might have seemed an alien environment. I have also been greatly helped – by advice, encouragement, gifts of publications and answers to importunate queries – by John Cowdrey,

Vera von Falkenhausen, Laurent Feller, Peter Herde, Jean-Marie Martin, Valerie Ramseyer, Trish Skinner, Hiroshi Takayama, Lucia Travaini, Chris Wickham, Thomas Wiedemann, my former pupil (now Professor) Joanna Drell, my present research students Christine Bonniot and Craig Cant, and two distinguished historians sadly no longer with us, Norbert Kamp and Léon-Robert Ménager. Peter Llewellyn and Prescott Dunbar kindly sent me copies of their translations of Amatus of Montecassino, which I found extremely helpful, although the versions quoted in this book (as of the other chronicle sources from south Italy) are my own. And without the exceptional medieval holdings of the Brotherton Library at Leeds, my work could never have approached whatever level of competence it has now reached.

Bernard Hamilton read and commented upon the entire manuscript as it was written, saved me from many a slip, and reassured me that what I was writing actually made sense. But the greatest debt of all is owed to Diane Milburn, despite her total, and inexplicable (not to say downright peculiar), lack of interest in medieval history.

ABBREVIATIONS

Acta SS	*Acta Sanctorum*
Amari, *BAS*	M. Amari, *Biblioteca Arabo-Sicula* (2 vols, Turin 1880)
Amatus	*Storia de' Normanni di Amato di Montecassino*, ed. V. de Bartholomeis (Fonti per la storia d'Italia, Rome 1935)
BISIME	*Bollettino del istituto storico italiano per il medio evo*
Cava	Archivio della badia di S. Trinità di Cava
Chron. Cas.	*Chronica Monasterii Casinensis*, ed. H. Hoffmann (*MGH SS* xxxiv, Hanover 1980)
Chron. Vult.	*Chronicon Vulternense del monaco Giovanni*, ed. V. Federici (Fonti per la storia d'Italia, 3 vols, Rome 1925–38)
Cod. Dipl. Aversa	*Codice diplomatico normanno di Aversa*, ed. A. Gallo (Naples 1927)
Cod. Dipl. Barese	*Codice diplomatico barese* (19 vols, Bari 1897–1950)
Cod. Dipl. Caiet.	*Codex Diplomaticus Caietanus* (2 vols, Montecassino 1887–92)
Cod. Dipl. Cavensis	*Codex Diplomaticus Cavensis*, ed. M. Morcaldi *et al.* (8 vols, Milan 1876–93: vols ix–x, ed. S. Leone and G. Vitolo, Cava dei Tirreni 1984–90)
Cod. Dipl. Tremiti	*Codice diplomatico del monastero benedettino di S. Maria di Tremiti 1005–1237*, ed. A. Petrucci (Fonti per la storia d'Italia, 3 vols, Rome 1960)
Conquerors and Churchmen	G.A. Loud, *Conquerors and Churchmen in Norman Italy* (Aldershot 1999)
Falco	*Falcone di Beneventano, Chronicon Beneventanum*, ed. E. D'Angelo (Florence 1998)
Gregory, *Reg.*	*Registrum Gregorii VII*, ed. E. Caspar (Berlin 1920–3)
Italia Pontificia	*Italia Pontificia*, ed. P.F. Kehr (10 vols, Berlin 1905–74: vol. ix ed. W. Holtzmann, 1963; vol. x ed. D. Girgensohn, 1974)

Loud, 'Calendar'	G.A. Loud, 'A Calendar of the diplomas of the Norman Princes of Capua', *PBSR* xlix (1981), 99–143
Malaterra	*De Rebus Gestis Rogerii Calabriae et Siciliae Comitis auctore Gaufredo Malaterra*, ed. E. Pontieri (*RIS*, 2nd edn, Bologna 1927–8)
MEFR	*Mélanges de l'Ecole Francaise de Rome – Moyen Age–Temps Modernes*
Ménager, *Recueil*	*Recueil des Actes des Ducs Normands d'Italie (1046–1127)* i *Les Premiers Ducs (1046–1087)*, ed. L.-R. Ménager (Bari 1981) [only vol. published]
MGH	*Monumenta Germaniae Historica*, following the usual conventions: *SS* = *Scriptores*, *SRG* = *Scriptores Rerum Germanicarum*, etc.
MPG	*Patrologia Graeca*, ed. J.P. Migne (161 vols, Paris 1857–66)
MPL	*Patrologia Latina*, ed. J.P. Migne (221 vols, Paris 1844–64)
Orderic	*The Ecclesiastical History of Orderic Vitalis*, ed. M. Chibnall (6 vols, Oxford 1968–80)
PBSR	*Papers of the British School at Rome*
Pirro, *Sicula Sacra*	R. Pirro, *Sicula Sacra*, 3rd edn by A. Mongitore (2 vols, Palermo 1733)
QFIAB	*Quellen und Forschungen aus italienischen Archiven und Bibliotheken*
Reg. Neap. Arch. Mon.	*Registrum Neapolitani Archivii Monumenta* (6 vols, Naples 1854–61)
RIS	*Rerum Italicarum Scriptores*
Roberto il Guiscardo	*Roberto il Guiscardo e il suo Tempo* (Relazioni e communicazioni nelle prime giornate normanno-sveve, Bari maggio 1973) (Rome 1975)
Romuald	Romuald of Salerno, *Chronicon sive Annales*, ed. C.A. Garufi (*RIS*, 2nd edn, Citta di Castello 1935)
Trinchera, *Syllabus*	F. Trinchera, *Syllabus Graecarum Membranarum* (Naples 1865)
Ughelli, *Italia Sacra*	*Italia Sacra*, 2nd edn by N. Colletti (10 vols, Venice 1717–21)
W. Apulia	*Guillaume de Pouille. La Geste de Robert Guiscard*, ed. M. Mathieu (Palermo 1961)

INTRODUCTION

In or about the year 1046 two young men travelled from their homes in Normandy to southern Italy in the hope of making careers for themselves. Both had the advantage of powerful and influential relatives who had already settled in that region. Indeed, by the time of their arrival men whom the contemporary sources describe as 'Normans' (the validity of that label will be discussed later) had been coming to the south of the Italian peninsula for at least a generation. During the course of the eleventh century these Normans first infiltrated, and then finally conquered, almost the whole of that area, south of a line running diagonally from Terracina in the west north-eastwards to the Adriatic coast just north of Teramo. But of the people responsible for this significant change in the history of Italy and of medieval Europe, the two who arrived in 1046, along with one other who appeared a decade or so later, were undoubtedly the most important. Any study of the Norman conquest of southern Italy must therefore devote close attention to their careers, and particularly to that of the longer-lived and most successful of these two earlier arrivals.

We ought therefore to begin by introducing our protagonists. The first, Richard, came from near Dieppe in the Pays de Caux in eastern Normandy. His uncle Rainulf, who had died a year or so earlier, had been the most important leader among the considerable number of his compatriots who had already settled in southern Italy, and had been the ruler – the count – of their first permanent settlement there, at a newly founded town called Aversa, a few miles north of Naples. He had been succeeded in that position by his nephew Asclettin, Richard's elder brother, but he too had died soon afterwards. We know very little about Richard's background in Normandy, though he was probably from the ranks of the minor nobility, but he appears to have journeyed south in some style. The contemporary historian who was best informed as to his career tells us that:

> Richard son of Asclettin was a fine figure of a man and a lord of good stature. He was a young man with an open countenance and strikingly handsome, and he was held in much affection by all who saw him. He was followed by many warriors and people. By deliberate choice, he rode so

small a horse that his feet could not avoid touching the ground. He was held in honour and respect by everyone, out of respect both for his uncle and brother, and for his own youth and extraordinary good looks.[1]

Though he had to wait three or four years before succeeding to his uncle's and brother's position, Richard's career in Italy was very soon successful. He acquired influential friends and patrons, soon obtained a lordship for himself, and by 1050 had become count of Aversa. From there he sought energetically and successfully to extend his dominions.

The other emigrant, Robert, whose career was to be even more spectacular, came from the Cotentin peninsula at the western end of Normandy, where his father was lord of a village called Hauteville (not far from Coutances), from which the family derived their name. He was, as an Anglo-Norman monk writing some eighty years later said, 'born of middling parentage in Normandy, neither from very low nor from on high, and a few years before the coming of [Duke] William to England, he went to Apulia along with fifteen knights, to remedy his straitened circumstances by employment with the unworthy people there'.[2]

We may be sceptical about the fifteen knights who allegedly accompanied him – the south Italian sources which briefly mention his arrival certainly do not imply that he had much of a following. But this account seems to have been correct about the 'middling parentage' and, especially, the 'straitened circumstances'. Robert was a younger son. His father, Tancred, had in the course of two marriages sired no less than twelve male children who grew to manhood, of whom Robert was the sixth, the eldest born of Tancred's second wife, Fressenda. At least three and possibly four of his elder brothers had already emigrated to southern Italy to seek their fortunes. In the words of another monk, writing at Catania in Sicily in about 1100:

> They saw that their own neighbourhood would not be big enough for them, and that when their patrimony was divided not only would their heirs argue among themselves about the share-out, but the individual shares would simply not be big enough. So, to prevent the same thing happening in future as had happened to them, they discussed the matter among themselves. They decided that, since the elders were at that time stronger than those younger to them, they should be the first to leave their homeland and go to other places seeking their fortune through arms.[3]

1 *Amatus*, II.44, p. 110.
2 William of Malmesbury, *Gesta Regum Anglorum*, ed. R.A.B. Mynors, R.M. Thomson and M. Winterbottom (Oxford 1998), pp. 482–3 (my translation).
3 *Malaterra*, I.5, p. 9.

Robert's two oldest brothers, William and Drogo, and perhaps a third, Humphrey (the sources conflict on this), went to southern Italy in the mid-1030s. They served as mercenaries in the invasion of the island of Sicily – at that time under Muslim rule – by the forces of the Byzantine empire in 1038. There William was alleged to have distinguished himself by a notable feat of arms, killing a Muslim emir in single combat.[4] He and Drogo were among the leaders of the Normans when they turned against their erstwhile paymasters and invaded the Byzantine province of Apulia, in the heel of Italy, in 1041. Eighteen months later William was chosen as the overall leader of the loose confederation of warlords who by that time (September 1042) had inflicted several serious defeats on the Byzantine forces and had overrun substantial parts of inland Apulia.

By the time of Robert's arrival in southern Italy William was already dead, and had been succeeded by Drogo as leader of the Apulian Normans. The latter appears to have been less than overjoyed by the appearance of his ambitious half-brother, and flatly refused (or maybe was simply unable) to provide any landed endowment for him, leaving him to make his own way in the world. And by fair means, and more frequently foul, Robert did so. For a time he was little more than a bandit, whose ingenuity, deviousness and lack of scruple soon gained him the nickname *Guiscard* ('the cunning' or 'the weasel'). In the end his career was to surpass those of all his brothers, of whom at least seven others either had already or were later to come to southern Italy. Only his youngest sibling, Roger, who joined him in Italy in about 1056, was to come near to rivalling him. Robert's destiny was closely linked both to him and to that of Richard of Aversa, who soon after he became count married Robert's sister, named Fressenda after her mother. These three men were to be the greatest of the Norman leaders in Italy, and between them they were to rule all the Norman conquests in the southern part of the peninsula. Richard took over the principality of Capua, stretching from just north of Naples to the border with the lands of the papacy half-way between Naples and Rome. Robert created a new principality, comprising Apulia, Calabria (the toe of Italy), the principality of Salerno on the west coast, and the overlordship of Sicily. Direct rule over the island was, however, delegated to Roger, who had been mainly responsible for its conquest in the years after 1061. By the time of his death in 1085 Robert had launched an invasion of the Byzantine empire and humiliated the German emperor – who, like the ruler of Byzantium, claimed to be the

---

4 *Malaterra*, I.7, p. 11. *Amatus*, II.8, p. 67, said that in 1038 William, Drogo and Humphrey had all recently arrived from Normandy, but *Malaterra*, I.9, p. 12, wrote that in 1041 only the first two were present, 'for none of their other brothers had yet followed them'.

rightful successor to the power of Imperial Rome – by forcing him to an ignominious retreat from that city. He thus became a figure of European consequence, famous (or infamous) throughout Christendom. The same Anglo-Norman monk who described his arrival, William of Malmesbury, claimed that William the Conqueror himself used to rouse his courage by thinking of the mighty deeds of Robert, 'saying that it would be disgraceful to show less bravery than one whom he so surpassed in rank'.

This anecdote may of course have been – indeed probably was – just an invention of the chronicler, though it shows how high Robert's reputation had risen, even in far-away England, by the 1120s. William of Malmesbury also recorded the epitaph on Robert's tomb at the abbey of Venosa, which read:

> Here lies the Guiscard, the terror of the world.
> From the City, the king of the Italians and Germans he hurled.
> Neither Parthians, Arabs, nor the army of Macedon, could Alexius free,
> Only flight: for Venice could prevail neither flight nor the sea.[5]

There was an element of exaggeration in this flowery verse, but only a small one. By 1085 Robert had become the greatest warlord in Latin Christendom; his support and alliance was courted by popes and emperors, and his armies could threaten the heirs to Charlemagne and Constantine.

The spectacular and successful careers of Robert Guiscard, Richard of Capua and Roger of Sicily make them in their own right worthy of study, not least as noteworthy examples of medieval social climbing. The consequences of their actions were even more significant, in that they left a new and very different Italy behind them, and in the long run substantially altered the history of Europe. Certainly their contemporaries thought them worthy of record, because from an age which left relatively few narrative sources (certainly less so than the immediately succeeding century), we possess no less than three works dedicated to the careers of this trio, all written in southern Italy within about twenty years of their deaths.

Soon after 1080 a monk called Amatus of Montecassino wrote a 'History of the Normans' from their first arrival in Italy (which he dated 'before the year 1000') up to the death of Richard of Capua in 1078. He was moved to do this, as he said in his final chapter, by the benefactions they had so generously bestowed on his own monastery, though earlier sections show that he was also influenced by his dislike of the (as he saw it) wickedness and impiety of some of the indigenous local rulers. He recounted at one point a

---

5   *Gesta Regum Anglorum*, pp. 484–5 (my translation).

story of how a local archbishop was told in a dream by St Matthew that 'God has given this land to the Normans on account of the wickedness of those who hold it'.[6] Amatus dealt in considerable detail with the careers of both Robert and Richard. Unfortunately his work survives only in a French translation of *c.* 1300–30, which must be treated with some care.

Secondly, between 1095 and 1099 a certain William of Apulia, about whom nothing is known except his name, dedicated a long poem in Latin hexameters about 'The Deeds of Robert Guiscard' to the latter's son and successor as duke, Roger *Borsa* ('the purse'). The coverage of this work is uneven: indeed, despite the title, its first book is devoted to the early history of the Normans in Italy before Robert arrived there; but a number of key military episodes are described in detail, including his expedition against Byzantium after 1081. Though there was less overt emphasis than by Amatus on the divine plan that the Normans were fulfilling, William too undoubtedly felt that God had ordained their conquest.[7]

Finally, a year or two after William wrote his poem, Geoffrey Malaterra, a monk in the recently founded Benedictine monastery of St Agatha at Catania, wrote his 'Deeds of Count Roger of Calabria and Sicily, and of Robert Guiscard his brother'. As the title suggests, Roger was the principal hero of this account, though Robert's activities received their fair share of attention. (Writing from Sicily, Geoffrey had little or no interest, or knowledge, of the career of Richard of Capua.) His particular theme was the *strenuitas* of the Normans, and especially of their leaders, a quality that can best be translated as a combination of energy and resolution, particularly in adverse circumstances, which enabled them to conquer the indigenous peoples of the region.[8] God helped them certainly, but only because they helped themselves – in both senses of that phrase – for Geoffrey had no illusions about the lust for power to which he saw the Normans as a whole, but particularly the Hauteville brothers, as prone: 'for the natural and customary inclination of the sons of Tancred was always to be greedy for rule, to the very utmost of their powers'.[9]

We have therefore a fair amount of information about the leaders of the Norman conquest of southern Italy and Sicily, and in particular about

6 *Amatus*, III.38, pp. 151–2.
7 There is a useful discussion of William's poem by K.B. Wolf, *Making History. The Normans and their Historians in Eleventh-Century Italy* (Philadelphia 1995), pp. 123–42. Though its approach is limited, this book is the fullest introduction to the contemporary chroniclers of the conquest.
8 O. Capitani, 'Specific motivations and continuing themes in the Norman chronicles of southern Italy in the eleventh and twelfth centuries', *The Normans in Sicily and South Italy. The Lincei Lectures for 1973* (Oxford 1977), pp. 1–46.
9 *Malaterra*, II.38, p. 48.

Robert Guiscard. In addition, the Normans played a significant role in a number of other historical narratives from southern Italy and the Byzantine empire, and were at least occasionally mentioned in the contemporary historiography from Germany, Rome and northern Italy. The voluminous history of Montecassino by Leo Marsicanus and his continuators, and the considerably later, but still valuable, history of the abbey of St Clement at Casauria in the Abruzzi by the monk John Berard may in particular be cited. Leo's chronicle, covering the history of Montecassino from its foundation in the sixth century up to 1072, but with far the greater emphasis on the eleventh century, is certainly very much a contemporary document, for it was begun on the instructions of Abbot Oderisius I of Montecassino (1088–1105), and Leo's section must have been concluded when he became cardinal bishop of Ostia about the time of the abbot's death. The continuation, most of which was by a monk called Guido, was written at the latest in the 1120s, some of it more or less contemporaneously with the events it describes.[10] The casual reader, if there can be such a person of a work which in the modern printed edition runs to some 600 pages in Latin, may be stupefied into insensibility by the frequent and lengthy lists of pious donations to the abbey which intersperse the narrative, and less edified than a medieval monk by the miraculous appearances of St Benedict which show the saint's concern to defend his abbey, but we are also told a great deal about the relations of the Normans with the richest and most influential monastery in southern Italy.

Yet despite this relative abundance of contemporary historical evidence, one cannot write a biography, in the conventional sense, of Robert Guiscard, or indeed of any other early medieval layman. The works about him were, as has already been implied, self-consciously literary ones, in which reality was, to some extent at least, subsumed by the authors' purposes and their wish to please their patrons or audience. Even such a learned and (relatively) sophisticated monastic chronicler as Leo of Ostia had parameters more or less strictly limited to the interests of his own house, and what might affect its welfare. We have only a little other evidence which directly concerns Robert Guiscard with which to supplement the narrative sources. Documentary evidence for any eleventh-century individual is inevitably very thin. We have only some forty charters issued in Robert's name, nearly

---

10   See especially Leo's introduction to the chronicle as a whole and to Book III, *Chron. Cas.*, pp. 3, 362. For the composition of this chronicle and the problems of authorship Hoffmann's introduction to his edition is fundamental, along with his 'Studien zur Chronik von Montecassino', *Deutsches Archiv für Erforschung des Mittelalters* xxix (1973), 59–162. Anglophone readers may find a convenient summary in H. Bloch, *Montecassino in the Middle Ages* (3 vols, Rome 1986), i.113–17.

all of them donations of property to churches, and not all of them by any means in complete or absolutely authentic texts. For Richard of Capua the situation is far worse, for we have only sixteen surviving genuine charters, and a couple of very dubious forgeries. For Richard's son Jordan, who ruled the principality of Capua between 1078 and 1090, there are only twenty-four genuine and two forged charters known.[11] Above all, and most frustratingly, one can do very little to approach the actual personality of these men. What we are told of this by the narratives is largely conventional, and once again subordinated to the author's literary purposes. Only for a very few churchmen who have left correspondence or extensive writings (Gregory the Great, Hincmar of Rheims, Gerbert of Aurillac, Gregory VII, St Anselm) might one actually write a medieval 'biography', certainly before the explosion of record-keeping and contemporary historical writing that were among the most significant features of the so-called 'twelfth-century Renaissance'.

What one can do, however, is to produce, if not a 'Life', at least a 'Life and Times' of Robert Guiscard, and there is indeed good reason to do this. We do have the means to describe the 'times', if not the 'life'. If the documentation for particular individuals may be deficient, that for south Italian society in the age of the Normans is surprisingly good, certainly for much of mainland southern Italy. (The situation is less satisfactory for Calabria and, until some way into the twelfth century, for Sicily.) Our documentation is, inevitably, almost all of ecclesiastical provenance. But it *is* extensive, particularly from the more important monastic houses. Thus the so-called 'Register of Peter the Deacon', the Montecassino chartulary from the early 1130s, contains more than 600 charters, the majority from the eleventh century, and this is only a part of the surviving documentation from the abbey of St Benedict. The massive chronicle–chartulary of Casauria (written *c.* 1175) copied some 2,100 charters, albeit that many of these are from the pre-Norman period. The archives of the abbey of the Holy Trinity, Cava, near Salerno, founded before 1025 and still in existence, contain over a thousand original charters from the eleventh century, and more than 3,500 from the twelfth. Another still-surviving medieval monastery, that of Montevergine, near Avellino, has preserved just over a thousand pre-1200 charters. The bad news is that only a part of this rich heritage is available in print. Neither the 'Register of Peter the Deacon' nor the Casauria chartulary

---

11 See Ménager, *Recueil* i (the only volume so far published); Loud, 'Calendar', pp. 119–27 nos 1–44. This calendar is now in some need of updating, but not for the reigns of the first two princes. Ménager's proposed edition of the charters of Roger I has never appeared, and with his death in December 1993 its eventual publication must be considered problematic.

(now Paris, B.N. MS lat. 5411) has been fully edited.[12] The Cava charters have been published in full up to 1080, but it was only after that date that the Normans really had much impact on the abbey and its surrounding area. Thereafter what editions there are of its documents are scattered and difficult to obtain, and cover only a small proportion of the riches that exist. Only for Montevergine, where all the documents up to 1196 have been published, with a photograph of every charter included in the edition, is the situation as one would wish.[13]

None the less, one should not dwell for too long on such evidential problems. There are a fair number of blessings to be counted. In particular almost all known Norman-era documents – indeed virtually all pre-1250 documents – from Apulia have been published. If there were no monastic houses of the size and importance of the great Campanian abbeys in this region, the survival of quite considerable documentation from, for example, the Benedictine establishments on the Tremiti islands, at Conversano, and the new shrine of St Nicholas, Bari (established in 1087), as well as from the important cathedrals of Bari and Troia, tells us much about the society of Norman Apulia. To complain about the paucity of sources is never a very fruitful exercise for historians, even though undergraduates writing essays all too often display a trusting faith in this ploy as a substitute for informed thought! Compared with those studying the period between the fall of the Roman empire and the first millennium, the historian of eleventh- and early twelfth-century southern Italy is fortunate, as the above – all too brief – survey shows.

Perhaps more to the point is the historical significance of the subject. Though the lands conquered by the Normans in the eleventh century were only later united and consolidated into a single kingdom by Guiscard's nephew, Roger II of Sicily, in the years after 1127, that kingdom lasted as a political unit until 1860. The consequences of the Norman conquest were therefore to last until the age of Cavour and Garibaldi, and were thus of very great importance for the long-term history of Italy. Yet this was not the only aspect of the conquest's significance. The Norman take-over of southern Italy and Sicily was only part of a much wider movement of

---

12 For detailed guides to their contents, H. Hoffmann, 'Chronik und Urkunden in Montecassino', *QFIAB* li (1971), 96–163, and C. Manaresi, 'Il Liber Instrumentorum seu chronicorum monasterii Casauriensis della nazionale di Parigi', *Rendiconti del istituto lombardo. Classe di lettere e di scienze morali e storiche* lxxx (1947), 29–62.

13 *Codice diplomatico verginiano*, ed. P.M. Tropeano (10 vols, Montevergine 1977–86). The later contents of this archive can be consulted through the printed calendar by G. Mongelli, *Abbazia di Montevergine: Regesto di pergamene* ii–iii (Pubblicazioni degli archivio di stato, 27, 29, Rome 1956–7).

European expansion, both internal and external, at this period; a process which was fuelled to a considerable extent by demographic imperatives. Internally this was marked by the clearance of land, the extension of settlement, the development of trade and the growth, albeit from a very low base, of towns. Southern Italy was, as we shall see, by no means isolated from such a general European movement. But the coming of the Normans, and their conquest of Byzantine Apulia and Calabria and Islamic Sicily, was in addition part of a process of external expansion which also embraced, not merely the Norman conquest of England, but the Reconquista in Spain, the German *Drang nach Osten* – 'the push to the east' along the Baltic coast which was to take German settlers as far as Latvia and Estonia by the thirteenth century, and the most spectacular manifestation, though in the long run probably the least productive in terms of concrete results: the Crusades. At the self-same time as the Normans conquered Lombard and Greek southern Italy and Islamic Sicily, the Christian Spaniards, hitherto penned in their northern mountains by the power of Islam, were pushing southwards along with their French allies into the Duero valley and the plains of Castile, while from the 1060s Saxon knights were once again pressing forward against the Slav tribes to their east, taking up once more the first efforts of conquest and colonisation which the Ottonians had abandoned eighty years earlier, not least because of their preoccupation with Italy. Sailors from the Italian mercantile ports began to reverse centuries of Islamic domination of the Mediterranean. Their trade expanded, and their fleets on occasion launched attacks on Islamic ports, as the Pisans did to Palermo in 1063 and Mahdia in 1087. Viewed as one pan-European whole, the chronology of this movement is striking. Duke William of Normandy conquered England in 1066, Robert Guiscard took Palermo in 1072, Toledo fell to Alfonso VI in 1085, the conquest of Sicily was finally completed in 1091, El Cid captured Valencia in 1094, and the First Crusade Jerusalem only five years later; all of these events therefore easily within the course of a single lifetime. Indeed, if Robert Guiscard died a decade before the preaching of the First Crusade, his younger brother Roger I of Sicily survived until 1101.

The eleventh century marked the watershed between the Europe of the Dark Ages and the much more confident and assertive Europe of the central and later Middle Ages. Dark Age Europe was inward-looking, on the defensive, backward, and overshadowed by the much more advanced civilisations of Islam to its south and Byzantium to the south-east. The Europe of the second Christian millennium expanded outwards to its natural geographic frontiers and beyond them, exporting its goods, its people and its religion, and presaging the early modern era in which western Europe was to be the major force in the world, remaining as such until the era of the World Wars and the rise of America, Japan and now China, in the twentieth century. The Norman take-over of southern Italy and Sicily was only one part of this watershed, but it was by no means an unimportant component, helping to end the Islamic dominance of the Mediterranean and greatly facilitating Christian ability to trade and communicate across that sea. However, the south Italian Normans also played an important part in destabilising the traditional Christian 'great power' in the eastern Mediterranean, the Byzantine empire, contributing to the decline of Greek Christendom to the profit of the west.

Furthermore, historians of the Middle Ages have in recent years become much more interested than hitherto in such issues as frontiers, 'frontier' or 'colonial' societies, the acculturation of subject peoples by dominant or invading forces, even if these were often, or indeed usually, numerically inferior, and the accommodations which the conquerors had to make due to such an inferiority and the physical and social differences between their new lands and their original homeland. Settlement and trading patterns, military obligation, ethnic relations as expressed especially through law and language, religious organisation and toleration, customs of marriage and inheritance – even such specialist areas as palaeography, diplomatic and coinage – are all now grist to the historian's mill in his (or her) analysis of these new colonial societies developing in the wake of the expansion of Latin Christendom during the central Middle Ages.[14] But all these are seen to be significant, not just as factors worthy of study with regard to any society of the past, but precisely because the widening of Christendom's boundaries produced hybrid societies, grafting the habits and assumptions of post-Carolingian western Europe onto indigenous stocks that up to that point had produced a very different variety of social structure.

Southern Italy and Sicily had never been part of that Carolingian world, despite the best efforts of Charlemagne and his great-grandson Louis II, and later on of the Ottonians, to extend their sway there. The Germanic society of Lombard south Italy had remained very much on the periphery, both geographically and socially, of the mainstream Christian west. However, the newcomers of the eleventh century came into contact not just with these indigenous Latin Christian inhabitants who were a part, albeit a notably distinct one, of their own society, but also with those whose language, culture and religious practices were alien: Greek Christians on both the mainland and Sicily, and Muslims on the island. Some historians have

---

14 See especially R. Bartlett, *The Making of Europe. Conquest, Colonisation and Cultural Change 950–1350* (1993). But among many other examples, the earlier essay by E. Lourie, 'A society organized for war: medieval Spain', *Past and Present* xxxv (1966), 54–76 may be cited as a model.

tended to overestimate the significance of the cultural fusion which resulted, but equally one cannot ignore the presence of groups who remained as substantial minorities within the new 'Norman' lands long after the conquest had run its course.

The chapters which follow will devote considerable attention to the actual process of the conquest, to the careers of the principal protagonists, and to the exegesis of the chronicles which are our principal sources for those events. They are whenever possible based on direct study of the sources, and rely on the secondary literature primarily to interpret these texts. But this book will also seek to place the conquest within the context of south Italian society in the eleventh century, and thus to provide a rather different treatment from the only studies of Robert Guiscard previously to have been published – and since these two recent books were in French and German, they will anyway not be accessible to many linguistically challenged Anglophone readers.[15] The first step towards providing that context is to examine its historical background, for without an understanding of the profound differences and divisions within southern Italy from long before the Normans arrived, one cannot comprehend the lengthy and complex process of the conquest.

---

15 Huguette Taviani-Carozzi, *La Terreur du Monde. Robert Guiscard et la conquête normande en Italie* (Paris 1996); Richard Bünemann, *Robert Guiskard 1015–1085. Eine Normanner erobert Süditalien* (Cologne 1997). I had largely completed this study before I was aware of this latter book.

CHAPTER I

Southern Italy before the Normans

When the first Normans arrived in southern Italy early in the eleventh century, the region to which they came was already very fragmented: divided not only politically but ethnically, religiously and culturally. There were three principal and contrasting areas. Apulia and Calabria were part of the Byzantine empire, ruled from Constantinople. The island of Sicily had been conquered from Byzantium by the Arabs during the ninth century, and remained under Islamic rule. The Campania, the western coastal region, along with the mountainous centre of the peninsula, was ruled by princes, and inhabited by people who considered themselves to be Lombards – descendants of the Germanic invaders of the peninsula in the sixth century. How many of them really were of Lombard blood is immaterial: not least because modern scholarship views the Germanic tribes who invaded the Roman empire as themselves cultural rather than ethnic units, united by language and law rather than race or common descent. But by the eleventh century these 'Lombards' had long since been assimilated, linguistically and socially, with the indigenous inhabitants, rule over whom they had seized from the Roman empire of Justinian. A chronicler writing in the later tenth century referred, significantly, to 'the Germanic language which the Lombards once spoke'.[1] By the year 1000 they may therefore be considered as, in our terms, native Italians.

However, all three of these regions were themselves divided. The provinces ruled by the Byzantine emperors Basil II and his brother Constantine VIII had a mixed population, partly Greek-speaking but also in part (and

---

1 *Chronicon Salernitanum*, ed. U. Westerbergh (Stockholm 1956), *c.* 38, p. 39.

in some areas almost entirely) Lombard, and that Lombard population was often extremely restive under Byzantine rule and apparently growing more so by the early eleventh century. Sicily was not only subject to frequent internecine disputes among its Arabic rulers, but religiously divided. A combination of immigration from north Africa and the conversion of many of the existing inhabitants meant that by now the majority of the island's population was indeed Muslim, but there remained a substantial Christian minority, perhaps still as much as a third of the total population. These Greek-speaking Christians were concentrated in the north-east of the island, in the area known as the Val Demone, with a few also in the Palermo area. They were to provide a very useful fifth column to the Normans when they invaded the island in the early 1060s. And while the Lombard area proper was culturally and linguistically more united than the other two regions, it was far from being so politically, being split into three contending principalities, based at Benevento, Capua and Salerno, whose rulers were often at odds with each other. In addition, there were several small duchies on the west coast which had never been conquered by the Lombards and retained an at times precarious independence, playing off the Lombard princes against each other and sometimes looking to Byzantium for political and military support. These duchies, from north to south Gaeta, Naples and Amalfi, had only very restricted (and in Amalfi's case extremely moun-tainous) territories, but derived much of their considerable wealth from commerce, including trade with the Muslim world. To the north of the principality of Benevento in the mountains of the Abruzzi were a number of more or less independent counties, theoretically subject to the duke of Spoleto in central Italy, and thus to the ruler of the north Italian kingdom (from 951 onwards the German emperor). The rulers of this area lying to the north of the River Trigno did occasionally interfere in the southern principalities, and a few southern monasteries (notably Montecassino) had dependencies or held land in the Abruzzi, but it was essentially a barrier region, geographically, politically, and to some extent socially, distinct from the south proper.

We shall return later to the situation at the start of the eleventh century. But to understand the complex political and social divisions of the region on the eve of the Normans' arrival we need to look briefly at its history in the early Middle Ages, to explain how and why the society of the year 1000 had developed. In particular one needs to understand why Lombard Italy was so divided, how Sicily had fallen into the hands of Islam and the way in which Byzantine rule over its south Italian provinces had evolved. The roots of these developments went back a very long way, and it is to these distant origins which we need now to look.

The evolution of southern Italy

The Lombards who had invaded Italy in 568 soon spread through much of the peninsula. In addition to their kingdom of Italy in the north, they had created two other political units, the duchy of Spoleto in the centre and the duchy of Benevento in the south. By the middle of the seventh century the Lombard dukes of Benevento already ruled most of southern Italy. Though the Byzantines seem to have put up a determined resistance in Apulia, the Lombards continued to push slowly southwards, and by the middle of the eighth century the duchy of Benevento comprised virtually all the southern third of Italy. Byzantium was left in possession only of the tip of the Salento peninsula in Apulia, central and southern Calabria, and Sicily. Northern Calabria and all of Apulia north of Otranto was by this stage held by the Lombards. The existing population, probably not very numerous after the plagues of the sixth and early seventh centuries and the economic disloca-tion of the invasion period, was rapidly assimilated by the newcomers and became 'Lombard', though they in turn exercised a considerable influence on their conquerors in facilitating their speedy conversion to Christianity. However, during this period the hitherto relatively dense urban network of Roman Apulia largely disappeared. Only a small number of coastal towns remained of any importance, and then more as centres of defence and administration than as genuine urban settlements. The contrast between the late Roman and Lombard periods can be seen quite clearly from the Church, for towns of any significance were almost invariably the seat of a bishopric. In the sixth century there had been at least fifteen bishoprics in Apulia; in the ninth century there were only six.[2]

The duchy of Benevento remained separate and distinct from the Lombard kingdom of northern Italy, and though the two ruling dynasties frequently intermarried, the dukes managed to avoid any effective subordina-tion to the northern ruler. The fact that the Lombards never conquered Rome and its surrounding region, and thus never had control of the easiest and least mountainous route between north and south, was undoubtedly an important factor here. Benevento remained independent when the northern kingdom was overrun by Charlemagne and his Franks in 774, and the then duke, Arichis, not only resisted Charlemagne's attempts to enforce his lordship but proclaimed his independence by adopting the title of prince, a style which remained in

---

2 J.-M. Martin, *La Pouille du VIe au XIIe siècle* (Rome 1993), pp. 248–50, and more generally pp. 116–250.

use by his successors. The late ninth-century chronicler Erchempert claimed, with perhaps more local pride than strict attention to the truth, that:

> Charles and all his sons whom he had now appointed as kings marched to attack Benevento with a great army of warriors, but God, under whose rule we were then prospering, was on our side. After a little while almost all of his men had died of disease and he beat an ignominious retreat with the few survivors.

He then recorded approvingly that when Charlemagne's son Pepin demanded the subjection of Arichis's son Grimoald on the grounds that the latter's father had allegedly been subject to the last Lombard king, Grimoald had indignantly refused, saying that he had been born free and intended to remain that way.[3] Erchempert was a monk of Montecassino, a monastery on the northern edge of the Beneventan zone which benefited both materially and in prestige from the Carolingians' favour, but retained a strong sense of local patriotism. Similar sentiments were to be found at another monastery equally favoured by the rulers of northern Italy, St Vincent on Volturno.[4] Indeed contemporary south Italian Lombard writers often referred to the Franks in terms very little different, and equally unflattering, from those which they used to describe Muslims or Greeks.[5] This sense of local Lombard identity, and not just geographical distance or political allegiance, also helps to explain the clear distinction between Lombard south Italy and the Abruzzi counties to the north: part of the nobility in this latter region were Frankish settlers, and the perception of their Frankish descent remained for a long time.[6] Indeed this sense of 'separateness', not just from the Frankish intruders but between northern and southern Lombards, was to endure: in the eleventh and twelfth centuries it was made clear by an important etymological distinction – the *Longobardi* were the inhabitants of southern Italy, the *Lombardi* the people of the north.

However, the period of relative stability in the south after *c.* 750, which the Carolingians did very little to disturb, lasted only some three-quarters of a century. It was shattered first by the Islamic invasion of Sicily in 827, and then by the break-up of the duchy of Benevento into first two, and then

---

3 Erchempert, *Historia Langobardorum Beneventanorum*, *c.* 6, *MGH SS Rer. Lang* (1878), pp. 236–7.
4 M. del Treppo, 'Longobardi, franchi e papato in due secoli di storia vulternense', *Archivio storico per le provincie napoletane* lxxiii (1953–4), 55–6.
5 S. Palmieri, 'Un esempio di mobilità etnica altomedievale: i saraceni in Campania', *Montecassino dalla prima alla seconda distruzione. Momenti e aspetti di storia cassinese (secc. VI–IX)*, ed. F. Avagliano (Miscellanea Cassinese 55, 1987), pp. 604–6.
6 Thus a charter of Abbot Roffred of St Vincent on Volturno in 988 described Count Rainald of Marsia as 'ex nacione Francorum', *Chron. Vult.* ii.335.

three separate units. The opportunity for the Arabs to land on the island was provided by a revolt there against the Byzantine authorities led by a disaffected officer called Euphemios; and this precedent was repeated in their subsequent attacks on the mainland. Though the completion of the conquest of Sicily was to take a long time – the last Byzantine fortresses in the east did not fall until as late as 902 – the Muslims soon overran much of the island. Palermo was captured in 831 and Messina in 842, and by then some Muslims had already turned their attention northwards. A group of them had been hired as mercenaries by the duke of Naples as early as 832, but the real opportunity for interference on the mainland came when the murder of Prince Sicard and the disputed succession which ensued led the principality of Benevento to dissolve into civil war in 839. Two rival princes emerged: Sicard's former treasurer Radelchis who ruled at Benevento, and his surviving brother Siconulf who made his base at Salerno, the fortified town on the coast south of the Amalfitan peninsula built by Arichis some sixty years earlier. Both sides sought Muslim assistance, but the erstwhile mercenaries soon ran out of control, seized coastal bases for themselves and launched devastating raids deep into the peninsula. Contemporaries were all too aware of this fatal combination of internecine dispute and external threat. Another chronicler from Montecassino, writing perhaps twenty years earlier than Erchempert, commented: 'If a reader in the future wishes to know the reason why the Saracens ruled over the lands of the Beneventans, the circumstances are like this. Prince Sicard of the Beneventans was killed by his own men . . .', and he went on to recount the succession dispute, and how one of Radelchis's officials invited Muslims to Bari who then seized the town for themselves. Meanwhile the prince was reducing areas loyal to his rival to ashes, and as the chronicler dryly and laconically recorded, 'from then onwards everything rapidly got worse'.[7]

How far the Muslims were seriously intent on the conquest of mainland southern Italy, and how far they were simply intent on plunder, and above all the capture of slaves, is a good question. The chroniclers' references to them 'depopulating' the countryside may well be significant, and a Frankish pilgrim to Jerusalem in the 860s claimed to have seen some 9,000 newly enslaved Christians at Muslim-held Taranto in the process of being sent to North Africa.[8] The raiders also extorted substantial sums in 'protection money', as for example when c. 861 the wealthy abbeys of Montecassino and St Vincent on Volturno each paid out some 3,000 gold coins to avoid

---

7 *Chronica Sancti Benedicti Casinensis, c.* 5, *MGH SS Rer. Lang.,* pp. 471–2.
8 F. Avril and J.R. Gaborit, 'L'itinerarium Bernardi monachi et les pèlerinages d'Italie du sud pendant le haut moyen-age', *MEFR* lxxix (1967), 273–4. For 'depopulation', e.g. Erchempert, *Historia, cc.* 20, 47, pp. 242, 255.

being burned down.[9] Obtaining ransoms for the return of Christian captives was another profitable enterprise. At the end of the century, by which time the monks of St Vincent were living in exile in Capua, they were able to build only a very modest new monastery there, for much of the money which they had obtained from donations or the lease of property was being used for the redemption of prisoners held by the Muslims.[10] Furthermore it has been suggested that most of the Muslims who ravaged the mainland, as opposed to the invaders of Sicily, were men who were themselves marginalised in the Muslim world, many of them outsiders of low status such as Berbers, acting without the knowledge or approval of the established powers within Islam, and without their help.[11] But given the divisions among the Lombards, and their distrust of outside interference, even when the Carolingian ruler of northern Italy, Louis II, was anxious to assist them, these Muslim raiders were singularly hard to drive out.

The consequences of this period of instability were considerable. The split in the principality of Benevento was formally recognised in 849 when the contending parties came to an agreement mediated by Louis II, then on the first of what was to be a number of campaigns in the south. (One may note that in one of the most significant clauses of this treaty the two princes agreed to expel all Saracens from their lands and not to employ them in future.)[12] Yet, just like the Treaty of Verdun of 843 among the Carolingians and innumerable externally negotiated treaties of more recent ages, this agreement was simply the prelude to further dispute and division. In particular, the gastaldate of Capua, which in the treaty of 849 had been assigned to Salerno, rapidly became detached from its nominal prince, and under its energetic ruler Landulf – described by Erchempert as 'a conqueror most anxious to wage war, by inclination and descent with the cruelty of a snake'[13] – emerged as an independent, and extremely disruptive, political unit. Furthermore the coastal duchies, all of whom were apparently trading with the Muslims, had every reason to welcome the progressive enfeeblement of their potentially threatening Lombard neighbours, and were markedly reluctant to join in proposed anti-Saracen alliances. They may indeed sometimes have profited directly from Muslim

---

9 *Chron. Vult.* i.357. Erchempert, *Historia*, c. 29, p. 245. Cf. *Chron. Cas.* I.35, p. 97.
10 *Chron. Vult.* ii.7–8.
11 N. Cilento, *Italia meridionale longobarda* (Milan/Naples 1971), pp. 150–2; B.M. Kreutz, *Before the Normans. Southern Italy in the Ninth and Tenth Centuries* (Philadelphia 1991), pp. 48–9. A century later (c. 977), Ibn Hawkal had a very low opinion of the *ribat* (colonies of volunteers for the *Jihad*) at Palermo: 'men of bad conduct, people of sedition, trash', Amari, *BAS* i.5.
12 *MGH Legum* iv, ed. G.H. Pertz (Hanover 1868), 221–5, at p. 224, c. 24.
13 Erchempert, *Historia*, c. 14, p. 240.

raids on the Lombard principalities, trading in booty and buying prisoners as slaves.[14]

After being held by the Muslims for almost a quarter of a century, Bari was eventually recaptured by the Emperor Louis II in 871. But the sequel to his success was indicative of south Italian attitudes and particularism. A few months later he was arrested by the prince of Benevento, and forced to swear as the price for his release never again to return to that city. The message was very clear: outside interference, however beneficial, was not wanted. Local patriot as he was, Erchempert was scandalised by this outrage to 'the saviour of the Beneventan province', and sagely quoted the Old Testament proverb, 'Smite the shepherd, and the sheep shall be scattered'.[15] This was indeed more or less what happened, for the Muslims still retained a number of other bases, and among other lesser outrages a major attack from Sicily was launched on Salerno in 871–2. When after a year's unsuccessful siege the Muslims retired through Calabria, 'they entirely depopulated it, so that it was like a desert rather than a well-watered land'.[16] More than forty years were to elapse before the Muslims were driven off the mainland completely. In the early 880s other groups of raiders who had established bases at Saepino in the Matese mountains (inland) and on the coast at the mouth of the River Garigliano destroyed both the abbeys of St Vincent on Volturno and Montecassino, whose surviving monks were forced to establish communities in exile, in which state they remained for many years, the monks of St Vincent at Capua until 914, and those of St Benedict first at Teano and then at Capua until 950.

That the Muslims were forced back on the defensive and eventually defeated was due to four related factors. In the first instance there was the determined resistance put up by the handful of Sicilian strongpoints still in Byzantine hands which engaged the attentions of the bulk of Muslim forces up to 902. Secondly there was a resurgence of Byzantine power on the mainland after 870, which was to be extremely significant in that it extended imperial authority over a much more extensive area than hitherto, and more or less fixed the territorial boundaries which were to last until well into the eleventh century. The Lombard garrison of Bari handed the town

---

14 P. Skinner, *Family Power in Southern Italy. The Duchy of Gaeta and its Neighbours, 850–1139* (Cambridge 1995), p. 285. Palmieri, 'Un esempio di mobilità etnica', p. 624. Cf. also Kreutz, *Before the Normans*, pp. 51–2. However, it is by no means always clear whether such people as the *coloni* purchased from the Muslims by the Bishop of Gaeta in 867, *Codex Diplomaticus Caietanus* (2 vols, Montecassino 1887–92), i.22 no. 13, were being ransomed or bought as slaves.

15 Zachariah xiii.7; Erchempert, *Historia*, c. 34, p. 247. Cf. for this episode *The Annals of St Bertin*, trans. J.L. Nelson (Manchester 1991), pp. 175–6.

16 Erchempert, *Historia*, c. 35, pp. 247–8.

over to the Byzantines in 876, apparently because they distrusted their own ability to defend it against the Muslims.[17] Taranto was recaptured in 880, and in the next few years under the governorship of Nikephoros Phokas the Byzantine forces in Italy were heavily reinforced, their hold in southern Apulia was consolidated (the creation of a new province called *Langobardia* was a feature of this process), and Byzantine rule extended into northern Calabria, including areas which had previously been part of the principality of Salerno. Settlers were also introduced from Asia Minor and the Balkans to consolidate these gains. Gallipoli, in southern Apulia, was for example repopulated with immigrants from Heraclea on the Asia Minor coast of the Black Sea. In the wake of the military conquests several new bishoprics were set up in Calabria after 886, with an archiepiscopal see at Santa Severina.[18] A mark of this new Byzantine influence was the visit to Constantinople by Guaimar I of Salerno in 887. Indeed, in 891 the Byzantines captured Benevento itself, and although they only retained this for less than four years[19] – it was too far inland to be easily reinforced or, as is obvious, for their naval power to have any effect – it was a potent sign of how much the empire's power in southern Italy had developed.

The immediate consequence of this Byzantine resurgence was to focus Muslim attentions on the west coast and the Lombard principalities, and hence the renewed raiding there in the 880s, which led to the destruction of the monasteries of Volturno and Montecassino. But the relative impunity with which the raiders had operated was largely a product of local disunity, of that spirit which was expressed in the tale Erchempert repeated of the deathbed of Landulf the Elder of Capua, on which he urged his sons to ensure their future profit by never permitting there to be any peace between Benevento and Salerno,[20] and which led Athanasius, the prince-bishop of Naples, so often to ally with the Muslims in the 880s, despite his own clerical position and repeated excommunications by the pope. However, by the turn of the century that situation, which the chronicler roundly and rightly condemned as 'an insane civil war between brothers', was changing.[21] The most important development was the bloodless coup which in 900 installed Count Atenulf I of Capua as prince of Benevento. Capua and

---

17 Erchempert, *Historia*, c. 38, p. 249.
18 V. von Falkenhausen, *Untersuchungen über die byzantinische Herrschaft in Süditalien vom 9. bis ins 11. Jahrhundert* (Wiesbaden 1967), pp. 18–25, provides an excellent summary. For Gallipoli, Martin, *Pouille*, pp. 224–5.
19 *Chron. Vult.* ii.6 says three years, nine months and twenty days.
20 Erchempert, *Historia*, c. 22, p. 43.
21 Erchempert, *Historia*, c. 47, p. 256. For Athanasius, *ibid.*, cc. 44, 49, 56, pp. 251, 254–5, 257.

Benevento were to be ruled together as one political unit for the next eighty years. Furthermore the local rulers were now more prepared to work together, and also to co-operate with the Byzantines, against the Muslim threat. Landulf I of Capua visited Constantinople in 910 and in 915 dispatched the abbot of Montecassino for a further visit there on his behalf.[22] Indeed up to 920 he even dated his documents by the regnal years of the Byzantine emperor in an implicit acknowledgement of Byzantine overlordship. Admittedly a first attempt to destroy the Muslim colony at the mouth of the Garigliano in 903 had been frustrated by the recalcitrance of the duke of Gaeta. However, in 915 a second attempt was more successful, not least because pressure from both the papacy and Byzantium had forced the rulers of Amalfi and Gaeta not to assist the Muslims.[23]

It might have seemed that with the capture of the last Byzantine stronghold in Sicily, Taormina, in 902 there might be renewed pressure on the mainland. But though the fall of Taormina was followed by an immediate invasion of Calabria, the death of the Sicilian and north African ruler Ibrahim-Abd-Allah at Cosenza in October of that year marked a watershed. Not only did the Muslims withdraw back to the island, but within a year his son had been murdered and his followers were at loggerheads.[24] Thereafter internal instability was to be almost as much of a problem for Islamic Sicily in the tenth century as it had been for the Lombard principalities in the ninth, and the rulers of north Africa had continuing problems in enforcing their rule on the island. Raids on Calabria continued intermittently throughout the tenth century, often being bought off by the payment of ransoms or 'protection money', and they even occasionally affected southern Apulia, but there was no longer the danger that these attacks might provide bridgeheads for further conquest. There were a number of quite lengthy truces negotiated between the Byzantine authorities and the rulers of Sicily (for example between 918 and 922, and again between 952 and 956) and at periods when internal dispute in Sicily was really marked, as in the late 930s and early 940s when there was a genuine civil war on the island, even the payment of tribute money from Calabria ceased. In the period after 964 Sicily's Fatimid overlords were anxious not to become

---

22 *Le Pergamene di Conversano*, ed. G. Coniglio (*Codice diplomatico pugliese* xx, Bari 1975), pp. 8–10 no. 4. Surprisingly this visit was not mentioned by the Montecassino chronicle of Leo of Ostia.

23 O. Vehse, 'Das Bundnis gegen die Sarazenen vom Jahre 915', *QFIAB* xix (1927), 181–204, remains the best account of this.

24 Ibn-al-Athir, in Amari, *BAS*, i.103. Though writing three centuries later, Ibn-al-Athir based his account on contemporary sources, and was extremely well informed about events in Sicily in the tenth and eleventh centuries.

embroiled with Byzantium while they strove to take over Egypt, and for more than a decade Calabria was left in peace.

Of course when raids on the mainland did take place their effects could be extremely unpleasant. In 925, for example, the Muslims attacked southern Apulia and captured Taranto and Oria, along with the Greek governor of Calabria who had taken refuge there. A later Jewish chronicler from Oria recorded that they 'made havoc of the land, and reduced it to the extremity of distress'.[25] In 950, after internal peace had finally been restored in Sicily, Reggio was captured and Muslim forces reached as far north as Cassano in the Val di Crati. Two years later the governor of Calabria was killed fighting against a renewed Muslim attack. But despite such successes, the incidence of these raids was sporadic, and most of the Calabrian towns were strongly established on hilltop sites and by no means easy to capture. The Muslims besieged Gerace, for example, in both 950 and 952, and on both occasions were unable to take the town and consented to be bought off. The same thing happened when they attacked Cosenza in 976.[26] The most significant long-term effect of these attacks was to push the Greek population of Calabria to move from the coastal areas onto stronger natural sites inland or in some cases to emigrate further north away from the most immediate danger. A later Calabrian chronicler suggested that the fortification of hilltop sites inland was a deliberate policy initiated by the Emperor Nikephoros Phokas (963–9).[27]

Though in the early years of the tenth century Byzantium was undoubtedly exercising considerable influence, at least indirectly, on the Lombard principalities, relations were by no means smooth. In 915 a contingent of Byzantine troops had aided Landulf I of Capua to destroy the Muslim base at the mouth of the Garigliano. But the princes of Capua–Benevento found it difficult to forget that their predecessors before the 840s had ruled over most of what was now the Byzantine province of *Langobardia*. The development of coastal towns like Bari and Siponto which benefited from trade in the Adriatic also made northern Apulia a desirable target for the Lombard princes, and the fiscal demands of the Byzantine government undoubtedly caused dissatisfaction among its subjects. Since in northern Apulia these

---

25 *The Chronicle of Ahimaez*, trans. M. Salzman (Columbia 1924), p. 98. Oria had what was probably the most important Jewish colony in the region in the tenth century. Ibn-al-Athir (Amari, *BAS*, i.105) said that an epidemic among the Muslim army brought this expedition to a halt.

26 Ibn-al-Athir, in Amari, *BAS*, i.109, 110.

27 E. Caspar, 'Die Chronik von Tres Tabernae in Calabrien', *QFIAB* x (1907), 35. The authenticity of this source has been disputed, but Caspar concluded that it was a genuine, if minor, chronicle.

were almost all Lombards, the princes could hope to find them sympathetic to their incursions. Landulf I invaded Apulia in 921, the governor Ursoleon was killed fighting at Ascoli on the frontier, and the prince then occupied much of the area, apparently with the support of the inhabitants. He sought to justify his invasion by accusing Ursoleon of misgovernment and persuading the imperial government to appoint him as the *strategos* of the province, a suggestion which they were understandably reluctant to fulfil, demanding rather that he evacuate the fortresses which he had captured and send his eldest son as a hostage to Constantinople (in addition to another son who was apparently already there).[28] The Byzantines did succeed in restoring their position in Apulia for a time after 921, but a second invasion in 926 had more serious effects, not least because at the same time Guaimar II of Salerno abandoned his previous neutrality and tried to take over the border regions of Lucania and Calabria which had once belonged to his principality. In addition the Beneventans received military assistance from Spoleto. It took some seven years for the Byzantines to restore their rule, and they did this only by securing the help of the north Italian king Hugh, as well as sending cavalry reinforcements to Apulia.

The real problem for Byzantium when faced with such threats to its south Italian dominions was that the empire had many other calls on its resources. Byzantium was a contemporary 'super-power', but for its rulers southern Italy could be no more than a minor priority compared with the importance of defending the eastern frontier of its Asia Minor provinces against the Arabs, and its European frontier in Thrace against the Bulgarians. In the 920s, for example, it faced a very difficult situation in Thrace, with the Bulgarian ruler Symeon very much on the offensive and at times posing an actual threat to Constantinople itself. It was only some years after his death in 927, when relations with Bulgaria had been put on a reasonably even keel, that troops could be spared for Italy, and then not in very substantial numbers. The force dispatched to Apulia in 934 comprised fewer than 1,500 mounted troops, more than half of whom were new recruits, and 400 Russian infantry.[29] The problem of greater priorities elsewhere was to reoccur later, and indeed was to be an important factor in the final collapse of Byzantine Italy before the Normans. While for much of the tenth century Byzantine power was in the ascendant, aggressive warfare

---

28 *The Letters of the Patriarch Nicholas Mysticus*, ed. R. Jenkins and L. Westerink (Dumbarton Oaks 1975), pp. 338–42 no. 82.

29 Details of this force are given in Constantine Porphyrogenitus, *De Ceremoniis*, ed. J. Reiske (Bonn 1829), lib. II *c.* 44, pp. 660–1. Cf. J. Gay, *L'Italie méridionale et l'empire Byzantin depuis l'avènement de Basile Ier jusqu'à la prise de Bari par les Normands (867–1071)* (2 vols, Paris 1904), i.210.

on the eastern frontier was usually the principal claim on the empire's troops. A substantial expedition was sent to Italy in 956 which seems to have been directed mainly against Naples, and a major attack on Sicily was launched in 964 (which failed disastrously). Otherwise the local authorities in Apulia and Calabria were generally left to get by as best they could.

However, for a considerable period after 934 the position in southern Italy remained relatively stable, even if there were periodic border skirmishes with the Beneventans, especially in the later 940s. The princes of Capua–Benevento were not by themselves sufficiently powerful to destabilise Byzantine rule in Apulia, particularly since their relations with Salerno could at times break down into open warfare (even if on nothing like the scale and frequency of the previous century), and they faced problems themselves in maintaining their authority over the whole of their principality. For a time after 935 charters at Benevento (though not Capua) even used the regnal years of the Byzantine emperors once more, though this practice did not continue very long. However, the coronation of the German king, Otto I, as Roman emperor in the west in 962, and his claims therefore to be the legitimate ruler over the whole of Italy, including the south, did pose a significant potential threat, and for a time appeared to have greatly altered the situation in southern Italy.

Otto based his policy in the south on a close and mutually advantageous alliance with the prince of Capua–Benevento, Pandulf I 'Ironhead' (961–81), to whom he granted the duchy of Spoleto and march of Camerino, that is to say authority over central Italy as well. From the emperor's point of view this arrangement had obvious advantages. Given the extent of his dominions he could devote only limited attention to central and south Italian affairs, and a reliable lieutenant was therefore a necessity. Furthermore the control over Rome and the papacy which he had established in 962 was fragile, and greatly resented by the hitherto independent Roman nobility, to such an extent that in 966 they expelled his appointee as pope, John XIII. Pandulf Ironhead was apparently the most powerful, and certainly the most energetic, of the local south Italian rulers. It was thus very much in the emperor's interest to have him on his side, and for him to recognise imperial overlordship. Furthermore he even had some sort of legitimate claim to his new dignities since a quarter of a century earlier King Hugh had, it seems, granted to his grandfather titular rule over Spoleto (though apparently without concrete effect since neither Hugh nor Landulf I then had the means to put this into practice).[30] From Pandulf's point of

---

30 *Chron. Vult.* ii.60: 'in ipso tempore Landulfus princeps marchio efficitur', which undoubtedly refers to Spoleto.

view the advantages were equally clear. Alliance with the emperor would consolidate his position as the strongest of the south Italian rulers, and since the rulers of Rome and Spoleto had launched an attack on his lands in 961, Pandulf had every incentive to assert his control over these areas if he could, and prevent this happening again. Above all the formidable military and political assistance of the emperor enabled him to revive his ancestors' claims over northern Apulia with what seemed like a real chance of success. Otto himself came to Benevento for the first time in February 967.[31] A year later he and the prince invaded Apulia.

However, in fact the Ottonian intervention accomplished very little, even though the imperial army got as far as Bari in 968. Without a fleet the town, by now the most important and almost certainly the capital of Byzantine *Langobardia*, could not be captured, and the allies withdrew. A further expedition into northern Calabria in the spring of 969 was equally inconclusive, and soon after Otto's withdrawal to northern Italy the prince of Capua was captured while besieging the border fortress of Bovino and sent a prisoner to Constantinople. The Byzantines, aided by troops from Naples, invaded Pandulf's dominions and briefly reached the Capuan plain, but then withdrew. After another year's inconclusive fighting peace was made on the basis of the original frontiers. Pandulf Ironhead had played an important part in securing this and was released.[32] In 972 this peace was sealed by the marriage of the emperor's son and heir, Otto II, with a Byzantine princess, Theophano.

By 970 therefore Byzantine rule over Apulia and Calabria had shown itself to be strong enough to resist powerful external pressure, and indeed while the Byzantines continued to hold the key border fortresses like Ascoli and Bovino any incursions were likely to be only temporary. The German emperor was never likely to be in southern Italy long enough to make much difference to this situation. On the other hand periodic Byzantine expeditions into the Lombard principalities, as in 956 and 969, even though they penetrated deep into enemy territory, were equally unlikely to accomplish more than the most temporary and nominal recognition of the eastern emperor's authority. Indeed the north–south border between the Byzantine and Lombard-ruled areas barely changed during the course of the tenth century.

What did appear to change in the 970s – though that appearance was to prove deceptive – was the balance of power in the non-Byzantine area. In the summer of 973 there was an abortive coup in Salerno which led to

---

31 *MGH Diplomatum* i (1879–84), 460–2 no. 338.
32 The most detailed account of these events comes in the *Chronicon Salernitanum, cc.* 170–4, pp. 173–7, which is our only significant contemporary chronicle from tenth-century southern Italy.

Prince Gisulf being taken off as a prisoner to Amalfi, and replaced as prince by his maternal uncle Landulf (an exiled member of the princely family of Capua–Benevento). However, within six months he was restored to his throne through the intervention of Pandulf Ironhead of Capua. But that intervention had a price: Gisulf was childless, and in return for the prince of Capua's support he associated one of the latter's younger sons with him as his co-ruler and designated successor. When Gisulf died in November 977 that son, also called Pandulf, became the nominal ruler of the Salernitan principality, but since he was still a child in fact his father now ruled – and was named as prince in the dating clause of Salernitan documents. Thus for a brief period the unity of the old principality of Benvento, comprising virtually all of non-Byzantine southern Italy, seemed to have been restored.

Yet in fact this proved entirely illusory. The only real link between the principalities was Pandulf himself, and when he died in March 981 not only did Salerno revolt, but the two principalities of Benevento and Capua split as well. The Beneventans installed as their prince Pandulf Ironhead's nephew, the son of his brother and co-ruler Atenulf (d. 968/9). The Salernitans looked first to Duke Manso of Amalfi, whom the Emperor Otto II, who was then in southern Italy, was forced reluctantly to accept as prince. But when Otto died in December 983 Manso was displaced in Salerno by a palace official, John of Spoleto, though the precise circumstances of how and why are unknown. John succeeded in holding on to power until his death in 999, and founding a dynasty which lasted until his great-grandson Gisulf II was driven out by Robert Guiscard in 1077.[33]

The events of 981–3 were extremely significant for a number of reasons. First and most obviously, they confirmed the final split of the old Beneventan principality into three separate units, and these three principalities remained split (apart from a very brief period between 1008 and 1014 when Capua and Benevento were temporarily under one ruler again) until the eventual Norman take-over. Secondly, they clearly showed the limitation of the German emperor's power in southern Italy, even when actually there in person. With his attention preoccupied with a renewed dispute with Byzantium, he

---

33   Pandulf the younger was briefly associated with Gisulf's widow, but from August 978 documents were dated by the regnal years of him and his father. See H. Taviani-Carozzi, *La Principauté lombarde de Salerne (IXe–XIe siècle). Pouvoir et société en Italie lombarde méridionale* (2 vols, Rome 1991), i.327–34. That Otto II tried and failed to displace Manso is suggested by *MGH Diplomatum* ii (1888), 308–10 no. 266, at p. 310 (= *Chron. Vult.* ii.271–5, at p. 275), written 'super Salernitanam civitam, in qua residebat supradictum imperatorem cums suis honoratibus ostiliter'. Cf. the much later *Romuald*, p. 168. Damage done by the 'Frankish', i.e. German, army is mentioned by *Cod. Dipl. Cavensis*, ii.289–95 no. 422 (986), at p. 289. John, Count of the Palace, son of Count Lambert (i.e. the later prince), is recorded by *ibid.*, ii.152–3 no. 328 (980).

was unable to prevent either the displacement of Pandulf Ironhead's son in Salerno or the breach between Capua and Benevento, even though Pandulf Ironhead's eldest son and successor at Capua, Landulf IV, remained his principal ally in the south. And finally, Otto II's renewed invasion of Byzantine territory led to a catastrophic military setback.

Quite what Otto II's intentions were in 982 is unclear, though it is worth noting that at least one contemporary commentator believed that he did intend the annexation of all the Byzantine territory in the peninsula, whereas the normally well-informed Thietmar of Merseburg stated that his primary motive was to free Calabria from the Muslim menace.[34] The circumstances for a renewed attempt to make his imperial claims over the south a reality may well have seemed favourable. From 976 onwards there had been a resumption of Muslim attacks on Calabria and southern Apulia, on a serious scale – Taranto had, for example, been sacked in 977. There appears also to have been serious trouble in some of the Apulian coastal towns, including Bari and Trani, quite possibly linked with the fiscal and military demands of resisting the Muslims.[35] But having invaded Lucania in January 982 and besieged – but failed to capture – first Matera and then Taranto, the imperial army marched south into Calabria. There, on 13 July 982 at Cape Colonna near Stilo, it encountered a Muslim army led by the ruling emir of Sicily, Abu 'al Qasim, and after a desperate battle, with heavy casualties on both sides, the Germans and their allies were utterly defeated. The emperor himself only just escaped – Thietmar gave a vivid, indeed melodramatic account of how he swam to safety to a Byzantine ship, and among the dead were Landulf IV of Capua and his brother Pandulf, the former prince of Salerno.[36]

The Muslims failed to follow up their victory; not least because their commander had been killed. But the disaster at Cape Colonna, and the premature death of Otto II at the age of twenty-eight just over a year later, leaving a small child as his heir, marked the end of any German threat to Byzantine Italy, and indeed of any western imperial involvement in the south for some seventeen years. Future imperial interventions in southern Italy, in 999, 1022, 1038 and 1047, were to be brief and almost entirely

---

34 *Annales Sangallenses, MGH SS* i (1826), 80. Cf. *Die Chronik von Bischofs Thietmar von Merseburg*, ed. R. Holtzmann (*MGH SRG*, Berlin 1935), lib. II *c*. 20, p. 122.

35 Lupus Protospatharius, *Annales*, ad. an. 982, *MGH SS* v (Hanover 1845), 55. A charter of August 983 from the Catepan (the governor of Byzantine Italy) to the Bishop of Trani refers to the latter's help during a recent siege of the town, A. Prologo, *Le Carte che si conservano nello archivio dello capitolo metropolitano della città di Trani* (Barletta 1877), pp. 32–5 no. 7.

36 *Die Chronik von Bischofs Thietmar*, III.21–2, pp. 124–7. Cf. Ibn-al-Athir, in Amari, *BAS*, i.110 for an account of the battle from the Muslim side, and also *Chron. Cas.* II.9, pp. 186–7.

confined to the Lombard principalities. The Ottonian defeat also ensured that the division of Lombard south Italy after Pandulf Ironhead's death would continue, and in particular that the principality of Salerno would remain independent of Capua. No future ruler would dominate this area as Pandulf I had done. His rule over Spoleto was granted to others, and after 982 the principality of Capua was left in the hands of a minor, with his mother as regent. Not only this but power in both this principality and that of Benevento became increasingly decentralised, and princely authority correspondingly reduced. In the 990s the cohesion of the principality of Capua broke down almost completely. In April 993 Prince Landenulf was murdered in Capua as he left a church after mass, apparently with the connivance, or at least the knowledge, of his younger brother Laidulf who succeeded him as prince.[37] Capua was soon afterwards besieged, first by the counts of Chieti and Marsia and then by Hugh, Margrave of Tuscany, acting apparently on imperial orders to catch and punish the murderers.[38] But though a number of those allegedly responsible were handed over and executed, this did nothing to restore order in the principality. Soon afterwards Archbishop Aion of Capua was also murdered, and the north of the principality degenerated into open warfare between the counts of Aquino and the powerful abbey of Montecassino. In November 996 Abbot Manso of Cassino, who was a relative of the princely family, was seized during a visit to Capua, despite coming there under a sworn safe-conduct, and then blinded.[39] The intervention of the Emperor Otto III in 999 did little to mend the situation and showed once again how ineffectual were such brief imperial forays into the south. Prince Laidulf of Capua was deposed on the grounds of his involvement in his brother's murder, and the emperor installed his own nominee, Ademarius, as prince. But almost as soon as the emperor had withdrawn, his protégé was expelled and the Capuans invited the brother of the prince of Benevento to rule them. When Otto returned to the south in 1001 he laid siege to Benevento, but was unable to take it and withdrew, dying soon afterwards.[40]

If the situation in the Lombard principalities (with the exception of Salerno which remained relatively coherent and peaceful) was by no means happy by the year 1000, that in the Byzantine lands was also growing difficult.

---

37 'Chronaca della dinastia Capuana', in Cilento, *Italia meridionale longobarda*, pp. 306–7.

38 *Chron. Cas.* II.10, p. 188.

39 There is a long account of this episode in *Chron. Cas.* II.16, pp. 196–200.

40 *Chron. Cas.* II.24, 208–9. For the dating, *Annales Casinenses ex annalibus antiquis excerpta*, *MGH SS* xxx.1409; *Annales Beneventani*, ad. an. 1001, ed. O. Bertolini, in *BISIME*, xlii (1923), 129. Cf. M. Uhlitz, *Jahrbücher des Deutschen Reiches under Otto II und Otto III* ii *Otto III 983–1002* (Berlin 1954), 302–3.

The resumption of Muslim raids from Sicily after 976 was only briefly interrupted by Otto II's 982 campaign, and thereafter the attacks intensified in both frequency and scope, penetrating not just into Calabria but deep into Apulia as well. In 986 a thrust into Calabria reached as far north as Cosenza in the Val di Crati. The outskirts of Bari were raided in 988, Taranto was attacked in 991, and Matera captured after a long siege in 994. In 1003 Bari itself was besieged for nearly five months, and rescued only by the arrival of a Venetian fleet. Cosenza was attacked once again in 1009, and this time sacked. The destabilisation of the area can be seen reflected in contemporary documents. In 992 an inhabitant of Conversano in central Apulia lamented that he had come to old age 'at a time of barbarism', and whereas previously when things were peaceful he had made financial provision for his two eldest sons on their marriages, he could not now do this for his youngest son. In 994 a judge in Conversano sanctioned a property sale by a child (something normally forbidden under Lombard law) because of necessity 'in this time of hunger'.[41] Nor could the Byzantine authorities necessarily rely on the loyalty of the Lombard population, among whom discontent was growing at this difficult period. The acting Byzantine governor was murdered at Oria in 997, and a year later one of the men responsible for his death offered to betray Bari, the capital of Byzantine Italy, to the Muslims, though he then double-crossed his erstwhile allies.[42] Given these circumstances, we may not be too surprised by a document of 999, in which the new governor of Byzantine Italy praised an officer at Taranto who had remained loyal to the emperor where others had not.[43] Another charter, written some years after the event, recorded that at the time 'when the wicked Saracens were besieging the city of Bari' (that is, 1003) a senior Byzantine officer who had come to Conversano – it is not clear from the context whether as the city's governor or just to take refuge there – had been seized by an armed group who wanted to expel him from the town.[44] Round about the same time a band of Christian renegades joined up with some Muslims to plunder the Tricarico region in Lucania.[45]

The most serious manifestation of this internal dissent within the Byzantine provinces came in May 1009 when there was a full-scale revolt in Bari.

---

41 *Cod. dipl. pugliese*, xx.56–61, nos 27–8.
42 Lupus Protospatharius, *Annales*, ad. an. 997–8, *MGH SS* v.56. For the murdered *excubitor* Theodore as acting governor, von Falkenhausen, *Untersuchungen*, p. 122.
43 Trinchera, *Syllabus*, p. 9 no. 10.
44 *Cod. dipl. pugliese*, xx.78–9 no. 35 (April 1019).
45 A. Guillou and W. Holtzmann, 'Zwei Katepansurkunden aus Tricarico', *QFIAB* xli (1961), 7, 12–13, 17 (partial English translation in R. Morris, 'Dispute settlement in the Byzantine provinces in the tenth century', in *The Settlement of Disputes in the Early Middle Ages*, ed. W. Davies and P. Fouracre (Cambridge 1986), pp. 136–7).

The Muslims who penetrated deep into Calabria and sacked Cosenza in August of that year probably capitalised upon the preoccupation of the Byzantine authorities with that rebellion. The revolt lasted for a considerable period, probably a year or more, during which the then governor, John Curcuas, died (seemingly of natural causes). It was only suppressed after the city had been besieged for two months by reinforcements sent from Constantinople under a new governor, Basil Mesardonites. The leader of the uprising, a local noble called Melus, fearing betrayal, fled first to Benevento and then to Capua.[46]

Nor were the non-Byzantine parts of Italy immune from the renewed attacks from Muslim Sicily. The duchy of Amalfi, whose trading links with the Islamic world had hitherto protected it, was attacked in 991, and in August 1002 an Arab raiding party is recorded as having reached as far inland as Benevento.[47] It is difficult to gauge the scale of these attacks, though clearly that on Bari in 1003 was an extremely serious attempt by a powerful army to seize a base, rather than just a raid aimed, as clearly many others were, at securing booty and prisoners. Thus when the first Normans arrived in Italy both the Byzantine provinces and, to a lesser extent, the Lombard principalities were threatened by this renewal of Muslim pressure, and in addition the Byzantines faced considerable internal disaffection within those areas of largely Lombard population over which they ruled. Both these factors were to play their part in the coming of the Normans.

Government

There was a fundamental contrast between on the one hand those areas of the south Italian mainland ruled by Byzantium and on the other the Lombard principalities and the duchies of the west coast. The former were part – albeit a peripheral part – of an organised and relatively centralised empire, with (by the standards of the Middle Ages) a sophisticated administrative apparatus. Government of the latter was a much more informal and personalised affair, even if the sources at our disposal are too meagre to identify all the mechanisms by which they were ruled.

---

46 *Annales Barenses*, ad. an. 1011, 1013, Lupus Protospatharius, *Annales*, ad. an. 1009, 1010, *MGH SS* v.53, 57. The *Anonymi Barensis Chronicon*, which does not mention the rebellion, agrees with Lupus in dating the death of John Curcuas and the arrival of his successor to 1010, *RIS* v.148. For Melus, *Chron. Cas.* II.37, p. 238.

47 *Annales Beneventani*, ed. Bertolini, p. 129.

THE AGE OF ROBERT GUISCARD

From the 880s onwards the area under Byzantine rule was divided into two θεματα (themes) or provinces: *Langobardia*, comprising northern and central Apulia, and the anachronistically named *Sicilia*, which included not only those few places in Sicily still in Byzantine hands up to 902 but also Calabria and the Terra d'Otranto. Only later was this last area transferred to the province of *Langobardia*, and only *c.* 950 was the southern province renamed (more accurately) *Calabria*.[48] The administrative centre of the two themes were Bari and Reggio respectively, though it has been suggested that had the Byzantines been able to retain control of Benevento, which they briefly held in the 890s, that would have remained as the provincial capital.[49] Each province was in turn divided into a number of τουρμα, though the officials in charge of these, the *turmarchs*, were downgraded during the course of the later tenth or early eleventh centuries into no more than governors of the principal towns.

During the first half of the tenth century the two Byzantine provinces remained administratively separate, each under the command of its own governor, the *strategos*, usually a relatively senior officer holding the court rank of *patrikios*. The *strategos* was, as the name implies (its literal translation is 'general'), both the civil governor and the military commander of the province. The south Italian provinces were therefore administratively no different from the other parts of the empire, composed in the tenth century of some thirty separate *themata*, although surviving lists of court precedence from this period show that *Langobardia* and *Calabria* were among the most junior commands in the provincial hierarchy as a whole. This accurately reflects their relatively low priority to the central government in Constantinople compared with the all-important *themata* in Asia Minor (still at this period the heartland of the Byzantine empire).[50]

The two provinces were by no means alike. The population of Calabria was largely Greek, that of *Langobardia* mainly Lombard, except in its most southerly part. They faced different external foes: Calabria was threatened by the attacks of the Sicilian Muslims while it was the Lombard princes of Capua–Benevento who were the more serious danger to the integrity of *Langobardia*. But there were strong pragmatic arguments for a unified command structure in southern Italy, particularly given the distance which separated it from the capital and the time which it would therefore take to send reinforcements, assuming that these would be available. Both

---

48   von Falkenhausen, *Untersuchungen* [see n. 18 above], pp. 27–8.
49   von Falkenhausen, 'Die Städte im byzantinischen Italien', *MEFR* ci (1989), 407–8.
50   The classic study of middle-Byzantine government is still J.B. Bury, *The Imperial Administrative System in the Ninth Century* (London 1911); see also A. Toynbee, *Constantine Porphyrogenitus and his World* (Oxford 1973), pp. 224–74.

provinces were therefore sometimes under the rule of the same man, as in 955 when Marianos Argyros was sent to Italy with reinforcements to coerce the Lombard principalities and the coastal duchies back to obedience, or at least quiescence, and in 965 when Nikephoros Hexakionites was appointed as 'governor of Calabria and Italy'.[51] (It was not in fact unknown elsewhere in the Byzantine empire for neighbouring provinces to be ruled by the same governor, but as a temporary expedient only, not as a permanent arrangement.) However, during the reign of the Emperor Nikephoros Phokas, who seems to have taken a much closer interest in Italian affairs than his immediate predecessors, and probably also in response to the renewed threat from the west with the alliance between Otto I and Pandulf Ironhead, there was a significant reorganisation of the Italian provinces. From c. 969 these were henceforth to be under the overall charge of a single officer, known as the Catepan, who was based in Bari. Calabria remained administratively separate, with its own governor and hierarchy of officials, but (though this has been disputed) almost certainly under the overall authority of the Catepan. It also seems probable that a third province, that of Lucania, was created at the same time or only very slightly later, for the relatively thinly populated region in the heel of Italy, into which Greek emigrants moving northwards from Calabria were beginning to penetrate in some numbers (although the population of this area was never to be entirely Greek). New bishoprics were founded in this area in the 970s, and a new ecclesiastical province set up, subject to the metropolitan see of Otranto. The administrative centre of the new province appears to have been Tursi, which also became the seat of a Greek bishopric.[52]

That the governor of the northern province now became the overall ruler of Byzantine Italy reflected that province's greater strategic importance, since its ports controlled the mouth of the Adriatic and provided the easiest communications route to the European mainland of the empire. Furthermore, after the death of Pandulf Ironhead in 981, with the Lombard principalities increasingly prey to internal problems, the Byzantines were able to extend their rule northwards into the thinly settled borderland

---

51 Trinchera, *Syllabus*, p. 5 no. 6; Theophanes Continuatus, *Chronographia*, ed. I. Bekker (Bonn 1838), pp. 453–4; *Vita S. Nili Iunioris*, c. 9, *MPG* cxx col. 105; von Falkenhausen, *Untersuchungen*, pp. 38–9, 81–2.
52 The evidence for the Lucanian province is extremely thin: the only express mention of its *strategos* comes as late as 1042, *St. Nicolas de Donnoso (1031–1060/1061)*, ed. A. Guillou (Corpus des actes grecs d'Italie du sud et de Sicile 1, Vatican City 1967), pp. 33–49 no. 3. This led von Falkenhausen, *Untersuchungen*, pp. 66–8, to suggest that the province had then only recently been founded and lasted for no more than a very few years. However, Guillou, 'La Lucanie byzantine: étude de géographie historique', *Byzantion* xxxv (1965), 119–49, especially pp. 127–34, has produced a convincing case for a foundation c. 970.

behind the Gargano peninsula which had hitherto been disputed with the princes of Benevento. Up to this period the northern frontier of Byzantine Apulia, or at least of the area securely under Byzantine control, had been the River Ofanto, the mouth of which is just north of Barletta. By *c.* 1000 it was the River Fortore some 90 km to the north, and the few small towns in the region such as Siponto, Lucera and Lesina were firmly in Byzantine hands. Lucera, the one settlement of any size in the inland part of this area, had fallen under Byzantine rule as early as January 983.[53] Subsequently, and significantly, this region became known as the 'land of the catepans', or as it became corrupted the Capitanata (a clear reflection of the relatively late date when it was incorporated under Byzantine rule).

The provincial governors, and at least some of the other senior administrative personnel, were Greeks dispatched from Constantinople. As elsewhere in the empire, both the governors before 970 and the later Catepans generally held office for fairly brief periods, about three years on average. The extended tenures of office by two eleventh-century Catepans, Basil Mesardonites who ruled Byzantine Italy from March 1010 until early in 1017, and Basil Boiannes, from December 1017 until the summer of 1028, were wholly exceptional.[54] The former's suppression of the rebellion of Melus and his influential connections (coming as he did from one of the great Byzantine noble families, distantly related to the imperial dynasty) may explain this,[55] as probably does the latter's success in defeating first the renewed rebellion led by Melus in 1017–18 and then the attempted invasion of the German Emperor Henry II in 1022.

However, many of the more junior officials were local men, and in Apulia, where the majority of the population were Lombards, they too might be drawn from this section of the population. Of the eleven turmarchs who can be identified at Bari in the late tenth and first half of the eleventh century, eight were Lombards. However at Taranto, where the bulk of the population were Greeks, nine out of the ten turmarchs attested between 1028 and 1063 would appear to have been Greek and only one a Lombard.[56] (These officers too clearly held office for relatively short periods.) Officials in Byzantine Apulia were indeed sometimes called by the Lombard title of *gastald*, probably reflecting their role as judges administering the Lombard law which was still in force even under imperial rule. In 992, for example, the leading inhabitants of Polignano (on the coast some 30 km south of

---

53 *Cod. Dipl. Cavensis*, ii.181–2 no. 358.
54 von Falkenhausen, *Untersuchungen*, p. 104.
55 A. Guillou, 'Un document sur le gouvernement de la province. L'inscription historique en vers de Bari (1011)', in his *Studies on Byzantine Italy* (London 1970), essay VIII, pp. 6–9.
56 V. von Falkenhausen, 'Taranto in epoca bizantina', *Studi medievali*, Ser. III.ix (1968), 162–3.

Bari) included three gastalds, two of whom held the rank of *spatharocandidatus* in the imperial hierarchy, as well as a turmarch with a Lombard name and another apparent Lombard who appears to have been a senior military officer, holding the higher rank of *protospatharius*.[57] However, there seems to have been a contrast between Apulia proper and Lucania, as against the Capitanata region only incorporated under Byzantine rule in the last years of the tenth century. Even if there were sometimes officials with Lombard titles, in those former areas, which had been part of the empire since the 880s, the fiscal organisation of the countryside seems to have followed the standard Byzantine pattern. Villages and their dependent territories formed taxable units (*khoria*), within which the inhabitants were collectively respons- ible for the dues which they owed to the imperial administration. Thus as Lucania became more populated towards the end of the tenth century and new settlements developed, new *khoria* were set up and boundaries of exist- ing ones redefined. But the more recently conquered Capitanata may never have been fully incorporated within the imperial administrative and fiscal system.[58] A vivid illustration of this comes in a charter from Lucera, dated by the regnal years of the emperors Basil and Constantine, from 997. Not only did the officials who supervised a sale carry the title 'gastald', but they appear to have modelled the document which was drawn up on Beneventan princely practice, even down to referring to the *palatium* from which they carried out their duties. However, this was in a place which less than twenty years earlier had still been under Beneventan rule.[59]

The Byzantine government did thus both employ local men as officials – Lombards as well as Greeks – and make concessions to the peculiar nature of its Italian provinces by sanctioning the operation of indigenous legal practices. Lombard law always prevailed in northern and central Apulia, and its rituals were recognised and expressly validated by imperial officials. Hence, to give but one example among many, at Bari in 969 an imperial *protospatharius*, who to judge by his name (Basil) was a Greek, witnessed a woman's donation to a local monastery which followed the forms laid down in the law code of King Liutprand, with the judge questioning the donatrix to ensure that she had not suffered violence or was otherwise acting under compulsion.[60] Furthermore the document recording this transaction raises

---

57 *Cod. dipl. pugliese*, xx.54–6 no. 25; von Falkenhausen, *Untersuchungen*, pp. 128–9.
58 Holtzmann/Guillou, 'Zwei Katepansurkunden aus Tricarico', 12–28; but cf. Martin, *Pouille*, p. 699.
59 V. von Falkenhausen, 'Zur byzantinischen Verwaltung Luceras am Ende des 10. Jahrhunderts', *QFIAB* liii (1973), 395–406.
60 *Cod. dipl. pugliese*, xx.44–6 no. 20. Cf. K. Fischer Drew, *The Lombard Laws* (Philadelphia 1973), pp. 155–6.

another interesting issue. The woman's legal guardian (*mundoald*), a relation of hers with a characteristic Lombard name (Tasselgardus), signed the charter in Greek. This was by no means an isolated example. About a quarter of the signatures appended to documents at Bari in the eleventh century were in Greek (the number of charters extant from before 1000 is too small for statistics to be meaningful). Admittedly the proportion from other places is much less – in Conversano it was only about 5 per cent but even that is not entirely negligible. Many, if not most, of those so signing were, like the Tasselgardus of the 969 charter above, not themselves Greeks but Lombards. There is a striking example of this in a charter recording a division of family property at Bari in 962. The document was drawn up in Latin, and witnessed by the two brothers of the man responsible for the transaction. One brother's name was signed, or perhaps recorded by the notary, in Latin. The other signed in Greek.[61] Though there was no attempt to Hellenise the Lombard population by the authorities, there were clearly at least some people in its ranks (and by definition those who appeared in property transactions would be from among the better-off) who showed their loyalty to the Byzantine regime, and perhaps also exhibited their own cultural vanity, by so demonstrating a rudimentary veneer of Greek forms. That this tendency was most marked at Bari, the Byzantine capital, is hardly surprising. But it is clear that, though the Lombard population of Apulia was volatile, and often restive under Byzantine rule, by no means all its members were intrinsically hostile to rule from Constantinople.

Indeed the problems which the Byzantines faced in southern Italy may have had almost as much to do with the nature of their regime as with the make-up of the subordinate population. The defect of such an organised government was the pressure which its exactions, both fiscal and military, placed upon its subjects. This may well have been enhanced if a fundamental distinction in Byzantine provincial administration revealed by the 'Book of Ceremonies' of Constantine Porphyrogenitus (compiled probably in the 940s) remained in force into the later tenth century. Constantine stated that the governors of the western provinces did not have fixed salaries (ρογα) from the imperial treasury, although the governors of the eastern provinces, which were far more important to the government in Constantinople, did. 'The *strategoi* of the west do not receive *roga* since each of them levies customary dues from his own province.'[62] The exaction of such taxes might, however, prove decidedly unpopular, particularly if there were sudden

---

61 *Codice diplomatico barese* iv *Le Pergamene di S. Nicola di Bari, periodo greco (939–1071)*, ed.
    F. Nitti de Vito (Bari 1900), 5–6 no. 2. Cf. Martin, *Pouille*, pp. 515–18.
62 *De Ceremoniis*, II.50, p. 697; Gay, *L'Italie méridionale*, p. 402.

demands for extra money, whatever the reason, or if the governor were seeking to exploit his greater independence from the centralised imperial fiscal system by profiting unduly from his office. After the death of the *strategos* of *Langobardia*, Ursoleon, in 921 the government at Constantinople, faced with a very difficult situation in southern Italy, was at some pains to conciliate the local population, more or less admitting that Ursoleon's misgovernment may have contributed to his fate, or at least (since he was actually killed fighting the prince of Capua–Benevento) to the unpopularity of his regime.[63] But such difficulties were by no means confined to the Lombard population of Apulia, nor were they necessarily the result of malgovernment by officials. John Muzalon, the *strategos* of Calabria, where the population was very largely Greek, was assassinated near Reggio only a few months after Ursoleon's death, apparently because of resentment caused by his attempts to raise the tribute needed to maintain the truce then in force with the Arabs of Sicily.[64]

That the exactions of the Byzantine regime might prove just as unpopular with the Greeks of southern Italy as with Lombards under imperial rule is also shown by a local revolt at Rossano in Calabria *c.* 965. This was caused by the attempts of the then governor, Nikephoros Hexakionites, to build a fleet. 'He planned to build those ships called *chelandia* from each of the towns of Calabria, through which not only would those cities be safe from the incursions of the enemy but Sicily, close by and the enemy (there) would be attacked.' (This either implies that the failure of the 964 expedition had not deterred the Byzantines from designs of reconquering Sicily, or alternatively should be interpreted that they intended to replace the considerable naval losses suffered during that campaign.) However, the inhabitants of Rossano so resented the demands placed upon them that they burned the ships and attacked the ships' captains, and then, fearful of the reprisals that the authorities might take, sought the mediation of a prominent and respected local holy man, St Nilos, to protect them from the governor's wrath.[65] A contemporary description of these *chelandia*, which confirms that their construction was set on foot during the reign of Nikephoros II, said that they were 'ships of wonderful length and speed, holding two banks of oars on each side and 150 sailors', and equipped with Greek

63   *Letters of Nicholas Mysticus*, pp. 343–7 nos 83 (to the archbishop of Otranto) and 85 (to the people of *Langobardia*).
64   George Cedrenus, *Historiarum Compendium*, ed. I. Bekker (2 vols, Bonn 1838–9), ii.355; Gay, *L'Italie méridionale*, pp. 202–3. His unpopularity was also attested by a confused anecdote in the Life of St Elias the Speleote, *c.* 8, *Acta SS Sept.* iii (1868), 870.
65   *Vita S. Nili Iunioris*, *c.* 9, *MPG* cxx.105–7. For the 964 campaign, Gay, *L'Italie méridionale*, pp. 290–1.

fire.[66] But the expense and labour of constructing and manning them must have been considerable, and hence the evident unpopularity of the measure.

These locally built ships may not have been very numerous – Thietmar of Merseburg thought that only two were demanded from Calabria 'as tribute' (surely an underestimate, or did he mean that two were built every year?). None the less, the possession of a fleet, and of course the Byzantine navy was much more extensive than just whatever ships were built locally, was of the utmost importance, even if on occasion, as when Bari was besieged in 1003, the imperial government was forced to look elsewhere for additional naval help. Above all it permitted, when other commitments allowed, the reinforcement of the locally raised forces in Italy, many of whom may have been light troops, *conterati*, by elite soldiers from the imperial guards regiments at Constantinople (the ταγματα) or men from the Asia Minor provinces whose troops were hardened by regular fighting on the empire's eastern frontier. The 400 Russians who accompanied the cavalry troops who came to Italy in 934 almost certainly came from the elite Varangian Guard, as did some of the troops who helped Basil Boiannes defeat the 1017–18 revolt. Both for the expedition which recaptured Taranto in 880 and in that sent to Naples in 956 troops were sent from the Thrakesion and Makedonion themes of Asia Minor.[67] However, it must once again be stressed that the availability of such reinforcements was dependent upon the situation on the empire's other frontiers being sufficiently stable to permit their absence.

In addition the principal towns of Byzantine Italy were strongly fortified. The defences of Taranto were rebuilt after the Byzantines recovered the town in the 880s, and once again between 965 and 969.[68] Though the town was captured and sacked by a Muslim force in 977, this was because the inhabitants fled and left it undefended, and it was strong enough successfully to resist a two-month siege by the army of Otto II in the spring of 982.[69]

---

66 *Die Chronik von Bischofs Thietmar*, III.23, p. 127. On the *chelandion* and other types of galley cf. J. Pryor, *Geography, Technology and War. Studies in the Maritime History of the Mediterranean 649–1571* (Cambridge 1988), pp. 57–63.

67 *Conterati*: Lupus Protospatharius, *Annales*, ad. an. 1040, *MGH SS* v.58. Russians: *De Ceremoniis*, II.44, p. 660; Adhemar of Chabannes, *Chronicon sive Historiae Francorum*, ed. J. Chavanon (Paris 1897), p. 178. For the 880 expedition, Gay, *L'Italie méridionale*, pp. 112–13, though his estimates of troop numbers need to be divided by at least half. 956: Theophanes Continuatus, *Chronographia*, pp. 453–4.

68 A. Jacob, 'La reconstruction de Tarante par les Byzantins aux IXe et Xe siècles. A propos de deux inscriptions perdues', *QFIAB* lxviii (1988), 1–19, especially 14–17.

69 Though *Die Chronik von Bischofs Thietmar*, p. 122, said that Taranto was taken after a short time, this is contradicted by the charter evidence. *MGH Diplomatum* ii.315–16 no. 272 (16 March 982), 'actum iusta civitatem Tarantum'; *ibid.* 318–20 nos 274–5 (18 May), 'actum foras muros Tarenti civitatis', 'actum iuxta Tarantum foras muros'.

Bari was able to resist the Muslims for five months in 1003 before being relieved. When Basil Mesardonites recovered that city from the rebels in 1011 he immediately set to work to build a citadel within the town (or at the very least substantially to strengthen an existing fortress; the inscription which records his work may suggest the latter, but we have no reference to this *praitorion* before that date).[70] And it should be noted that one of the obligations to the state to which the inhabitants of the Byzantine lands in Italy, even the clergy, were subject, and from which exemption was very rarely given, was the repair of the fortifications of their towns.[71] In Calabria a number of towns were established in, or transferred to, more easily defensible locations, generally on mountainous sites, during the later tenth and early eleventh centuries, and often provided with citadels. The local chronicle which attributed this initiative to the Emperor Nikephoros Phokas said that he ordered 'that the governor rebuild all the towns of Calabria not in the coastal regions, but he move them and their dignities to the most safe places, and restore to each of them their own boundaries'.[72] But in fact this process was a lengthy one and continued long after the 960s, as will be discussed later.

The Byzantines were also concerned to ensure that the Church in its south Italian provinces remained loyal to Constantinople. Obviously this was not a problem in those areas where the clergy and congregations were Greek. But in most of Apulia and parts of Lucania and northern Calabria the population was wholly or partly Lombard, and the liturgical and cultural language of the Church remained Latin. There was thus always a danger that churchmen and their flocks would look to Rome rather than Constantinople, particularly since the papacy had never been fully reconciled to the enforced subordination of the south Italian churches in the areas under Byzantine rule to the patriarch of Constantinople during the Iconoclast dispute of the eighth century.[73] After the imperial coronation of Otto I in 962, with the papacy little more than a client of the German emperor and the latter closely allied with the prince of Capua–Benevento, this became more than just a potential problem. In 966 Pope John XIII fled from the hostile Roman nobility into temporary exile in Capua. There he raised the town's see to be a metropolitan archbishopric, with its own

---

70 Guillou, 'Un document sur le gouvernement de la province', especially pp. 4–5, 12; *Anonymi Barensis Chronicon*, ad. an. 1011, *RIS* v.148. But the first charter reference does not come until as late as 1033, *Cod. Dipl. Barese*, iv.43–6 no. 21.
71 Prologo, *Le Carte di Trani*, pp. 37–8 no. 8 (999); A. Guillou, 'Notes sur la société dans le katépanat d'Italie au XIe siècle', *MEFR* lxxviii (1966), 461.
72 Caspar, 'Die Chronik von Tres Tabernae', pp. 35–6 [above, note 27].
73 For which see J. Herrin, *The Formation of Christendom* (Oxford 1987), pp. 349–52, and E. Pontieri, *Tra i Normanni nell'Italia meridionale* (2nd edn, Naples 1964), pp. 3–26.

province of subordinate bishops. This was not an overtly anti-Byzantine measure. Rather it marked the recognition of Capua as Prince Pandulf Ironhead's *de facto* capital and centre of government and was an attempt to consolidate his authority over his principality – the first archbishop was the prince's younger brother, John. But two years later, just at the time when Otto and Pandulf were attacking Byzantine Apulia, Pope John created a second archbishopric at Benevento, and this initiative was aimed much more directly against Byzantine interests, for the new archiepiscopal province stretched deep into Byzantine territory in northern Apulia and among the suffragan sees which were now made subject to the new archbishop were those in key strategic places such as the border fortresses of Ascoli and Bovino. The creation of the archbishopric of Benevento was therefore part of an attempt to destabilise the loyalty of Lombard Apulia. It ushered in a period of intense ecclesiastical competition between Rome and Constantinople within southern Italy. New archbishoprics, some with dependent provinces but most (to begin with) autocephalous, were created in the areas of Byzantine jurisdiction: Otranto (969), which became the metropolitan of a province comprising four Latin sees and one Greek in southern Apulia and Lucania, Taranto (978) and Trani (987). (The see of Bari had apparently already been raised to archiepiscopal rank before the papal initiatives, and this was anyway normal Byzantine practice for a town which was the headquarters of a theme.) The process continued into the eleventh century, with new archbishoprics at Lucera (1005), Oria/Brindisi (*c.* 1007) and Siponto (1023).[74] Similarly new bishoprics were created to provide suffragans for these archbishops, as at Tursi (*c.* 969), Polignano (before 992) and, much later, Monopoli (1033).[75] Meanwhile the papacy moved to promote the see of Salerno to archiepiscopal rank (probably in the summer of 983). While the new archbishopric had only a single suffragan see (Paestum) within the principality of Salerno itself, a number of bishoprics in Lucania and northern Calabria, in areas once part of the principality (before 850) but now actually under Byzantine authority, were declared to be subject to it. In practice this remained a dead letter, both for political reasons and because of the northward shift of the Greek population in Calabria. At least one of the sees which the papacy wanted to subordinate to Salerno, Malvito, had probably already been converted to the Greek rite, and the Byzantines

---

74 von Falkenhausen, *Untersuchungen*, pp. 148–55; Cilento, *Italia meridionale longobarda*, pp. 184–207; C.G. Mor, 'La Lotta fra la chiesa greca e la chiesa latina in Puglia nel secolo X', *Archivio storico pugliese* iv (1951), 58–64 (though his suggestion that some sees had for a time rival Greek and Latin incumbents appears unlikely).
75 Polignano: *Cod. dipl. pugliese*, xx.54–6 no. 25. Monopoli: *Codice diplomatico brindisiano* i, ed. G.M. Monti (Trani 1940), 6–7 no. 3.

reacted to this papal action with further ecclesiastical changes of their own, including the promotion of one of Salerno's theoretical suffragans, Cosenza, to be an archbishopric.[76]

The intention behind such changes to the ecclesiastical structure in the Byzantine zone was to safeguard the independence of the Latin clergy from Roman jurisdiction (and hence Ottonian influence), and to ensure their loyalty to imperial rule. But the policy was not as such anti-Latin: given that most of the population of Apulia, part of that in Lucania and a minority in northern Calabria were Lombards (and therefore Latin Christians) this would have been counter-productive. The claim made by the Ottonian ambassador to Byzantium in 968, Liutprand of Cremona, that Nikephoros Phokas and the Patriarch of Constantinople Polyeucht wished to forbid the Latin rite in southern Italy was ludicrous, and on a par with some of Liutprand's other dishonest and propagandist assertions.[77] Though demographic shifts were causing a degree of Hellenisation in northern Calabria during the tenth century and this led to changes in one or two Calabrian bishoprics, Apulian sees with Latin bishops and cathedral staffed by Latin clergy remained Latin, even if, as in the case of Taranto, much of the local population and most of the local clergy were Greek.[78] What the Byzantine authorities were trying to do was to bind the Latin churches more closely to imperial rule, and the churches in Apulia in particular were closely supervised by those authorities. The choice of archbishops and bishops was vetted by the government: on at least one occasion, at Bari in 1035, a newly elected archbishop was sent into exile at Constantinople and replaced by another candidate more acceptable to the authorities. Furthermore, Byzantine officials acted as the advocates (legal representatives) of churches, and the jurisdictional rights of prelates over their clergy remained strictly controlled. So too did exemptions from taxation, which while occasionally conceded were limited and specific in their application (not least to safeguard the fiscal base of the regime). Loyalty was, however, rewarded: a privilege from the Catepan extending the jurisdiction of the see of Trani in 983 was in recompense for the bishop's loyalty during the recent siege of the town.[79]

76 Taviani-Carozzi, *Principauté lombarde de Salerne*, ii.672–4. The papal bull confirming the new archbishopric of Salerno in 989 is clearly retrospective, but the promotion must have occurred after June 983 when the see was still only a bishopric, *Cod. Dipl. Cavensis*, ii.188–9 no. 355.

77 Liutprand, *Legatio*, c. 62, *Die Werke Liudprands von Cremona*, ed. J. Becker (3rd edn, *MGH SRG*, 1915), p. 209.

78 von Falkenhausen, 'Taranto in epoca bizantina', pp. 149–56.

79 Prologo, *Carte di Trani*, pp. 32–5 no. 7. For fiscal exemption, see above, note 71; von Falkenhausen, *Untersuchungen*, pp. 155–7. For the archbishop, *Annales Barenses*, ad. an. 1035, *MGH SS* v.54.

These policies seem to have worked – certainly the Latin bishops of Troia and Acerenza were to be killed fighting for Byzantium and against the Normans in 1041.[80]

If we are to believe Liutprand of Cremona, the Emperor Nikephoros II claimed in 968 that the Lombard princes of Capua–Benevento and Salerno were no more than his slaves.[81] Clearly we cannot take this assertion, in a text designed to traduce and belittle the Greek emperor, too literally, even if the latter may have used a term such as δουλοι in the heat of anger. Though the Byzantines would undoubtedly have liked the Lombard princes to obey their authority, in practice the latter were independent rulers, and Byzantine overlordship was only acknowledged on rare occasions when imperial power was more than usually strong or the princes required imperial assistance. There were certainly diplomatic contacts: Guaimar I of Salerno visited Constantinople in 887 and was granted the court title of *patrikios*, while the count of Capua (as he then was) sent an envoy in the following year. Landulf I of Capua went there seeking military assistance in 910 and was made a *patrikios*, and one of his sons was apparently resident there as an (ineffectual) guarantee of his good behaviour in 921. Guaimar II of Salerno was also given the title of *patrikios*, probably about the same time as Landulf.[82] But such diplomatic contacts and favours had no more than a very short-term effect. The regnal years of the Byzantine emperors were used only sporadically in princely documents, in the early years of the tenth century up to 920, and occasionally at Benevento (but not Capua) for a few years after 935. Thereafter signs of submission were conspicuous by their absence, except for two occasions in Salerno, during the expedition of the *strategos* Marianos Argyros to the west coast in 956 and when the Catepan Basil Mesardonites visited the city in the autumn of 1011.[83] Where the link with Byzantium was important was in the coastal duchies, which sought imperial protection as a counterweight to the Lombard princes who threatened their independence. The regnal years of the Byzantine emperors continued to be used in documents at Naples right through into the eleventh century, and the rulers of Amalfi received Byzantine court titles on a fairly regular basis after 907. Duke Manso I proclaimed his rank of *patrikios* on his seal after 966. (As a usurper seeking to found a new ruling dynasty there

80 *Annales Barenses*, MGH SS v.55.
81 *Legatio*, cc. 15, 27, pp. 184, 189.
82 Erchempert, *Historia*, cc. 67, 80, pp. 260, 264; *Chron. Cas.* I.52, p. 133. For use of their titles by the princes of Salerno, *Cod. Dipl. Cavensis*, i.139–40 no. 111 (899), 170–2 no. 133 (917).
83 For 1011, T. Leccisotti, *Le Colonie cassinesi in Capitanata* I *Lesina* (Miscellanea Cassinese 13, 1937), pp. 68–9 no. 21 (also published by Trinchera, *Syllabus*, p. 14 no. 14).

were good domestic reasons for stressing this prestigious connection.) Only at Gaeta did the Byzantine connection seem to decline as the tenth century wore on, and though Gaeta retained close political and familial links with Naples the use of imperial regnal years in its documents was abandoned after 934.[84] But after the elimination of the Saracen base on the River Garigliano in 915 the Lombard princes had no further need of Byzantine assistance, and sought rather to take advantage of imperial problems to extend their power into Apulia, albeit with virtually no long-term success.

The Lombard principalities were undoubtedly much more stable in the tenth century than they had been in the ninth. The union of Capua and Benevento for much of the century, and the close family relationship between the princes even after the two principalities split away from each other in 981, undoubtedly made a major contribution to this stability. Dynastic continuity was ensured by the nomination of sons as co-rulers in their fathers' lifetimes; indeed Gisulf I of Salerno was made co-prince with his father at the tender age of three.[85] This practice of associating sons with their fathers' rule was also followed in the duchies of Naples and Amalfi. There was, however, a significant contrast between Capua–Benevento and Salerno in the tenth century. While in the latter principality the personal property of the princely family was held in common between brothers, the princely title was passed down on a system of strict primogeniture and never shared between brothers. In Capua–Benevento, for a considerable period anyway, it was. Landulf I and his younger brother Atenulf II appear to have ruled together from their father's death in 910 until Atenulf's death in 940, not as separate princes of Capua and Benevento but as joint rulers of both principalities.[86] Similarly Pandulf Ironhead and his younger brother Landulf III were recorded by a strictly contemporary source as ruling both principalities *bifarie* in the 960s.[87] Since Landulf I associated both his sons with his rule, there was even a brief period in 939/40 when there were no less than four princes ruling jointly – father, uncle and two sons – though this was exceptional. After 943, when Atenulf III was exiled, according to the Salerno chronicle 'for his cruelty' but perhaps also as a consequence of fraternal rivalry, there were never more than two princes at the same time,

---

84 Skinner, *Family Power*, pp. 99–101; U. Schwarz, *Amalfi im frühen Mittelalter (9–11. Jahrhundert)* (Tübingen 1978), pp. 31–5, 37.
85 *Chron. Salernitanum*, c. 159, p. 166.
86 *Chron. Cas.* I.52, pp. 133–5; R. Poupardin, *Les Institutions politiques et administratives des principautés lombards de l'Italie méridionale (IXe–XIe siècles)* (Paris 1907), pp. 92–7, 144–5.
87 *Chron. Salernitanum*, c. 166, p. 170. Cf. *Chron. Vult.* ii.158 (965), 162 (967).

either brothers or after 969 only father and son. Pandulf Ironhead associated only his eldest son with him as co-ruler, and that only after his brother's death in the winter of 968/9.[88] After that date therefore the practice of designating only the eldest son as co-prince and successor was the same in both (or after 981 all three) principalities, except for a very brief period 1008–14 when the two principalities of Capua and Benevento were once again briefly united, under the rule of cousins.

But by the last years of the tenth century the character and effectiveness of princely rule were very different in Salerno from those in Capua and Benevento. Princely power remained a reality in Salerno, effective throughout the principality, until well into the eleventh century. The princely palace in Salerno remained as the focus for political and legal activity within the principality, justice was a princely monopoly, and legal cases which had first been heard before princely officials in outlying parts of the principality were often concluded in the palace itself.[89] Cases involving Amalfitans holding property within the principality were also heard in the princely palace, even though both plaintiff and defendant might still actually be resident in the duchy.[90] The Church within the principality was kept firmly under princely control: the only two episcopal sees in the principality, those of Salerno and Paestum, and a number of other important churches and monasteries throughout the region remained under the *mundium* or legal protection and control of the prince (just as women were in Lombard law under the *mundium* of their husbands or other male relations); in effect therefore as private princely churches. Any privileges granted to churches were strictly limited in extent, and never included the alienation of judicial rights. The choice of bishops (and after 983 archbishops) remained in the hands of the prince.[91] The city of Salerno was a real capital and focus for the principality: princely relatives and the aristocracy generally continued to reside there, and most of the other main centres of habitation were no great distance away. Economically and socially the city of Salerno played a greater role in its principality than Benevento and Capua did in theirs: not least because of its greater size – something which, if it cannot be measured exactly, can be seen reflected in the twenty-nine notaries, all of them

88 *Chron. Salernitanum*, cc. 159, 169–70, pp. 167, 173. Similarly John II of Salerno associated his younger son Guaimar with him as prince only after the death of his eldest son Guido in 988.
89 Taviani-Carozzi, *Principauté lombarde de Salerne*, pp. 572–6; and her general remarks on the princes, *ibid.*, pp. 441–4, 616.
90 E.g. *Cod. Dipl. Cavensis*, ii.61–2 no. 259 (969), 79–80 no. 274 (973).
91 Taviani-Carozzi, *Principauté lombarde de Salerne*, pp. 611–76; especially pp. 614–21, 662–4, 674. The archbishop's role as a litigant in the princely palace like any other is well illustrated by *Cod. Dipl. Cavensis*, ii.117–19 no. 302 (978).

laymen, who were active there during the last twenty years of the tenth century.[92] Above all, territorial lordships did not develop in the principality of Salerno until some time after the arrival of the Normans. Admittedly it has been suggested that there is evidence for a count at the frontier town of Nocera in 947. Nocera was an obvious strategic point when the princes were at war with Capua–Benevento, as they were *c.* 950, and the town was certainly fortified in the early to mid-tenth century (a charter of 998 referred to the 'old *castellum*'). But no comital dynasty was ever established there. The *comitatus* of Nocera (a term which is found only towards the end of the century) was probably never more than a normal administrative district, and the count in 947 seems actually to have been a princely relative who held some property there, not the lord of the place.[93] A son of the exiled Atenulf III of Benevento was given a lordship at Conza on the eastern frontier of the principality by Gisulf I. But he did not have any comital title, and he soon fell out with the prince and was exiled to Naples, so his lordship had only the most ephemeral existence.[94] The title of count *was* used in the principality of Salerno, but only as a mark of personal status; it did not denote the semi-independent local territorial rule that it came to do in Benevento and Capua.

For by *c.* 1000 the government of these two – by now separate – principalities was markedly less effective than that of Salerno. Ironically it was during the very period when princely rule was seemingly at its apogee, after 950 and more especially during the reign of Pandulf Ironhead, that symptoms of future difficulty first became apparent. More charters survive from the twenty years of his rule than from the sixty years before he became the senior prince. Nearly all of them embodied gifts or concessions. Moreover while the ninth-century princes of Benevento, for all the problems that they faced (or perhaps because of them), were careful to limit the scope of their grants, avoiding alienations from the princely fisc and of regalian rights, giving out instead property newly acquired by judicial confiscation or through such rights as inheritance from men lacking heirs, their successors adopted a very different policy. Not only land but regalian and judicial rights were granted out, both to nobles and to churches. Thus in 964 Pandulf I and his brother granted the county of Isernia (in the hilly inland area north of the Monti di Matese which is now known as Molise) to their cousin Landulf

---

92 Taviani-Carozzi, *Principauté lombarde de Salerne*, pp. 541–2.
93 *Cod. Dipl. Cavensis*, i.224–5 no. 174, misinterpreted by C.G. Mor, *L'Età feudale* (2 vols, Milan 1952–3), ii.139–40. For the *castellum*, *Cod. Dipl. Cavensis*, iii.54 no. 495. See Taviani-Carozzi, *Principauté lombarde de Salerne*, pp. 492–6.
94 *Chron. Salernitanum*, cc. 161, 175, pp. 168, 178; *Cod. Dipl. Cavensis*, ii.62–3 no. 260 (July 969).

with an extensive immunity which effectively withdrew the area from their jurisdiction.[95]

A keystone of the policy of both Pandulf I and his father Landulf II was his alliance with the two great Benedictine abbeys in the north of the principality of Capua: St Benedict of Montecassino and St Vincent on Volturno. These monasteries had been sacked by the Muslims in the 880s and both communities had remained in exile for long periods before returning to the mother-house. The monks of St Vincent had remained at Capua until 914, those of Montecassino had taken refuge first at Teano and then at Capua, and had only gone back to their original monastery in 950. During the intervening period neighbouring aristocrats had made significant inroads into the monastery's block of lands in the Liri Valley plain to the south and east of Monte Cassino itself, the *Terra Sancti Benedicti*. However, after 950 the support of the princes enabled Abbot Aligern (949–86) to regain the alienated property, coercing the gastalds of Aquino and counts of Teano into surrendering their ill-gotten gains and holding a series of land pleas in 960 and 963 to recover Montecassino property in a variety of other places in the north of the principality.[96] Similarly Landulf II vindicated Volturno's claims to its property against the counts of Venafro in 954, and Pandulf I gave it a substantial donation of land belonging to the princely family in the Capuan plain in 964.[97] The princes intended the two abbeys to be foci of support and counterweights to the power of the nobles in the north of the principality, and hence Landulf's decisive action when Abbot Aligern of Montecassino was kidnapped by the gastald of Aquino, forcing the latter to a humiliating public display of submission. But the very fact that Atenulf of Aquino's first reaction to princely pressure had been to rebel rather than submit showed the need to create powerful allies for princely authority in this northern area.[98] Not only did the princes confirm existing fiscal immunities, but in 967 Pandulf granted both monasteries the right to erect fortifications on their lands, thus sanctioning within these extensive blocks of property the beginnings of that process known to modern-day historians as *incastellamento*: the grouping together of peasants in fortified villages, which served both as a means of defence and to facilitate the effective economic

95 Poupardin, *Institutions*, pp. 105–6 no. 112.
96 *Chron. Cas.* I.1–2, pp. 166–71; *I Placiti cassinesi del secolo X con periodi in volgare*, ed. M. Inguanez (4th edn, Miscellanea Cassinese 24, 1942).
97 *Chron. Vult.* ii.64–8, 216–33.
98 *Chron. Cas.* II.2, pp. 168–9. Atenulf of Aquino had added injury to insult by exhibiting the captive abbot in the main square at Aquino dressed up in a bear-skin, and then setting dogs on him.

exploitation of the land by allowing the landowner more easily to impose and collect rents and exact services.[99]

One should not exaggerate the extent of the initial *incastellamento* on the monastery lands – it was to be far more extensive in the mid-eleventh century than earlier – and Pandulf's charter of 967 mentioned only three sites by name, one of which (Rocca Janula) was a fortress pure and simple, defending the road up to the monastery itself. But what was significant was that the prince was sanctioning and encouraging his ecclesiastical allies to participate in a process that was already under way elsewhere in his dominions, and which was in the long term seriously to undermine princely authority. *Castella* became the focal points for nascent territorial lordships, where aristocratic dynasties became established and engrossed for themselves judicial and fiscal rights that had hitherto been the prerogative of the prince. By the later tenth century the princes were themselves sanctioning such a process, as with Pandulf Ironhead's cession of Isernia to his cousin in 964. The process continued after the split of the two principalities of Capua and Benevento in 981; indeed it appears to have been particularly marked in the principality of Benevento, where Pandulf II conceded his regalian rights over Greci in 988 and Trivento in 992 to local counts.[100] Whether such concessions were actually giving away princely rights, or merely recognising alienations which had already taken place, is by no means clear. But their effect was to devolve much of the prince's authority on local nobles, and undermine the unity of the principality.

A further symptom of this was the emergence and proliferation of comital dynasties. The comital title had begun as a personal title, signifying membership of the princely kin. It evolved into a territorial designation. But the tenth-century counts in the principalities of Capua and Benevento did not merely replace the gastalds as local representatives of the prince. The change of title implied a change in function, with the increasing privatisation of authority in the hands of hereditary dynasties of local nobles. Gastalds exercised delegated princely authority; counts exercised their own power. The early counts were indeed almost all princely relatives. Two of Landulf III's sons became counts at S. Agata and Larino in the eastern part of the principality of Benevento. The early tenth-century counts of Teano in the

---

99   L. Tosti, *Storia della badia di Montecassino* (3 vols, Naples 1843), i.226–8; *Chron. Vult.* ii.162–4. The peculiarities of south Italian terminology should be noted here: a *castrum/castellum*, used interchangeably, usually denoted a fortified village or small town (as opposed to *casalis/villa* for an open settlement), although *castellum* might also be used, as by Geoffrey Malaterra, to describe an urban citadel. But a castle in the north European sense was usually called a *rocca*, as with Rocca Janula.

100 Poupardin, *Institutions*, pp. 117–18 nos 140–1.

principality of Capua descended from a younger son of Atenulf I. They were replaced by a son of Pandulf Ironhead, and when he became prince in 993 his younger brother took over the county of Teano. But this process of the entrenchment of princely relatives in the localities did not therefore signify any enhancement of princely power – rather the reverse, particularly after a generation or two had elapsed. This was especially the case because the Carolingian practice of vassalage had never become established in the south. Links between prince and aristocracy remained essentially personal, not in any sense institutional. Furthermore, local authority became increasingly fragmented. There were by the later tenth century far more counts in the two principalities than there had been gastalds in the ninth century. Partible inheritance led to the fragmentation of existing counties. Thus one branch of the family of the counts of Teano remained as counts there, but in the eleventh century, other descendants of the same family became counts of Venafro and Presenzano, *castella* in the upper Volturno valley a few kilometres to the east of Teano. New counties were also set up in the northern and eastern parts of the principality of Benevento, sometimes as we have seen with express princely sanction, as at Greci and Trivento, though the *castella* that were the bases of these new counts were never quite as numerous in these more mountainous and thinly settled regions as they were in the more low-lying and fertile areas.[101]

Thus by the year 1000 there was a clear contrast between the principalities of Benevento and Capua, where the princes exercised an increasingly tenuous control of their principal nobles, and that of Salerno, where authority was still retained in the hands of the prince. Hence, while there was in Salerno an hereditary dynasty of princely treasurers, descended from a younger brother of Guaimar I, this lineage never enjoyed any territorial lordship. But in Benevento by the end of the tenth century even the prince's authority over the Church was being eroded. Certainly in August 980 a legal case involving a dispute between the monastery of St Vincent on Volturno and two laymen was heard before the archbishop of Benevento, where in Salerno such matters would have been reserved to the prince.[102]

---

101   J.-M. Martin, 'Eléments préféodaux dans les principautés de Bénévent et de Capoue (fin du VIIIe siècle–début du XIe siècle): modalités de privatisation du pouvoir', *Structures féodales et féodalisme dans l'Occident méditerranean (Xe–XIIIe siècles)* (Rome 1980), pp. 553–86, especially pp. 571–80; H. Taviani-Carozzi, 'Pouvoir et solidarités dans la principauté de Salerne à la fin du Xe siècle', in the same volume, pp. 587–606. There is a useful chart of the Lombard counties in Capua and Benevento in Mor, *L'Età feudale*, ii.185.

102   *Chron. Vult.* ii.186–90; H. Taviani-Carozzi, 'Caractères originaux des institutions politiques et administratives dans les principautés lombardes de l'Italie méridionale au Xe siècle', *Settimane di studio del centro italiano di studi sull'alto medioevo* xxxviii *Il Secolo di ferro: mito e realtà del secolo X* (1991) 273–326, at pp. 299, 312, 323.

Admittedly this case confirmed an earlier princely judgment about the same property. But after 980 the lands of St Vincent, and the Molise region as a whole, became entirely divorced from princely jurisdiction, and princely diplomas for this monastery ceased.

This tendency towards fragmentation even manifested itself in the little duchy of Gaeta. Towards the end of the tenth century castral foundations multiplied in its hinterland and cadet branches of the ducal house became established as counts at Fondi, Traetto and Sujo, which became increasingly independent of ducal authority, particularly after 1012 when the duke was a minor.[103] If the duchies of Naples and Amalfi seem to have escaped this process, this reflected both the limited extent of their territory (or in Amalfi's case of the territory that was actually cultivatable) and their relatively em- battled position in the face of their more powerful neighbours, which placed a premium on ducal leadership.

In terms of dynastic succession the southern principalities and the coastal duchies displayed relative stability after 900. The descendants of Atenulf I remained as princes of Capua and Benevento until the Norman take-over of Capua in 1058 and the death without direct heir of the last prince of Benevento in 1077. If there were succession problems at Salerno in the decade after 973 this was because of Gisulf I's childlessness, and John the Spoletan successfully entrenched his new ruling dynasty after 983. The descendants of Docibilis I ruled Gaeta from 867 until 1032, and here too failure of heirs rather than revolution appears to have ended the dynasty's rule. At Naples the same family ruled from 840 until 1137. Only in Amalfi, where Duke Mastalus II was murdered in 958, was there a change of dynasty through violent means, and even here the usurper's family con- tinued in power until long after the arrival of the Normans.[104] But after 981 the internal cohesion of two of the three Lombard principalities broke down. The principality of Capua was in disorder in the 990s, while in 1003 Pandulf II of Benevento was temporarily driven from his throne, and only restored after two years in exile.[105] But in addition to such obvious prob- lems there was a subtler threat to the established regime, in the haemorrhage of authority in those areas more distant from the princely capitals into the hands of aristocrats basing their rule around their *castella*. With this fragmentation of power the Lombard region became ripe for destabilisation, and early in the eleventh century the Normans arrived to do precisely that.

---

103 J.F. Guiraud, 'Le réseau de peuplement dans le duché de Gaète du Xe au XIIIe siècle', *MEFR* xciv (1982), 498–501; Skinner, *Family Power*, pp. 149–51.

104 Schwarz, *Amalfi im frühen Mittelalter*, pp. 36–7, who suggests that the murdered prince may have been a minor, thus facilitating the coup.

105 *Annales Beneventani*, ed. Bertolini, p. 129.

Society

Southern Italy in the early Middle Ages may have been politically divided: it was none the less wealthy, and by the early eleventh century its economy was growing and diversifying. Amatus of Montecassino wrote that when attempts were made to persuade the Normans to come to the region as mercenaries, they were told that 'they ought to come to the land which flowed with milk and honey and so many good things'.[106] The context of this story suggests that this description was intended particularly to refer to the principality of Salerno, but the relative stability of the tenth century, even if less marked after 980, meant that by 1000 southern Italy as a whole might be considered prosperous.

Such an opinion might seem paradoxical, not to say ironic, given the unenviable reputation which the *Mezzogiorno* has acquired in more recent times for poverty and backwardness, something which even the considerable efforts of successive Italian administrations since 1945 to boost the southern economy have not yet eradicated. Yet there are good reasons to suggest that in the early to central Middle Ages the south of the peninsula was just as, if not more, prosperous than the north. Parts of the south are, after all, extremely fertile, even if much of the interior is hill or relatively high plateau (300 m or more). The lowland parts of the Campania – the volcanic plain of Capua and the alluvial plain from Salerno southwards – had been one of the chief granaries of the Roman empire, praised for their fecundity by among many others Pliny the Elder.[107] The Apulian coastal plain around Bari with its *terra rossa*, already heavily settled by the tenth century, the Salento peninsula around Lecce, the south-western coast of Calabria running north from Reggio, and in Sicily the lower slopes of Mount Etna, the Catania plain and the Conca d'Oro round Palermo were other potentially rich agricultural areas. Water is certainly a problem, especially on the eastern side of the peninsula where the rainfall is lower than on the west and virtually entirely in the winter months. There are few rivers in Apulia – only the Ofanto in the north is of any real significance – and in Lucania even fairly major ones like the Bradano tend to flood in winter and dry up in the summer. But one should not exaggerate these difficulties given that the land supported a population much smaller than in the modern era. Certainly there are parts of the south with poor soil, particular problems of

---

106 *Amatus*, I.19, p. 24.
107 Pliny, *Natural History* v, ed. H. Rackham (London 1940), pp. 258–9. Cf. G. Rickman, *The Corn Supply of Ancient Rome* (Oxford 1980), p. 102.

water supply or retention and an unsuitable microclimate, and most of these were still thinly populated, even semi-deserted at the start of the Norman era: notably the Gargano peninsula, much of the hinterland of the Tavoliere of northern Apulia, the barren limestone Murge of inland south Apulia, and the swampy and malarial area at the mouth of the Bradano on the Apulian/Lucanian border. In the mountainous region of southern Lucania and northern Calabria probably only about 5 per cent of the land was ever cultivated.[108] But the population was growing during the tenth century, settlers were moving into hitherto deserted areas such as the Cilento region in the south of the principality of Salerno, and new settlements were being made in ones already populated, notably in the coastal belt north and south of Bari.[109] Nor were the problems of water supply that affected the drier areas insurmountable. On the edge of the Gargano massif and in southern Apulia around Conversano there were numerous cisterns in use, and already in the mid-tenth century there was a (admittedly isolated) reference to irrigation in this latter area. Aqueducts were also in use in Amalfi by the early eleventh century.[110] Islamic expertise in irrigation was undoubtedly of benefit in Sicily, although the geographer Ibn Hawkal, writing in 977, said that in the Palermo area only gardens were irrigated rather than fields as was the case elsewhere in the Islamic world. In the twelfth century another Arabic geographer, Edrisi, also remarked on the aqueducts and canals which brought water to these gardens. He noted too the many gardens and 'good and fruitful' countryside around Catania, and while he mentioned that there were many springs in this area, given that it usually has less rainfall than any other part of Sicily, this almost certainly implies irrigation as well.[111] Furthermore the still extensive tree cover of more mountainous regions such as the Abruzzi borderland, inland Lucania and the Sila and Aspromonte ranges in Calabria prevented winter rainstorms having the catastrophic erosive effect on the lower slopes that they have had in more recent times when such areas have been to a considerable extent deforested.

The wealth of southern Italy as early as the ninth century can be seen from the two great abbeys of the principality of Capua. Recent archaeological investigation has revealed that the early ninth-century monastery of

---

108 *Saint Nicolas de Donnoso*, ed. Guillou, p. 5.
109 Martin, *Pouille*, p. 261.
110 *Cod. dipl. pugliese* xx.84–8 no. 16 (963); *Codice diplomatico amalfitano*, ed. R. Filangieri di Candida (Naples 1917), pp. 48–9 no. 33 (1018). Martin, *Pouille*, pp. 68–87, provides an excellent discussion.
111 Amari, *BAS*, i.6, 16, 18. Edrisi noted that the River Amenano at Catania was sometimes full to overflowing but in other years dry.

St Vincent on Volturno (most of the building activity taking place between 808 and *c.* 830) was one of the largest in the medieval west, with perhaps as many as 300 monks. It was bigger therefore than all but one or two of the most prestigious monastic houses of the Carolingian world north of the Alps, as large as St Wandrille, bigger than Fulda, and appreciably bigger than St Gallen. The great size of this monastic complex and the high level of workmanship revealed there required a major economic infrastructure to have made it possible.[112] Montecassino may not at this period have been as large a community, or have had such an elaborate complex of buildings, but it was certainly extremely wealthy. In 842–3 Prince Siconulf of Salerno confiscated huge quantities of gold and silver, thousands of gold coins and a number of precious objects in gold and silver from the monastery, both to pay his Muslim mercenaries and to attempt to buy the friendship of the duke of Spoleto and the Carolingian king Louis II in the civil war against his rival Radelchis.[113]

The presence of such huge quantities of gold in southern Italy (some 23,800 ounces may have been involved in the transactions between the two rival princes and their potential allies in northern Italy in 843–4)[114] points to substantial trade with the Islamic world, even at this early date. Amalfi and Gaeta were the two principal ports for this trade, and their commercial contacts with Islamic Sicily and north Africa explain their reluctance to support military action against the Muslims who were attacking southern Italy.[115] Indeed it has been suggested, very plausibly, that it was his wealth derived from commerce which enabled Docibilis I to take over as ruler of Gaeta in 867. Certainly both his will of 906 and that of his grandson Docibilis II in 954 show that they possessed not just extensive lands within the duchy but also considerable movable wealth in gold, silver, silks and coinage.[116] But if Gaeta benefited from trade, the key entrepôt was probably Amalfi. Ibn Hawkal recorded that Amalfi was 'the richest city of southern Italy . . . the most affluent and the most opulent'. (Naples he regarded as less important, though he commented on the excellence of the textiles

---

112   *San Vincenzo al Volturno. The 1980–86 Excavations*, ed. R. Hodges (2 vols so far published, Archaeological Monographs of the British School of Rome 7 & 9, London 1993, 1995); see especially Hodges' essay 'San Vincenzo al Volturno and the plan of St Gall', *ibid.*, ii.153–75.

113   A.O. Citarella and H.M. Willard, *The Ninth-Century Treasure of Monte Cassino in the Context of Political and Economic Developments in South Italy* (Miscellanea Cassinese 50, 1983), especially pp. 88–9 for translated texts.

114   Citarella & Willard, *Ninth-Century Treasure*, pp. 72–3.

115   A.O. Citarella, 'The relations of Amalfi with the Arab world before the Crusades', *Speculum* xlii (1967), 299–312.

116   *Cod. Dipl. Caiet.* i.30, 87, nos 19 and 52; Skinner, *Family Power*, pp. 32–3, 66.

made there, especially linen. Charter evidence, however, suggests that Naples in the tenth century was already crowded and booming.)[117] Over a century later Guiscard's biographer described Amalfi as 'a wealthy and populous city, none richer in silver, gold and garments from innumerable places'.[118]

While Amalfitan merchants were undoubtedly active in trade with the Byzantine empire – there were a number of them at Constantinople in 944, and Liutprand knew of their purchase of high-quality silk cloths there[119] – the principal source of gold, which had to be imported for there were no mines anywhere in medieval Christendom, was Muslim Africa. That such imports were far from negligible is clear, for southern Italy was the only area in western Christendom between the seventh and the thirteenth centuries to possess a regularly minted gold coinage. Admittedly the sporadic minting of gold solidi at Benevento and Salerno ceased in the mid-ninth century, as one would have expected given the parlous state of those principalities at that strife-torn period, though Byzantine solidi continued to circulate in areas under imperial rule. But just over a century later the production of native gold coins commenced once more, and the nature of this was extremely significant. From the 960s coins known as tarì were minted, at Amalfi. These were imitations of Islamic quarter-dinar coins, modelled on those already being minted in Sicily (which sometimes themselves circulated on the mainland).[120] These tarì point conclusively to the importance of trade with the Islamic world during the tenth century, and from c. 1000 onwards they were also minted at Salerno, closely linked economically with Amalfi and where many Amalfitans were resident.[121] The spread of Amalfitans to other parts of the south (though it can be better documented in the Norman period than – Salerno apart – pre-1000) was integral to the city's trade, since the main commodities exported were agricultural, especially grain and timber, and neither Amalfi nor (probably) Gaeta was capable of producing a significant surplus from their restricted (and in Amalfi's case mountainous) hinterland.[122] Thus the Lombard

---

117 Amari, *BAS*, i.6–7 = R.S. Lopez and I. Raymond, *Medieval Trade in the Mediterranean World* (New York 1955), p. 54; P. Skinner, 'Urban communities in Naples, 900–1050', *PBSR* lxii (1994), 279–99, especially pp. 285–6.
118 *W. Apulia*, III, lines 475–9, p. 190.
119 *Legatio*, c. 55; cf. his *Antapodosis*, lib. V c. 21, *Die Werke Liudprands*, pp. 143, 205.
120 *Tarì cassimissimi*, i.e. of the caliph Abu'l Qasim (934–46) are mentioned in *Cod. Dipl. Cavensis*, i.246–7 no. 191 (July 956, from Nocera), 251–2 no. 195 (January 957, from Salerno).
121 L. Travaini, *La Monetazione nell'Italia normanna* (Rome 1995), pp. 19–22.
122 A.O. Citarella, 'The patterns in medieval trade. The commerce of Amalfi before the Crusades', *Journal of Economic History* xxviii (1968), 531–55.

principalities played a significant role in the coastal cities' trade with the Islamic world.

Furthermore, even at the height of the Muslim attacks in the ninth century there is evidence to suggest that not all contacts were hostile, not least because of the employment of Muslims as mercenaries. There must therefore have been some ability to communicate one with another, as indeed a couple of the anecdotes in the tenth-century Salerno chronicle suggest (and interestingly in a Salernitan, not an Amalfitan, context).[123] There may even have been some restricted Arabic settlement in Calabria. There were Muslims living at Reggio by the 1060s, and in the more than fifty documents after 1050 which survive from the bishopric of Oppido, about 40 km north of Reggio, some twenty of the personal names recorded (about 13 per cent of the total) are Arabic in origin, although these persons would appear to have been by then Christian.[124]

None the less, the Muslim impact on the mainland was for the most part profoundly negative, and the effects of the disorders of the ninth century and the continued, if sporadic, raids on Calabria in the tenth, were considerable and long-lasting. Thus while the monks of Volturno returned to their mother-house in 914, after thirty-three years of living in Capua, it was not until the beginning of the next century, under abbots John IV (998–1007) and Hilarion (1011–45), that any real attempt was made to reconstruct what was left of the great ninth-century monastic buildings after the sack of 881. Up to 998 the monks 'had dwelt at the church of the Saviour [one of the several smaller churches in the complex], where they had lived as best they could under difficult conditions'. Only then was the great basilica built by Abbot Joshua (791–817) repaired and put back into use.[125] In the wake of the sack the monks had clearly been desperately short of money and had leased many of their more outlying properties in return for cash downpayments. Subsequently they had lost control of probably the bulk of their lands in the Abruzzi, and deliberately abandoned what they had once held in northern Apulia, leasing (effectively in perpetuity, if not necessarily in theory) property such as the fisheries the abbey owned at Lesina. It was only after 950 that the monastery's economic base really began to recover,

123 *Chron. Salernitanum*, c. 110, pp. 122–3 (Prince Guaiferius encounters a Saracen while returning from the bath-house and on the latter's request gives him his hat); and c. 112, pp. 125–6 (a woman captive is about to be raped by a Muslim on the high altar of a church. She protests 'in his own tongue' – according to the chronicler (a monk, and of course male!) more about the sacrilege than the rape); Palmieri, 'Un esempio di mobilità etnica' [above, n. 5], pp. 602, 608–9.
124 *Amatus*, V.11, p. 234; *La Théotokos de Hagia Agathè (Oppido) (1050–1064/1065)*, ed. A. Guillou (Corpus des actes grecs d'Italie du sud et de Sicile 3, Vatican City 1972), pp. 29–30.
125 *Chron. Vult.* ii.342–3 (quote), iii.77–8.

and thereafter the monks' attention was concentrated on the land round the monastery on the Rocchetta plateau, the *Terra Sancti Vincenti* proper, and what could be salvaged or obtained anew in the Capuan plain.[126]

Similarly the monks of Montecassino had to reconstruct and redevelop the *Terra Sancti Benedicti* after their return to their mother-house in 950, and although they made sporadic attempts to vindicate their claims to properties once held in northern Apulia (Montecassino seems to have had closer links with the Byzantine authorities than Volturno) these do not seem to have been particularly effective.[127] But, as we have seen, princely support enabled Abbot Aligern to reclaim lands in the Liri plain alienated by the monastery's aristocratic neighbours during the monks' residence at Capua. Both Aligern and his contemporary Abbot Leo of Volturno (944–56), who had played a part in Aligern's election, imported settlers, mainly from the Abruzzi, to exploit their abbey lands. These newcomers were offered generous terms to encourage their settlement; on the Montecassino lands a render of one-seventh of grain and one-third of the wine harvest to the abbey was usual. Nevertheless the income secured was enough to permit Aligern to undertake significant rebuilding within the abbey precinct.[128] The beginnings of the *incastellamento* on these abbeys' property were just as much if not more to do with this economic redevelopment as they were with the needs of defence, though this aspect should not be over-emphasised since neither on the lands of Montecassino nor on those of Volturno were *castella* very numerous before the arrival of the Normans. Montecassino had no more than half a dozen *castella* before 1000, and the monks of St Vincent fortified villages only in the central part of their territory and along a little bit of its eastern border where they were in dispute with the counts of Isernia.[129]

Landowners in the principality of Salerno were also trying to develop the economic potential of their property in the second half of the tenth century, especially in the northern part of the principality around Salerno itself and Nocera, where a considerable number of *pastinatio* contracts survive from

---

126 C.J. Wickham, 'Monastic lands and monastic patrons', *San Vincenzo al Volturno*, ed. Hodges, ii.148–52. For Lesina, *Chron. Vult.* ii.183–5 (965).

127 G.A. Loud, 'Montecassino and Byzantium in the tenth and eleventh centuries', in *The Theotokos Evergetis and Eleventh-Century Monasticism*, ed. M. Mullet and A. Kirby (Belfast 1994), pp. 35–7, but cf. Martin, *Pouille*, pp. 659–60.

128 *Chron. Cas.* II.3, pp. 171–3. Cf. *Chron. Vult.* ii.61.

129 G.A. Loud, 'The Liri Valley in the Middle Ages', *Archaeological Survey in the Lower Liri Valley, Central Italy, under the Direction of Edith Mary Wightman*, ed. J.W. Hayes and I.P. Martini (British Archaeological Reports, International Series 595, Oxford 1994), pp. 55–7; C.J. Wickham, 'The *Terra* of San Vincenzo al Volturno in the 8th to 12th centuries: the historical framework', in *San Vincenzo al Volturno. The Archaeology, Art and Territory of an Early Medieval Monastery*, ed. R. Hodges (British Archaeological Reports, International Series 252, Oxford 1985), pp. 227–58, especially pp. 250–1.

THE AGE OF ROBERT GUISCARD

this period. These were leases to tenants with the obligation laid upon them to clear wasteland and plant crops, sometimes chestnut and fruit trees, and especially vines (with a delay of six to ten years before rent was due to allow these to become productive).[130] These contracts reveal therefore a country-side that, like the estates of the great abbeys in the north of the Capuan principality, was in the process of being developed, but was at a relatively early stage of that development, with landowners striving to encourage settlers and new cultivation. Interestingly the situation in the Salerno/Nocera region changed after about 1010; thereafter most leases were renewals rather than provision for fresh cultivation, suggesting that the region was begin-ning to be fully exploited.[131] However, *pastinatio* contracts were to play a significant role in developing cultivation in the Cilento region in the south of the principality in the first half of the eleventh century. In this more distant and less obviously attractive area (since it was much hillier) the pace of development was not surprisingly somewhat slower, although renewed colonisation had clearly begun in the tenth century.[132] Thus by 1000 the agrarian economy of the Lombard principalities was expanding. However, the fact that this development only gathered pace after 950 suggests quite how disruptive the troubles of the ninth century, and above all the *razzias* of Muslim raiders, had been.

Pressure from Islamic Sicily had a further significant effect on the south Italian mainland. The Islamisation of Sicily and the continuation of raids on Byzantine Calabria in the tenth century – there were at least a dozen major attacks, five in the first quarter of the century, and then after a rel-atively peaceful period five more in the last quarter – led to a considerable shift in the geography of population. Greeks from Sicily emigrated to Calabria, and the people of Calabria moved inland and northwards, and in turn spread into the hitherto underpopulated area of Lucania and even, to a limited extent, into the principality of Salerno.

The changing demographic balance of early medieval Calabria has engendered considerable scholarly debate. Epigraphic evidence, as well as the opinion of Procopius, suggests that in the late antique period Calabria was a largely Latin province.[133] By the tenth century the southern and central parts at least were more or less exclusively Greek. This may in part have

130   Taviani-Carozzi, *Principauté lombarde de Salerne*, pp. 414–19.
131   *Ibid.*, p. 415.
132   N. Acocella, 'Il Cilento dai longobardi ai normanni (secoli X e XI). Struttura amministrativa e agricola', in his *Salerno medioevale ed altri saggi* (Salerno 1971), especially pp. 409–41. One of the earliest *pastinatio* contracts in this region is *Cod. Dipl. Cavensis*, iii.17–18 no. 471 (994).
133   S. Borsari, *Il Monachesimo bizantino nella Sicilia e nell'Italia meridionale prenormanna* (1963), p. 16; Procopius, *History of the Wars*, ed. H.B. Dewing (Cambridge 1919), p. 154.

resulted from settlers from the mainland of the Byzantine empire, both refugees from the persecution of the Iconoclast era and planned settlement in the wake of the Byzantine *revanche* of the later ninth century: there was certainly some deliberate colonisation in the reign of Leo VI, although most of the exiguous evidence for this relates to southern Apulia. Other Greek settlers came from Sicily. How extensive this emigration was is problematic, for most of the evidence comes from saints' lives, and Christian monks, as all these saints were, may well have been under greater pressure from the Sicilian Muslims than ordinary laymen. Elias the Speleote (born *c.* 865), for example, left the island after his companion at his hermitage was killed by the Muslims.[134] On the other hand there is also evidence for toleration: Ibn Hawkal recorded that Christians were accustomed to visit the alleged tomb of the philosopher Aristotle in the main mosque of Palermo (a converted church) to pray for rain.[135] But whether or not there was any widespread persecution on the island, there was certainly the pressure, conscious or unconscious, of acculturation. Indeed a majority of the hitherto Christian population of Sicily probably did convert to Islam, even if a substantial Christian minority remained in the north-east.[136] However, some lay people as well as monks may have chosen to cross the Straits of Messina. Not surprisingly the evidence is fragmentary. There is, however, one late, but very interesting, charter from Salerno from 1068 which suggests that such emigration may have continued over a long period. This document was drawn up for a woman, now a nun, who was 'the daughter of Gisa the African and the widow of Basil the Sicilian goldsmith'. Her late husband was clearly a Greek from the island, and her father presumably a refugee from the Christian community in Tunisia which was still in existence in the eleventh century.[137]

Whether or not the immigration from Sicily into Calabria after the Arab conquest of the island was substantial must remain controversial. But it is abundantly clear that Muslim raids on Calabria played a significant part in the shifts of population that took place there. They led to changes in the

134 *Acta SS, Sept.* iii (11 September) 851; L.R. Ménager, 'La "Byzantination" religieuse de l'Italie méridionale (IXe–XIIe siècles) et la politique monastique des normands en Italie', *Revue d'Histoire Ecclésiastique* liii (1958), 747–74 (a most important discussion), at p. 763.
135 Amari, *BAS*, i.3.
136 Yâhût, in Amari, *BAS*, i.51: an early thirteenth-century account, but based on older sources now lost.
137 *Cod. Dipl. Cavensis*, ix.201–3 no. 67. Basil the Goldsmith's son Andrew made a donation to the Greek monastery of St Nicholas of Gallucanta (see below) in 1091, *Le Pergamene di S. Nicola di Gallucanta (secc. IX–XII)*, ed. P. Cherubini (Altavilla Silentina 1991), pp. 280–3 no. 111. For the Christians of north Africa, Gregory VII, *Reg.* I.22, p. 36 [English translation E. Emerton, *The Correspondence of Gregory VII* (Columbia 1932), pp. 16–17].

settlement pattern in southern Calabria, with the population moving from exposed coastal districts into more secure and easily defensible sites inland. This process may have begun in earnest with the official action in the reign of Nikephoros Phokas. But it certainly did not end there, nor were such movements always the consequences of deliberate planning by the Byzantine authorities. For example, in 976 the *kastron* of Sant' Agata, near Reggio, was surrendered by its inhabitants to a raid led by the emir Abu 'al Qasim. The inhabitants appear to have been allowed to leave unharmed, and they moved some 40–45 km to the north to the fertile Gioia plain. About 1044 they founded a new town of Oppido, on a fortified hill 342 m above sea level and over 200 m above the plain. The bishopric there was dedicated to their old patron, St Agatha.[138] (She was a Sicilian saint, so this may possibly suggest that the original settlement had been founded by émigrés from the island.) And at about the same time as Abu 'al Qasim's attack or maybe slightly earlier, a monk called Nicodemus took refuge from an Arab raid in the mountains to the east of Oppido, where he founded a new abbey on an almost inaccessible site over 700 m high, surrounded by woods. This monastery was still in existence when the Normans took over Calabria eighty years later.[139] Other monks fled further north, seeking both to avoid the Muslim danger and to find solitude for their monastic observances in a hitherto underpopulated region. Many of them moved into the Mercourion district on the border with Lucania, or into the neighbouring (and even further north) Latinianon. As its name implies, this latter region had once been part of the Latin/Lombard area – for much of the ninth century it had been within the principality of Salerno. But its absorption into the Greek area reflected not just Byzantine military pressure but the shifts in population that the attacks on southern Calabria had engendered. For the monks who moved into these areas were, whether they liked it or not, accompanied by numbers of other people. St Luke of Armento (d. 984) was born and became a monk in Sicily, moved first to Reggio and then to the Val di Sinni in the Latinianon. But after spending seven years there, he fled to escape back to solitude from the crowd of his would-be disciples.[140]

By the end of the tenth century the Greek population was in the majority in all except a few northerly parts of Calabria. But it is clear not just from the saints' lives but also from the charter evidence that this situation was the product of a displacement within the fairly recent past, and perhaps also of a degree of acculturation among the existing population. A quarter of

---

138 Ibn-al-Athir, Amari, *BAS*, i.110; *La Théotokos de Hagia Agathè*, ed. Guillou, pp. 17–23.

139 *Saint-Nicodème de Kellerana (1023/1024–1232)*, ed. A. Guillou (Corpus des actes grecs d'Italie du sud et de Sicile 2, Vatican City 1968), pp. 3, 8–10.

140 *Acta SS*, *Oct.* vi.339; Ménager, 'La "Byzantination" religieuse', pp. 767–8.

the place-names in the surviving eleventh-century documents from Oppido cathedral were of Latin origin, and 17 per cent of the personal names are Hellenised versions of Latin ones.[141] Hence even in this southern part of Calabria the Greek population were relative newcomers. Further north the evidence is more striking: in the Mercourion region only nine out of some fifty place-names identifiable in the documentation from this period are Greek; the remainder are in origin Latin names, albeit by then in Hellenised form. By the first half of the eleventh century the population of this region was overwhelmingly Greek, and within a few kilometres of the *kastron* of Mercourion there were no less than five Greek monasteries.[142] But the Latin origin of most of the place-names shows that this Greek population had arrived in the area at most three or four generations earlier.

Indeed so pronounced was this northwards demographic shift that quite a number of Greeks travelled further north into the Latin area proper. The Sicilian goldsmith mentioned in his daughter's charter of 1068 was by no means unique. Greek monks found new homes in the Lombard principalities, most famously St Nilos of Rossano, who left his native Calabria in the early 980s to escape both the Muslims and the pressures of his own fame and the hordes of would-be disciples which that engendered. His biographer claimed that 'he preferred to dwell among the Latins since he was unknown to them'.[143] He spent fifteen years at Valleluce, near Montecassino, before moving on once more, first to the duchy of Gaeta and then to Grottaferrata near Rome. But St Nilos was far from alone. There were several Greek monasteries in the vicinity of Salerno in the early eleventh century, one of which, St Nicholas de Gallucanta near Vietri, was still Greek when given to the Latin monastery of Cava in 1087. Another Greek monastery was founded at Pontecorvo, in the north of the principality of Capua in 999, and this also remained in the hands of Greek monks until shortly before it was given to Montecassino in 1075.[144] A few Greek monks also moved into southern Apulia, which was under Byzantine rule but the population of which was Lombard. The monastery of St Nicholas of Morbano, near Venosa, was founded in the later tenth century and this house was still inhabited by Greeks as late as 1267.[145] But this emigration was by no means confined to monks. Thus in 932 a younger son of Prince

141 *La Théotokos de Hagia Agathè*, ed. Guillou, pp. 29–31.
142 *St. Nicolas de Donnoso*, ed. Guillou, pp. 8–9.
143 *MPG* cxx.124.
144 S. Borsari, 'Monasteri bizantini nell'Italia meridionale longobarda (sec. X e XI)', *Archivio storico per le provincie napoletane* lxxi (1950–1), 1–16; Bloch, *Montecassino in the Middle Ages*, i.213–15.
145 H. Houben, *Die Abtei Venosa und das Mönchtum im normannisch-staufischen Süditalien* (Tübingen 1995), p. 193.

Guaimar I of Salerno leased a garden at Lauro in the south of the principality to a man 'who was a native of the land of the Greeks'.[146] In this case the man's name, Ursus, suggests that he was a Lombard who had moved north, but we need not assume that he was a refugee from Greek pressure. It is far more likely that he was an early participant in this general northwards shift, although if some Lombards were leaving northern Calabria this would have contributed to the Hellenisation of this area. But by the end of the tenth century a number of Greeks who were not monks had also settled in the principality. For example, the monks of the wealthy abbey of St Maximus, Salerno, leased land at Nocera to two Greek brothers, one of whom was a priest, in the year 1000, and a Latin abbot in Cilento leased land to 'Kallinus son of John the Greek' in 1008.[147] These Greek immigrants remained as a recognisable group into the Norman period. Thus 'Constantine son of Constantine, born of the Greek race', leased property at Avellino in 1063, and a Greek called Policarpus made a donation to St Nicholas de Gallucanta in 1069. Indeed the son of a Greek priest identified himself as such when he made his will at Avellino as late as 1113, although in his dispositions for his wife he specified that these should follow Lombard law.[148]

The presence of these Greeks seemingly playing a normal part in everyday life in the principality of Salerno suggests that, whatever the problems which the Byzantine authorities faced in Apulia, personal relations between Greeks and Lombards were amicable. Nor should we assume that the religious antagonism which was later to bedevil such relations was as yet present. Such changes as the conversion of the bishopric of Malvito to the Greek rite by c. 983 may in part have been occasioned by papal jurisdictional claims, but also were a natural consequence of the changing demographic composition of northern Calabria.[149] During the early 980s St Nilos had perfectly amicable discussions about differences of religious practice with the monks of Montecassino. But these talks were about matters of everyday observance; they were not the disputes over theological principle which were to embitter Graeco-Latin relations in later centuries. Indeed Abbot Aligern invited Nilos and his brethren to celebrate a Greek service in the abbey church at Montecassino, and Nilos responded by composing a hymn in honour of St Benedict.[150] There was as yet still one Church, not two separate ones. Hence a group of Amalfitans could establish their own

146   *Cod. Dipl. Cavensis*, i.194–5 no. 151.
147   *Cod. Dipl. Cavensis*, iii.98–9 no. 529; iv.122–3 no. 607.
148   *Codice diplomatico verginiano*, i.246–8 no. 63; ii.107–9 no. 125; *Pergamene di S. Nicola di Gallucanta*, pp. 238–41 no. 95.
149   *Italia Pontificia*, x.87.
150   *MPG* cxx.124–32; Loud, 'Montecassino and Byzantium', pp. 38–9.

Benedictine monastic house on Mount Athos in Greece in the early 990s, and a Latin prelate like the archbishop of Bari could co-operate with the Byzantine authorities by giving a church outside that city, built by the then Catepan, to two Greek monks in 1032.[151]

Southern Italy was therefore divided both politically and culturally. But we should not assume that it was the division between Latin and Greek that by itself made the region unstable. For all the border scuffles between the princes of Capua–Benevento and the Byzantines, the tenth century had been, at least up to *c.* 980, a time of stability and economic development. The region was by no means poor: and its position at the crossroads of the Mediterranean was economically advantageous. But after 981 weaknesses became apparent. Authority, and hence internal unity, within two of the three Lombard principalities declined, while a resurgence in Muslim attacks from Sicily placed strains upon the Byzantine provinces and also threatened the western coast of the southern peninsula. Byzantine Apulia became increasingly restive, and with the eastern empire locked in a climactic struggle with the neighbouring Bulgarian kingdom there were few resources to spare for southern Italy in the first years of the eleventh century. Similarly the German emperors, for all their claims to be the rulers of the whole of Italy, had never managed to enforce their authority south of Rome, save for those few brief years when Otto I had been allied with Pandulf Ironhead. The area was thus growing in prosperity, but something of a power vacuum existed in those first few years of the new millennium. There was potential for further disruption and thereby possibility for profit. Within a very few years the first Normans would arrive to exploit these very real opportunities, and exploit them to the hilt.

---

151 A. Pertusi, 'Monasteri e monaci italiani all'Athos nell'alto medioevo', *Le Millénaire du Mont Athos. Etudes et mélanges* (2 vols, Chevetogne 1963), i.222–5; *Cod. Dipl. Barese*, i.31–2 no. 18.

CHAPTER II

The coming of the Normans

First contacts

Quite how and when the Normans first came to southern Italy is obscure. That we cannot be sure of the circumstances in which their first contact with the area occurred is not because we lack information – far from it. But several different and seemingly contradictory traditions of their arrival emerged, to be preserved by the chroniclers of the Norman conquest when they wrote their histories between sixty and a hundred years after the event. Not surprisingly some scholars have tended to dismiss these later accounts as legends of little or no historical value.[1] None the less, it is possible to reconcile the various traditions, and to suggest a plausible (if ultimately unprovable) explanation for their arrival.

According to Amatus of Montecassino, whom it should be remembered was writing *c.* 1080–2, a group of forty Norman pilgrims were returning from the Holy Sepulchre in Jerusalem and had reached Salerno (by what route he does not make clear) 'before the year 1000'. The town was under attack by Muslims to whom it had formerly paid tribute. But because the tribute was no longer being paid, the Muslims had moved to attack the city, which was on the point of surrender. The pilgrims went to the prince, Guaimar, and asked him to furnish them with weapons and horses (as pilgrims they were of course travelling unarmed). Once they had obtained

---

1 Notably E. Joranson, 'The inception of the career of the Normans in Italy – legend and history', *Speculum* xxiii (1948), 353–96, and J. France, 'The occasion of the coming of the Normans to Italy', *Journal of Medieval History* xvii (1991), 185–205.

these weapons they attacked the Saracens, killed many of them and drove the rest off. So impressed were the prince and his subjects with their prowess that they begged the Normans to stay to defend them, and when the latter proved reluctant they sent them home laden with presents, asking them to recruit their compatriots to come to southern Italy, 'the land flowing with milk and honey and so many good things'. Amatus then passed on to describe how Count Robert of Normandy exiled a man called Gilbert Buatère for killing someone called William, how Gilbert and his four brothers came to Italy and at Capua met Melus, the leader of a previous rebellion against the Byzantine emperor in Apulia, who enlisted them in a renewed uprising against the Greek authorities.[2]

There are a number of problems with this account, not least with the dating. If the phrase 'before the year 1000' (*avan mille* in the surviving French translation) is taken literally, the attack on Salerno can only have taken place in 999, the year when Guaimar III of Salerno succeeded his father John as prince.[3] Yet even the first insurrection in Apulia under the command of Melus took place some years later, in 1009–11, while his renewed invasion of that province, accompanied by his Norman allies, can be securely dated to 1017.[4] Furthermore Robert only became count (or duke) of Normandy in 1028. It would appear therefore that even if one should take the account of Amatus at face value, he telescoped events which occurred over a number of years to imply that they followed in a rapid sequence.

William of Apulia, writing some fifteen years later than Amatus, told a completely different story. He made no mention of Salerno at all, though like Amatus he said that the first Normans to come to southern Italy were pilgrims. They had, however, gone to the shrine of St Michael on Monte Gargano, on the Adriatic side of the peninsula. There they had, seemingly by chance, encountered Melus who had begged for their assistance in his fight against the Greeks, and as a result they had gone home to recruit help,

---

2 *Amatus*, I.16–21, pp. 21–8; Eng. trans. by Joranson, *art. cit.*, pp. 356–8.
3 The numbering of the Lombard princes has hideous pitfalls for the unwary. Older studies have followed Michelangelo Schipa, *Storia di principato longobardo di Salerno* (Naples 1887) that there were five princes of Salerno called Guaimar. However, the only evidence for there being a 'Guaimar III' was one charter, *Cod. Dipl. Cavensis* i.172–3 no. 134, there misdated to 917. This would appear to be an eleventh-century document, and hence the early tenth-century 'Guaimar III' never existed. Thus the prince who ruled from 999 to 1027 should be Guaimar III, succeeded by his son Guaimar IV (1027–52). See Taviani-Carozzi, *Principauté lombarde de Salerne*, i.366–9.
4 *Annales Beneventani*, ed. Bertolini, p. 131; *Annales Cavenses, MGH SS* iii.189; *Annales Casinenses, MGH SS* xix. 305; *Annales Casinenses ab antiquis annalibus excerpta, MGH SS* xxx(2). 1410–11; Lupus Protospatharius, *Annales, MGH SS* v. 57.

and then returned to Italy, met Melus once again in the Campania and joined him in his attack on Apulia.[5]

Leo Marsicanus, in the original version of his chronicle of Montecassino, gave a third and briefer account, which was different again from those of Amatus and William. He described the original revolt of Melus in some detail, and then how he took refuge at Capua where he and his brother Dattus 'plotted with all the means at their disposal to overthrow the Greeks' rule and free their country from their tyranny'. There Melus encountered forty Normans, 'in flight from the anger of their lord, the Count of Normandy', whom he persuaded to take part in his proposed invasion. Leo listed the leaders of these Normans as Gilbert *Botericus*, Rodulf of Tosny, Osmund, Rufinus and Stigand. However, when Leo (or possibly someone else) came to revise his original chronicle, he clumsily inserted Amatus's story of the attack on Salerno, more or less verbatim, and omitted his original list of the Norman leaders, though he added confirmation of the date of the invasion of Apulia, the sixth year of Abbot Atenulf of Montecassino, which was 1017.[6]

While there are elements common to more than one of these accounts – the Normans as pilgrims, the role of political exiles, the naming of Gilbert Buatère, and the Normans' involvement in Melus's renewed insurrection in Apulia – the stories are discordant, and certainly those recounted by Amatus and William have unlikely or contradictory elements. William, for example, alleged that those who travelled out to take part in Melus's attack on Apulia came unarmed, and were only provided with weapons after they had arrived in Campania, which seems improbable. He also said that during the winter before their attack there was an unprecedented snowfall, which we know from the Bari and Benevento annals to have occurred in 1009, before the first rebellion of Melus.[7] Furthermore how likely was it that a wanted rebel such as Melus would have risked his life by visiting the Gargano shrine, in an area which was at this period firmly under Byzantine control? It is therefore not surprising that there has been a tendency to dismiss all these versions as legends, or alternatively to disregard those of Amatus and William and suggest that Leo's account is incomplete.

For whereas all three of the south Italian historians were writing towards the end of the eleventh century, and therefore long after the event, there was another chronicler writing much nearer to the time, probably *c.* 1030, the Burgundian monk Radulf Glaber, who gave yet another version of the

---

5 *W. Apulia*, I, lines 11–57, pp. 98–102; Eng. trans. by Joranson, *art. cit.*, pp. 359–60.
6 *Chron. Cas.* II.37, pp. 236–9; Eng. trans. of redaction 2, Joranson, *art. cit.*, pp. 356–8, redaction 1, *ibid.*, p. 372.
7 *Annales Beneventani*, ed. Bertolini, p. 130; Lupus, *Annales, MGH SS* v. 56–7.

Normans' arrival in Italy. He too referred to a man who had fallen foul of the count of Normandy, whom he correctly named as Richard (II, ruler of Normandy 996–1026). This man, whom Glaber called Rodulf, went with some companions to Rome where it was the pope, Benedict VIII (1012–24), who recruited him for an attack on Byzantine Apulia. Glaber also claimed that news of the initial victories secured by Rodulf and his friends led to many other Normans leaving their country, along with their families, and coming to join in the assault on Apulia, and he gave a highly coloured account of how they forced their way through the St Bernard Pass, refusing to pay the tolls demanded by the local lords.[8]

Glaber's suggestion that the pope was the instigator of, or at least a party to, the attack on Apulia in 1017, is supported by another near-contemporary French chronicler, Adehemar of Chabannes, and is not inherently implausible.[9] As we have seen, the papacy had since the 960s been making efforts to restore its authority over the bishoprics of Byzantine south Italy, and Benedict VIII and his family, the counts of Tusculum, were allies of the German ruler Henry II, whom Benedict had crowned as emperor at Rome in 1014. Henry, like his predecessors, regarded southern Italy as part of his dominions. Furthermore relations between the papacy and the patriarchate of Constantinople were at a particularly low ebb in the early eleventh century, principally because of disputes about the western addition of the *filioque* clause to the Creed; indeed they had deteriorated to such an extent that Byzantine sources refer to a schism.[10] Yet to suggest that Glaber's account, despite obvious omissions such as the role of Melus, was in the main accurate is not necessarily to disprove those of the south Italian writers. One can perhaps reconcile all these versions of the story of the Normans' arrival, for none of them is entirely implausible, even if equally clearly none is entirely complete.

Given the upsurge of Muslim raids on the mainland of southern Italy after 975, an attack on Salerno in or around the year 1000 is by no means unlikely. If a raiding party could reach as far inland as Capua and Benevento in 1002, one could certainly threaten Salerno in or about the same period. Furthermore such an attack is not entirely uncorroborated. One version of the Montecassino annals does indeed refer to an attack on Salerno in the year 999, but the manuscript in which this occurs was written in the twelfth

---

8 *Radulfus Glaber Opera*, ed. J. France, N. Bulst and P. Reynolds (Oxford 1989), pp. 96–101. Both Joranson and France argue strongly that Glaber's is the key and only trustworthy account.

9 *Chronicon*, ed. J. Chavanon (Paris 1897), p. 178; Eng. trans. by Joranson, *art. cit.*, p. 371.

10 H. Hoffmann, 'Die Anfänge der Normannen in Süditalien', *QFIAB* xlix (1969), 95–144, at pp. 124–5.

century, and the reference might therefore be dependent on Amatus.[11] However, in 1005 the archbishop of Salerno granted a privilege to a church at Vietri, on the coast just north of Salerno, which had been rebuilt after being destroyed by the Saracens.[12] Furthermore in 1009 Duke Sergius of Amalfi recorded how he, his father and grandfather had been taken prisoner by the Saracens because they had been unable to pay the tribute demanded from their city. Since his grandfather Manso died in 1004/5, this must have occurred at some period before then. Amalfi is only about 25 km from Salerno, and one might plausibly suggest that the seizure of its rulers was linked with the attack on Salerno, caused according to Amatus by the failure to pay the customary tribute.[13] Moreover, while the 'Chronicle of Amalfi', a fragmentary history of the city compiled c. 1100, has no direct reference to these events, it too mentions the year 999, claiming that Melus and the Normans attacked Apulia in that year. While this is clearly impossible, one might suggest that here a confused memory was preserved that 999 was indeed the year when the Normans first came to Italy.[14] In addition, the story of Norman pilgrims repulsing an attack on Salerno was also recounted by Orderic Vitalis, writing in Normandy c. 1115. The details included in his version may hardly be credible – he alleged, for example, that a hundred Normans defeated 20,000 Muslims whom they surprised while picnicking on the sea-shore, and the Drogo he claims was the Normans' leader is not otherwise attested.[15] But since Orderic is most unlikely to have known of Amatus's account, at the very least he shows that the tradition linking the Normans with an attack on Salerno was more than the invention of the Montecassino monk.

The story of Amatus that there was a Muslim attack on Salerno c. 999/1000 is therefore perfectly credible. One need not dismiss it as legend, nor does one have to redate it to c. 1016, on the eve of Melus's second attack on Apulia, as Chalandon and others have done.[16] But does believing the account of Amatus necessarily invalidate the other versions of the Normans' arrival? One might suggest that William of Apulia's account was equally plausible, although the group of pilgrims whom he described must be viewed as entirely separate from those who may have saved, or helped to save, Salerno c. 1000. Certainly pilgrims from north of the Alps had already made visits to the shrine at Monte Gargano, notably the Frankish monk Bernard on his

---

11 *Annales Casinenses ab antiquis annalibus excerpta*, MGH SS xxx(2).1409.
12 *Cod. Dipl. Cavensis*, vi.40–3 no. 898, there misdated to 1035.
13 Hoffmann, 'Die Anfänge', pp. 101–2.
14 Schwarz, *Amalfi im frühen Mittelalter*, p. 204.
15 *Orderic*, ii.56–7.
16 F. Chalandon, *La Domination normande en Italie et en Sicile* (2 vols, Paris 1907), i.48–50.

way to Jerusalem *c.* 868, and the monastic reformers Odo of Cluny and
John of Gorze in the middle of the tenth century. The Emperor Otto III as
an act of repentance went barefoot to the shrine during his expedition to
the south in 999, prompted either by the north Italian monk St Romuald,
or by the Greek holy man St Nilos (depending on which of their biograph-
ies one trusts).[17] Furthermore we should not underestimate the possible
links between the shrine of St Michael on the Gargano and Mont St Michel
in Normandy, particularly since another important monastic reformer, the
Burgundian William of Volpiano, who visited Monte Gargano *c.* 995, was
soon afterwards active in Normandy being entrusted with the important
abbey of Fécamp *c.* 1001 by Duke Richard II, and later overseeing the
reform of several other monasteries in the duchy, including Mont St Michel.[18]
Nor was the presence of Melus at Monte Gargano entirely impossible.
Although the Byzantines were firmly in control of the hinterland of the
Capitanata, the Gargano massif was an isolated and thinly populated region, with numerous places of concealment available in its caves, and the
risks of arrest there consequently much less than in the relatively thickly
populated, and entirely flat, coastal area further south. According to William
of Apulia, Melus was 'clad in the Greek manner', which might suggest
that he was travelling incognito (although equally this may have been the
normal dress for a well-born patrician from the Apulian coastal towns). It
is also perfectly feasible that Melus needed to contact supporters within the
Byzantine province to prepare for his renewed insurrection, which when it
occurred began in the Capitanata. Furthermore there were long-standing
and close historical links between the Gargano shrine and the bishopric (or
from 968 archbishopric) of Benevento. In 978 Prince Pandulf Ironhead had
confirmed the shrine as the property of the archbishop, and this concession
appears to have been recognised by the Byzantine authorities.[19] For how
long after their hold on the Capitanata had been firmly established in the

---

17 A. Petrucci, 'Aspetti del culto e del pelligrinagio di S. Michele Arcangelo sul Monte
    Gargano', in *Pelligrinagi e culto dei santi in Europa fino alla prima crociata* (Quattro convegno del
    centro di studi sulla spiritualità medievale, Todi 1963), pp. 145–80, especially 168–70;
    Sarah Hamilton, 'Otto III's penance: a case study of unity and diversity in the eleventh-
    century Church', *Studies in Church History* xxxii (1996), 83–94.

18 *Chronica Sancti Michaelis Monasterii in Pago Virdunensi, MGH SS* iv.82–3; for the date, *Chartes et
    Documents de St Benigne de Dijon*, ed. G. Chevrier and M. Chaume (2 vols, Dijon 1936–43),
    ii.243–4.

19 Ughelli, *Italia Sacra*, viii.66–7. The document was witnessed by the archbishop of Taranto
    (a see under Byzantine rule) and two senior Byzantine officers. Cf. von Falkenhausen,
    Untersuchungen, p. 165, and for an important discussion J.-M. Martin, 'La culte de saint
    Michel en Italie méridionale d'après les actes de practique (VIe–XIIe siècles)', in *Culto e
    insediamenti michelici nell'Italia meridionale fra tarda antichità e medioevo*, ed. C. Carletti and
    G. Otranto (Bari 1994), pp. 375–404, especially 388–93.

980s they continued to recognise the see of Benevento's claims over the Monte Gargano shrine is a good question, but it is possible that even *c.* 1015 it was still regarded as a Beneventan protectorate, which may also explain why Melus could have dared to appear there.

We may then reconstruct the process by which the Normans arrived in southern Italy as follows. The Muslim attack on Salerno *c.* 999 described by Amatus seems to be confirmed, and it is probable that there was therefore a kernel of truth in his story of the Norman pilgrims aiding the city, though one might be sceptical as to whether their role was as heroic or as important as he, and later Orderic, claimed. Norman mercenaries were probably already employed in southern Italy in the early years of the eleventh century. Hence Amatus described how after the early battles in Apulia in 1017 more Normans *from Salerno* joined Melus's army, which strongly suggests that they had been in service there.[20] Thus while the story of the meeting with Melus at Monte Gargano is not by any means impossible, this was unlikely to have been the first contact of the Normans with the south of the peninsula. Similarly it is perfectly feasible that Benedict VIII played a part in planning the attack on Byzantine Apulia in 1017 and encouraging Norman mercenaries to take part. Glaber suggests that the prince of Benevento (Landulf V) was also a party to this attempt, while Amatus and Leo agreed that Melus gathered his forces at Capua, which must have been with the connivance of its princes, the two cousins Pandulf II and Pandulf IV (the latter the brother of the prince of Benevento).[21] Given the traditional ambitions of the princes of Capua–Benevento to recover the lands their predecessors had once held in northern Apulia, the involvement of this close-knit princely kin-group is more than likely, even if it took the form of covert support rather than open military action. (One should also remember that the two principalities had been once again temporarily united between 1008 and 1014.)

One further point needs to be stressed with regard to the attack on Apulia in 1017. Whatever Glaber and William of Apulia might imply about this being a specifically Norman enterprise, in reality the Normans were only auxiliaries, albeit no doubt extremely useful ones, to a primarily Lombard enterprise. Leo Marsicanus said that Melus 'recruited many other people who either hated the Greeks or were following him personally', Amatus wrote of 'the small number of the Normans helping Melus' and suggested that to begin with, at any rate, the Normans numbered only 250.[22]

---

20 *Amatus*, I.23, p. 36.
21 For the numbering of these princes, see below, genealogical chart III (page 307), based on that in Cilento, *Italia meridionale longobarda.*
22 *Chron. Cas.* II.37, p. 239; *Amatus*, I.22, p. 30.

Infiltration and early settlement

The attack on Apulia commenced in May 1017 with an invasion of the Capitanata, probably because this was the region where Byzantine rule was least firmly established, and the invaders rapidly won a series of engagements which led the Byzantine forces to retire to the coast. But in contrast to the earlier revolt of 1009 the Byzantines retained control of the coastal towns, an attempt to capture Trani by a *coup de main* failed,[23] and there seems to have been a period of stalemate, during which both sides sought reinforcements. Both Glaber and Amatus imply that a second and larger group of Normans joined the original contingent; indeed Amatus suggests (surely with some exaggeration?) that they were by the autumn of 1018 some 3,000 strong. But the delay worked to the advantage of the Byzantines, and the new Catepan, Basil Boiannes, who arrived at Bari in December 1017, was accompanied by substantial fresh forces. Indeed the timing of the rebellion was singularly unlucky, for the Emperor Basil II had at last succeeded in his conquest of Bulgaria, and with its other frontiers at peace, Byzantium had for once troops to spare for the distant province of Langobardia. Boiannes seems to have begun by trying to undermine the support which Melus was receiving from the Lombard princes – it is difficult to know how else to interpret his privilege, allegedly granted on imperial orders, to Montecassino in February 1018 confirming the abbey's property rights in Apulia – for the abbot, Atenulf, was the younger brother of the prince of Capua.[24] Finally, in October 1018 the Byzantines won a decisive victory at Canne, a few miles north-west of Trani, and the few who were left from Melus's army were forced to flee to the Lombard principalities. The surviving Normans – only about eighty remained, according to Leo Marsicanus – took service with the Lombard princes, the abbot of Montecassino, and later even with the Byzantines, while Melus went north to Germany to enlist the help of the Emperor Henry II. His brother-in-law Dattus, along with a bodyguard of Normans, took refuge in a tower at the mouth of the River Garigliano near the border between the principality of Capua and papal territory, which was given to him by Benedict VIII.

Boiannes meanwhile took steps to consolidate his victory. His success had made the Lombard princes once more amenable to Byzantine diplomacy,

---

23   Lupus Protospatharius, *Annales*, *MGH SS* v.57. Boiannes granted the property of one of the Trani rebels to a loyal Lombard officer, who in turn gave it to Montecassino in 1021: Trinchera, *Syllabus*, p. 20 no. 19.

24   Trinchera, *Syllabus*, p. 18 no. 17, though the text as it was transmitted is defective: von Falkenhausen, *Untersuchungen*, pp. 176–7.

though it is possible that Guaimar III of Salerno was always reasonably well disposed towards the eastern empire.[25] Boiannes bribed Pandulf IV (who was already making overtures to him) to allow him to send a striking force to besiege the Garigliano tower and arrest Dattus. The pleas of Abbot Atenulf of Montecassino secured mercy for the Norman garrison (no doubt the abbot either wished to use these troops himself or was conscious of the feelings of the Normans already in his employment), but Dattus was taken back to Bari and executed.[26] Then, to consolidate his hold on northern Apulia, Boiannes began the construction of a series of fortified settlements on hilltop sites along the fringes of the Apulian plain: Troia, Fiorentino, Montecorvino, Dragonara and Civitate. None of these new towns was more than 20 km from another, all were established to a fairly regular plan with one main street running lengthways through the site, with not only a garrison but also farmers settled there, and fairly soon, if not quite immediately, they became the seats of bishoprics. Troia was probably established as early as the summer of 1019 (assuming that the corrupted copy which is all that survives of its foundation charter preserves the gist of a genuine text).[27] Further south Boiannes established another new town at Melfi on the border between Apulia and the principality of Salerno.[28]

However, these Byzantine successes led to the intervention of the western Emperor Henry II. Melus himself had died at Bamberg in April 1020, soon after his arrival in Germany, but the influence of Benedict VIII, who had also gone to visit the emperor, and the consciousness of his predecessors' claims to overlordship over southern Italy, impelled Henry to take action. In the spring of 1022 he marched into southern Italy with a sizeable army, Pandulf IV of Capua was deposed and – spared execution only by the pleas of the archbishop of Cologne – taken off a prisoner to Germany. His brother, the abbot of Montecassino, was drowned in the Adriatic as he fled to Constantinople. Pandulf was replaced by his cousin, Count Pandulf of Teano, and a pro-imperial abbot, Theobald, was installed at Montecassino. The loyalty and the prayers of the monks were secured by generous donations (including a magnificent Gospel Book with a gold-chased cover, written a few years before at Regensburg, now *Cod. Vat. Ottobon. Lat.* 74) and the traditional privilege confirming the abbey's rights and possessions. To

---

25 Hoffmann, 'Die Anfänge', pp. 123–4.
26 *Chron. Cas.* II.38, pp. 240–2.
27 Trinchera, *Syllabus*, pp. 18–20 no. 18; cf. von Falkenhausen, *Untersuchungen*, pp. 177–9. For the sites and their plans, J.-M. Martin and G. Noyé, 'La cité de Montecorvino et sa catédrale', *MEFR* xciv (1982), 513–49.
28 *W. Apulia*, I, lines 245–8, p. 112. *Cod. Dipl. Cavensis*, v.134 no. 793 (1027) is the first documentary reference.

this Henry added the grant of the nearby fortress of Rocca d'Evandro, prob-ably not just as a mark of favour but to strengthen the defences of the abbey lands.[29] Similar privileges were granted to a number of other important south Italian churches, notably the abbey of St Vincent on Volturno (which like Montecassino had strong historical links with the empire), and the abbey of St Sophia at Benevento.[30]

Yet for all this intensive propaganda campaign (and fostering the great abbeys of south-central Italy was of course a traditional imperial policy going back to the reign of Charlemagne), Henry's expedition was just as ineffectual in the long term as those of his predecessors. His attempted invasion of Apulia stalled before the new fortress of Troia, where after a three-month siege the summer heat and an outbreak of disease in the German army led to its withdrawal northwards. The garrison which defied him included 'Franks', some of whom may well have been Normans.[31] Soon after the Emperor Henry's death in 1024, his successor Conrad II released the imprisoned prince of Capua (according to Amatus on the request of the latter's brother-in-law Guaimar III of Salerno), and within a couple of years Pandulf IV had chased out his cousin and namesake and had regained control of his capital city and, to the extent to which the princes did now control it, his principality. His hapless relative took refuge in Naples. The abbey of Montecassino, far from profiting from the Em-peror Henry II's generosity, was now exposed to Pandulf's revenge. 'Not only', said its chronicler, 'did he not abandon his earlier wickedness, but rather every day he grew worse, venting his spleen in devastation of this monastery to satisfy his hatred of the emperor.'[32]

The next fifteen years saw bitter disputes, both between the different principalities and duchies of the west and centre of the peninsula, and to some extent within them as well (though the principality of Salerno re-mained appreciably more stable than its neighbours). Confusing as these quarrels are, certain themes can readily be identified: the struggle of Pandulf IV to reassert his control over the principality of Capua, the attempts by the Lombard principalities to absorb the hitherto independent coastal duchies, and the continued ambition of the princes (or at least those of Salerno

29   Bloch, *Montecassino in the Middle Ages* [above, introduction note 10], i.15–30.
30   *Chron. Vult.* iii.17–21; *MGH Diplomatum Regum et Imperatorum Germaniae*, iii (Hanover 1900–3), 596–7 no. 468 (for St Sophia).
31   Trinchera, *Syllabus*, pp. 21–2 no. 20 (1024) rewarding the Troians for their loyalty during the siege, though doubts have been expressed as to the authenticity of this document: von Falkenhausen, *Untersuchungen*, pp. 181–2. The Swabian chronicler Herman of Reichenau (*MGH SS* v.120) recorded the deaths from disease of the bishop of Konstanz and the abbot of Sankt-Gallen during the siege.
32   *Chron. Cas.* II.56, p. 276.

and Capua) to assert their pre-eminence within the 'Lombard' territories –
something which was to be triumphantly achieved by Guaimar IV of Salerno
in 1038. Above all, there was the growing use of Norman mercenaries, as
the means *par excellence* of enforcement in these disputes.

However, another feature of this period was the enhanced power and
prestige of the Byzantine empire within southern Italy. The relative peace
and stability of the empire in the last years of Basil II and under his immediate successors meant that for once there were sufficient troops to spare
from the rest of the empire if these should be needed in Italy. So in 1025
massive reinforcements were dispatched to southern Italy for an expedition
to reconquer Sicily, although this project was abandoned after the death
of the Emperor Basil in December, even though the advance guard had
already crossed the Straits of Messina.[33] None the less, the political and
military situation had been transformed from that of a decade earlier. Not
only was the Apulian frontier secure, but Byzantine influence stretched
even into the Lombard principalities. The Catepan, Basil Boiannes, provided troops to assist Pandulf IV's siege of Capua in 1025–6, and then
arranged the deal through which his defeated rival was guaranteed a safe
withdrawal in return for the town's surrender.[34] Indeed later on in the
century the Greek historian John Skylitzes could remember Basil Boiannes
(with some perhaps understandable exaggeration) as the man who had
subdued all Italy as far as Rome for the Emperor Basil.[35]

But at the same time the Byzantine authorities took care to defuse the
potential for conflict over religious issues within the area under their direct
rule. In 1025 the jurisdiction of the papacy (rather than the patriarch of
Constantinople) over the ecclesiastical province of Bari was finally recognised, a concession which must surely have eased papal grievances. (There
was anyway now more opportunity for compromise since Pope Benedict
VIII had died in 1024, and his successor, and brother, John XIX, was less
committed to a hard line against Constantinople.) Similarly direct papal
authority over the new bishopric of Troia was conceded *c.* 1030.[36] However, notwithstanding this greater readiness to tolerate papal claims, the
Byzantine governors continued to maintain a strict control over the Latin
churchmen in areas under their rule, and clearly there was good reason for

---

33 *Annales Barenses*, ad. an. 1027 (*sic*), *MGH SS* v.53; *Anonymi Barensis Chronicon*, ad. an. 1025, *RIS* v.149.
34 *Amatus*, I.34, p. 45; *Chron. Cas.* II.56, pp. 274–5.
35 *Synopsis Historiarum*, ed. H. Thurn (Berlin 1973), p. 426. [Also in George Cedrenus, *Historia Compendium*, ii.546.]
36 *Italia Pontificia*, ix.203, 317–18. For the background, K.J. Herrmann, *Das Tuskulaner Papsttum (1012–1046)* (Stuttgart 1973), pp. 63–8.

this concern. Relations between the Catepans and Archbishop Bisantius of Bari might seem to have been close, given that the archbishop co-operated with Pothos Argyros in the latter's foundation of a church outside Bari staffed by Greek monks in 1032, 'to pray daily for the holy emperor and for the lord Pothos who built it, and for the other catepans who shall rule this land'. Yet when Bisantius died in 1035, the Bari annals recorded that he was not only 'the guardian and defender of the whole city', but 'terrible and without fear against all the Greeks'. A successor, Romuald, was elected 'by all the people', but almost immediately summoned to Constantinople and kept in exile there, while a new archbishop was chosen. This suggests that there were still some tensions within Apulia, where a Lombard population lay under Greek rule. The defeat of Pothos Argyros by a Muslim raiding force in Calabria during the summer of 1031, shows that Byzantium also faced military difficulties in southern Italy.[37] But raids from Islamic Sicily were no more than an irritant, relations with the Lombard principalities appear to have been good (or at least stable), and there was as yet no real threat to Byzantine rule. By the late 1030s the authority of the eastern empire was recognised not just up to the River Fortore, which had been the frontier of the Byzantine Capitanata for at least a generation, but as far north as Termoli, in a region which until very recently had been at least nominally subject to the princes of Benevento. But in northern Apulia Byzantine rule rested on the loyalty of Lombard functionaries: men such as Vitalis, who in 1032 was the turmarch (town governor) of Vieste on the Gargano peninsula and who gave a church there to the (Latin) monastery on the Tremiti islands in the Adriatic, and Lando who in 1045 was turmarch of Lucera in the Capitanata (a town still acknowledging Byzantine rule even after the Norman invasion of Apulia).[38] But loyalty to Byzantine rule was not necessarily confined to such officials. The colonists in the new castral/town foundations of Basil Boiannes in the western Capitanata also had a vested interest in the regime which had established them as (albeit small-scale) independent landholders, and the continued operation of Lombard law under the supervision of Lombard officials meant that in everyday affairs such communities were largely self-governing.[39] One might indeed suspect that any tensions which did exist were more likely to be present in

---

37 *Cod. Dipl. Barese*, i.31–2 no. 18; *Annales Barenses, MGH SS* v.53–4.

38 *Cod. Dipl. Tremiti*, ii.38–42 no. 12, 63–7 no. 19; *Cod. Dipl. Cavensis*, i.162–3 no. 127 (there misdated to 911).

39 S. Borsari, 'Aspetti del dominio bizantino in Capitanata', *Atti dell'accademia Pontaniana*, n.s. xvi (1966/7), 55–66, especially pp. 61–2. For the use of Lombard law, an excellent example is a charter of Bishop John of Lucera of 1039, *Cod. Dipl. Cavensis*, vi.99–101 no. 938.

Bari and other coastal towns where the impact of Byzantine rule was greater, rather than in these more outlying areas.

Thus, whatever underlying tensions there may have been, the Byzantine provinces remained outwardly stable, at least until *c.* 1040, while in the meantime the Lombard principalities became increasingly involved in dispute. The most disruptive factor would appear to have been Pandulf IV of Capua, who was far from satisfied with the recovery of his principality in 1026. His ambitions were probably aided by the succession of a new prince of Salerno, Guaimar IV, in March 1027. While the latter may not actually have been a minor, he was still quite young (indeed his mother was named as co-ruler for the first few months of his reign), and he was anyway Pandulf's nephew. To begin with at least, he was prepared to allow Pandulf a free hand: 'he had made agreements with his uncle Pandulf and they got on well together. They were of one mind, and disposed of their possessions by common accord.'[40] One might interpret this last phrase to suggest that Guaimar consented, or at least did not interfere, in Pandulf's seizure of Naples in 1027. Although this success proved ephemeral, for the Capuans were driven out of that city within three years, this was not the end of the prince's ambitions, for in 1036 he tried to seize Benevento from his other nephew and homonym, Pandulf III, and soon afterwards he took over, for a brief period, the duchy of Gaeta.[41]

Yet, for all his seemingly aggressive intent, Pandulf IV faced problems within the principality of Capua, for, as we have seen, the effectiveness of princely rule had been in decline since the later tenth century. One of the traditional princely strategies for enhancing their authority in the north of the principality was an alliance with, or control over, the wealthy and powerful monasteries of Montecassino and St Vincent on Volturno – not least because both possessed an extensive and concentrated block of territory around the monastery, known respectively as the *Terra Sancti Benedicti* and *Terra Sancti Vincenti*. If he could control these two monasteries the prince had not merely access to their considerable incomes but bases in the Liri Valley to the north of the Roccamonfina barrier and in the mountainous north-eastern interior that could be a counterweight to the largely independent nobles of these more distant parts of the principality. To this end Pandulf now forced Abbot Theobald of Montecassino to live at the Cassinese cell in Capua, 'abbot indeed in theory, but in reality a prisoner who was

---

40 *Amatus*, II.2, p. 59; *Cod. Dipl. Cavensis*, v.131–3 nos 791–2. Guaimar IV had been co-prince with his father since November 1018, after the death of his elder brother John: *ibid.*, v.3–5 nos 709–10.

41 *Annales Beneventani*, ed. Bertolini, p. 154; *Amatus*, I.40, p. 52; Skinner, *Family Power*, p. 152. Pandulf was in his first year as duke of Naples in March/April 1028: *Chron. Vult.* iii.62, 66.

never allowed to go outside the city without guards' (according to Leo Marsicanus), while the abbey was administered by a lay official called Theodwin, with a force of Norman mercenaries to support him. Theobald eventually escaped, and took refuge in the abbey's daughter-house in the Abruzzi, the Holy Liberator on Monte Majella, which was far enough away to be outside the prince's control. But after his death in 1035 the prince installed one of his own creatures as abbot, a Greek called Basil who had previously had charge of the cell at Capua (and also therefore of Abbot Theobald while he was detained there). Indeed where the real power at Montecassino lay was made clear in 1032, when the Catepan Pothos Argyros issued a *sigillion* confirming Cassinese properties in Apulia, not to Abbot Theobald but to Basil as provost of St Benedict, Capua. (It also shows that relations between the prince and the Byzantine authorities remained good.)[42] After Pandulf had bullied the monks into electing him as head of the mother-house, Basil did not, according to the abbey's chronicler, 'behave as a real abbot, but acted rather as the prince's business agent (*procurator causarum*)'. There were similar, if less detailed, complaints about the prince's oppression of the monastery of St Vincent.[43]

The monks of Montecassino viewed their travails as simply the product of the prince's innate wickedness. The monastery's later abbot, Desiderius, summed up his house's view of Pandulf IV:

> through robbery and the shedding of blood Pandulf cruelly seized cities, towns and all the other lands round about [the monastery] and made them subject to his lordship, for a long time he insatiably committed all sorts of crimes, murders and thefts, and the seizure of churches. . . . Led on by his greed, he sacrilegiously took away all the *castra*, villages and estates of the monastery, to such an extent that he left to the monks hardly a single peasant to till the fields, or indeed any fields which might be tilled by the peasant.[44]

It is hardly surprising that the monks resented such treatment, and probably greatly exaggerated its impact. But there was a real political purpose to this policy, and to the prince's attempt to install his son Hildebrand as archbishop of Capua (again following earlier precedent, for Pandulf Ironhead had done the same thing). Abbot Theobald was a nominee of the emperor

42 Trinchera, *Syllabus*, pp. 24–6 no. 23 [also in *Le Colonie cassinesi in Capitanata i Lesina*, ed. T. Leccisotti (Miscellanea Cassinese 13, Montecassino 1937), 70–1 no. 22]; *Chron. Cas.* II.57–61, pp. 277–86, quote from p. 279; *Amatus*, I.35–7, pp. 46–50.
43 *Chron. Cas.* II.62, p. 286. Cf. *Chron. Vult.* iii.78; *Amatus*, I.38, p. 50.
44 *Dialogi de Miraculis Sancti Benedicti*, lib. I c.9, ed. G. Schwarz and A. Hofmeister, *MGH SS* xxx(2).1123.

who had deposed Pandulf, and hence clearly not reliable, and the control of the two abbeys would help him to assert his authority over the nearby nobles, such as the counts of Aquino and Teano whose lands lay on either side of the *Terra Sancti Benedicti*. But earlier on, while his brother had been abbot, Pandulf had been a generous benefactor to Montecassino, endowing it with substantial property along the northern border of his principality.[45]

However, by the early 1030s the prince of Capua had fallen out with his erstwhile ally Guaimar of Salerno. Amatus, keen to denigrate the prince, alleged that this was due to his sexual designs on a relative of Guaimar's wife. But Guaimar's own ambitions were undoubtedly a factor, for as William of Apulia wrote: 'a great desire for rule among these princes gave rise to wars. Each wished to be the most powerful and one strove to seize the rights of the other.'[46] In such a situation there was an obvious demand for mercenaries, and the Normans fulfilled this need. Indeed there had already been plenty of opportunities for employment in the immediate aftermath of the disaster of 1018. Some of the survivors had taken service with the prince of Benevento; Abbot Atenulf of Montecassino had stationed a garrison of Normans in a fortress at Pignetaro to oppose the depredations of the counts of Aquino; and Henry II had installed Melus's sons at Comino (in the foothills of the Abruzzi north of the *Terra Sancti Benedicti*) with a force of Normans in 1022. The troops furnished by Guaimar III to his brother-in-law Pandulf in 1025 were also Normans.[47] But the greatest opportunity came with Pandulf IV's expulsion from Naples in 1030. After Duke Sergius IV had recovered his duchy, and probably by prior arrangement, he installed a force of Normans at Aversa, on the edge of the Capuan plain about 15 km to the north of Naples in a newly built fortress, and with the right to levy tribute on the surrounding, and very fertile and prosperous, district. To seal the agreement he married his widowed sister to the Normans' leader Rainulf. The latter may just conceivably have been one of the brothers of Gilbert Buatère, who according to Amatus had accompanied him to Italy, though it would be unwise to place too much credence on this extremely confused account.[48]

The settlement at Aversa was the first real base that the Normans possessed in southern Italy; one which was under their own control rather than

---

45 In May 1017 he had granted the monastery the *castella* of S. Urbano and Vicalvi, near Sora, and a large block of territory in the Abruzzi: E. Gattula, *Accessiones ad Historiam Monasterii Casinensis* (Venice 1734), pp. 106–8; Bloch, *Montecassino in the Middle Ages*, i.373.

46 *W. Apulia*, I, lines 148–50, p. 106; *Amatus*, II.3, pp. 59–60.

47 *Chron. Cas.* II.38, pp. 240–1; *Amatus*, I.31, 34, pp. 41–2, 45.

48 *Amatus*, I.41–2, pp. 53–4; cf. *ibid.*, I.20, p. 25. Chalandon, *Domination Normande*, i.76–7, who dates the recovery of Naples (wrongly?) to 1029, plausibly suggests that Sergius had already come to an arrangement with the Normans.

that of a local ruler. (It should be noted that, despite Leo Marsicanus, who claimed that 'it was then that Aversa was first inhabited', this was more probably the fortification of an existing settlement than the utilisation of an entirely new site, for there is a reference to the church of St Paul of Aversa in a charter of Prince Pandulf V, the former count of Teano, in September 1022.)[49] Quite how independent the Normans of Aversa were was soon made clear, for after the death of his wife Count Rainulf (so Amatus styled him) changed sides and made an alliance with Pandulf of Capua. The narrative sources leave the chronology of these events vague, or disagree with each other. But if the Montecassino chronicle is to be believed, then Pandulf controlled Naples 'for nearly three years', and thus his loss of the city and the settlement of the Normans at Aversa should be dated to 1030 (something confirmed by a later charter, dated in the year of the Incarnation 1050 and 'now in the twentieth year that the Norman people have lived in Liguria at the city of Aversa').[50] How soon Rainulf reneged on his alliance with the Neapolitans cannot be established.

However, despite the establishment of Aversa and the apparent pre-eminence of Count Rainulf among the newcomers, the Normans were far from being united. Pandulf IV was already employing other Normans to subdue the lands of Montecassino, and others again were serving the prince of Salerno. When, probably in the mid-1030s, the elder sons of Tancred de Hauteville came to Italy, they enlisted first with the prince of Capua, then, dissatisfied with the rewards they were offered, they abandoned his service and entered that of Guaimar of Salerno, and thereafter fought against the Capuans. William of Apulia indeed suggested that the Normans deliberately prolonged such disputes:

> The Normans never desired any of the Lombards to win a decisive victory, in case this should be to their disadvantage. But now supporting the one, and then aiding the other, they prevented anyone being completely ruined. Gallic cunning deceived the Italians, for they allowed no one to be at the mercy of a triumphant enemy.[51]

Yet this passage smacks so clearly of hindsight that one may well doubt whether the men of the 1030s were quite so machiavellian. William's account appears to imply that the eventual take-over by the Normans was clearly in mind even from this early stage. One might suggest at the very most that

---

49 Napoli, Archivio di stato, pergamena 9.BB.III no. 3 (a nineteenth-century transcript), for the monastery of the Holy Saviour *in insula maris*, Naples.
50 *Amatus*, I.43–5, pp. 54–6; *Chron. Cas.* II.56, p. 275; *Cod. Dipl. Aversa*, pp. 390–2 no. 40.
51 *W. Apulia*, I, lines 156–61, p. 106. Cf. *Malaterra*, I.6, p. 10.

any deliberate fomenting of local quarrels was actuated by the need for continued employment rather than by any more long-term intentions.

However, in 1038 the political situation in southern Italy was transformed by two new developments: an expedition to southern Italy by the German Emperor Conrad II, and a renewed attempt by the Byzantines to reconquer Sicily, which began that summer. Both were to have profound consequences. Conrad undoubtedly wished to secure recognition of his overlordship over the Lombard principalities – and one should remember that every western emperor since Otto I had made at least one expedition to southern Italy. The Cassinese sources, not surprisingly, suggested that his journey was in response to their complaints about the iniquities of Pandulf of Capua, but we need not take this as being more than, at the most, a contributory factor, even though to the monks of Montecassino Conrad's expedition appeared to be a divinely inspired deliverance from their troubles. But to begin with at least the emperor was prepared to negotiate with Pandulf, who offered him hostages and a substantial bribe (or perhaps one should interpret this, as the emperor probably did, as payment of tribute). Only when Pandulf failed both to fulfil his promises and to attend his court in person did Conrad move to decisive action. In May 1038 he invested Guaimar of Salerno (who had prudently gone to meet the emperor with generous gifts) with the principality of Capua, and on the latter's request he also formally invested Rainulf as Count of Aversa. Amatus alleged that Guaimar needed the latter's support because 'without the agreement of the Normans, he could neither defend his own property nor conquer that of others'.[52]

We should be wary of taking such comments entirely at face value, for Guaimar's position after 1038 was at least outwardly strong, and not necessarily just dependent on Norman support. Pandulf IV remained for a while at his fortress on Monte Tifata, a few kilometres to the east of Capua, but soon left to seek aid from the Byzantine court at Constantinople – hoping that the good relations which he had previously maintained with the Byzantine authorities would now benefit him. He was, however, disappointed, and remained in exile (and Amatus suggested under arrest) for two years. In the intervening period the prince of Salerno rapidly extended his authority over the neighbouring city-states, taking over Amalfi in April 1039 and Sorrento four months later. The former duke of Sorrento was consigned to prison in Salerno, and Duke John of Amalfi fled to Constantinople, where he was to remain until Guaimar's death thirteen years later. Although initially he acquiesced in Guaimar's take-over, the archbishop of Amalfi soon went into exile as well, in Rome, where he died ten years later.

---

52 *Amatus*, II.4–6, pp. 60–5 (quote p. 64); *Chron. Cas.* II.63, pp. 288–93.

In 1040 Guaimar also gained control of Gaeta, albeit only briefly. But although Amatus suggested that Count Rainulf aided Guaimar in the take-over of Sorrento, it is by no means clear that these annexations were simply the result of Norman military aid. There were internal disputes within the ruling families at both Amalfi and Sorrento, while the duchy of Gaeta was already severely fragmented and the ducal family appears to have died out in the direct line in the mid-1030s when the city had fallen under the control of Pandulf IV.[53] Where the Normans were certainly important was in vindicating Guaimar's control over the principality of Capua, and especially the more northerly areas of the principality. When, for example, the abbot of St Vincent on Volturno appealed for the prince's help against incursions on their lands by the Borells (a family of Abruzzi nobles who were trying to extend their power south-westwards from their ancestral lands in the upper Sangro valley), Guaimar dispatched Rainulf and his Normans to his assistance. But even in the principality of Capua, Guaimar did not look only to the Normans for support; the Lombard counts of Teano were among his principal allies in asserting his control in the area around Montecassino in the early 1040s.[54]

Indeed, while Rainulf and his men at Aversa were the prince's close allies, other Normans may have posed problems for him. Whether those whom Pandulf IV had established on the Montecassino lands were ever fully under the new prince's control is doubtful. When the new German abbot whom Conrad had appointed, Richer, came to complain to Guaimar about their continued depredations, all the prince could do was to advise him to go to Germany and seek the emperor's help – unless this was a subtle way of removing, at least for a while, a potentially obstructive figure who was anxious to safeguard the independence of his abbey. (When Richer did eventually return after a two-year absence, the prince discouraged him from conducting a campaign against the Normans on the *Terra Sancti Benedicti* with the troops whom he had brought.)[55] Furthermore when the Byzantines requested Guaimar for troops to assist in their attack on Sicily, he was ready to accede to this by sending 300 Normans to join the expedition, and appears to have used this opportunity to rid himself of potential trouble-makers, including the Hauteville brothers William and Drogo.[56] Some at least of the Normans were clearly surplus to requirements.

53 *Amatus*, II.3, 7, pp. 59, 65; Schwarz, *Amalfi im frühen Mittelalter*, pp. 48–51, 98–104, 245–7; Skinner, *Family Power*, pp. 55, 151–3. For the dates of Guaimar's take-overs, *Cod. Dipl. Cavensis*, v.98–9 no. 937, 108–10 no. 946. For the archbishop (d.1049), W. Holtzmann, 'Laurentius von Amalfi, ein Lehrer Hildebrands', *Studi Gregoriani* i (1947), 207–36.

54 *Chron. Vult.* iii.79; *Chron. Cas.* II.67–8, pp. 302, 304.

55 *Chron. Cas.* II.69–70, pp. 306–8.

56 *Malaterra*, I.6–7, p. 10.

The Byzantine expedition to Sicily had begun in the late summer of 1038. (One suspects that they may have waited until the army of the German emperor had commenced its long march home before crossing the Straits of Messina, just in case Conrad had planned some aggression against Apulia.) However, the Byzantines had already been trying for several years to foment the internal quarrels among the Muslim emirs of Sicily, and given the tensions within the island between those Muslims who were native Sicilians and more recent arrivals from north Africa, this must have seemed a propitious moment for the attack. Substantial reinforcements had been sent from Constantinople including a contingent from the elite Varangian Guard – Scandinavian mercenaries who were under the command of Harold Hardrada (later to become king of Norway) – and an experienced general who had been extremely successful in campaigns on the empire's eastern frontier was appointed to take charge, Giorgios Maniakes. Although Messina was soon captured, progress thereafter was slow, and it took two years to conquer the north-east of the island, even though most of the population of this region were still Greek Christians, and thus presumably sympathetic to the invaders. But in 1040 Maniakes inflicted a bloody defeat on the Muslims in a pitched battle near Troina, to the west of Mount Etna, and then captured the important city of Syracuse on the southeast coast. The eastern half of Sicily was now in Byzantine hands. However, at this point the Byzantine generals began to quarrel among themselves, Maniakes was recalled, his successors were much less competent (so at least was claimed by the Byzantine historian Skylitzes), the Muslims recovered almost all the lost territory, and soon only Messina was left under Byzantine rule.[57]

Yet quite how quickly Byzantine affairs in Sicily went wrong after the recall of Maniakes is not at all clear, and the account of Skylitzes is too partial towards the former to be taken entirely at face value. It is probable that it was the crisis which developed in Apulia in the spring of 1041, and the subsequent withdrawal of troops to the mainland, rather than the incapacity of the Byzantine commanders, that led to the abandonment of the previous gains.[58] Furthermore, there are other aspects of the episode that need to be examined with a critical eye. Hence, while the later south Italian writers predictably ascribed the victories gained by the expedition to the courage and fighting skill of the Norman contingent, we may be sceptical

57 Skylitzes, *Synopsis Historiarum*, pp. 403–7; = Cedrenus, *Historia Compendium*, ii.520–5. Good secondary accounts in Chalandon, *Domination normande*, i.88–95, and S. Tramontana, *I Normanni in Italia. Linee di ricerca sui primi insediamenti* i *Aspetti politici e militari* (Messina 1970), pp. 131–59.
58 M. Amari, *Storia dei Musselmani in Sicilia*, 2nd edn by C.A. Nallino (3 vols, Catania 1933–9), ii.452–4.

as to whether this relatively small force of at most a few hundred men was quite so crucial to the Byzantine success as Malaterra, for example, suggested. Nor indeed were all the western troops necessarily Normans, at least according to William of Apulia. However, the sources do all agree (more or less) about the upshot of the Norman involvement. After the victory at Troina, or some other successful action, there was a dispute about booty, or perhaps concerning the wages agreed for the Norman forces. A north Italian from Milan, called Arduin, was attached to the Norman contingent, and may have been one of its commanders. Since he could speak Greek (and had therefore presumably been in Byzantine service for some time), he was sent to remonstrate with the Greek commander, either Maniakes (according to Malaterra and Amatus) or one of the generals who took charge after his recall, Michael Dokeianos (William of Apulia and Skylitzes). The general took exception to the terms in which he was addressed and had Arduin flogged, and the western contingent then abandoned the expedition.[59]

On balance, it may be more probable that the incident took place while Maniakes was still in command, given that shortly afterwards, and notwithstanding what had happened, Arduin was made the *topoterites* or garrison commander at Melfi, the fortress town founded by Basil Boiannes on the border between southern Apulia and the principality of Salerno, apparently by Michael Dokeianos who succeeded as Catepan of Italy in November 1040. Given that Maniakes was now in disgrace (and indeed according to Skylitzes had been imprisoned on his return to Constantinople), someone who had fallen out with him would quite probably have been regarded as trustworthy.[60] Arduin, however, was intent on treachery, or saw the opportunity which his new position gave him to create his own lordship, and ingratiated himself with the inhabitants of Melfi (according to Amatus) while secretly contacting the Normans of Aversa. In March 1041 he and his allies seized Melfi and launched a new invasion of Apulia.[61]

This tale told by the chroniclers is certainly dramatic, and there is enough agreement between them to suggest the basic truth of the account (especially since there is corroboration from the Greek history of Skylitzes). But the crisis which engulfed Byzantine Apulia was more complex than most of the narrative sources imply, for that province was already in turmoil even before Arduin's *coup de main* at Melfi. The incumbent Catepan, Nikephoros Dokeianos (presumably a relative of Michael), had died at Ascoli in January 1040, and the leaderless province was then shaken by a revolt in the Taranto

---

59 *Amatus*, II.14, pp. 72–3; *Malaterra*, I.8, pp. 11–12; *W. Apulia*, I, lines 206–21, p. 110;
    Skylitzes, *Synopsis Historiarum*, pp. 425–6 [= Cedrenus, *Historiarum Compendium*, ii.545–6].
60 As shrewdly pointed out by J.J. Norwich, *The Normans in the South* (London 1967), p. 58.
61 *Amatus*, II.16–18, pp. 74–6.

region in May, in which two senior Byzantine officials were murdered, and very soon afterwards by the seizure of Bari by Argyrus, the son of the former rebel leader Melus. Discharged light troops (*conterati*), recruited locally, were the principal culprits in these disturbances, until they were eventually dispersed by Argyrus (apparently double-crossing his former allies). When Michael Dokeianos landed at Bari in November his first action was to make an example by hanging or blinding some of the ring-leaders in these disturbances.[62] The underlying cause of these troubles was the ill-feeling caused by the demands of the Byzantine tax collectors and recruiting officers for the Sicilian expedition, something of which alone among the chroniclers Amatus realised: 'the Apulians and Calabrians were forced to this exhausting campaign by the *solidi* and pence of the emperor, and both nobles and people were stirred up by this'.[63] Hence when Arduin began the 1041 invasion, not only were most of the Byzantine troops still in Sicily but there were potential allies within a very restive province.[64] Indeed, we should probably view the campaigns of 1041–2 as far from being a purely Norman enterprise, rather a revolt in which the Normans played what may have been to begin with only a subordinate part. But that part was to turn into one of the decisive steps in their conquest of Italy.

Up to 1041 their activities had been limited mainly to the Lombard principalities on the western side of the peninsula, and their territorial possessions were limited to Aversa (still at this stage under the suzerainty of Guaimar of Salerno) and those villages on the Montecassino lands where they had been stationed by Pandulf IV and which they continued to hold after his deposition in defiance of the abbot.[65] The investiture of Count Rainulf by the emperor in 1038 had regularised his position at Aversa, had (as one might put it) made the Normans of Aversa 'respectable', but apart from linking them with the dominant local ruler of the Lombard area had contributed nothing material to the extension of their power. Otherwise the Normans were still interlopers, sometimes useful, at other times no more than a further source of disturbance in an already troubled region. The invasion of Apulia was to change all that. And by creating the conditions which made that attack possible – by denuding the province of troops and by undermining its internal stability – the Byzantine expedition to Sicily contributed materially to the Norman take-over.

---

62 *Annales Barenses* and Lupus, *Annales*, MGH SS v.54, 58; *Anonymi Barensis Chronicon*, *RIS* v.149–50 (which also identifies the office Arduin held).
63 *Amatus*, II.8, p. 66.
64 *W. Apulia*, I, lines 241–4, p. 112, although the suggestion here that the province was quiet must be modified in the light of the annalists' evidence.
65 *Chron. Cas.* II.65, p. 304.

Normandy and Italy

So far we have been content to follow the terminology employed by the contemporary sources (both narrative and from *c.* 1050 onwards increasingly charters), which describe the newcomers overwhelmingly as 'Normans' (*normanni*). But who were these *normanni* and why had they come to southern Italy? William of Apulia, for example, offered a purely etymological definition of the term:

> In the language of their native country the wind which carries them from the boreal regions from which they have departed to seek the frontiers of Italy is called 'north', and the word 'man' is used among them to signify *homo*; thus they are called 'Normans', that is 'men of the north wind' [*homines boreales*].[66]

But William never explained what their native country was, and in his poem frequently used 'Gauls' (*Galli*) or 'Franks/Frenchmen' (*Franci*) as synonyms for 'Normans'. Furthermore his definition of the term 'Norman' was virtually identical with that made by earlier writers to describe the Northmen or Vikings who had attacked the Carolingian empire – without there being any clear distinction between one sort of Viking and another – Dane, Norwegian or Swede.[67] The Byzantine writer Skylitzes described Arduin leading (or so he believed) 500 'Franks from Transalpine Gaul' as part of Maniakes' expedition to Sicily, and while the Byzantines tended to refer to all westerners indiscriminately as 'Franks', this phrase still raises an important question.[68] To someone from southern Italy, or indeed from the Mediterranean world in general, a 'northman' might well be simply anybody from north of the Alps, and if the newcomers came from France, as Skylitzes said, this does not establish that all, or even many of them, actually came from the duchy of Normandy. That early charters from Aversa, the quintessential 'Norman' town in southern Italy, could be drawn up in the name of men *de genere Francorum*, and refer to the 'custom of the Franks', and in one case to Richard I of Capua and his son as 'rulers of the Franks and Lombards', might also give us pause.[69]

---

66 *W. Apulia*, I, lines 6–10, p. 98.
67 E.g. *Rodulfus Glaber Opera*, p. 32. Cf. Adam of Bremen, *Gesta Hammaburgensis Ecclesiae Pontificum*, ed. R. Schmeidler (*MGH SRG*, Hanover 1917), lib. I *c.* 14, p. 19: 'For the Danes and the other peoples who are beyond Denmark are all called Northmen by the historical writers of the Franks.' See Tramantona, *I Normanni in Italia*, pp. 44–54.
68 *Synopsis Historiarum*, p. 425 [= Cedrenus, *Historiarum Compendium*, p. 545].
69 *Cod. Dipl. Aversa*, pp. 386–7 no. 43 (1068), 393–4 no. 48 (1070), 396–7 no. 50 (1073), 399–401 no. 53 (1073), all written by Peter, deacon and notary.

Yet while Malaterra and Amatus of Montecassino both repeated the standard etymological definition of what a Norman was – Malaterra adding that it was a term derived from the English language – they were both emphatic in linking the invaders of southern Italy specifically to the duchy of Normandy, and described them exclusively by the term 'Norman', and not French/Franks or Gauls. And while Malaterra was himself almost certainly a Norman, Amatus was a Lombard from the principality of Salerno – yet he began his history by giving a concise overview of Norman victories, beginning with the conquest of England by Duke William of Normandy, so he was clearly in no doubt as to where these Normans came from.[70] One should also remember that William of Apulia was writing a poem, and his terminology might be dictated more by the demands of scansion than any concern for ethnographic accuracy. Similarly, the use of French/Frankish terms did not recur in Aversan charters after the 1070s, and therefore might be dismissed as little more than a passing fad, or indeed as a peculiarity of the particular notary who wrote all four of the documents in question.

However, when medieval chroniclers wrote of a people, the concept they had in mind was an artificial one, based on ideas of common descent, language, law, behaviour and character, but not necessarily a reflection of reality – rather of how they perceived a people ought to be. Hence Malaterra's view of the Normans: 'a most astute people, eager to avenge injuries, looking rather to enrich themselves from others than from their native fields . . . unless they are held in thrall by the yoke of justice, they are a most unbridled people'. In this he repeated a theme, one might almost say a cliché, developed by a number of other writers, most notably (somewhat later) Orderic Vitalis.[71] Yet in practice most medieval 'peoples' were a construct, a product perhaps of common language and culture and of a sense of political identity, but certainly not of common descent, and often actively recruiting outsiders to their ranks, as indeed was the case in Normandy itself, where prominent families such as the Tosny and the Giroie were descended from immigrants (from the Ile-de-France and Brittany

---

70 *Malaterra*, I.1–3, pp. 7–8. Some of Malaterra's concern with the duchy was specific to the Hauteville family, such as the stories recounted about Tancred, the father of the clan, and his son Serlo, in *ibid.*, I.38–40, pp. 24–5, but from the earlier passage it is clear that he thought of the Normans as a people (*gens*) with a particular character and identity, who came from Normandy. Cf. *Amatus*, I.1–15, pp. 9–20, especially *cc.* 3–4, pp. 11–13.

71 *Malaterra*, I.3, p. 8. Cf. G.A. Loud, 'The *Gens Normannorum*. Myth or reality?', *Proceedings of the Fourth Battle Conference on Anglo-Norman Studies 1981*, ed. R. Allen Brown (Woodbridge 1982), 104–16, 204–9 [reprinted *Conquerors and Churchmen*]; H.D. Kahl, 'Einige Beobachtungen zum Sprachgebrauch von *Natio* im mittelalterlichen Latein mit Ausblicken auf das neuhochdeutsche Fremdwort «Nation»', *Aspekte der Nationbildung im Mittelalter*, ed. H. Beumann and W. Schröder (Sigmaringen 1978), pp. 63–108.

respectively).[72] Indeed William of Apulia noted of the early career of the Normans in Italy: 'if any malefactor from the neighbourhood fled to them, they freely received him. They taught their own language and customs to those who joined them, creating a single, seemingly united, people.'[73] Similarly Malaterra described one of Robert Guiscard's exploits during his days as a freebooter in Calabria, in which his companions were Slavs, themselves probably recent immigrants to southern Italy, 'so loyal to him that they might have been brothers'.[74] Above all, however, there were other Frenchmen, who shared a language and culture with people from the duchy of Normandy, and who would be all too easy for those in Italy to confuse with 'genuine' Normans from the duchy, and for the chroniclers to subsume under the generic term 'Normans', constrained as these writers were by artificial ideas of kinship and national identity (though of the south Italian writers only Malaterra referred expressly to the Scandinavian origins of the Normans, which was a topos of authors from Normandy itself).[75]

That people from other parts of France, and indeed from elsewhere in Christendom, were involved in the Norman conquest of southern Italy will become clear in the subsequent pages, while the extent to which southern Italy and Sicily were ever really 'Norman' will be discussed in the chapter on the society of Norman Italy [below, pp. 278–89]. But while there were certainly quite a few non-Norman Frenchmen who came to southern Italy in the eleventh century, some of whom became quite prominent, as well as north Italians such as Arduin, the majority of the incomers were actually from the duchy of Normandy. Of those who can be identified from south Italian charter evidence, L.-R. Ménager has calculated that between two-thirds and three-quarters (depending on the criteria for identification used) came from Normandy itself. Furthermore a substantial proportion of the non-Normans came from Brittany and Maine, areas bordering on Normandy and as the eleventh century wore on increasingly under its influence.[76]

But while the chroniclers' generic references to Normans thus largely (even if not completely) reflected the genuine origins of the invaders, this

72   L. Musset, 'Aux origines d'une classe dirigeante: les Tosny, grands barons normands du Xe au XIIIe siècles', *Francia* v (1977), 45–80; *Orderic*, ii.22.
73   *W. Apulia*, I.165–8, p. 108.
74   *Malaterra*, I.16, pp. 16–17.
75   While not emphasising the significance of the Normans' Scandinavian descent in the manner of Dudo of St Quentin and William of Jumièges, Malaterra correctly identified Rollo, the first 'duke', as a Norwegian (as opposed to Dudo, who alleged he was a Dane): cf. here D.C. Douglas, 'Rollo of Normandy', *English Historical Review* lvii (1942), 417–36.
76   L.-R. Ménager, 'Pesanteur et étiologie de la colonisation normande de l'Italie', *Roberto il Guiscardo*, pp. 189–214, and his 'Inventaire des familles normandes et franques émigrées en Italie méridionale et en Sicile (xi–xii siècles)', in *ibid.*, pp. 259–390.

still leaves a most important question unresolved. Why should it have been persons from the duchy of Normandy who came to southern Italy in the eleventh century? We should of course dismiss the chroniclers' remarks about the inherent qualities of the Normans, their skill at war and cunning, that desire for rule and *strenuitas* (dynamism, endurance, courage – the word is a difficult one to translate, but embodies all these ideas) so beloved of Malaterra.[77] These were part of the Norman 'national myth', propagated not just by south Italian writers but by those in Normandy and England as well, and reflect not historical reality – there is nothing to show that the Normans were any braver or more skilled at war than their neighbours – but how medieval intellectuals perceived a successful people ought to be distinguished. We must not confuse propaganda and reality. Yet that still leaves the question of why it was the Normans rather than, for example, Frenchmen in general who took over southern Italy.

The chroniclers also pointed to such factors as over-population in Normandy. 'The number of this people grew so great that neither field nor forest were sufficient to provide so many folk with the necessities of life.'[78] Malaterra pointed out how it was the impossibility of providing for so many sons from the family property that led the Hauteville brothers to emigrate to Italy, and the Hautevilles were by no means unique in facing this problem. Thus Giroie, the ancestor of the clan so well known to Orderic Vitalis as the founders and patrons of his own monastery of St Evroul, had seven sons, only one of whom became a cleric (and thus ought to have been disqualified from having children), though in this case the problems of inheritance were simplified by the premature death of several of the brothers before they married and had heirs of their own. Nevertheless, in the next generations five of Giroie's grandsons, two granddaughters and three great-grandsons ended up settling in southern Italy, while several other family members (including two of his sons) made more temporary visits.[79] Similarly of the eight sons of Guimund des Moulins, from near Mortagne on the border of the duchy, at least three and quite possibly more emigrated to Italy, as well as a daughter. While political miscalculation may have played a part in the destiny of this family, at least one of Guimund's sons was already prominent in southern Italy before he became involved in rebellion in Normandy.[80]

---

77 Capitani, 'Specific motivations and continuing themes in the Norman chronicles of southern Italy' [above, Introduction note 8], pp. 1–46, especially 6–11.
78 *Amatus*, I.1, p. 10.
79 *Malaterra*, I.5, p. 9 [above, p. 2]; *Orderic*, ii.30, 58, 98, 102–4, 126–8, iv.16, 32.
80 The eight sons are listed as witnesses to a ducal confirmation of a donation of their father (1040 x 1050), *Recueil des actes des ducs de normandie (911–1066)*, ed. M. Fauroux (Caen 1961), pp. 280–1 no. 117. Cf. Ménager, 'Inventaire', pp. 332–6.

Furthermore, while over-population in Normandy, and the problems of providing an adequate endowment at home for the members of such large families as these, undoubtedly played a part in the Norman diaspora, such factors were hardly a peculiarity of Normandy. There was a general demographic increase in eleventh-century France, and pressure of population alone can hardly explain why it should be Normans in particular who took the road to southern Italy. Pilgrimage also played a part in this. Whether or not one takes either or both of the 'Salerno' and 'Gargano' stories of the Normans' arrival in Italy as trustworthy, they were agreed that Normans first came to the south as pilgrims. There is good evidence for the activities of Normans as pilgrims in the first half of the eleventh century; indeed Duke Richard II, while remaining in the duchy himself, sponsored and financed others to go to Jerusalem, while his younger son Duke Robert died on his way back from the Holy Sepulchre in 1035.[81] Southern Italy was a focal point on the pilgrimage routes of Christendom. It contained the important, if poorly documented, shrine on Monte Gargano, was relatively close to Rome, and despite the opening up of a feasible land route through the Balkans in the 1020s, many pilgrims to Jerusalem still preferred (as indeed they continued to do in the twelfth century) to travel through Italy to one of the ports of the Adriatic coast, make the short sea-crossing to Durazzo, and then follow the Via Egnatia to Constantinople.[82] But again, pilgrimage was hardly a phenomenon confined to Normandy, and while it may have led to the first contacts between the duchy and southern Italy it does not explain why Normans in particular went to settle there.

Admittedly there might be other destinations available for those from other parts of France wishing to seek opportunities abroad. Above all, for those from areas such as Aquitaine and Burgundy there was Spain, where the southward advance of the Christian frontier during the eleventh century was materially aided by the participation of French knights in the military expeditions of the Spanish kings. But even here we should not assume too much. Though Frenchmen were going on pilgrimage to Compostella from before the millennium, their first large-scale military involvement in the peninsula came only with the expedition against Barbastro in 1063–4 (in which some Normans were also involved), and by this date

---

81 Hugh of Flavigny, *Chronicon, MGH SS* viii.393–4, 398–9; *Rodulfus Glaber Opera*, pp. 36, 202–5; *The Gesta Normannorum Ducum of William of Jumièges, Orderic Vitalis and Robert of Torigny*, ed. E.M.C. van Houts (2 vols, Oxford 1992–5) [henceforth GND], ii.81–5 [lib. VI cc. 11–12].

82 *Orderic*, iii.166, reported the death in Apulia of a Norman noblewoman on her way to Jerusalem in the early 1100s. Cf. more generally, G.A. Loud, 'How "Norman" was the Norman conquest of southern Italy?', *Nottingham Medieval Studies* xxv (1981), 18–19 [reprinted *Conquerors and Churchmen*].

most of mainland southern Italy had already been conquered by the Normans. French involvement in Spain was anyway very much limited by and under the control of the local Spanish rulers, and not the product of spontaneous and large-scale immigration. While one cannot ignore the significance of the links of marriage and kinship between, for example, the kings of Castile and the dukes of Burgundy, and the kings of Navarre and various prominent Gascon nobles, in directing men from these areas to Spain, it would appear that the most significant phase of such immigration came after 1100.[83]

The most plausible answer comes from the social and political conditions within Normandy itself. Though they differed as to names and details, all the chroniclers who described the Normans' arrival in Italy were agreed that some of those involved, including the leaders, were men exiled from their native land. As we have already seen, both Amatus and, later, Orderic described the exile of an early Norman leader, whom Amatus named as Gilbert Buatère and Orderic called Osmund Drengot, by Duke Robert after the killing of a certain William – one assumes that they referred to the same incident or story, but whether (assuming there was a basis in fact) the duke was correctly named must be more dubious since Amatus connects this with the attack on Apulia in 1017 (a decade before Robert became duke).[84] However, Amatus was writing a long way from Normandy and probably sixty to seventy years after the event, and if Orderic was in Normandy he was writing a century later, so errors about chronology and names were perfectly possible. However, the fact that an early leader was a political exile is attested also by the much more contemporary account of Glaber, and may therefore be taken as inherently likely. Certainly Duke Richard II was quite prepared to exile the disobedient, including his own nephew and namesake whom (perhaps c. 1020) he deprived of the county of Avranches and sent abroad.[85]

But at least under the rule of Richard II Normandy was relatively peaceful. After his death in 1026 law and order rapidly broke down. The duchy was close to civil war in the late 1020s, and if Duke Robert may have prevented this by diverting the attention of his nobles to aggressive campaigns against Normandy's immediate neighbours (or perhaps to defending

---

83   M. Bull, *Knightly Piety and the Lay Response to the First Crusade. The Limousin and Gascony, c. 970–1130* (Oxford 1993), pp. 70–114.

84   It was clearly not a mistake of the French translator since the second redaction of the Montecassino chronicle, which copied this section of Amatus, also named Robert as the ruler of Normandy: *Chron. Cas.* II.37, p. 237.

85   C. Potts, 'The earliest Norman counts revisited: the lords of Mortain', *The Haskins Society Journal* iv (1992), 29–31.

the duchy against the attacks of these neighbours), conditions became much worse after his death in 1035. His son and successor William was only seven years old and born outside wedlock, and during his long minority his nobles 'immediately hatched plots and rebellions, and fierce fires raged all over the country . . . Mars was raging and numerous troops of warriors were being killed', as one contemporary put it.[86] In the words of the duke's biographer, 'unrestrained lawlessness then prevailed everywhere'.[87] As an adult, Duke William had to reassert his authority by waging a series of campaigns against rebels, particularly in western Normandy in 1047, and then in the central and eastern parts of the duchy in the early 1050s, when he also faced external attack, including from his erstwhile ally King Henry of France. Only with his victory over the latter at Varaville in 1057 was Normandy once more relatively orderly and secure.

A number of explanations have been advanced for the scale and duration of the political crisis in Normandy in the second quarter of the eleventh century. A generation or more ago this was seen as the result of the rise of new aristocratic families. More recently it has been suggested that what was occurring was rather the consolidation of territorial lordships (quite possibly by already prominent families) at the expense of the duke, the Church and of lesser landowners, and the competition which resulted from such pressures, particularly with the intrusion into western Normandy of nobles from the east of the duchy. Alternatively the key has been sought in rivalries within the extended ducal kin-group, brought to a head by the succession of a child of doubtful legitimacy who was challenged by relatives who felt that they had as good if not better a claim to rule.[88] One might indeed suggest that all these factors played their part in undermining the peace and stability of the duchy. But whatever the cause, it seems undoubted that the breakdown began soon after 1026 and internal dispute, plundering of ecclesiastical land and unauthorised castle-building were rife c. 1030 under Duke Robert.[89] Internal feuding reached a peak in the late 1030s/early 1040s with a series of revenge murders involving some of the leading aristocratic

---

86 GND, ii.92 [lib. VII.1].

87 *Guillaume de Poitiers, Histoire de Guillaume le Conquérant*, ed. R. Foreville (Paris 1952) [henceforth WP], lib. I *c.* 6, p. 14.

88 D.C. Douglas, 'The rise of Normandy', *Proceedings of the British Academy* xxxiii (1947), 101–30 [reprinted in *Time and the Hour. Some Collected Papers of David C. Douglas* (London 1977), 95–119]; D.C. Douglas, *William the Conqueror* (London 1964), pp. 83–104; D.R. Bates, *Normandy before 1066* (London 1982), especially pp. 99–128, 172–82; E. Searle, *Predatory Kinship and the Creation of Norman Power* (Berkeley, CA, 1988), pp. 159–234.

89 Hugh of Flavigny, *Chronicon, MGH SS* viii.401, even if some of the details adduced here are highly unlikely. Cf. for the theft of Church lands under Duke Robert, *Recueil des actes des ducs de Normandie*, pp. 214–16 no. 74.

families and the young duke's own household, and though Duke William began to restore order from the mid-1040s onwards, the use of such expedients as the Truce of God, enforced by ecclesiastical sanctions (something hitherto unknown in Normandy), shows how much need there was to reinforce central authority.[90] However, once Duke William began to reassert control he acted decisively and ruthlessly, and while his sycophantic biographer William of Poitiers praised the duke's supposed mercy to those who opposed him, there was little or no sign of this in practice. Indeed other sources suggest that William the Conqueror was renowned rather for his severity, keeping those who fought against him in prison rather than ransoming them, and (as William of Poitiers himself admitted) deliberately massacring the French army which opposed him at Varaville.[91] Though William of Poitiers alleged that the duke forgave the two relatives who led the rebellions of 1047 and 1051–4, Count Guy of Brionne and William of Arques, it was notable that both these counties were suppressed and the counts concerned immediately and completely disappeared from Normandy.[92] Indeed, elsewhere in his account, William of Poitiers himself praised the severity of ducal justice: 'they [the rebel inhabitants of Domfront] knew all too well how brigands and robbers were hated in Normandy, and rightly handed over to justice, to be rarely if ever acquitted', and he claimed that 'by his [the duke's] efforts and laws Normandy was cleansed of robbers, murderers and evil doers'.[93]

For these 'robbers' and 'evil doers' we may just as easily read 'rebels' or 'political opponents', many of whom were either deliberately sent into exile by the duke (perhaps invoking the custom of *ullac* or banishment once exercised by his distant Scandinavian ancestors), or decided to flee rather than face the decidedly uncertain prospect of his mercy. Some at least of these men can be shown to have chosen southern Italy as their destination. These included the duke's cousin William Warlenc, count of Mortain, exiled *c.* 1055 or a little later, according to Orderic Vitalis for little more than loose or disloyal talk, but more probably either because as a relative in the male line he was perceived as a threat by the duke, or so that his property and position could be used to endow the latter's half-brother Robert. William left for Apulia, allegedly with only a single attendant, but

90   M. de Bouard, 'Sur les origines de la trêve de Dieu en Normandie', *Annales de Normande* ix (1959), 169–89. For the murders, GND, ii.92–7 [lib. VII.2–3].

91   WP, I.25, 34, pp. 58, 82. Cf. *Self and Society in Medieval France: the Memoirs of Guibert of Nogent*, trans. J.F. Benton (New York 1970), p. 69. *Orderic* ii.78 on the sufferings of the prisoners captured at Mortemer in 1054.

92   WP, I.9, 28, pp. 20, 62.

93   WP, I.17, 48, pp. 38, 118. Cf. *Orderic*, ii.284.

some years later his daughter Eremburga became the second wife of Count Roger of Sicily.[94] In 1061 the abbot of St Evroul fled from Normandy, 'knowing that the duke was raging against him and all his kindred, and was out for their blood, and being warned by friends that the duke's fury would not stop short of violence to him', and he too ended up in Apulia, dependent on the patronage of Robert Guiscard.[95] The fact that as yet there were no clear rules governing the hereditary succession to property in Normandy may also have been a factor here. Thus after his involvement in the rebellion of the early 1050s, Guimund des Moulins's lordship ended up in the hands of his son-in-law, while his sons were left to seek their fortune elsewhere, which several of them did in Italy, along with at least one loyal vassal from Normandy.[96] Indeed the departure of rebels and troublemakers from Normandy to southern Italy can be attested into the early twelfth century – one of those to suffer then at the hands of King Henry I was (ironically) the son of the man who had gained Guimund des Moulins's lordship and daughter.[97]

Ducal wrath might not be the only factor here. So too could family competition. One of the reasons why so many of the Giroie family ended up in southern Italy was the pressure upon that kin-group by their powerful rival Roger of Montgomery, one of the aristocrats most favoured by Duke William, who seems to have turned a blind eye to the harassment of his neighbours in central Normandy by Roger and more particularly by his formidable wife Mabel of Bellême, 'that cruel woman, who had shed the blood of many and had forcibly disinherited many lords and compelled them to beg their bread in foreign lands'. When the latter's enemies finally succeeded in murdering her in 1077, they too fled to Apulia.[98]

In periods of disorder, some people inevitably lost out, especially given that property was changing hands through external pressure, and that successful aristocrats were enforcing their lordship over others, and as a corollary of this demanding services and renders from them, and enforcing (a hitherto absent?) judicial control.[99] And in particular, in the period of

---

94   GND, ii.126–8 [lib. VII.19]. Cf. *Orderic*, ii.312; *Malaterra*, IV.94, p. 93.

95   *Orderic*, ii.90–1, 99–103.

96   *Recueil des actes des ducs de Normandie*, pp. 432–4 no. 225; Ménager, 'Inventaire', pp. 332–6.

97   *Orderic*, iii.134–5. Cf. the case of Robert de Montfort in 1107: *Orderic*, vi.100–1.

98   *Orderic*, ii.54–5, 90–1, iii.122–7, 134–6 (quotation). Orderic loathed Mabel for her attacks on St Evroul.

99   E.g. the knight summoned to the court of the abbot of St Evroul and deprived of the lands he held from the monastery, and the vassals of the same monastery whom Abbot Robert handed over to his cousin Arnold of Eschauffour, who 'piled all kinds of oppressive services upon them and their men, and forced them to perform castleguard': *Orderic*, ii.62–4, 80–2.

crisis after 1035, with internecine violence rife for the best part of a decade, there were those who were forced out or who sought to avoid the very real dangers of life in the warrior class. The cloister was one means of escape – taken, for example, by Herluin, the minor noble who retired from the world to found what became the influential monastery of Bec, either as the result of a vow when he was in mortal danger in the midst of a battle (if we are to believe Orderic), or because of his increasing dissatisfaction with the sinfulness of secular knighthood (as his biographer would have it).[100] Others also found the pressures of secular life intolerable: such as a man called Gilbert who had tried unsuccessfully to prevent the murder of Duke William's cousin and steward Osbern *c.* 1040, or Robert de Grandmesnil who at about the same time entered St Evroul after his father had died of wounds received in a family feud.[101]

Yet such an escape was only likely to appeal to a minority of the knightly class, certainly while they were physically able and still relatively young. Furthermore entry to the cloister was almost invariably accompanied by a landed endowment, and for families like the Hauteville or the Moulins with an abundance of sons and limited property (in the latter case thanks to their falling foul of the duke), this might not be feasible. Hence emigration in search of new opportunities was perhaps a more plausible alternative, especially for those brought up to warfare as a way of life, and particularly if they already had kin or acquaintances in southern Italy. Furthermore, there is a very striking, if unprovable, relationship between the chronology of events in Normandy and the expansion of the Normans in the south. The breakdown in order in the duchy in the later 1020s was followed by the first permanent settlement of the Normans in Italy at Aversa in 1030. The crisis after 1035 came a few years before the Normans' expansion into Apulia in 1041–2. Then, as we shall see later, the first rebellion against Duke William and its suppression in 1047 came just before the Normans moved into Lucania and northern Calabria, and the crisis of the early 1050s and William's great victory at Mortemer in 1054 (accompanied as it was by the proscription of leading rebels) was followed by the conquest of the rest of Calabria and further gains in Apulia in the late 1050s and early 1060s. In each case problems in Normandy preceded by a very few years an important stage in the expansion of the Normans in the south. It seems very probable that exiles, voluntary or involuntary, from Normandy swelled the ranks of those in Italy, and facilitated new gains there.

---

100   *Orderic*, ii.12; C. Harper-Bill, 'Herluin, Abbot of Bec, and his biographer', *Studies in Church History* xvi (1978), 15–25, especially 16–18.
101   *Cartulaire de l'Abbaye de St. Trinité du Mont de Rouen*, ed. A. Deville, in the appendix to *Cartulaire de l'Abbaye de St. Bertin*, ed. M. Guérard (Paris 1840), pp. 423–5 no. 6; *Orderic*, ii.40.

But we should also not underestimate the positive attractions of southern Italy, especially for those whose relatives were already established and prospering there. Once the first Normans had settled in Italy, there was good reason for those who had connections there to take advantage of them. This was the case with the Hautevilles:

> the younger brothers, who had up to now been forced by their youth to remain at home, heard rumours of how their elder brothers, who had gone before them, had by their valiant behaviour raised themselves to the heights of honour and lordship, and as soon as age permitted they followed after them . . . a great multitude of their relatives and compatriots, and even people from the surrounding regions, followed them in the hope of gain.[102]

Similarly, some sixty or more years later, Arnulf de Montpincon set off for Apulia, 'mindful of the acquisitions of his uncle, William de Grandmesnil'.[103]

After 1066 there were of course the counterattractions of England as a land of opportunity and profit. But it should be remembered that the conquest of England was an enterprise organised under ducal leadership, in which the greatest gains were made by a small number of leading aristocratic families, most of whom were related to the duke himself, and their immediate vassals. For those outside this charmed circle, southern Italy was probably still a more attractive proposition; certainly emigration there continued until the early years of the twelfth century. Nor was the perception of southern Italy as the land of opportunity entirely confined to Normans. A charter from Chartres, from perhaps the 1070s, tells an interesting tale. A certain Geoffrey the Black had 'laid down the belt of knighthood' and retired to the cloister, abandoning also his wife and two small sons. When they had grown to adolescence (their late teenage years, perhaps?), they had set off 'to the unknown lands of Apulia', though not before one of them had fathered an illegitimate child whom he had left with his hapless mother. The family was not penniless, for she was able to provide an endowment for that boy, who had been taught his letters, to become an eight-year-old child oblate in the monastery where his grandfather was a monk. But with no doubt restricted opportunities at home (and how much had the family's property suffered without an adult to protect it?), a life of adventure abroad had beckoned invitingly.[104] The document reminds us that not only Normans, but also their neighbours might look to the 'new frontier' of southern Italy. But, as we have seen, there were good reasons why the conquest of the south should have been a primarily Norman enterprise.

---

102 *Malaterra*, I.11, p. 14.
103 *Orderic*, iii.166.
104 *Cartulaire de l'Abbaye de Saint-Père de Chartres*, ed. B.E.C. Guérard (2 vols, Paris 1840), i.221–2.

CHAPTER III

The conquest of the mainland

Apulia and Aversa in the 1040s

Arduin and his Norman allies seized Melfi, with the connivance (or at least the acquiescence) of the inhabitants, in the early part of March 1041. Within a few days they had also taken over the neighbouring towns of Venosa and Lavello, a few kilometres to the east, and Ascoli, some 25 km to the north. A few days later, on 17 March, the Normans defeated a hastily gathered Greek force, apparently under the personal command of the Catepan Michael Dokeianos, in a battle fought beside the River Olivento, between Melfi and Lavello.[1] This success consolidated their hold on the frontier region around the Upper Ofanto valley, and the invaders then moved down the valley towards the coast. Seven weeks later, on 4 May 1041, they fought a second battle, this time against a considerably larger Byzantine army near Canne, 50 km to the north-east, not far from the coastal town of Barletta, and either on or very close to the site of their predecessors' disastrous defeat in 1018. Despite outnumbering the invaders several times over, the Greek forces were once again defeated with heavy casualties.

Estimates of numbers by medieval writers are notoriously untrustworthy. But while those given by the near-contemporary chroniclers for the Norman army in this Apulian campaign show some variations, they are not

---

1 Skylitzes, *Synopsis Historiarum*, p. 426 [= Cedrenus, *Historiarum Compendium*, p. 547], confused the first two battles of 1041, but plausibly ascribed the initial defeat to the Catepan's failure to collect sufficient troops before engaging the enemy. For the date, *Annales Barenses*, *MGH SS* v.54.

inherently improbable (unlike Malaterra's estimate of the 60,000 Greeks who opposed the invaders). Amatus suggested that before his *coup de main* at Melfi Arduin had used the excuse of going on a pilgrimage to Rome to make a discreet visit to Aversa and there enlist the support of Count Rainulf, or at least his permission to recruit among the latter's followers, some 300 of whom returned with the Milanese soldier to Apulia.[2] In addition there were those Normans who had served with him in Sicily, some of whom may have been part of the Melfi garrison. In all there may have been 500–700 knights, and William of Apulia would suggest about 500 infantry as well, though William added that they were poorly equipped, and only a few (apparently even among the knights) had chain-mail hauberks and shields. The Bari Annals estimated the total number of the invading army at the second battle as some 2,000 – again a not unreasonable figure since the initial successes probably led to local recruits joining the Norman forces.[3]

Although medieval armies were not generally very large, the relatively small number of the invaders (and perhaps the deficiencies of their equipment) may explain why, despite their initial victories, the campaign appears to have stalled after this second defeat of Michael Dokeianos. Alternatively, the Normans' casualties in these two encounters may have been more numerous than the chroniclers imply. Both sides devoted the summer of 1041 to building up their strength. The Byzantines hastily transferred troops from their army in Sicily and from Calabria. The hapless Dokeianos was superseded, and sent in the reverse direction to Sicily (though he was not completely disgraced since he was eventually to be killed some years later fighting the Pecheneg nomads in the Balkans). He was replaced as Catepan by the son of the former governor Basil Boiannes. But while Amatus suggested that the latter arrived along with soldiers from the elite Varangian Guard, the Greek historian Skylitzes was adamant that no reinforcements accompanied him, and he had to make do with the troops who were already in Italy. It is probable therefore that these Varangians were among the forces brought from Sicily.[4]

Meanwhile their opponents sought local allies, and to secure these they decided on a change of leadership, inviting Atenulf, the younger brother of the prince of Benevento, to be their lord. Amatus wrote that this was 'because it strengthened the resolution of the inhabitants of this land' – an explanation that is much more convincing than William of Apulia's suggestion that Atenulf bribed the Normans to become their leader, though

2   *Amatus*, II.17–18, pp. 75–6.
3   *W. Apulia*, I, lines 255–9, p. 112; *Malaterra*, I.9, p. 12; Bari Annals as note 1 above.
4   Skylitzes, *Synopsis Historiarum*, pp. 426–7, 470 [= Cedrenus, *Historiarum Compendium*, pp. 546, 601].

no doubt any money or valuables he could provide were very useful.[5] What happened to Arduin thereafter is unclear – he simply disappears from the story. Furthermore, Amatus continued that:

> the Normans did not cease to scour the principate [*of Benevento? or did this mean the area of Apulia under their control?*] for men strong and capable of fighting. They gave them, and had distributed, horses from the wealth of the Greeks whom they had conquered in battle, and they promised to give those who helped them against the Greeks a share in what they acquired in future. And so the people took heart and wished to fight against the Greeks.[6]

This again suggests that the Normans were as yet relatively few in number, and the campaign was certainly not one conducted by them alone. It was only in September 1041 that they once again took the offensive, moving south-eastwards along the flank of the Murge ridge to attack the Byzantine forces which had been gathered near Montepeloso (modern-day Irsina) on the River Bradano. There they secured a complete victory, routing the Greek army and capturing the Catepan. As a result the coastal towns abandoned the empire and threw in their lot with the Normans. But once more the terms in which this was described (this time by William of Apulia) are significant: 'All the fortified towns of Apulia, Bari (the most important), Monopoli, Giovenazzo, and several other cities, abandoned their alliance with the Greeks and came to an agreement with the Franks.'[7]

This was not therefore a conquest – rather towns which were already restive under Byzantine rule, and in practice only loosely subject to it, decided to change sides and join the insurrection, of which the Normans were a very important, but by no means the only, part.

Nor were the Normans very united, as was to become very apparent over the winter of 1041–2. Once again, as earlier in Sicily, a dispute about the profits of victory had a corrosive effect on the victors. Prince Atenulf decided to ransom the prisoners captured at Montepeloso (including presumably the Catepan), but rather than sharing the money with his Norman allies retired to Benevento and kept it for himself. Not surprisingly, the disappointed Normans decided to find a new leader. But whereas those who had come from Aversa looked to their existing overlord, Guaimar of

---

5   *Amatus*, II.23, pp. 84–5, followed by *Chron. Cas.* II.66, p. 299; *W. Apulia*, I, lines 318–25, p. 116. William may, however, have been correct to place the choice of Atenulf as leader *after* the second battle, whereas Amatus implies that it was between the two encounters, i.e. in April.
6   *Amatus*, II.25, p. 88.
7   *W. Apulia*, I, lines 398–401, p. 120. The *Annales Barenses* added Matera to the towns specifically named.

Salerno, and he himself was actively soliciting support among the Normans as a whole, we are told that 'those who held land in Apulia' preferred to have Argyrus son of Melus as their leader, and in February 1042, after a meeting with their envoys in Bari, he became their commander.[8]

William of Apulia explained this decision in a suitably poetic, if rather unlikely, manner: the Normans loved Argyrus and wanted him as their leader because his father had been their benefactor. Yet given that Melus had died twenty years earlier, and few if any of the handful of Normans who had survived his defeat could still have been alive, the real explanation must be rather different, and more prosaic. Argyrus had already taken control of Bari in 1040, albeit that (since the Catepan Michael Dokeianos had been received there a few months later) he must at that stage still have acknowledged imperial rule.[9] The agreement with him was a necessary part of the defection of the coastal towns to the side of the invaders. Who were 'those who held land in Apulia', who preferred him to Guaimar? Both Amatus and William of Apulia suggest that even before Melfi was captured the Normans involved had chosen twelve of their number as leaders, call-ing them counts – Amatus adding that Count Rainulf of Aversa was largely responsible for who was chosen. The Normans clearly must have been divided into contingents under various leaders, men either from families of some status in Normandy or who had already distinguished themselves in Italy like William de Hauteville, 'the Iron Arm'. But it may be that these authors writing years after the event anticipated the division of territories, which we know from Amatus to have occurred in the autumn of 1042. Anyway, those among the Norman leaders beholden to Rainulf of Aversa were unlikely to have been antagonistic to Guaimar, to whom Rainulf remained loyal and closely linked. The real division at the start of 1042 may have been between those like William 'the Iron Arm' who had taken part in the Sicilian expedition and those recruited from Aversa. We have already suggested that Guaimar IV had used the Sicilian expedition as an oppor-tunity to rid himself of potential trouble-makers, and Malaterra wrote that those who had returned with Arduin from Sicily were reluctant to take service once again with the prince of Salerno, 'knowing the untrustworthi-ness of Guaimar'.[10] But the need for an alliance with the patriciate which dominated the coastal towns was probably the key factor recommending Argyrus, who controlled (or was the most influential figure in) Bari, the most important of these towns. The consequence was that by the spring of

---

8   *W. Apulia*, I, lines 414–40, pp. 120–2. Date: *Annales Barenses* and Lupus, *Annales, MGH SS* v.54, 58.
9   Above, p. 80.
10 *Malaterra*, I.8, p. 12.

1042 only Taranto and the Salento peninsula, the most southerly part of Apulia, and the isolated port of Trani, were left in Byzantine hands.

It was not only the Normans and their allies who were affected by internal disputes. So too were the Byzantines. The death of the Emperor Michael IV in December 1041 and the succession of his nephew Michael V had led to the return to favour of the disgraced Giorgios Maniakes, who was then sent to Apulia to retrieve the disastrous situation there. (In addition the former prince of Capua, Pandulf IV, was allowed to return to Italy, doubtless in an attempt to destabilise the Lombard principalities of the Campania.) Maniakes arrived at Taranto in April 1042. Argyrus and the Normans tried to force a further pitched battle, but were unsuccessful, and as soon as their forces withdrew northwards Maniakes launched a counter-offensive which recovered both Matera and Monopoli in June. It should be noted that this was directed not so much against the Normans as against those towns which had thrown off Byzantine rule, and the disloyalty of their inhabitants was punished by mass executions when these towns surrendered. At the same time the citizens of Giovenazzo were persuaded to change sides and abandon their alliance with the Bariots and the Normans. After the failure of their attempt to bring Maniakes to battle, Argyrus and his Norman allies concentrated on the coastal region north of Bari, first recapturing Giovenazzo and then at the end of July besieging Trani, the last town in Byzantine hands in northern Apulia.[11]

Yet by this time loyalties in Apulia were becoming increasingly confused, not least as a result of events in Constantinople. The Emperor Michael V proved unpopular and was deposed and blinded in April 1042. If we are to believe William of Apulia, his successor, Constantine Monomarchos (Constantine IX), sent large sums of money to Argyrus in Bari to lure him back to loyalty to the empire. However, Constantine's accession placed Maniakes once again in a tricky position, since he was disliked and distrusted by Constantine and his advisers (a number of lurid explanations were advanced by different sources to explain this).[12] Thus while in August 1042 Argyrus abruptly called off the siege of Trani (having the siege engines burned to make certain of this), abandoned his Norman allies and retired to

---

11   For the chronology, *Annales Barenses* and Lupus, *Annales, MGH SS* v.55–6, 58. *W. Apulia*, I, lines 511–57, pp. 126–8, suggests that the Norman incursion into southern Apulia followed Maniakes's counter-attack, but his narrative is so confused as to make little sense, whereas the annalists actually date these events. For Pandulf, *Amatus*, II.12, p. 70.

12   Both *W. Apulia*, I, lines 469–70, and Skylitzes, *Synopsis Historiarum*, p. 427 [= Cedrenus, *Historiarum Compendium*, pp. 547–8] suggest that a sexual scandal was at the root of this enmity. Psellus in his *Chronographia* ascribed the rift simply to the new emperor's carelessness and contempt for his general: *Michael Psellus: Fourteen Byzantine Rulers*, trans. E.R.A. Sewter (Harmondsworth 1966), p. 194.

Bari, soon afterwards Maniakes arrested and executed two imperial officials who had been sent out to supersede him, declared himself emperor and began preparations for an expedition to Constantinople.

Disentangling both the sequence of events, and more importantly the reasons for these tergiversations is by no means easy, given the confusions within individual sources and the disagreement between them. Whatever role imperial blandishments and bribery may have played in Argyrus's change of side, equally important may have been his realisation that the Normans were potentially more of a threat to the interests of the Apulian coastal towns than were the Byzantines. Not only were the economic interests of the towns linked to Byzantium – Bariot ships were already trading as far afield as Constantinople itself[13] – but the emperor was prepared to allow the larger towns, and particularly Bari, at least a measure of self-government. Argyrus himself was to be left in effective control of Bari until he was summoned to Constantinople in 1045 or 1046, not to be disgraced but to become an important member of the imperial court.[14] And the coastal towns of Apulia, in particular Bari and Brindisi, henceforth remained obstinately attached to Byzantium and opposed to the Normans.

But the defection of Argyrus, which was greatly resented – Amatus indicated that one prominent Norman leader, Peter son of Amicus, had to be restrained from killing him[15] – also had very clear and momentous consequences for the Normans themselves. Hitherto, just as in the earlier attack on Apulia in 1017–18, they had served under native leaders, and there is evidence which suggests that they were in fact only a part (albeit perhaps the most important part) of a coalition against Byzantine rule. But in September 1042 they decided to choose a leader for themselves, and elected as their commander William 'the Iron Arm', who had played a prominent role both in the Sicilian expedition and in the earlier stages of the Apulian campaign – according to Malaterra he had risen from his sickbed to play a decisive part in the victory over the Byzantines in May 1041, and he had been one of the leaders of the foray towards Taranto in May 1042.[16] At the same time the other prominent Normans arranged a share-out of the conquests they had made or expected to make in the fairly near future. This division was to shape the development of Norman Apulia right through the period of conquest and well into the rule of Robert Guiscard as duke, and

---

13   The *Anonymi Barensis Chronicon*, *RIS* v.151, recorded the loss at Bari of a ship from Tarsus in 1045, and of one loaded with oil intended for Constantinople in 1051.
14   *W. Apulia*, II, lines 14–20, p. 132.
15   *Amatus*, II.28, p. 93. The *Pierre de Gautier* here must be a copyist's or translator's error. For this family, see Genealogical Chart VI, below, p. 304.
16   *Malaterra*, I.10, p.13; *W. Apulia*, I, lines 520–6, 543–6, pp. 126–8.

thus needs to be examined in detail. While not all the men mentioned in Amatus's account can be traced thereafter, some of them, or their descendants, were to retain the lordships created for a long period.[17]

Though Count Rainulf of Aversa had played no more than a very indirect part in the attack on Apulia, he was not forgotten, no doubt because of his senior status among the Normans as a whole, as well as his role in the preparation of the original attempt on Melfi. He was assigned the Gargano peninsula and the town of Siponto. Of the frontier towns seized by the Normans at the outset of the campaign, Count William (as he was now styled) received Ascoli, and his brother Drogo Venosa, while Lavello was assigned to a certain Arnolin. Melfi was to be held in common by all the Norman leaders. Peter son of Amicus was to have Trani, and his brother Walter Civitate in the northern Capitanata (to the west of the Gargano peninsula). A certain Rodulf, otherwise unknown, was given Canne, while further south Monopoli (on the coast *c.* 40 km south of Bari) was allocated to Hugh Toutebove, who had played a prominent part in the first battle with the Byzantines near Lavello in March 1041.[18] Other Normans were assigned lordships on the western side of the Murge ridge at Minervino (about 25 km north-east of Venosa), Acerenza (18 km south of Venosa) – which was given to Rainulf of Aversa's nephew Asclettin – and at Montepeloso. Two further lordships were established some way further south, on the River Agri in the border region between Apulia and Lucania, at Grumento and Sant'Arcangelo.

The Normans may have penetrated into this last area very soon after their original capture of Melfi. Certainly a Greek abbot from the Latinianon region of Lucania, between the Agri and the Sinni rivers, had referred to 'the invasion of the heathen' (by which he surely meant the Normans) when he made his last will and testament in May 1041. (The document also involved property near Bari, so it is possible that he may simply have meant the main attack on northern Apulia. But if that was the case, then those in Lucania were already well informed about events further north and of their potential danger.)[19] These bases on the Lucanian border were strategically significant, not least because they offered a potential barrier to Byzantine reinforcements marching north from Calabria. A Norman lordship at Grumento also acted as a defence for the southern part of the principality of Salerno, and given the renewed involvement of Prince Guaimar in Apulian affairs (which will be discussed more fully below) this may also have been a

---

17   *Amatus*, II.30–1, pp. 95–6.
18   *Malaterra*, I.9, p. 12.
19   G. Robinson, 'The history and chartulary of the Greek monastery of St. Elias and St. Anastasius of Carbone', *Orientalia Christiana* xv (1929), 138–44 no. 2.

factor in establishing a Norman lord and his followers here.[20] However, while it is quite possible – even probable – that these southern bases were already in Norman hands, this was not the case with all the places assigned in the share-out of September 1042. It is unlikely that the Normans had as yet penetrated into the Gargano region or the northern part of the Capitanata. The coastal towns of Siponto, Trani and Monopoli were still in Byzantine hands, and remained so for some years to come. So the division in the autumn of 1042 was not just a share-out of what the Normans actually held, but a plan for, and assignment of, future conquests. It would appear that the intention was to circle the main Byzantine stronghold at Bari from both north and south before moving in for the kill. But even where the lordships distributed were as yet unconquered, the arrangements of 1042 provided a strong claim for the future – thus a generation later the Gargano region (which may well only have been conquered in the 1050s) was indeed held by a junior branch of the family of Count Rainulf.[21]

However, while the Normans of Apulia now sought to have an overall leader of their own, they still needed some local allies, and in addition they hoped to legitimise their conquests. Furthermore those from Aversa at least still recognised Guaimar of Salerno as their overlord. Hence the Normans requested Guaimar to sanction the arrangements made, and to recognise Count William as their leader, and it was only after securing Guaimar's sanction that the latter was formally recognised as their count. To ensure the smooth working of this arrangement Guaimar gave William his niece as his wife (in what was to be the first in a whole series of diplomatic marriages between Salernitan princesses and members of the Hauteville kin). The corollary was that Guaimar now claimed to be the duke (i.e. the overlord) of Apulia, and from January 1043 onwards he so styled himself in his charters. In that same month, with Maniakes about to set off across the Adriatic in his bid for the imperial throne and thus in no position to intervene, the prince of Salerno joined with the Normans in a full-scale attack on Bari. (For all the more cautious strategy outlined above, the circumstances doubtless seemed propitious to try a *coup de main*.) But after a five-day siege they abandoned the attempt and retreated.[22] This was Guaimar's one and only military intervention in Apulia, but he continued to style himself as duke for several years to come, and the Apulian Normans to recognise some sort of lordship from him.

---

20   D. Clementi, 'Stepping stones in the making of the "Regno" ', *BISIME* xc (1982/3), 259–61.
21   W. Jahn, *Untersuchungen zur normannische Herrschaft in Unteritalien (1040–1100)* (Frankfurt 1989), pp. 53, 322–3.
22   *Amatus*, II.29, pp. 93–5; *Cod. Dipl. Cavensis*, vi.225–6 no. 1016; *Anonymi Barensis Chronicon*, *RIS* v.151.

Yet for some years after 1043 the Norman advance in Apulia was relatively slow. The confusion created in the Byzantine ranks by the revolt of Maniakes was short-lived, for the latter was killed soon after he landed in the Balkans in February 1043. Even as he was crossing the Adriatic, his successor as Catepan, Basil Theodorokanos, was welcomed in Bari, and he and Argyrus were then able to launch an expedition against Maniakes' base in Otranto without Norman interference. While there are some indications in the annalistic sources for the next few years of internal dispute within Bari, that town and coastal Apulia south of Bari remained under Byzantine control (or, as long as Argyrus was present, perhaps one should say in alliance with Byzantium). The defence of the Byzantine province certainly did not rely merely on Greek troops – given the growing problems of the empire in the 1040s there may not have been many of these to spare for southern Italy. Thus in December 1045 the new Catepan, Eustatios Palatinos, granted a village near Bari with a fiscal exemption to a Lombard judge in return for his loyalty both against the Normans and 'when affairs went badly under the rebel Maniakes', and for more recent military service.[23] In northern Apulia Peter son of Amicus tightened his grip on the area round Trani, fortifying the coastal towns of Barletta and Bisceglie to the north and south of the town, and founding two new settlements inland from it at Andria and Corato to complete the encirclement, but he seems to have been unable to capture Trani itself. Similarly Siponto was still in Byzantine hands in 1052, even if by that stage it was only accessible to them by sea.[24] Nor, despite defeating the Catepan in a battle near Taranto in the spring of 1046, were the Normans able to make more than a very temporary and ephemeral penetration into the Salento peninsula in the south. The key to this situation would seem to be twofold. The Byzantines retained possession of most of the larger towns: Bari itself, Trani, Brindisi, Taranto, Matera and Otranto. It was only the smaller settlements, most of them inland, which had fallen to the invaders. Those towns which remained under Byzantium may well have been in practice largely autonomous – certainly in the period between the autumn of 1043 and that of 1045 when there was no Catepan in office and Argyrus was probably functioning in that role, in fact if not in name.[25] But they had no wish to be ruled by the Normans. Secondly, one may suspect that the latter were still relatively few, and that – as was shown at Bari early in 1043 – the siege of a major town was still beyond them.

23 J. Lefort and J.-M. Martin, 'Le Sigillion du Catepan d'Italie Eustathe Palatinos pour le juge Byzantinios (décembre 1045)', *MEFR* xcviii (1986), 525–42 (edition at pp. 527–9, also in *Cod. Dipl. Barese* iv.67–8 no. 32).
24 *W. Apulia*, II, lines 30–1, p. 132 *Anonymi Barensis Chronicon*, *RIS* v.152.
25 von Falkenhausen, *Untersuchungen*, p. 92; Lefort & Martin, 'Le Sigillion du Catepan', p. 535.

Hence the Norman advances in the mid- to late 1040s were in the more peripheral areas. In 1044 Count William (significantly along with Prince Guaimar) led an expedition into northern Calabria and established a base at Scribla. By 1045, when Drogo de Hauteville captured Bovino, the Normans were beginning to penetrate into the Capitanata, and by 1047 Count Walter son of Amicus held Lesina, on the Adriatic coast to the north-west of the Gargano peninsula.[26] By 1050 one of Walter's vassals was established in a lordship at Devia, some 15 km along the coast to the east.[27] So by that stage, if not yet established in the Gargano itself, the Normans were a fair way towards surrounding it. But we cannot assume that there was as yet a complete take-over, even of areas into which the Normans had penetrated. Although, given notarial conservatism and the fact that even the invaders would sometimes acknowledge nominal (and clearly quite meaningless) imperial rule, dating clauses in charters cannot be taken as an infallible guide, it would appear that, for example, the Troia/Lucera region of the Capitanata remained independent of the Normans well into the 1050s.[28] And in 1045, in a charter issued at Serracapriola, not far from Lesina on the other bank of the River Fortore, a Lombard count, Tasselgardus of Larino, made a grant to a monastery but reserved the right to raise as many cavalrymen as he might need from the property concerned 'to fight against the Greeks or Apulians or neighbouring towns'.[29] By 'the Apulians' in this document we should probably understand 'Normans'. Indeed, the River Fortore probably marked the effective northern boundary of Norman penetration in the east of the peninsula at this period. But it is also interesting that the Byzantines were still considered a potential factor in the northern Capitanata in the mid-1040s.

By 1045 the Normans were also making incursions into the principality of Benevento. In or shortly before June of that year a Beneventan count was killed fighting 'the most wicked Normans' in the Caudine Valley to the south-west of the town.[30] It cannot have been very long afterwards that the father of Desiderius, the future abbot of Montecassino, who came from a

---

26 Lupus, *Annales*, *MGH SS* v.58; *Romuald*, p. 179; *Le Colonie cassinesi in Capitanata* i *Lesina*, 71–2 no. 23.

27 Jahn, *Untersuchungen zur normannische Herrschaft*, p. 362 no. 1.

28 E.g. *Cod. Dipl. Cavensis*, i.160–3 nos 126–7 (1045/6, wrongly dated by the editors to 910/911); *Les Chartes de Troia (1024–1266)*, ed. J.-M. Martin (*Cod. Dipl. Pugliese*, xxi, 1976), pp. 96–103 nos 9–11 (1050, 1053, 1059). However, n.b. *Cod. Dipl. Tremiti*, ii.159–63 no. 51 (1054), a document of the Norman Robert, lord of Devia, dated by the regnal years of Constantine IX.

29 *Cod. Dipl. Tremiti*, ii.111–15 no. 35.

30 Pergamene Aldobrandini [formerly, to 1990, on loan to the Biblioteca Apostolica Vaticana, now at Frascati], Cartella I no. 36.

family of Beneventan nobles, was also killed in battle against the Normans.[31] By the early 1050s much of at least the southern part of the principality had been taken over by the invaders, though those who came along the Caudine and Calore valleys must have derived from Aversa rather than the newer Norman power centres in Apulia. However, on this western side of the peninsula the progress of Norman expansion was still relatively slow, and subject to check. Thus, although in the early 1040s all but a very few strongpoints in the Montecassino lands were in the hands of the Normans, the vigorous action taken by Abbot Richer, helped by troops he had brought from northern Italy and by Lombard nobles from the Abruzzi who had long-standing links with the monastery, enabled the monks to expel the intruders from almost the whole of the *Terra Sancti Benedicti* in 1045. The decisive moment seems to have come when a Norman count (so he was described) called Rodulf from Aversa and a small party of knights imprudently came to pray in a church in S. Germano (the town immediately below Montecassino), and were promptly ambushed by the irate populace. Most of the party were massacred, and Rodulf was kept a prisoner for nearly a year until he swore not to molest the abbey's lands in future. Emboldened by this, the monks and their troops and allies attacked and captured all the strongpoints remaining in the Normans' hands. Those of the enemy they captured were deprived of their horses, armour and weapons before being sent back to Aversa (or in Rodulf's case ransomed). To consolidate this success, Abbot Richer set in train a comprehensive programme of fortification on the abbey lands, gathering the inhabitants together in fortified villages (*castella*) to protect them from any renewed incursions. By 1059 there were some twenty of these *castella* on the *Terra Sancti Benedicti*, the majority of them either founded or (in the case of existing settlements) provided with walls and towers in the late 1040s.[32] These measures, combined with a degree of restraint exercised by Guaimar IV over the Normans of Aversa, proved effective, and the abbey lands remained largely safe from the Normans thereafter.

Furthermore, while Count Rainulf of Aversa, with Guaimar's agreement, took over Gaeta in the autumn of 1042, after the Gaetans had rejected the prince's own rule, this lordship proved ephemeral. In the summer of 1045 the citizens took advantage of Count Rainulf's death to invite the Lombard count of Aquino to become their lord, according to

---

31 *Chron. Cas.* III.2, p. 364.
32 *Chron. Cas.* II.71–3, pp. 309–15; G.A. Loud, 'The Liri Valley in the Middle Ages', *Archaeological Survey in the Lower Liri Valley, Central Italy under the Direction of Edith Mary Wightman*, ed. J.W. Hayes and I.P. Martini (British Archaeological Reports, International Series 595, Oxford 1994), pp. 57–8, 123–4.

Leo Marsicanus because they hated Guaimar's rule. Count Atenulf remained as duke thereafter, and his rule over Gaeta was unchallenged until the final take-over of the principality of Capua by the Normans in the early 1060s.[33]

The failure to keep control of Gaeta is explicable. This was (by contemporary standards) a large and populous town, at some distance from the Normans' base at Aversa (about 70 km by the most direct route), and separated from it by the barrier of the extinct volcano of Roccamonfina and the Monti Aurunci. But, just as in Apulia, one may suspect that in the Campania shortage of numbers was also a factor. That the death of only fifteen Normans (albeit combined with the capture of a prominent leader) gave such a decisive encouragement to the defenders of the Montecassino lands is surely significant.[34] Furthermore, while the opportunity for Norman expansion was provided primarily by divisions among the rulers of the indigenous population, as with the tensions between the Lombard upperclass and the Byzantines in Apulia, between Pandulf IV and Guaimar of Salerno in the west, and within the towns of southern Italy such as Gaeta, neither in Apulia nor on the west coast were the Normans themselves united. This became apparent in Apulia after the death of Count William 'the Iron Arm' in the winter of 1045–6, when the claims of his brother Drogo to succeed him as the overall leader of the Apulian Normans were challenged by Count Peter son of Amicus, and there appears to have been some actual fighting between the two factions.[35] At almost exactly the same time similar tensions came to a head among the Aversan Normans, following the death of Count Rainulf in the summer of 1045 (perhaps on 1 May), and then that of his nephew and successor Ascletin not long afterwards. Here the succession was disputed by another of the old count's nephews, called Rainulf like his uncle, and another (unrelated) Norman called Rodulf who was supported by Guaimar. (It is possible that this Rodulf was the same man whose capture so aided the monks of Montecassino, but we cannot be certain, and the chronology of these events must make this doubtful.) The other candidate, Rainulf, was backed by the former prince of Capua, Pandulf IV, returned from his exile at Constantinople and anxious to recover his former principality. While the representative of the established comital line was successful, and Guaimar's candidate driven from Aversa, matters were then complicated by the arrival of yet another nephew

---

33 *Chron. Cas.* II.74, p. 315; Chalandon, *Domination normande*, i.87. Atenulf was in his thirteenth
   year as duke in August 1057: *Cod. Dipl. Caiet.*, ii.15–17 no. 203.
34 *Chron. Cas.* II.71, p. 310.
35 *W. Apulia*, II, lines 27–37, pp. 132–4.

of Count Rainulf I, Richard, with a substantial following and some support at Aversa for his claim to the countship. Not surprisingly the incumbent count did not welcome him, and for a time he had to make his way in Apulia, where his brother's former followers recognised him as lord of Genzano (10 km north-east of Acerenza). But he then fell out with Count Drogo, who 'captured Richard and put him into prison'.[36]

Amatus's account of the comital succession at Aversa after 1045 is complicated enough, but other evidence shows that in fact it was even more difficult and problematic than he suggested. According to Amatus, it was while Richard was a prisoner that his cousin died, and it was then the influence of Guaimar IV which persuaded Drogo to release him, and led to his succession as count of Aversa. All this may well have been true, but it was certainly not the whole story, for either Count Asclettin or Count Rainulf II had left a young son called Herman, who in March 1048 was nominally ruling Aversa under the tutelage of a certain William Bellabocca, whom Leo Marsicanus alleged was a family connection of the Hautevilles (*de cognatione Tancredi*). Subsequently the Aversans expelled this William, and according to Leo, 'summoned Richard son of Asclettin from Apulia, and appointed him as their count'.[37] And indeed a charter of 1050 from Aversa was dated in the fourth year of 'the young boy [*puerulus*] Herman and the first year of his uncle [*avunculus*] Count Richard'. No month is given, but from Richard's regnal years given in subsequent Aversa charters, it seems probable that this document must date from November or December 1050, and that Richard must have become count no earlier than November 1050.[38] There is no further mention of the child Herman.

One might therefore plausibly suggest that Count Drogo deliberately kept Richard a prisoner to enable his relative William to act as co-count and actual ruler of Aversa, and that it was not just the persuasion of Prince Guaimar but the Aversans' expulsion of William in favour of the representative of the 'legitimate' line of their original count, Rainulf I, that led to Richard's release. Furthermore we know that at some stage no later than the early 1050s Richard married Drogo's sister Fressenda. Might

---

36 *Amatus*, II.32–4, 36–7, 39, 44–6, III.12, pp. 97–101, 103–4, 106, 110–12, 126; *Il Necrologio di Cod. Cassinese 47*, ed. M. Inguanez (Rome: FSI 1941), p. 58. The source cited by Chalandon, *Domination normande*, i.109, to place Rainulf's death in June is an eighteenth-century forgery.

37 *Amatus*, III.12, pp. 126–7; *Chron. Cas.* II.66, p. 301; *Cod. Dipl. Aversa*, pp. 395–6 no. 49.

38 *Cod. Dipl. Aversa*, pp. 390–2 no. 46. (One should note that the chartulary of St Blaise, Aversa, from which these documents have been taken, is not in chronological order.) If Herman was the son of Rainulf II, then in fact Richard was his cousin, not his uncle: however, again strictly speaking, *avunculus* meant mother's brother, and if Herman was Asclettin's son then Richard would have been his paternal uncle (*patruus*).

this have been part of the agreement that secured Drogo's consent to his succession?[39] Whatever the case here, this period of instability at Aversa had been a lengthy one, nearly five and a half years from the death of Count Rainulf until the eventual accession of his nephew Richard, and had been exacerbated by the interference of the prince of Salerno (still at this stage at least the nominal ruler of the Capuan principality) and of the leader of the Apulian Normans. These problems surely contributed to the slackening of Norman pressure on the abbey of Montecassino.

Thus both in Aversa and in Apulia the Normans were divided. Nor should we be surprised that members of the Aversan comital family were potential or actual rivals to one another. For when, following the example of his older brothers, Robert de Hauteville came to southern Italy, soon after his half-brother William's death and at about the same time as Richard of Aversa (1046/7 therefore), Count Drogo gave his half-brother a distinctly unsympathetic welcome. He refused to endow him with a landed base, and he then shunted him off to Calabria – as much to get him out of the way as anything. Siblings were potential competitors as well as allies (as was to be the case among the sons of Tancred in the years to come when Robert was their leader), and in the mid-1040s Drogo may well have not had much to give. Nor at first did Robert find northern Calabria very profitable, for Amatus continued:

and then Robert returned to his brother and told him of his poverty. And what he said with his mouth was shown by his face, for he was extremely thin. But Drogo turned his face away, and all those of his household turned their faces away.[40]

One more factor affecting the Normans in southern Italy at this period was the relationship of their leaders with Guaimar IV of Salerno. One modern scholar has recently suggested that the Emperor Conrad II's investiture of Rainulf as Count of Aversa rendered the Normans legally independent of any overlord; that therefore the relations between Guaimar and the Normans who aided him after that date were those of paymaster and mercenaries, not lord and vassals; and furthermore that Guaimar's involvement in Apulia after 1042 was simply as the representative of the western

<hr>

39 The account of Richard's marriage in *Amatus*, II.45, p. 112, is confused by the translator's substitution of 'Count of Aversa' for 'Count of Apulia' (which the sense clearly implies). However, *Amatus*, VII.1, p. 292, and *W. Apulia*, III, lines 637–40, p. 198, make clear that the mother of his son Jordan was Guiscard's sister, although they do not name her. She was, however, identified in several of Jordan's charters between 1079 and 1089: Loud, 'Calendar', nos 21, 26, 27, 30–1, 36, 38, for full references. She was clearly named after her mother, Tancred de Hauteville's second wife.
40 *Amatus*, III.9, p. 122; cf. *ibid.*, II.46, III.7–8, pp. 112–14, 120–2.

emperor, and thus once again no formal overlordship there was recognised.[41] However, such suppositions are implausible. Whatever problems there may be in interpreting the phraseology of Amatus, given that his account only survives in a much later French translation, his description of the relations between Guaimar and the Normans appears unequivocal. Thus when Guaimar's candidate as count was driven from Aversa, 'Drogo hastened to punish the injury done to his lord'. When Guaimar agreed to recognise the rival claimant, Rainulf II:

> Rainulf was summoned in front of Prince Guaimar and in front of Drogo. He came as soon as he was summoned, and under oath he put himself under the lordship of the prince. And so he was invested from the prince's hand with the banner and [received] many gifts.[42]

Certainly the western emperors used banners to invest men who had sworn fealty to them with fiefs, especially those on the borderlands of their empire. Indeed Conrad II had used a banner as the symbol of his lordship when investing Guaimar himself as Prince of Capua and Rainulf I as Count of Aversa in 1038.[43] But Guaimar's use of the same instrument cannot therefore be taken as proof that he saw himself simply as the emperor's south Italian representative, however Conrad or his son Henry III (ruler from 1039 onwards) may have regarded his status. The earliest surviving charter from Norman Aversa, and the only one known from before Henry III's south Italian expedition of 1047, was dated by Guaimar's regnal years, both as prince of Salerno and, separately, as prince of Capua.[44] Furthermore, Guaimar's assumption of the title of Duke of Apulia in January 1043 (again calculating his regnal years as duke separately from those relating to his other dominions) cannot be interpreted other than as a claim to full lordship – and one should note that his rule was expressly recognised (or at least his regnal years used to date a charter) at Melfi in 1044.[45] Guaimar was then recognised as their overlord both at Aversa and in that part of Apulia controlled by the Normans, at least up to 1047.

However, his assumption of such authority was probably not what the western emperor had envisaged, either in 1038 or thereafter. Hence when Henry III came to Italy in the winter of 1046, although his primary concern was to sort out the chaos of rival claims which then enveloped the

---

41   Clementi, 'Stepping stones in the making of the "Regno"', pp. 252–7, 263–74.
42   *Amatus*, II.36, 39, pp. 104, 106.
43   *Amatus*, II.6, pp. 63–5; J. Deér, *Papsttum und Normannen. Untersuchungen zu ihren lehnsrechtlichen und kirchenpolitischen Beziehungen* (Cologne 1972), pp. 22–30.
44   *Cod. Dipl. Aversa*, pp. 389–90 no. 45.
45   Ughelli, *Italia Sacra*, vii.196–8.

papacy, he also took steps to regulate the political balance in southern Italy. During his very brief journey south of Rome in January and February 1047, he deprived Guaimar of his title as Prince of Capua, and reinstated the former prince Pandulf IV. Since his return from Byzantium in 1042, Pandulf had been a significantly disruptive element within the principality, whom the prince of Salerno, despite his Norman allies, had been unable to overcome (not least because some Normans had entered the former prince's service). By restoring Pandulf, the emperor hoped to re-create something of a balance of power in the Lombard principalities. But in addition, he invested both Count Rainulf II of Aversa and Count Drogo with the land which they held. Then, after being refused entry to Benevento, and in response burning down the suburb outside the city walls, the emperor set off northwards through the Abruzzi, having been in southern Italy little more than a month.[46]

The emperor's intervention, brief as it was, considerably altered the status of the various parties active in south Italian affairs. Guaimar henceforth abandoned his claims to be Duke of Apulia – the last reference to him with this title came, significantly, in a charter of January 1047.[47] It therefore seems clear that his use of this title was without imperial sanction, and very probable that it was the Emperor Henry's irritation with this usurpation of imperial rights that led him to clip Guaimar's wings in 1047 by depriving him both of this dignity and of his title over the Capuan principality as well. Furthermore, the status of the county of Aversa altered, at least in theory. Aversan charters no longer used the regnal years of Guaimar, but rather those of the Normans' own counts (in addition the dating clause of the charter which first refers to Count Richard, in December 1050, acknowledged the emperor's rule).[48] One might assume, therefore, that it was the imperial recognition of 1047 which first sanctioned the Norman dominions as independent entities.

However, one might also suggest that some of these changes were more cosmetic than really significant. Guaimar's control over the principality of Capua had always been fragile and incomplete, and it is doubtful whether Pandulf IV exercised much more after he regained his position. The north of the principality, notably Montecassino and its lands (ruled by the German Abbot Richer), those of the counts of Aquino (by now also ruling Gaeta) and of the counts of Teano, who had formerly supported Guaimar,

---

46 *Amatus*, III.1–3, pp. 116–18; *Chron. Cas.* II.77–8, pp. 320–3; *Annales Beneventani*, ed. Bertolini, p. 136. Henry was at Colonna, south-east of Rome, on 7 January. He then went via Montecassino to Capua, where he was on 3 February. By 1 March he had already reached the River Sinello in the Abruzzi on his way north.

47 *Cod. Dipl. Cavensis*, vii.26–8 no. 1073.

48 *Cod. Dipl. Aversa*, pp. 395–6 no. 49 (March 1048), 390–2 no. 46 (Nov./Dec. 1050).

were all outside his effective control. He probably now ruled over no more than the plain immediately round the town of Capua and the hills to its east. In reality therefore, the balance of power in the Campania may not have been greatly altered by the emperor's action, for the destabilisation of the Capuan principality was too far advanced for 'legal' claims to have much significance. But the impact of these changes on the Norman possessions took some time to have any effect, because whatever the theoretical status of the Norman counties of Aversa and Apulia, their leaders remained closely linked to Guaimar. Amatus indeed would suggest that little had been changed by the imperial investiture of the Norman counts. His description of how Richard became count of Aversa in 1050 employed terminology little different from that used for the relations between the prince and the Normans before 1047:

> Prince Guaimar requested Drogo to hand Richard over to him, and Drogo, as a loyal count, willingly surrendered him. And Richard was brought to Salerno. There Guaimar had him clad in silk and brought him to Aversa, and with the consent and agreement of all the people made him count. And Richard humbled himself in fealty to the prince, and the prince rejoiced in Richard's prosperity.[49]

The reality, as we have seen, may have been more complex and drawn-out than this idealised description – and Richard's captivity at Drogo's hands and the latter's interference in Aversan affairs explains why the new count was prepared still to recognise the prince of Salerno as his superior. It was part of the price of his succession. But the episode shows how much more important actual political circumstances were than any theoretical 'legal' status such as that established by the occasional (and as we have seen, very brief) imperial interventions in southern Italy. Much the same might be said about the relationship between Guaimar and the Normans of Apulia. Mutual self-interest explained their co-operation before 1047, reinforced by the marriages of Count William to Guaimar's niece and of Drogo, soon after he succeeded his brother, to Guaimar's daughter Gaitelgrima. But while Amatus was at great pains to stress Drogo's loyalty '[he] had such devotion and fealty to the prince that Guaimar many times acted against him but he could never make him abandon his fealty. Nothing could make Drogo do anything against Guaimar's wishes'[50] – careful reading of his account suggests that the reality was rather different, even before 1047. Thus when Drogo

---

49 *Amatus*, III.12, pp. 126–7.
50 *Amatus*, II.35, pp. 101–2. Gaitelgrima's name is known from only one later charter, Jahn, *Untersuchungen zur normannische Herrschaft*, pp. 377–8 no. 7 (1087), in which Drogo was named as the first of her three husbands.

decided to acquiesce in the take-over of Aversa by Count Rainulf II at the expense of Guaimar's candidate Rodulf, and persuade the prince to follow his lead: 'Drogo asked on Rainulf's behalf. But it was not a request but a command, for he bent the will of the prince to what he wanted.'[51] Yet even after 1047 Amatus portrayed Drogo as Guaimar's 'loyal count', and they remained closely allied in the fast-changing south Italian political situation after 1047.

However, one might suggest that whereas up to 1047 the Normans of both Aversa and Apulia remained theoretically subordinate to Guaimar, self-interest was always more important than status, and that did not change with the Emperor Henry's intervention. What *did* change was the relative power of the protagonists. For while Guaimar IV was pursuing his ambitions to be the ruler of Capua and the coastal towns, and the overlord of Apulia, his own ancestral principality was beginning to lose the cohesion which had hitherto made it more stable than the other two Lombard principalities and his princely authority was beginning to erode. Before Guaimar's reign, the prince had retained a monopoly over public authority, and had been careful not to share this even with the members of his immediate family. Guaimar, however, created semi-independent seigneuries for his brothers, at Sorrento in the west and at Capaccio in the south-east of the principality. In the years 1047–9 he divided the family's personal lands (hitherto held in common, but under the prince's direction) with his two brothers, henceforth to be inherited separately. And in addition his reign saw the growth of legal and fiscal concessions, and even of the alienation of parts of the Salerno town defences, to private individuals (by no means all of whom were princely relations) and sometimes to *consorterie*, groups of private owners holding in common. The princely fisc was diminishing and his exercise of authority was being diluted.[52] Meanwhile, by the later 1040s the Normans were expanding and growing in strength, advancing north into the Capitanata, south into Calabria, and into the principality of Benevento both east from their bases in Apulia and west from Aversa. Admittedly the Normans themselves were often disunited. But while that may sometimes have hampered their advance, it also meant that their leaders (and up to 1047 their nominal overlord Guaimar) were often powerless to control them, as in the attacks on the Montecassino lands. By the late 1040s it was becoming all too clear that the Normans were far more than a useful adjunct to the existing powers in the west and centre of southern Italy, and a destabilising force in Byzantine Apulia. The erstwhile mercenaries were already a long way down the road to becoming masters. And it was into this promising situation (for the newcomers) that, either just before or perhaps just after the imperial

---

51   *Amatus*, II.39, p. 106.
52   Taviani, *Principauté lombarde de Salerne*, ii.846–7, 856–97.

expedition of 1046–7, there arrived the man who was to make the Norman conquest of southern Italy a reality – Robert Guiscard.

The Battle of Civitate and its aftermath

The Emperor Henry III's investiture of the Norman leaders in 1047 may have had little real impact upon their power or status, at least in the short term. But in two further respects the imperial expedition of 1046–7 had profound and lasting consequences for the Normans of southern Italy. The first of these stemmed from the changes to the papacy that occurred in the wake of the synod of Sutri of December 1046, when Henry appointed a German bishop as Pope Clement II. Not only did the series of German popes who followed him embark on a campaign of Church reform that was to have momentous and far-reaching results for Christendom as a whole, but from the time of Leo IX (1048–54) onwards they took a much greater interest than had their predecessors in events in southern Italy. Secondly, the refusal by the citizens (and presumably the prince) of Benevento to submit to the emperor had led him to instruct Pope Clement to excommunicate the inhabitants, and to punish them further by giving the Normans his permission to continue their attacks on the principality.[53] Given this encouragement, it was hardly surprising that their ravages increased, but within a very few years this was to bring them into serious conflict with the new reforming papacy.

Furthermore, as we have already suggested, it is probable that the flow of emigration from Normandy increased in the late 1040s as a consequence of Duke William's efforts to restore order and increase his authority within his duchy. This in turn facilitated the Norman expansion in the south. However, not all the incomers were political exiles, and in particular there is no indication whatsoever that the Hauteville brothers came to Italy for this reason. Rather, to them it was the land of opportunity, made so in particular by the pre-eminence of their brother Drogo. The latter's growing power *vis-à-vis* his fellow Normans was shown when he appointed his younger full-brother Humphrey as count at Lavello, thus either succeeding or displacing the former holder Arnolin.[54] Soon afterwards, probably in 1048, Drogo

---

53 *Chron. Cas.* II.78, p. 323.
54 *Malaterra*, I.11–12, p. 14. However, Arnolin's son Ernulf was later (in 1072) to be count of Lavello: H. Houben, *Die Abtei Venosa und das Mönchtum im normannisch-staufischen Süditalien* (Tübingen 1995), pp. 252–3 no. 18. Was Humphrey's appointment because in 1047/8 he was still a child?

sent his newly arrived half-brother Robert to the base that the Normans had already established at Scribla in northern Calabria, on a hilltop site overlooking the Val di Crati and the Roman Via Popilia, the main inland north–south communications route in the region.[55] However, the locality proved unhealthy – the plain of Sybaris just to the east was marshy and malarial. Some time later (the sources are difficult to reconcile – it may have been only a few months or perhaps as much as several years after-wards) Robert shifted his base some 20 km to the south-west to S. Marco Argentano, on a mountain site (428 metres/1,380 feet above sea level) to the west of the Crati Valley, which because of its height was a considerably healthier location. From these two successive headquarters he raided as far south as Cosenza. To begin with, at least, he had only a few Norman followers, and so he attracted to his side a group of Slav settlers, who acted as light infantry, scouts and plunderers. As yet there was no real conquest – indeed Robert was little more than a bandit, subsisting on booty and the profits of kidnapping, sometimes purchasing food from the local inhabitants but more often stealing it, and as his power waxed making nearby towns and settlements pay tribute. The turning point, and one of the defining moments of Robert's career, came when he arranged a parley with Peter, the governor (or perhaps simply one of the leading inhabitants, the sources disagree here) of Bisignano, just on the other side of the River Crati from S. Marco. He used his great strength to drag the other man from his horse, and carried him off to pay a large ransom.[56] Quite *when* this took place is hard to determine – indeed the whole chronology of Robert's early career in Calabria is vague – but the impact of such depredations was undeniable. A later charter (written in 1071) gave a retrospective but none the less bleak view of the coming of the Normans to Lucania and northern Calabria, as it sketched the history of a local Greek monastery:

> Not long afterwards our whole country was seized and occupied by heathen hordes, and everything came to complete ruin. And moreover they made a complete end of the army of the emperor and the whole was chaos. . . . As

---

55 A.-M. Flambard-Héricher, 'Un instrument de la conquête et du pouvoir: les chateaux normandes de Calabre. L'Example de Scribla', *Les Normands en Méditerranée*, ed. P. Bouet and F. Neveux (Caen 1994), pp. 89–109.

56 *Amatus*, III.7–10, pp. 120–5; *Malaterra*, I.16–17, pp. 16–18. Most commentators, e.g. Chalandon, *Domination normande*, i.118–20, Taviani-Carozzi, *La Terreur du Monde*, pp. 184–92, place these events before the Battle of Civitate (following Amatus), rather than after (as Malaterra). On the literary depiction of the kidnapping, G.A. Loud, 'Anna Komnena and her sources for the Normans of southern Italy', *Church and Chronicle in the Middle Ages. Essays Presented to John Taylor*, ed. I.N. Wood and G.A. Loud (London 1991), pp. 54–6 [reprinted in *Conquerors and Churchmen*].

time went by and the disorder increased, the whole place became waste land.[57]

Amatus's account implies that Drogo was unable or unwilling to endow Robert in Apulia – and Robert had already shown his independent tendencies by offering to take service with the newly restored Prince Pandulf of Capua, before very quickly falling into dispute with him about the rewards for his assistance.[58] Furthermore, Drogo would have been unwilling to renew dispute with the other Norman leaders of Apulia by unduly favouring newly arrived members of his family. But by c. 1048 Norman parameters were expanding, and it was precisely in what to them were peripheral areas – such as Calabria, where resistance was more disorganised than in what to the Byzantines was the key region (central and southern Apulia), where the larger towns were situated – that gains were to be made. Just as vulnerable was the principality of Benevento, where the defiance of Henry III by the prince and the people of his principal town had allowed the Normans an 'open season' to seize the surrounding area. By the early 1050s two powerful leaders had established themselves not far from Benevento: a certain Count Hugh, otherwise unidentified but who we are told was the commander of 'the Beneventans [i.e. the Beneventan Normans]'; and Gerard who led 'the men of Telese' (on the River Calore about 20 km west of Benevento) and also held Buonalbergo (20 km to the north-east of that town). A third Norman, Radulfus des Moulins, had established himself further north in the vicinity of Boiano, in an upland valley to the north of the Monti del Matese.[59]

Gerard of Buonalbergo was to prove a staunch ally of Robert Guiscard and founded one of the main aristocratic dynasties of Norman Italy. According to Amatus, Guiscard's early career in Calabria was difficult – no doubt the unhealthy conditions at Scribla did not help – and he twice returned to Apulia, looking for reinforcements or (certainly the first time) for some other more attractive opening. 'His knights were few, he was poor in the necessities of life, and he lacked money in his purse. Indeed he lacked everything, except that he had plenty of meat. As the children of Israel survived in the desert, so Robert lived on his hilltop.' None the less his half-brother Drogo proved unsympathetic. However, on his second return to Apulia Robert encountered Gerard – and indeed it was the latter who,

---

57 Robinson, 'Carbone', 171–5 no. 8 (date of the charter established by A. Guillou, 'Notes sur la société dans le Katépanat d'Italie au XIe siècle', *MEFR* lxxviii (1966), 451).

58 *Amatus*, III.6, pp. 119–20.

59 *W. Apulia*, II, lines 133–6, p. 138.

apparently on hearing of his exploit at Bisignano, first referred to him by the famous nickname, Guiscard – 'the cunning'. Gerard offered him his aunt Alberada (his father's presumably much younger sister) as a wife and then proposed to serve under him, or at least as his ally, with some 200 knights. With this substantial reinforcement Robert made immediate gains in Calabria and 'ate up the land'.[60]

There are, however, some puzzling features to this account. Why was Gerard so willing to help Robert? Furthermore Drogo was extremely reluctant to sanction the marriage: 'he said that in no way would he allow this relationship', and it took a great deal of persuasion both from Robert and from the count's chief men before he changed his mind. This may have been due to his reluctance to see the power of his potentially troublesome half-brother so materially enhanced. Similarly, if we follow Amatus's chronology, Gerard's offer of alliance came after Robert had extracted the ransom from the hapless Peter of Bisignano, and had thus begun to make real progress in Calabria. He may therefore have wished to link his fortunes with a 'coming man'. However, there is a further possibility. Some years later Guiscard repudiated his wife, despite the fact that she had borne a son to him, on the grounds of consanguinity. Most historians have assumed that this was simply an excuse, and that his real motive was political, to allow him to marry a Lombard princess to facilitate his continued take-over of the south. Yet it is notable that Gerard of Buonalbergo remained loyal to him – he was never involved in any of the revolts that Robert faced in Apulia, and when Guiscard set off to attack Byzantium in 1081 he associated Gerard, 'his most faithful friend' as William of Apulia called him, with his son by his second wife in the government of southern Italy. Furthermore, both Amatus and Malaterra reported the alleged consanguinity in the most matter-of-fact terms, as though there was no doubt in the matter.[61] One might suggest therefore that Gerard and Robert were actually related. This would certainly explain why Gerard was apparently so anxious to help Robert. One might indeed go further. Was Drogo's reluctance to sanction the marriage explicable not just because he felt little for Robert, or even distrusted him (they were after all only half-brothers, and Drogo was probably ten years or more older), but because Gerard was perhaps a relation of Robert's mother, Tancred de Hauteville's second wife? He would thus have been related to Robert, but not to Drogo, Tancred's son by his first marriage. This must remain a speculation, but such a hypothesis does make sense of Amatus's

---

60   *Amatus*, III.7, 11, pp. 121–2 (quote), 126.
61   *Amatus*, IV.18, p. 194; *Malaterra*, I.30, p. 22; *Chron. Cas.* III.15, p. 378 (perhaps dependent on Amatus). Cf. *W. Apulia*, IV, lines 193–7, p. 214.

story, and reminds us that there were tensions among the incoming Normans, and even among the Hauteville kin.[62]

None the less, by 1050 the invaders' advance was manifest. And in the early months of that year Pope Leo IX came to southern Italy, visiting Capua and Salerno before going on pilgrimage in April to the shrine of St Michael on Monte Gargano. What he saw profoundly shocked him. His contemporary biographer recorded that:

> He journeyed on pilgrimage to the frontiers of Apulia, to repair the
> Christian religion which seemed almost to have disappeared there; and
> in particular he sought to bring about peace between the local inhabitants
> and the Normans. The princes of the area had formerly recruited the latter
> to help them against foreign peoples, but now they suffered them against
> their will as savage tyrants and plunderers of their native land.[63]

By this time there is every indication that the Normans were cordially hated by many of the local inhabitants, above all for their brutal and destructive methods of warfare. The theft of foodstuffs, seizure of plough teams, cutting down of vines and olive trees (which might take years to become fruitful again) and destruction of crops – all actions well attested by the chroniclers – brought misery and the spectre of starvation to the indigenous population. Amatus wrote that Leo 'begged them [the Normans] to cease their cruelties and to abandon their oppression of the poor', while Leo himself accused them of burning churches and indiscriminately slaughtering non-combatants.[64] Similarly from the 1040s onwards charters complain that cultivation or the payment of rents have been made impossible because of the depredations of the 'cursed Normans'.[65] Not surprisingly local people loathed the invaders. The monks of Montecassino had the greatest difficulty rescuing the Norman leader Rodulf from the angry populace of S. Germano who had massacred his followers in 1045, and a couple of weeks later had similar problems saving from their own troops the Norman garrison of Sant'Andrea which had surrendered to them on terms.[66] Indeed, the hatred

---

62 I owe this perceptive suggestion to my doctoral student Christine Bonniot.
63 *Pontificum Romanorum Vitae*, ed. J.M. Watterich (2 vols, Leipzig 1862), i.157–8. Cf. Herman of Reichenau, *Chronicon, MGH SS* v.132, for very similar sentiments – again strictly contemporary, for Herman died soon after 1054.
64 *Amatus*, III.16, p. 130; Chalandon, *Domination normande*, i.123–4. For the damage wrought by the Normans, e.g. *Malaterra*, I.24, p. 20; *Amatus*, II.45, III.9, IV.14, V.23, VI.4, pp. 112, 122, 193, 243, 265; *Pontificum Romanorum Vitae*, ed. Watterich, pp. vc–ivc (*sic*).
65 E.g. *Reg. Neap. Arch. Mon.*, iv.299–301 no. 380 (1043); Taviani-Carozzi, *La Terreur du Monde*, pp. 179–80.
66 *Chron. Cas.* II.71, pp. 310–11.

felt for the incomers by many of the native population extended beyond southern Italy proper. At about this time an abbot from Normandy, John of Fécamp, was travelling to Rome, apparently to visit the pope, when he was attacked and robbed in papal territory. His letter of complaint to Leo IX alleged that:

> Hatred by the Italians for the Normans has now developed so much and become so inflamed throughout the towns of Italy that scarcely anyone of the Norman race may travel safely on his way, even if he be on a devout pilgrimage, for he will be attacked, dragged off, stripped, beaten up, clapped into chains, and often indeed will give up the ghost, tormented in a squalid prison.[67]

But what brought matters to a head in the south was the situation in Benevento. The city and its rulers had refused to submit to Henry III in 1047, and Prince Pandulf III proved equally recalcitrant when Leo came to the city in 1050, seeing the pope as the agent and ally of the emperor (who was his cousin). In reply the pope renewed his predecessor's excommunication of the Beneventans. But by that stage, with the Normans seizing territory only a short distance from Benevento itself, the townspeople had had enough. They expelled the prince and his officials and sent a delegation to the pope asking him to take on the rule of the city. Some lengthy negotiations ensued, but in April 1051 the citizens swore fealty to the pope, and in July Leo himself visited Benevento, freed its inhabitants from excommunication and took over the city in the emperor's name (that is made very clear both because the contemporary Beneventan annals thereafter dated their entries by the regnal years of Henry III and by the express testimony of the contemporary German chronicler Herman of Reichenau).[68] Drogo and Prince Guaimar were summoned, and the pope insisted that Norman attacks on Benevento and its territory should cease forthwith, something to which Drogo agreed. However, this promise proved a dead letter, because however much the count of Apulia may have been in earnest he was unable to control his fellow Normans, who continued their attacks on Benevento and its immediate territory. The pope, by now at Salerno, tried once more to persuade Drogo to control his associates (and that they were prepared to ignore any agreement with the pope shows how limited the authority of the count of Apulia still was, despite the pre-eminence of the Hauteville family). But on 10 August 1051 Drogo was assassinated at Montillaro, near Bovino,

---

67 *MPL* cxliii.798–9.
68 *Annales Beneventani*, ed. Bertolini, pp. 137–8; Herman, *Chronicon*, ad. an. 1050, *MGH SS* v.129. Cf. *Chron. Cas.* II.46, p. 254.

by some of the local inhabitants, perhaps (if we can believe Malaterra) led by a Lombard member of his own household. Several other prominent Normans were similarly murdered at the same time.[69]

Drogo's murder was a clear sign both of how unpopular the Normans were and of how far the situation in southern Italy was, from the pope's point of view, out of control. Drastic action was needed to restore order, and Leo – who in his youth had been active as a leader of his church's troops – now decided that a military solution was needed. But there was also a further factor involved, for the Byzantine empire was actively seeking assistance against the Normans. Constantine IX had already dispatched an embassy to the German court to explore the possibilities of an alliance in 1049. His chosen agent in southern Italy was Argyrus, the Bariot leader who had played such an important part in Apulian affairs in the early 1040s. He had spent some five years at Constantinople, where he had played a prominent part in the suppression of a serious revolt in 1047. In March 1051 he arrived back in Italy as the new Catepan and opened negotiations with the pope for an anti-Norman coalition. It is unlikely that Argyrus brought many reinforcements from Constantinople with him, for with the Pecheneg nomads attacking across the Danube and Turkish raiders beginning to threaten the eastern frontier of Byzantine Asia Minor the empire can have had few if any troops to spare at this time. But Argyrus was well supplied with money. William of Apulia suggested that this was to buy off the Normans, or hire some of them as mercenaries to use against the Turks – but far more significant was its use to finance an anti-Norman alliance. His first step was to send an embassy to the pope laden with presents to canvass the possibility of joint action.[70] Furthermore, from the pope's viewpoint such contacts were desirable for other, and indeed more significant, reasons than just the restoration of order in southern Italy, desirable as that might be. Leo and his advisers were above all concerned with the reform of the Universal Church. The restoration of good relations with Constantinople, after half a century of little or no contact between the papacy and the eastern empire and its patriarchate, would be a major step towards the unity and renewal of the Church under papal leadership.

Yet taking concrete measures against the Normans took a long time, not least because when the pope returned to southern Italy in the spring of 1052, accompanied by troops from Gaeta and the Abruzzi region, Guaimar

---

69 *Malaterra*, I.13, p. 14; cf. *W. Apulia*, II, lines 79–80, p. 136. More generally, *Amatus*, III.15–19, pp. 128–33.

70 *W. Apulia*, II, lines 46–74, pp. 134–6. For a very helpful discussion of Argyrus's role, E. Petrucci, 'Rapporti di Leone IX con Constantinopoli', *Studi medievali*, Ser. III.xiv (1973), 771–96.

IV of Salerno (still very closely linked with the Normans) flatly refused to co-operate, and as yet aid from the imperial court was not forthcoming. However, in April 1052 Guaimar's rule was rocked by a revolt in his restive subject city of Amalfi, perhaps brought on by the tribute he customarily exacted from it. His puppet ruler Manso was expelled, and envoys were sent to Constantinople to recall the former prince John, who had been there in exile since 1039. Then, on 3 June 1052 Guaimar himself and his younger brother Pandulf were both assassinated. The prince of Salerno's death was not directly connected with his links with the Normans (so far as we know); rather he fell victim to a conspiracy at his own court, triggered by, and apparently in alliance with, the Amalfitan revolt. The ringleaders and potential beneficiaries were his four brothers-in-law, who appear to have been members of the kin-group of the Lombard counts of Teano (from the principality of Capua).[71] But they were part of a wider group which included the brothers of the future archbishop of the city, Alfanus, and the former duke of Sorrento, another town which Guaimar had seized. The ramifications of the conspiracy suggest that there was considerable dissatisfaction in Salerno with Guaimar's rule, and it is notable that one of the first actions of the conspirators after the murder was to promise to restore property which the prince had confiscated.

However, they had made the mistake of allowing the prince's brother Guido to escape. He promptly appealed for help to Humphrey de Hauteville, who had succeeded his brother Drogo as leader of the Apulian Normans, and whose forces had already been gathered to oppose those raised by Pope Leo. In little over a week the dead prince's son Gisulf, who had held the princely title in association with his father since 1042, had been installed as prince. The Normans wreaked their vengeance on the conspirators – killing the four ringleaders and thirty-six of their associates. According to Amatus, the Normans then 'became Gisulf's knights and were invested by the hand of Prince Gisulf with the lands which they held'. Presumably what this meant was not that the Apulian Normans any longer recognised any bond of dependence from Gisulf for their lands there (this seems inconceivable after the arrangements made by Henry III in 1047), but that a number of Normans either already held or were now granted land in the principality of Salerno.[72] But more important in the short term was that the principality of Salerno would remain neutral in the approaching showdown with the pope.

---

71 Taviani-Carozzi, *Principauté lombarde de Salerne*, i.402–3.

72 *Amatus*, III.23–35, pp. 138–49; quote from *c.* 32, p. 148. There had been Normans in the region of Nocera as early as 1041; but this may have been simply a group of freebooters: *Cod. Dipl. Cavensis*, vi.170–3 no. 985.

Meanwhile, and despite the potential threat facing them, the Normans continued their attacks elsewhere. It was probably in 1052, perhaps after the pope had departed to seek assistance from Germany, that Richard of Aversa besieged Capua, but allowed himself to be bought off with a substantial money payment. And although we cannot be certain of the exact dating – this may have been early in the next year – Count Humphrey and Peter son of Amicus launched a pre-emptive strike against the forces of Argyrus and inflicted a heavy defeat upon them at Siponto.[73] All this can only have strengthened Leo in his determination to do something about the Norman 'problem' as he spent Christmas 1052 with the emperor at Worms.

The campaign of 1053 was the only concerted effort made to defeat the Normans in southern Italy, and as such its failure marked a decisive step in their conquest of the region. But widespread as the anti-Norman coalition was, it was the failure fully to combine its forces which ensured its defeat. Crucially, while Henry III had promised, and indeed dispatched, a substantial force to help the pope, once Leo had returned to Rome in March 1053, the emperor was persuaded by his advisers, and especially Bishop Gebhard of Eichstätt, to recall the troops dispatched. The only reinforcement that arrived from Germany was a force of several hundred Swabian troops, drawn from Leo's own relations and connections. Indeed, the expedition may not have been popular in Germany. Herman of Reichenau (a Swabian himself) wrote sourly that those of his compatriots who aided the pope went 'some at the order of their lords, some influenced by hope of gain, many of them wicked and depraved, driven from their country because of their various crimes'.[74] None the less, by the time he travelled to southern Italy at the end of May, the pope had assembled a substantial army, recruited partly from the principality of Capua, and partly from the Abruzzi and the Lombard counties of the northern Capitanata still nominally part of the principality of Benevento, as well as some troops from Benevento itself. If we can believe William of Apulia, there were also men recruited from the marches and the duchy of Spoleto. The south Italian leaders included Duke Atenulf of Gaeta and his brother Count Lando of Aquino, and the count of Teano, from the principality of Capua; from the Abruzzi the counts of Chieti and various members of the Borell family who dominated the region south of the Sangro Valley, as well as the counts of Guardia and Campomarino from the Biferno Valley further south on the Adriatic coast.[75]

---

73 *Amatus*, IV.8, p. 188; *Chron. Cas.* III.15, p. 378; *Anon. Barensis Chron.*, *RIS* v.152 (which suggests that Argyrus had some Lombard troops under his command).
74 *MGH SS* v.132.
75 *Chron. Vult.* iii.85–7; *W. Apulia*, II, lines 149–76, p. 140.

The intention was to march into Apulia and join forces with the Byzantine troops under Argyrus.

But, faced with this threat, the Normans were also forced to unite, whatever differences and tensions there may have been among them in the past. Under Count Humphrey's overall command, there were not only the combined forces of the Apulian Normans, including those of the Hautevilles' principal competitors Peter and Walter the sons of Amicus, but also those from the Benevento region who had done so much to spark the conflict, Count Richard of Aversa and his troops from the west coast, and Robert Guiscard and his forces from Calabria. William of Apulia estimated that they had in all some 3,000 cavalry, although only a few infantry. They intercepted the pope's army near the small town of Civitate, just south of the River Fortore on the edge of the Capitanata plain. (It was clearly vital to prevent Leo's forces joining with the Byzantine forces and their Apulian auxiliaries further south.) None the less, when the two armies approached each other, the Normans tried to negotiate. The size of the papal army, perhaps some reluctance to fight directly against the vicar of St Peter, as well as a serious shortage of food, induced them to avoid battle if they could. Their main ploy was an offer to hold the lands which they then possessed as papal vassals. However, these overtures were spurned: William of Apulia blamed the arrogance of the Germans for this, Amatus more specifically the papal chancellor Frederick of Lorraine, but it was probably inevitable. The Normans were so short of food that they had no time to spend in prolonged discussion – they had to fight immediately or disperse – and so on 17 June 1053 they attacked the papal army. The German contingent, fighting on foot, put up a bitter resistance to the Apulian Normans and to Guiscard and his troops from Calabria. But Richard of Aversa on the right wing of the Norman army charged through the Italian forces who opposed him, most of whom immediately fled. When he managed to rally his men and attack the Germans in the rear, a massacre ensued. The result was one of the very few decisive military victories of the age.[76]

The disaster at Civitate spelled the end of any hope of expelling or taming the Normans and paved the way for their conquest of the rest of southern Italy. It marked the ruin of Pope Leo's policy in southern Italy, and the catastrophic results of his military expedition were long remembered as a tragic denouement of an otherwise distinguished pontificate and a dire warning against the papacy becoming directly involved in secular

---

76   The most detailed account was by *W. Apulia*, II, lines 82–266, pp. 138–46, but is largely supported by *Amatus*, III.39–41, pp. 152–8, Herman of Reichenau and others.

warfare. Even those who otherwise admired the pope such as Peter Damian, later to be cardinal bishop of Ostia and one of the leaders of the reform party in Rome under his successors, felt that he had gravely erred by causing such bloodshed, however righteous his cause might have been.[77] Yet even though the citizens of Civitate promptly surrendered Leo to the victorious Normans, it took some time for the effects of the defeat to become fully apparent, and for papal policy towards southern Italy to change. Indeed the Normans appear to have been almost embarrassed by the capture of the pope, who was treated with the utmost respect and escorted to Benevento. Admittedly Geoffrey Malaterra claimed that in the aftermath of the battle Leo invested them with their present lands, and what in future they could conquer in Calabria and Sicily, to be held 'as an hereditary fief [haereditalis feudum] from St Peter'.[78] But there is no corroborative evidence for this assertion, and it seems clear that the Catania chronicler was here anticipating what in fact occurred six years later. Nor did the battle prevent negotiations continuing between the pope, the German emperor, the Catepan Argyrus and the imperial court at Constantinople in an attempt to revive the anti-Norman alliance. At the beginning of 1054 Leo dispatched a high-level legation to the Greek emperor, headed by Humbert, cardinal bishop of Silva Candida, while at about the same time Argyrus sent envoys to the German court, and in response to this the emperor issued a privilege protecting his father Melus's tomb in Bamberg.[79] But any chance of agreement and some new anti-Norman initiative was fatally compromised by the bitter opposition of the patriarch of Constantinople, Michael Cerularius, who distrusted Argyrus and his negotiations with the westerners, and with whom the legation became embroiled in bitter dispute concerning differences in religious observances. The embassy ended in recriminations, and accomplished nothing except a widening of the religious divide between east and west. Anyway, Leo died in April 1054, and there was a considerable delay before his successor was elected. Then Constantine IX died in January 1055, and his passing ushered in a long period of internal instability and dispute at Constantinople. Finally any prospect of a further expedition by the western emperor was ended by the premature death of Henry III in October 1056, leaving a small boy as his heir with a long minority in prospect.

---

77   Die Briefe von Petrus Damiani, ed. K. Reindel, ii (MGH Briefe der deutsche Kaiserzeit iv, Munich 1988), no. 87, at pp. 514–15.
78   Malaterra, I.14, p. 15.
79   Henrici III Diplomata, ed. H. Bresslau and P.F. Kehr (MGH Diplomatum Regum et Imperatorum Germaniae V, Berlin 1931), p. 440 no. 322. It was doubtless the same embassy that led Henry to grant a privilege to the monastery of Tremiti two days later: ibid. no. 323.

Meanwhile the Normans had an almost free hand to extend their dominions in southern Italy. One of their first successes was the capture of Conversano, 25 km south-east of Bari, in 1054, but for the most part they were content to exact tribute from the strongly defended Apulian towns.[80] Elsewhere, and especially in the principality of Salerno and Calabria, they now went on the offensive. Indeed, immediately after Leo's death, Count Humphrey laid siege to Benevento (clearly the pope's presence there for almost nine months after Civitate had up to that point protected the town). However, he was unable to capture it – the Normans still appear not to have been able to act successfully against the larger towns. Soon afterwards, and presumably because the count of Apulia's attack showed that the papal/imperial protectorate was no longer functioning successfully, the citizens looked once again to the leadership of their former prince, Pandulf III, who was allowed to return in January 1056.[81] But in other areas the Norman aggression proved more profitable, and in the years 1055–60 they conquered a substantial proportion of those areas of the south Italian mainland that had hitherto escaped their clutches.

One of the most marked features of the years after Civitate was the difference in the Normans' attitude to the principality of Salerno, whose prince had hitherto been their main local ally. Even if any formal link had ended in 1047, relations had remained very close during the lifetime of Count Drogo, who, it will be remembered, was Guaimar IV's son-in-law. At the very end of his life Guaimar had sought to perpetuate such links by marrying off his now widowed daughter to Robert, the younger brother of Count Richard of Aversa, who had recently arrived in Italy.[82] (Drogo's brothers Humphrey and Robert were both already married, and thus not available.) The Normans had also, as we have seen, been responsible for Gisulf II's installation as prince, though here self-interest had played just as big a part as any loyalty to Guaimar's memory, for all that, according to Amatus, Guaimar's surviving brother had appealed to that sentiment when seeking their aid. In 1052 the Normans could not risk the principality being in hostile hands. Yet there are signs that the relationship was changing even before Guaimar's death, or at least that it was already one in which strictly material considerations predominated. After Amalfi had rebelled against

---

80 *W. Apulia*, II, lines 293–6, p. 148: 'The inhabitants of Troia paid tribute to the count, those of Bari, Trani, Venosa, Otranto and the city of Acerenza obeyed him'. Of these only Venosa, and perhaps Acerenza, were actually in Norman hands.
81 *Annales Beneventani*, ed. Bertolini, pp. 139–40.
82 *Amatus*, III.36, pp. 149–50. Here *fille* must be a translator's or copyist's error for *veuve*; Jahn, *Untersuchungen zur normannische Herrschaft*, p. 323.

him, Guaimar could not employ Norman troops against it, because with the loss of his tribute money from that city he was unable to raise the cash to pay them. Similarly, whatever appeals Guido may have made to Count Humphrey and other Normans to aid his nephew, he was forced to hand over his own and his family's valuables to reward them, and it would appear that Gisulf granted (or had to grant?) lands to some of the Normans who had helped him.[83]

After the Battle of Civitate such payments became simply 'tribute', with both Richard of Aversa and Count Humphrey demanding 'the customary gifts' that Guaimar had given them, and attacking the principality when they were denied them. Humphrey's ally in this was his half-brother William, the seventh of Tancred de Hauteville's sons, who with two other siblings had relatively recently come to the south. He indeed was the main profiteer from these attacks on the principality of Salerno – one wonders whether Humphrey's intention here was above all to create a lordship for his brother. In or about 1055 they captured the *castellum* of S. Nicandro in the valley of the River Sele about 40 km east of Salerno and a number of other places in the surrounding area, which became the basis for the county held by William and his descendants, known as the county of the Principate. (By the end of the decade William also held Scalea, considerably further south, on the border between the principality and Calabria.) In response, the Salernitans, like the monks of Montecassino a decade earlier, fortified their settlements.[84] Thus here, as in other areas, Norman depredations greatly extended that process known to historians as *incastellamento* – the clustering of the rural population into relatively large defended villages (which is what, rather than 'castle', the Latin term *castellum*, which one encounters in the sources, usually meant).

The ability of the Salernitans to respond to this aggression was hampered by the growing internal weakness of the principality. In particular, relations between Prince Gisulf and his uncle Guido of Sorrento became very strained, but this was by no means the only tension within the upper class. The decision of the Salernitan cleric Alfanus to become a monk at Montecassino in 1056 was spurred on by the news that he and his brothers were suspected of involvement in the murder of Guaimar IV – four years after the event this was still a destabilising factor.[85] Amatus blamed the tensions between the prince and his uncle entirely on the former's ingratitude, and expressly contrasted the prince's malevolence with his uncle's

---

83   *Amatus*, III.28, 30, 33, 35, pp. 143, 146–9.
84   *Amatus*, III.45–6, pp. 161–3; *Malaterra*, I.24, p. 20.
85   *Chron. Cas.* III.7, p. 368.

selflessness. But we cannot take such a judgement at face value, in a work which consistently sought to blacken Gisulf's character (and thus to justify the eventual conquest of Salerno itself by Robert Guiscard). This intra-familial tension was rather the product of Guaimar's endowment of his brothers with their own territorial lordships – something which previous rulers had avoided – and probably of Gisulf's efforts to reassert his haem-orrhaging princely authority. He was also at pains to limit the judicial privileges that his father had granted to the archbishop, or that the latter had simply asserted without previous princely contradiction.[86]

The most spectacular Norman advances in the later 1050s were those made by Robert Guiscard in Calabria. By 1056, or possibly earlier, several of the more important places of northern Calabria – Bisignano, Martirano and Cosenza – were paying tribute to him, although it is probable that at this stage he only directly controlled the region north of the Val di Crati. However, after the death of his brother Humphrey early in 1057,[87] Guiscard succeeded him as the overall leader of the Apulian Normans, and as a result had command of greatly enhanced military strength – both from those areas which his brother had held and from an ability to recruit other Apulian Normans with the inducement of potential gains to be made. He also had the help of his youngest brother Roger, who arrived in Italy at about the time of Humphrey's death. Guiscard's first step (probably in late spring/early summer 1057) was a daring reconnaissance in force which took him first to Squillace, half-way down Calabria at the point where the peninsula is at its narrowest, and then right round the east coast as far as Reggio, the capital of Byzantine Calabria, at its extreme tip. The real gains of this expedition were made on the return journey with the submission of Nicastro and Maida, on the south-west of the Sila Mountains and some 70 km further south than S. Marco Argento. Then, while Robert returned to Apulia, where his new authority was under challenge from the Hautevilles' old rival Count Peter son of Amicus, his brother forced the inhabitants of the Val di Saline in central Calabria into submission, and fortified a base at Nicefola. In the autumn of the same year (though the chronology cannot be entirely certain) Guiscard returned to Calabria and launched a more serious attack on Reggio, but was frustrated by shortage of supplies, most of the foodstuffs from the surrounding area having been gathered up by the

---

86 Taviani-Carozzi, *Principauté lombarde de Salerne*, ii.960–9. For Guido, *Amatus*, III.44, pp. 159–61.

87 Humphrey's death can only be dated approximately from the chronicles, and surprisingly was not recorded in any of the surviving south Italian necrologies. But cf. *Les Chartes de Troia*, pp. 111–14 no. 18 (February 1083), dated in the twenty-sixth year of Robert's rule.

defenders. But his determination to complete the conquest of Calabria was shown by his remaining at Maida over the winter of 1057–8.

However, at this point (again the chronology is vague, but probably in the early months of 1058) Guiscard and Roger fell into dispute, largely because of the former's reluctance to grant the latter what he considered to be an adequate share of the gains in Calabria. Malaterra's account, our only source for this disagreement, is very partial towards Roger, and suggests that Guiscard was being thoroughly unreasonable. 'He acted in an ill-advised manner towards him, and while generous to others began to be stingier with him than was proper', and Malaterra implied that one motive for this was Robert's jealousy of Roger's growing military reputation.[88] However, it would be unwise to take this view entirely at face value. Not only was Guiscard facing problems in Apulia, but as yet the Normans held only a part (largely on the western side) of northern and central Calabria. It is not clear that as yet Guiscard had a great deal with which he could endow his brother. The Norman tactics appear to have been to seize a fortified base, or themselves to fortify a strong natural position, use it to devastate the surrounding region and to terrorise the other settlements in the area into submission, thereby paying tribute and handing over hostages, but not necessarily surrendering the town into the hands of a Norman garrison – nor indeed is it clear that Robert had the manpower to garrison all the settlements in the region under his general control. Given his difficulties in Apulia, where several of the more important towns were still in Byzantine hands, and the fact that his fellow Normans – or at least the powerful 'sons of Amicus' kin-group – resented his authority, he was naturally reluctant to weaken his own property and powerbase in Calabria, even in favour of a brother.

Furthermore in the spring of 1058 parts of Calabria suffered an extremely serious famine, caused partly by Norman ravages and partly by drought. Malaterra graphically described the sufferings of the populace, reduced to eating roots and bread made from bark, nuts, millet and wheat husks. That his account was by no means exaggerated is confirmed by a roll copying the charters of the bishopric of Oppido, in central Calabria, between 1050 and 1065: contained therein are forty-one documents for the years 1050 to 1057, and a single one thereafter in 1065. The abrupt cessation of document production in an area which up to that point had been prosperous is surely suggestive; here the impact of the famine was prolonged by the damage done during Roger's siege of the town early in 1059.[89] A

---

88 *Malaterra*, I.23, p. 20.
89 *Malaterra*, I.27, p. 21; *La Théotokos de Hagia Agathè*, ed. Guillou [above, ch. I, n. 124], esp. p. 28.

combination of the famine – which must have made supplies scarce for Norman garrisons as well, even if they doubtless plundered what foodstuffs were available – Guiscard's concerns in Apulia, his dispute with Roger, and his marriage to Sichelgaita of Salerno in the later part of 1058, all prevented much further advance in Calabria for about a year. We know, for example, that Robert was in Apulia in April 1058,[90] and the negotiations for his marriage required his presence in Apulia and Salerno through late summer and autumn 1058. Given these circumstances, it is hardly surprising that he gave way in his dispute with Roger, and promised him half of Calabria, albeit the southern part which had not yet been conquered, giving him in the meanwhile a base at Mileto (which in 1058 was probably the furthest point south in Norman hands). From here Roger advanced southwards once more in the early months of 1059, decisively crushing an attempted counter-attack led by the governor of Gerace and the bishop of Cassano (presumably in exile from his northern Calabrian see). Finally, late in 1059 or perhaps more likely in the early months of 1060, when Guiscard and substantial reinforcements were again free to join him, the two brothers besieged and this time captured Reggio, and Calabria was more or less completely under their control. The last town to remain loyal to Byzantium was Squillace, to which some of the garrison of Reggio fled when its surrender was imminent. But when Roger approached the town, they evacuated it and sailed off to Constantinople.[91]

The speed with which Calabria was conquered can be attributed to a number of factors. First and foremost, the defenders lacked outside support. There were still contacts between Byzantine Calabria and the motherland in the 1050s, but given the parlous position of the eastern empire, in the grip of an internal crisis and under attack both by the Pechenegs on the Danube and increasingly by the Turks from the east, there was no chance of any but the most minimal reinforcement being sent to southern Italy. Indeed, the Byzantine historian Cedrenus admitted as much when he discussed the career of Robert Guiscard, contrasting the limited numbers of the defending forces compared with the superior resources of 'horses, money and weapons' that Guiscard possessed.[92] There were few attempts to launch counter-attacks or to fight the Normans in the open; and the one attempt to do this in 1059 ended disastrously. But the Normans themselves were still not that numerous: Roger, for example, had only sixty knights when he

---

90 *Chron. Cas.* III.9, p. 371.
91 *Malaterra*, I.32, 34–7, pp. 36–9. For the dating, Chalandon, *Domination normande*, i.173–4; Taviani-Carozzi, *Terreur du Monde*, p. 255. Gay, *L'Italie méridionale et l'Empire byzantin*, ii.560–1, suggests late 1060.
92 *Historiarum Compendium*, p. 721.

raided into the Mileto region in 1057, even if Guiscard deployed considerably larger forces in his various attacks on Reggio (and in 1060 the city surrendered when he brought up his siege engines). Norman tactics, directed above all at securing the surrender of towns and strongpoints by destroying the crops and livelihoods of the inhabitants, were especially effective in a mountainous region where cultivatable land was limited, and thus easily targeted. Furthermore vines (and the trees which supported them), and the olive and mulberry trees of southern Calabria, made the communities which depended upon them especially vulnerable, since once cut down they would take years to regrow or be replaced from cuttings. But the Normans also facilitated surrenders by allowing them to be made, at least at first, on relatively lenient terms, involving the payment of tribute but often not direct occupation. In some areas, notably at Gerace and Stilo in central Calabria, the local Greek patriciate was left in place. Indeed one suspects that local collaborators who preferred a peaceful life under Norman rule to defending their independence in a state of permanent warfare considerably aided the Normans. One local source suggested that division among the Greeks was a major factor in the conquest. Norman garrisons were unpopular. When one was installed at Nicastro about a year after the town submitted to Guiscard, the inhabitants promptly massacred it, and c. 1062 the inhabitants of Gerace went to great pains to make Guiscard (who had rashly entered the town without an escort) promise not to install a citadel there 'which would make them entirely subject to his wishes', and then to promise Count Roger a substantial sum of money to the same end. Inevitably, as time went on and Robert sought to consolidate his hold over the region, more garrisons were installed – while at key strategic points such as Reggio they clearly were from the start. But this was a slow process – there was, for example, no citadel at Cosenza until as late as 1091, even though a French bishop had been installed there by 1059.[93] Immediately after the conquest the Normans were probably, for many Calabrians, relatively distant overlords, and this made it easier for them to reconcile themselves to the new regime. Tribute in return for peace was a price worth paying.

While Guiscard was subduing Calabria, other conquests were under way. The most significant was Richard of Aversa's capture of Capua in June 1058. Richard secured the town's surrender through blockade, starving it into submission after a long siege, and he had to promise to leave its defences in the hands of its inhabitants before they acquiesced in his takeover.

---

93   *Malaterra*, I.28, II.26, 28, IV.10, 17, pp. 22, 38–9, 91, 96; 'Die Chronik von Tres
     Tabernae' [above, ch. I, n. 27], *c.* 11, p. 38; *Italia Pontificia*, x.110. More generally,
     G. Noyé, 'Féodalité et habitat fortifié en Calabre dans la deuxième moitié du XIe siècle
     et le premier tiers du XIIe siècle', *Structures féodales* [above, ch. I, n. 101], pp. 607–28.

But by doing so, he displaced the old Lombard princely family, usurped their title and authority (such as it was), and thereafter was in a position to extend his rule, more or less legitimately, away from his restricted territory around Aversa and over the whole of the principality, stretching up to where it bordered the lands of the papacy to the north of the Monti Aurunci and along the upper Liri Valley, and towards the mountains of Marsia. A key sign of his new status was his reception at Montecassino by its new abbot, Desiderius, in November 1058:

> He was received in procession like a king. The church was decorated as though it were Easter Day. The lamps were lit and the choir resounded with chants and the princely *laudes*. He was led into the chapter house, and was seated, though unwillingly, in the abbot's place. His feet were washed by the abbot's own hands, and the care and the defence of the monastery were entrusted to him. . . . He granted peace to the church and promised to fight its enemies.[94]

He had, in a word, become respectable. From an interloper, he had become a ruler; from the Normans being the main threat to southern Italy's richest abbey, they had become its protectors.

The final step in the legitimisation of both the new prince of Capua and Robert Guiscard as ruler of most of the rest of mainland southern Italy came with their recognition by the papacy. But before that, in the later months of 1058, Guiscard took another move towards cementing his position, through his marriage to Sichelgaita, the sister of Prince Gisulf II of Salerno. As has been suggested above, his repudiation of his first wife, Alberada, on grounds of consanguinity (that they were related, and thus that the marriage was therefore unlawful and invalid), should not necessarily be dismissed as a mere excuse – it may in fact have been true. Furthermore, the eleventh-century clerical reform movement, which had been established at Rome by the German popes after 1046, was already beginning to make some headway, albeit very tentatively, in southern Italy.[95] That movement sought not merely to reform the clergy, but also to improve the morality of the laity, and the enforcement of the Church's rules against marriage to even quite distant relations (those within the seventh degree of kinship) was an important element of this. Whether such a prohibition would really have had much effect on Guiscard is arguable; though Amatus suggested that he did become conscious of the sinfulness of the union. But if he was married to someone related to him, then the dissolution

---

94 *Amatus*, IV.13, pp. 191–2.
95 Cf. Taviani-Carozzi, *Principauté lombarde de Salerne*, ii.963–9, 973–80.

THE AGE OF ROBERT GUISCARD

of this union might well seem desirable as he sought legitimisation by the Church (and we cannot assume that what happened in 1059 was entirely unforeseen). In that case his repudiation of Alberada was certainly well timed. It also enabled him, through his marriage to Sichelgaita and relationship with the old princely family, to secure a degree of acceptance and legitimacy in the eyes of Lombards as well as Normans. There were as well obvious advantages for Gisulf. The *quid pro quo* for his sister, and according to Amatus the lands which formed her dowry, was Robert's protection against the aggression of Richard of Capua on the northern border of the principality, and restraining influence exercised on his brother Count William, whose ruthless aggrandisement was posing a real threat to Gisulf's position. It also bolstered Gisulf's position within the principality against his uncle Guido.[96]

This was not of course the first such marriage between one of the Hautevilles and a woman from the Salernitan princely family. Count William had married a niece of Guaimar IV, Drogo had married one of his daughters, and shortly after Guiscard's marriage to Sichelgaita, Guido of Sorrento (far from pleased with this union) married off another of his daughters to Count William of the Principate. Yet Guiscard's marriage may have marked a new development. It seems probable that Gaitelgrima, the daughter of Guaimar whom Drogo had married (and who after his death went on to marry two other Norman leaders), was illegitimate. If that was so, then Guiscard's marriage was qualitatively different, in that he was the first of his family to marry the legitimate daughter of an actual prince. When he eventually conquered Salerno in 1076, this gave him (and more particularly his son born from Sichelgaita) a claim to rule that he would not have otherwise possessed.[97] But by that date Guiscard was already well established as the ruler of most of mainland southern Italy. Here the decisive step was his adoption of the title of 'duke', and the recognition of that dignity by the papacy. Here both Robert, and Richard of Capua who was similarly recognised as prince of Capua, profited from a radical and sudden reorientation of their policy towards southern Italy by the reformers who had been installed at the Roman Curia by Leo IX and the other German popes.

---

96 *Amatus*, IV.18–25, pp. 194–9; *W. Apulia*, II, lines 416–46, pp. 154–6, who stresses how much more acceptable this made Robert to the Lombards. There is, however, no need to follow the wilder flights of fancy of Taviani-Carozzi, *Principauté lombarde*, ii.918–45, that such marriages led to the 'spiritual adoption' of Normans by the princes. Here she reads far too much into Amatus's phraseology (as rendered by the later translator).

97 Guaimar had another daughter called Gaitelgrima, born shortly before his death to his wife Gemma. She married (*c.* 1075?) Prince Jordan I of Capua. Guaimar is most unlikely to have had two daughters of the same name by the same wife: however, he was married to Gemma as early as 1032, so the chances of his having had an earlier first wife are remote.

As we have seen, the disaster at Civitate had not in the short term altered Leo's policy towards the Normans, nor had this changed under his immediate successors. Amatus claimed that Victor II (1055–7), the former bishop of Eichstätt whose advice had helped sabotage the 1053 campaign, was not intrinsically hostile to the Normans; but his successor, the former papal chancellor Frederick of Lorraine (Stephen IX) certainly was.[98] However, Frederick's death in March 1058 left the reform group at the Curia in a difficult position. The death of the Emperor Henry III had already removed the imperial protection that they had hitherto enjoyed, and while Godfrey, duke of Lorraine and margrave of Tuscany, the dominant figure in northern Italy, was prepared to support his brother Frederick as pope, he was not necessarily prepared to render much assistance to his successors. Furthermore the Roman nobility resented the reformers' intrusion into an institution which they had previously dominated, and saw this as their opportunity to reassert control over the papacy. The result was a schism. The Romans chose one pope (Benedict X), the reformers retaliated by electing their own candidate (Nicholas II). Duke Godfrey helped Nicholas to establish himself in Rome, but when he then retired to northern Italy the reformers needed to look for help elsewhere. The papal archdeacon, Hildebrand, travelled to Capua in the spring of 1059, and persuaded Prince Richard to provide 300 knights, with whose aid Nicholas defeated and captured his rival for the papal throne.

Obviously this timely aid had its price, and indeed the *Annales Romani* suggest that Hildebrand recognised the new Norman prince and accepted the latter's oath of fealty to the Roman Church before the troops were dispatched northwards to help the reform pope.[99] There were a number of reasons why a settlement with the Normans was desirable, which will be discussed in more detail at a later point (see Chapter V). But above all, there was the recognition of reality that the Normans were in southern Italy to stay, and that the interests of the Church would benefit from acknowledging this fact. Hence, once he was securely established in Rome, Pope Nicholas set off for southern Italy, where in August 1059 he held a council at Melfi, one of the Apulian towns held by Guiscard himself. We know that Richard of Capua was present at this council, but there is no evidence that he was formally invested with his dominions (or at least no record of such a ceremony has survived); perhaps whatever had transpired between him and Archdeacon Hildebrand a few months earlier was deemed

---

98 *Amatus*, III.47, 50, pp. 163, 166; H.E.J. Cowdrey, *The Age of Abbot Desiderius. Montecassino, the Papacy and the Normans in the Eleventh and Early Twelfth Centuries* (Oxford 1983), pp. 111–12.

99 *Annales Romani*, in *Le Liber Pontificalis*, ed. L. Duchesne (2 vols, Paris 1886–92), ii.335.

sufficient warranty for his new status. But Robert Guiscard swore fealty to the pope, and was then invested 'by the grace of God and St Peter Duke of Apulia and Calabria, and in future, with the help of both, of Sicily'.[100]

Robert would still have to work hard to make this title a reality. So too would Richard of Capua, who as yet held only a part of his nominal principality. Similarly there was still quite a substantial area of Apulia outside Guiscard's control, and not only the Byzantines and native Apulians, but also some of his fellow Normans were reluctant to recognise his authority. None the less, the papal investiture of 1059 marked a decisive step. He was no longer simply an adventurer, or even a conqueror. He was now the ruler of southern Italy.

A conquest completed?

By the time of Guiscard's investiture in 1059 most of southern Italy was in the hands of the Normans. The conquest of Calabria was completed a few months later with the capture of Reggio and Squillace. However, at that time Bari and much of southern Apulia were still in Byzantine hands – or perhaps one should better say loyal to Byzantium. Among the towns which still had Greek garrisons and acknowledged imperial rule were Brindisi, Oria, Taranto, Otranto and Gallipoli.[101] It was to take Guiscard and the Normans twelve years to overcome these remaining bastions of Byzantine power, and even then there were still isolated enclaves on the mainland which remained independent of the Normans. Indeed, the conquest was, arguably, never quite completed. Some explanation is clearly needed of why this should have been the case.

To begin with, it took some time for Robert, and Richard of Capua, to consolidate their authority even in those areas under their theoretical control. Hence in 1059 Richard only really possessed the plain around Capua itself, and as yet his authority in his nominal capital was limited by the agreement which had secured the city's surrender a year earlier. It was only in 1062 that he forced the citizens to hand over their defences to him, and he was forced to besiege the town a second time to secure this. Very shortly afterwards he captured Teano, 20 km to the north of Capua. But it was only in the spring of 1063 (between March and June), and after the death of

---

100 *Le Liber Censuum de l'Eglise Romaine*, ed. P. Fabre and L. Duchesne (3 vols, Paris 1889–1952), i.421–2; *W. Apulia*, II.400–5, p. 154.
101 Cedrenus, *Historiarum Compendium*, ii.722.

Duke Atenulf, that he brought Gaeta under his rule. Very soon afterwards he faced a serious rebellion from the remaining Lombard nobility, headed by the counts of Aquino and Teano, aided by Richard's own son-in-law and lieutenant William of Montreuil. His authority in the north of the principality was not finally secured until 1065, despite his alliance with the abbey of Montecassino (which profited considerably from the lands of the rebel Lombards). How much the Normans were still resented by the local population was demonstrated in 1065 when the garrison which William of Montreuil had installed at Piedemonte, not far from Aquino, was massacred in an uprising by the peasants of the surrounding area.[102]

Guiscard meanwhile began by extending his authority in inland Apulia. In 1060 he captured Troia, and built a citadel and installed a garrison there. This town, the only one of any size in the Capitanata, had hitherto remained independent, albeit paying tribute to the Normans. Henceforth it was to be a key centre of ducal authority.[103] A year later he captured Acerenza: though from whom is unclear (we have only the barest reference to the event). This town had been part of the original share-out among the Norman leaders in 1042 when it had been assigned to Asclettin, the later count of Aversa. But we do not know if he had ever obtained possession of it, or whether, if he had, the inhabitants may later have regained their independence. It is even possible that Guiscard may have gained it from some other Norman lord.[104] Indeed, we are very badly informed about events in Apulia throughout this decade. The chronicler's concerns were with other matters – particularly with the commencement of the conquest of Sicily. William of Apulia's poem entirely ignores the period between the synod of Melfi and the beginning of the siege of Bari (i.e. 1059–68), while the relevant section of Amatus (Book V) not only has little to say about Apulia but is more than usually disorganised. One is left therefore with the exegesis of some cryptic annalistic sources, and the use of these by past scholars has been vitiated by their reliance upon the so-called *Breve Chronicon Nortmanicum*, which is in fact an eighteenth-century forgery, and must therefore be disregarded.[105]

One may, however, suggest that the continued resistance of the Byzantine towns in southern Apulia owed as much to extraneous factors as to any very

---

102 *Amatus*, VI.1–6, pp. 258–66; Chalandon, *Domination normande*, i.215–20; G.A. Loud, *Church and Society in the Norman Principality of Capua, 1058–1197* (Oxford 1985), pp. 38–51.
103 *Amatus*, IV.3, V.6, pp. 185, 228–9 (two separate mentions of the same incident). The date is given by the 'Chronicon Amalphitanum', in Schwarz, *Amalfi im frühen Mittelalter*, pp. 211–12.
104 Lupus Protospatharius, *Annales*, MGH SS v.59.
105 This is still the matter of some dispute, but the arguments of A. Jacob, 'Le *Breve Chronicon Nortmanicum*: un veritable faux de Pietro Polidori', *QFIAB* lxvi (1986), 378–92, are very convincing.

vigorous or coherent response by the eastern empire. In particular, for much of the 1060s Guiscard was preoccupied by events elsewhere. In 1061 and again in 1064 he was in Sicily, on both occasions accompanied by a substantial force of troops (who were not therefore available for use in his absence against what was left of Byzantine *Langobardia*). Early in 1062 Robert captured Brindisi and Oria, but most of the campaigning season that year was taken up by a recurrence of his dispute with Count Roger, caused once again by his reluctance to fulfil his promises to provide his youngest brother with an adequate endowment in Calabria. In 1062 this led to actual fighting between their rival forces. Malaterra noted that 'the duke, while generous with money, was stingy in giving out the smallest portion of land, and made use of all sorts of roundabout ways to drag matters out'. As has been suggested already, this may have been because as yet Robert had no very large landed endowment himself, even in Calabria where the conquest had often been by agreed surrender rather than outright seizure. None the less, his continued delay in satisfying the very justified claims of his brother and principal ally was far from wise. In the end he agreed to abide by the terms of their earlier agreement, by which Roger was to have the southern half of the province. But in the interim both time and lives had been wasted in fruitless dispute. Indeed Guiscard's recklessness had put his own life in considerable danger – and Roger (who despite their dispute clearly retained a fondness for his elder brother) had to rescue him from the hostile Greek inhabitants of Gerace. Nor indeed was this the end of Robert's difficulties in Calabria, for in 1064–5 there was a revolt in the Cosenza region, which took several months to suppress.[106] Given these preoccupations, Guiscard was unable for some years to turn his attention to completing the Apulian conquest. He made a brief appearance in that area in 1064, probably early in the year before going to Sicily, and made an agreement with the people of Bari – presumably based on a continuation of their payment of tribute – a sensible enough move given that his other commitments precluded any major offensive operations in Apulia at this period.[107]

There *were* gains made in Apulia during the early part of the 1060s, but these were made not by Robert but by other Norman lords. In 1063 Godfrey, a son of Count Peter of Andria (part therefore of the 'sons of Amicus' kin-group), captured Taranto, one of the main Apulian ports. In 1064 the duke's nephew Robert of Montescaglioso gained Matera, and at about this time also the nearby town of Montepeloso. These victories effectively

---

106 *Malaterra*, II.21 (quote), 23–8, 37, pp. 35–9, 47; Lupus, *Annales*, *loc. cit.*
107 *Anon. Barensis Chron.*, *RIS* v.152. Cf. *Malaterra*, II.40, p. 48, who claimed that the inhabitants had been for a time in revolt against the emperor and in alliance with Robert (perhaps reading too much into the agreement?).

eliminated the Byzantine presence on the Apulia/Lucania border – the 'instep' of Italy. Meanwhile, at the other end of Apulia, Guiscard's brother Geoffrey, and after his death his son Robert (who became known as the count of Loritello) pressed northwards across the Biferno and Trigno rivers and into the Abruzzi. By 1064 Robert's incursions had begun to destabilise the lands of the abbey of St Clement of Casauria in the Pescara Valley, almost 100 km to the north of the village of Rotello from which he drew his title. Robert Guiscard had *c.* 1060 appeared briefly in this region to help his brother, but thereafter these operations, like the successes of the other Normans in Apulia, appear to have been carried out independently.[108] Similarly Guiscard was unlikely to have done more than just turn a blind eye to the continued aggression of his brother William and his allies in the principality of Salerno – though Pope Alexander II was less complacent, excommunicating Count William and two other Normans, Guimund des Moulins and Turgisius of Rota, for their depredations on the property of the archbishopric of Salerno in 1067.[109]

Nor indeed, despite the problems they faced in other, and to them more important, parts of their empire were the Byzantines entirely passive. At some point after 1062 they recaptured Brindisi, and it is probable that in 1065/6 they also retook Vieste on the Gargano peninsula. Certainly we know that Vieste was in the hands of Richard of Capua's younger brother Robert, who had inherited his family's claims to the Gargano region, in August 1065, but Duke Robert was recorded as capturing the town and a (apparently) Greek officer called Kyriakos a year later. One is tempted to link this brief Byzantine counter-attack with the arrival of a contingent from the Varangian Guard at Bari in 1066.[110] But, if so, it was short-lived, for in 1066 Robert was finally able to devote his attention to Apulia, captured Vieste (as we have seen) and also Otranto, where a Latin-rite (and presumably French) archbishop called Hugh was in office by January 1067.[111]

However, soon afterwards Guiscard was faced with a much more dangerous development: a widespread revolt among the Normans in Apulia, including some members of his own family, stirred up and financed by the Byzantines. The ringleaders of this conspiracy were Amicus, son of Count Walter of Lesina, and his father-in-law Joscelin of Molfetta, Roger Toutebove (probably the son of the man to whom Monopoli was allocated in the

---

108   *Anon. Barensis Chron.*, *loc. cit.*; *Malaterra*, I.33, II.39, pp. 23, 48; *Chronicon Casauriense*, *RIS* ii(2).863.

109   *Italia Pontificia*, viii.351–2 nos 23–5 [= *MPL* cxlvi.1335–9 nos 54–5].

110   *Cod. Dipl. Tremiti*, ii.231–5 nos 77–8; 'Chronicon Amalphitanum', p. 213; *Anon. Barensis Chron.*, *RIS* v.154.

111   *Amatus*, V.26, p. 247; *Italia Pontificia*, ix.409.

division of 1042), and Guiscard's own nephews Geoffrey of Conversano and Abelard. Geoffrey was the son of Guiscard's sister, Abelard that of his elder brother Humphrey. Here Robert's own chickens were coming home to roost – for when his brother had died back in 1057 Robert had ignored the claims of the latter's (then very young) son and taken for himself the overall leadership of the Apulian Normans. A decade later Abelard, by now in his teens, was anxious for revenge. Although Robert, who was in Calabria when the rebellion broke out, moved extremely fast and caught the rebels before they were ready, the suppression of this revolt occupied the autumn of 1067 and early months of 1068. Joscelin and Roger Toutebove fled to Constantinople. Count Amicus and the duke's nephews were forgiven, albeit at the cost of some of their lands.[112]

Hence it was not until August 1068 that Guiscard was ready to begin the most ambitious military operation that he had yet undertaken: the siege of Bari. For a number of reasons this was a very difficult enterprise, and could only be attempted when Robert could rely on the full support of his Norman vassals. Indeed, according to Malaterra it was precisely Robert's demand for military service that had previously provoked his nephew Geoffrey to rebellion. Similarly, Count Roger temporarily abandoned his operations in Sicily to take part in the later stages of the attack on Bari. The necessity of such a wide-ranging mobilisation was clear. Bari was a trading port, with its own ships, situated on a peninsula, with its landward side strongly defended. The Normans of Italy were by this stage well versed in the techniques of siege warfare – Guiscard had, for example, used siege engines against Reggio in 1060. But here the defenders were demoralised and the town had surrendered on terms soon after the Normans' arrival. In other cases, such as the two sieges of Capua in 1058 and 1062, and that of Troia in 1060, victory was secured by blockading the town until hunger forced its inhabitants to capitulate, while early in 1068 Robert had only been able to overcome his nephew Geoffrey's stronghold of Montepeloso by bribing the castellan to surrender. Only at Messina in 1061 had the Normans actually forced an entry into a strongly fortified city, and then most of the garrison had already been killed in a rash sortie and only a handful of defenders were left. Even then, the Normans had been lucky to catch them by surprise.[113] But the inhabitants of Bari were not prepared to surrender: 'the people of the city resisted and said that they would not abandon their

---

112 *Amatus*, V.4, pp. 224–7; *W. Apulia*, II, lines 444–77, pp. 156–8; *Malaterra*, II.39–40, pp. 48–9. Dating: Jahn, *Untersuchungen zur die normannischer Herrschaft*, pp. 100–9 (*contra* Chalandon and other older authorities, who believed the rebellion to be much more prolonged).

113 *W. Apulia*, II, lines 459–77, pp. 156–8; *Malaterra*, II.5–10, pp. 29–30.

loyalty to the emperor whatever attacks he might make upon them'.[114] The land wall was easily manned, and supplies could be brought in by sea from the Byzantine territories on the other side of the Adriatic. Furthermore, although the mid-eleventh-century Byzantine emperors had neglected their navy, it was still by no means negligible, and the Normans were relatively inexperienced in naval warfare. Bari was therefore a formidable obstacle. Where Guiscard did have an advantage was in the timing of the operation. For by 1068 the situation on the eastern frontier of the Byzantine empire had become critical, with Turkish raids penetrating through Armenia into Asia Minor proper. The new emperor, Romanus IV, was determined to do something about this. Thus, however serious the position of the few remaining Byzantine possessions in southern Italy might be, that was only a minor priority for the government in Constantinople. We cannot be sure whether Duke Robert was aware of this situation, but given that western mercenaries were already serving in some numbers in the Byzantine army, including Normans such as Robert Crispin and Roussel of Bailleul (the second of whom had played a prominent part in the early stages of the invasion of Sicily), it is more than likely that he was.[115]

Once it became clear that, despite the employment of siege engines and towers, the town could not be stormed, it became imperative to blockade it by sea. Robert had recruited ships and sailors from Calabria. The chroniclers claimed that he sought to link his ships together with chains and walkways, to create a sort of pontoon bridge right around the seaward sides of the city, but the defenders still managed to break through. The siege continued for two years and eight months – testimony both to Guiscard's determination and to his ability to mobilise and maintain his forces over a long period, though we know nothing of how this was managed. He also did his best to exploit divisions within Bari, which may have been caused by familial and factional rivalries, but which the chroniclers (and especially Amatus) present as a dispute between those prepared, however reluctantly, to reach an accommodation on favourable terms with the Normans and those determined to resist to the bitter end. And despite their other preoccupations, the Byzantines made two serious efforts to relieve the city by sea. The first in 1069 was partially successful; some ships were lost but supplies were brought in, and the siege prolonged. The second, early in 1071, by which time Bari was in desperate straits, was commanded by Joscelin of

---

114 *Amatus*, V.27, p. 248.
115 J. Shepard, 'The uses of the Franks in eleventh-century Byzantium', *Anglo-Norman Studies* xv *Proceedings of the Battle Conference 1992* (1993), 274–305, especially pp. 296–8; *Malaterra*, II.33, p. 48. For the defects of the Byzantine fleet, *Michael Psellus: Fourteen Byzantine Rulers*, p. 201.

Molfetta, the former rebel who had fled to Constantinople in 1068. Amatus alleged that he was carrying considerable sums of money and other valuables to use as bribes to undermine the loyalty of Robert's army. However, his squadron was intercepted and defeated by Count Roger, who had arrived from Sicily with fresh ships, and Joscelin himself was captured. William of Apulia was in no doubt about the significance of this success:

> The Norman race had up to this point known nothing of naval warfare. But by thus returning victorious they very much enhanced their leader's confidence, for he knew that the Greeks had been unable to carry enough help to the citizens of the town to hinder the siege. At the same time he greatly rejoiced at the novelty of this naval victory, hoping in consequence that he and the Normans might in future engage in battle at sea with more hope of success.[116]

William was undoubtedly right to emphasise this victory, for, with no further hope of relief and food supplies exhausted, it led directly to Bari's surrender, on 16 April 1071. The loss of the supply convoy was probably more significant than the disputes within the ruling class in procuring the surrender, for while these quarrels had come to a head with the murder of the leader of the pro-imperial (or anti-Norman) party in July 1070, it still took another nine months before Bari yielded. This suggests that Amatus's emphasis on the internal quarrels among the Bariots may be misleading. Yet even though Bari was near starvation when it finally surrendered, Robert still offered generous terms. William of Apulia claimed that he returned most of the property of the inhabitants that had been seized (presumably lands outside the walls), freed them from tribute which they had in the past paid to other Normans, and refrained from imposing any new burdens on them himself. Argyritzus, the leader of the 'peace party' before the surrender, remained as the leading inhabitant, and in a later passage William even claimed that Robert had 'entrusted the city' to him.[117] There is no other confirmation of this, and a charter of 1075 shows the town to have been under the charge of two officials, one of whom, Lizius the viscount, was probably a Norman. But the other, Maurelianus the Catepan, was probably a prominent local man, who claimed to hold the Byzantine rank of patrikios. (One should note that the title of Catepan was henceforth downgraded to mean simply an urban or local official, and was no longer used for

---

116 *W. Apulia*, III, lines 132–8, p. 170.
117 *W. Apulia*, III, lines 145–6, 537–8, pp. 172, 194. Other accounts of the siege: *Amatus*, V.27, pp. 248–55; *Malaterra*, II.40, 43, pp. 48–51. The dates are given by the *Anon. Barensis Chron.*, *loc. cit.*

a provincial governor.) Other contemporary documents from Bari, which acknowledge Robert's rule, show another man with a Byzantine rank, calling himself 'imperial protospatharius and *krites* [judge] of Italy', validating property transactions 'according to the law and custom of the city'.[118] This suggests therefore that the local patriciate was largely left in charge, and probably Robert had little choice in this. Given that Bari was, by contemporary standards, a large and populous town with a diversified economy which he needed to remain prosperous, and that his own troops were still not that numerous, coercion was not really an option. This was especially the case since he needed the help of Bariot ships and sailors in his attack on Palermo, which he launched only a few months after Bari surrendered.

The fall of Bari meant that the whole of Byzantine Apulia was now in Norman hands, for Brindisi – by 1068 the only other significant town left under imperial rule – had been captured shortly before Bari's capitulation. It is more than likely that Guiscard always intended to seize, or secure the submission of, all the other places on the mainland outside the principality of Capua which were still independent of his rule. But there was a considerable delay before he undertook such operations there. His first priority after the surrender of Bari was to transfer his forces to Sicily and undertake the siege of Palermo. Here he was successful relatively quickly and Palermo surrendered in January 1072 (see below, Chapter IV). But thereafter Guiscard was distracted by another revolt among the Normans of Apulia in 1072–3, this time encouraged by Richard of Capua, and subsequently by the breakdown in his relations with the papacy (see Chapter V), and continued problems both with the prince of Capua and with his troublesome nephew Abelard.

Admittedly Amalfi and its little duchy voluntarily submitted to his rule in the autumn of 1073, after the death of Duke Sergius IV, agreeing to pay tribute to Robert in return for his protection against his brother-in-law Gisulf of Salerno, who had never forgiven the Amalfitans for their involvement in his father's murder – and would doubtless have liked to recover his father's former lordship over the wealthy trading city.[119] However, Robert did not capture Abelard's stronghold of Santa Severina in northern Calabria until 1075. A peace treaty with Richard of Capua was brokered, with

---

118 *Cod. Dipl. Barese*, v *Le Pergamene di S. Nicola di Bari, periodo normanno (1075–1194)*, ed. G.B. Nitto de Rossi (Bari 1902), 3–5 no. 1; *Cod. Dipl. Barese*, i *Le Pergamene del duomo di Bari (952–1265)*, ed. G.B. Nitto de Rossi and F. Nitti di Vito (Bari 1897), 49–52 nos 27–8 (1073).

119 *Amatus*, VIII.2–3, 6–8, pp. 339–49; *W. Apulia*, III, lines 412–20, p. 186. Both imply that this was very shortly before 1076, but for the correct dating: Schwarz, *Amalfi im frühen Mittelalter*, pp. 58–60, 248–50. Sergius's widow Purpura was the abbess of a Salernitan nunnery in 1087: *Pergamene del monastero benedettino di S. Giorgio (1038–1698)*, ed. L. Cassese (Salerno 1950), pp. 60–2 no. 7.

some difficulty, by Abbot Desiderius of Montecassino early in the next year. It was only then that Robert was able to move against what was left of the principality of Salerno. Prince Richard agreed to aid him in besieging Salerno itself, and in return Guiscard would then help the prince to capture Naples – above all by providing the naval force that the Capuan Normans lacked – and also aid him in his efforts to extend the northern frontier of his principality.[120] Notwithstanding this agreement, the chroniclers all argued that the attack on Salerno was entirely Prince Gisulf's fault, provoking the long-suffering Norman duke by his continual aggression and brutality. Amatus, in particular, portrayed Gisulf as a sadistic tyrant, who ignored all warnings to moderate his behaviour, from the pope, Abbot Desiderius, and from his own sister, the duke's wife Sichelgaita:

> The iniquities of the most ferocious Prince Gisulf of Salerno continually increased and worsened, and the insatiable rage of this man appeared to surpass the cruelty of Nero and Maximian. He reduced the people of his city to poverty. His fury was seemingly without remedy.

Finally (so Amatus claimed) he provoked the tolerant duke beyond endurance. 'While the duke searched for peace, the prince looked rather to have hatred and enmity.'[121] Similarly Malaterra described how Robert tried to appease the prince:

> [He] bore this patiently. He sent envoys to arrange a meeting, to persuade Gisulf to adopt a more prudent course than the one he had adopted. But when he realised the evil that was lodged in the prince's heart, and that the more he tried to be conciliatory the worse the prince's behaviour became, then he renounced the treaty between them and prepared for inexorable hostilities.[122]

Yet we must surely be extremely sceptical about this story propounded by such pro-Norman apologists, and indeed Amatus's denunciations of Gisulf are so extreme and extended as to suggest that he had a strong personal motive. The most plausible identification of Amatus is that he was a former bishop of Paestum (in the south of the principality of Salerno), who had resigned his see to become a monk at Montecassino in the late 1050s. Why

---

120 *Amatus*, VII.16–21, 28–9, pp. 307–14, 322–3. *Malaterra*, III.4–6, pp. 58–60, whose chronology is very confused, places this after the siege of Salerno. Dating by the 'Chronicon Amalphitanum', Schwarz, *Amalfi*, pp. 214–15, and cf. here Chalandon, *Domination normande*, i.241.
121 *Amatus*, VIII.1–14, pp. 339–54 (quotes from pp. 339–40, 354).
122 *Malaterra*, III.2, p. 58.

he should have done this is unknown, but if it was a consequence of dispute with, or ill-treatment by Gisulf – and we do know that the prince was trying to limit ecclesiastical privileges in the later 1050s – then his hostility towards Gisulf is understandable.[123] But given Guiscard's record of aggression, and the internal weakness of the principality that had been growing for at least a generation, it was not so much a question of *if* Robert was going to attack Salerno, but rather *when*.

The siege of Salerno began early in May 1076 and lasted for seven months. By December the populace within was starving – Amatus graphically described their suffering, which he compared to that of the people of Jerusalem when besieged by the Romans in AD 70. He claimed that the duke was well aware of how enfeebled the garrison and inhabitants were, and that he could capture the town whenever he wished, but preferred to avoid the bloodshed that would inevitably ensue if it were taken by storm. Anyway, this proved unnecessary. On the night of 12/13 December a collaborator within the city opened a postern gate for the duke's army, his troops entered and quietly took over a section of the walls, and the next morning the town surrendered.[124] Gisulf and his brothers took refuge in the citadel, on the hill overlooking the town, and held out there for some months longer, but that merely delayed the inevitable end. Gisulf and his immediate family were allowed to leave unharmed, once his brothers had surrendered their lordships (though Robert threatened to imprison the prince for life if this was not done). But in fact he had no real interest in them – his concern was the principality and its wealthy capital. Henceforth Salerno, rather than as previously Melfi and Venosa, became the centre of his power. And, as earlier at Bari, it was important to reconcile the local population to his rule. While Gisulf and his brothers were expelled, otherwise Guiscard went out of his way to stress the benevolence of his rule. Amatus implied that such measures as opening a market as soon as the city was taken and bringing in supplies to be sold cheaply, and allowing the citadel's garrison to remain unharmed and retain their property, were due to the duke's innate mercy.[125] But they were also good policy. Furthermore, while the prince's brothers Landulf and Guaimar were forced to surrender their lands, other more distant members of the princely kin-group were more fortunate. The descendants of Gisulf's uncles Guido and Pandulf were allowed to keep their lordships at Giffoni and Capáccio, and indeed these dynasties

---

123   A. Lentini, 'Ricerche biografiche su Amato di Montecassino', *Benedictina* ix (1955), 183–96.
124   *Amatus*, VIII.14–24, pp. 354–65, especially *c.* 20 (Amatus obviously knew his Josephus). A much briefer account in *W. Apulia*, II, lines 424–61, pp. 186–8. Dates: *Annales Casinenses ex annalibus antiquis excerpti, MGH SS* xxx(2).1420–1; *Annales Beneventani*, ed. Bertolini, p. 144.
125   *Amatus*, VIII.24, 28, pp. 365–6, 369.

remained, the Capáccio branch in particular intermarrying with local Normans, until well into the twelfth century.[126] Similarly the local establishment within the town of Salerno remained undisturbed. The transition from Lombard to Norman rule was undoubtedly facilitated by the adherence of Archbishop Alfanus to Guiscard from before the siege began – an adroit change of side by a man who in one of his poems had once sycophantically praised Gisulf as the 'new Caesar' who had loaded the Gallic leaders with chains, as had been done in antiquity.[127] But Guiscard took other steps to emphasise the legitimacy and benevolence of his rule over the principality. He continued the coinage of the Lombard princes, including the new copper coinage issued by Gisulf, although one issue in 1077 or shortly afterwards was stamped with the word 'victory' to mark his triumph.[128] Lombard officials remained in office, such as the Sico 'count and judge', who witnessed Salernitan charters from 1065 until after Guiscard's death.[129] Since there is unlikely to have been any significant Norman immigration into Salerno itself, Robert clearly wished to maintain and enhance its economic prosperity, and since Lombard law remained in force, there were obviously strong pressures working in favour of continuity. But Robert also employed Lombard officials within his household, notably his *vesterarius* Gratian to whom, at Sichelgaita's request, he gave a house in Salerno in 1079. He took over the patronage of the abbey of Holy Trinity, Cava, just outside Salerno, much favoured by Gisulf II in his later years, and whose abbots had been important spiritual advisers to the last two Lombard princes. And in some diplomas granted to recipients within the principality after 1077 Robert adopted the tactful style 'Robert, duke of the Normans, Salernitans, Amalfitans, Sorrentines, Apulians, Calabrians and Sicilians'.[130] He also, as a very visible sign of his beneficent rule, played a major part in the rebuilding of Salerno cathedral, which was commemorated in an inscription (taken from a poem by Archbishop Alfanus) installed in a prominent position on the atrium of the building.[131] Furthermore, the comments

---

126   G.A. Loud, 'The abbey of Cava, its property and benefactors in the Norman era', *Battle* ix (1987), 159–63, and 'Continuity and change in Norman Italy: the Campania during the eleventh and twelfth centuries', *Journal of Medieval History* xxii (1996), 324–31 [both reprinted in *Conquerors and Churchmen*]. See below, chart IV.

127   *Amatus*, VIII.17, pp. 357–8; *I Carmi di Alfano I, arcivescovo di Salerno* (Miscellanea Cassinese 38, Montecassino 1974), no. 17, p. 144.

128   P. Grierson, 'The Salernitan coinage of Gisulf II (1052–77) and Robert Guiscard (1077–85)', *Papers of the British School of Rome* xxiv (1956), 37–59.

129   *Pergamene del monastero benedettino di S. Giorgio*, pp. 15–59 nos 4–6 (1065, 1073, 1085); *Nuove pergamene del monastero femminile di S. Giorgio di Salerno* i *(993–1256)*, ed. M. Galante (Altavilla Silentina 1984), pp. 18–19 no. 7 (1077).

130   Ménager, *Recueil*, pp. 95–8, 105–8, nos 27–8, 33.

131   *I Carmi di Alfano*, no. 53, p. 216, lines 7–10.

made by William of Apulia about the Lombards being more willing to serve him once he had married Sichelgaita, were surely especially relevant after the conquest of Salerno, since the princes from whom she was descended (and to whom William alluded) were the rulers of that principality.[132] With her aid, Guiscard could indeed appear as the quasi-legitimate successor to the former princely dynasty.

The acquisition of the city of Salerno and the remaining parts of its principality not already occupied by the Normans was the most significant and successful step towards the consolidation of the whole of mainland southern Italy in Norman hands. But it did not mark the end of attempts to further that end. Even while Salerno was still under siege, Richard of Capua, with Robert's support, made a foray into the papal Campagna. Owing to bad weather and shortage of supplies, this achieved little, except to earn both prince and duke excommunication by Gregory VII – in Robert's case a renewed sentence since he was already under anathema.[133] Then, in May 1077 Richard began the siege of Naples, with the city blockaded from the sea by Duke Robert's ships, as the two had agreed before the attack upon Salerno was undertaken. However, Naples proved a tougher nut to crack than had Salerno (probably because it was internally much more cohesive). The city was still resisting almost a year later when Richard of Capua died on Easter Thursday, 5 April 1078. His son Jordan, who had been at odds with his father for some time and had already made his peace with the pope, then abandoned the operation, though it would appear that the price of his withdrawal was the payment of tribute and a *de facto* Capuan protectorate over Naples. Furthermore, outlying parts of the already small duchy, such as Pozzuoli, Acerra and the northern slopes of Monte Vesuvio, were henceforth under Capuan rule.[134] Meanwhile Duke Robert had turned his attention to Benevento, where Prince Landulf VI had died on 17 November 1077. His only son had been killed fighting against the Normans three years earlier, and there was no heir – although Landulf had, some years before his death, recognised papal overlordship over the city – all that was by now left of the old principality of Benevento. A month after the prince's death Robert laid siege to the city. This lasted for some five months, but Benevento was saved by the death of Richard of Capua. Jordan I was perhaps anxious to cement his good relations with the papacy, perhaps simply detemined not to allow Guiscard any further increase in his power

---

132 *W. Apulia*, II, lines 436–41, p. 156.
133 *Amatus*, VIII.22, pp. 361–2; *Chron. Cas.* III.45, p. 423 (see below, Chapter V).
134 M. Fuiano, *Napoli nel medioevo (secoli xi–xiii)* (Napoli 1972), pp. 16–31; Loud, 'Calendar', nos 28, 67, 112, 126; *Reg. Neap. Arch. Mon.*, v.119–20 no. 445 (1087), 378–9 no. 551 (1113), vi.44–5 no. 575 (1119).

(and also, according to the Montecassino chronicle, received a hefty bribe from the Beneventans). His interference, only a few days after his father's death, led Robert to abandon the siege.[135] Thereafter a further revolt in Apulia over the winter of 1078–9 which took more than a year to suppress, his reconciliation with the papacy in 1080 and his preoccupation with the Byzantine empire in his last years all combined to prevent Robert from again threatening Benevento, or taking further action to extend his territories northwards. In addition the principality of Capua was more obviously on the defensive under Jordan I than it had been under Richard, although there were still sporadic forays into papal territory – thus Jordan's younger brother Bartholomew attacked the lands of the abbey of Subiaco in the Sabina in 1087.[136] But these had no lasting results.

However, there was one area where Norman aggression was by no means discontinued, in the mountains of the Abruzzi where a group of Lombard counties lay under the nominal sovereignty of the western empire, but were in practice independent. Here Norman pressure did have some more permanent consequences. As we have seen, Guiscard's nephew Count Robert of Loritello was already threatening this region in the mid-1060s, probably as yet more in the county of Chieti than further north – Robert may have at this stage been rather stirring up the unruly vassals of the monastery of Casauria than seizing its lands himself. But the Capuan Normans were also probing northwards into the inland county of Marsia, into which Richard I led an expedition in 1067, albeit more for plunder than for conquest.[137] By 1074, when Gregory VII excommunicated the Normans who were seizing the property of Casauria and the abbot was fortifying his villages against them, they were actively menacing the Pescara Valley. The papacy also had claims over this part of central Italy, and it was no doubt for his incursions here that Robert of Loritello was excommunicated (along with his uncle) by Gregory VII at the Lenten synod of 1075, both of them as 'invaders of the properties of St Peter'. But such spiritual sanctions had little or no effect. In the later part of that decade a vassal of Robert of Loritello called Hugh Mamouzet was creating havoc in the Abruzzi, not least when he captured and imprisoned the abbot of St Clement's. For a time this monastery was abandoned by all except a handful of monks. Count Robert

---

135 *Annales Beneventani*, ed. Bertolini, p. 145; *Chron. Cas.* III.45, p. 423. For the background, O. Vehse, 'Benevent als Territorium des Kirchenstaates bis zum Beginn der Avignonesischen Epoche, I, Bis zum Ausgang der normannischen Dynastie', *QFIAB* xxii (1930–1), 87–160, esp. pp. 99–111.

136 *Chronicon Sublacense*, ed. R. Morghen (*RIS*, 2nd edn, Bologna 1927), p. 14.

137 *Amatus*, VI.8, pp. 266–70; *Chron. Cas.* III.23, p. 390. Date: *Annales Casinenses ex annalibus antiquis excerpti, MGH SS* xxx(2).1419.

himself led a major expedition into the county of Chieti *c.* 1076/7 which captured its count, Transmund, besieged Ortona (on the Adriatic coast 20 km east of Chieti) and defeated an army raised by Transmund's family in a pitched battle. At much the same time the prince of Capua's son Jordan led a second expedition into the county of Marsia. Indeed by the late 1070s the Normans may have been penetrating even further north. In the Lenten synod of 1078 Pope Gregory excommunicated those who had invaded the march of Fermo and the duchy of Spoleto. It is a good question what was meant by this geographical description; he may simply have lumped the Abruzzi counties under this broad definition, but the mention of Fermo suggests that some Normans may have reached as far as the county of Aprutium and even crossed the River Tronto.[138]

Guiscard's peace with the papacy in 1080 did something to restrain this pressure, certainly insofar as his nephew Robert was involved. But it did not entirely cease, not least because this was a region at the very periphery of Norman Italy and those involved were largely outside the effective control of the Norman rulers. This was all the more the case after Guiscard's death. Robert of Loritello subsequently ignored the rule of his cousin Duke Roger Borsa, and he and (after his death in 1096) his son proudly styled themselves 'Count of Counts'.[139] There was a renewed wave of Norman pressure in the Abruzzi in the 1090s, the prime movers in which were Robert I of Loritello's younger brother Tassio and Hugh Mamouzet. (Count Robert II of Loritello concentrated his activities in the Capitanata rather than the Abruzzi.) Hugh Mamouzet created a lordship which comprised much of the lower Pescara Valley, and a Norman bishop was installed at Chieti. Almost all our information concerning this period is derived from the later chronicle of Casauria, and the monks regarded Hugh Mamouzet in particular with loathing since he tried to intrude one of his chaplains as abbot. Yet Hugh was well regarded at the nearby monastery of St Bartholomew of Carpineto as 'a magnificent nobleman and a particularly generous benefactor of this church'.[140] We should be cautious about giving too much credence to monastic cries of woe, especially since Casauria had for a long time had very difficult relations with its Lombard vassals and tenants, who did their

---

138 *Amatus*, VII.30–3, pp. 323–32; *Chron. Casauriense*, *RIS* II(2) (Milan 1726), cols 864–6; Gregory, *Reg.* II.52a, VI.5b, pp. 197, 403. Cf. for a detailed account of the whole period, C. Rivera, 'Le Conquiste dei primi normanni in Teate, Penne, Apruzzo e Valva', *Bollettino della reale deputazione abruzzese di storia patria* xvi (1925), 7–94.

139 Ughelli, *Italia Sacra*, vi.702 (1095) *Cod. Dipl. Tremiti*, iii.262–4 no. 90 (1111); Jahn, *Untersuchungen zur die normannischer Herrschaft*, 400–1 no. 16; Rivera, 'Le Conquiste', p. 51.

140 Ughelli, *Italia Sacra*, x.360. For Bishop Rainulf (fl. 1095–1101), *Regesto delle pergamene della curia arcivescovile di Chieti* i *(1006–1400)*, ed. A. Balducci (Casalbordino 1926), pp. 4–5, 92–6.

best to escape the abbots' claims over them and were often as guilty as the Normans of usurping its property. Anyway Mamouzet's lordship collapsed after his death *c.* 1097, and Tassio's son William abandoned his Abruzzi lands to go to the Holy Land *c.* 1103. The ultimate profiteer from these changes was another Norman, Richard, who established a new county of Manopello within the territory of the old Franco-Lombard county of Chieti – but he in fact brought a degree of order to the region, and became a benefactor and protector of the abbey of Casauria.[141] Nor was the native aristocracy entirely displaced – the Norman advance from Apulia largely followed the obvious route along the coast, and in the interior to the west of the Monti di Maiella the Lombard counts of Valva remained in power until the end of the century, and probably thereafter.[142] By the early twelfth century a degree of coexistence seems to have evolved in the Abruzzi. The region remained unstable until its conquest by King Roger of Sicily in the early 1140s, but rather through the lack of any central authority to enforce order than because of overt Norman expansionism.

Hence the capture of Salerno did not mark the end of the period of conquest. The Normans continued to press northwards into the Abruzzi until *c.* 1100, before their impetus in this region petered out. By then, however, the internal cohesion of their dominions was breaking down. After Guiscard's death, and that of Jordan I in 1090, both the dukes of Apulia and the princes of Capua faced challenges to their authority. One symptom of this was the revolt of Amalfi, which threw off ducal overlordship in 1088. Although Roger Borsa reasserted his authority there for a time *c.* 1100, the Normans had little or no impact upon Amalfi, and the little duchy remained effectively independent until its conquest by King Roger in 1131.[143] Indeed, one of the most notable features of the Norman conquest of the mainland was how small an effect it had on the larger towns of the region. These were for the most part overcome only fairly late in the conquest – something explicable both because of the Normans' relative paucity of numbers, and due to the difficulties in prosecuting successful sieges. When such towns as Bari and Salerno were captured few Normans settled

---

141 *Chronicon Casauriense*, cols 868–76. Important discussion by L. Feller, 'Casaux et *castra* dans les Abruzzes: San Salvatore a Maiella et San Clemente a Casauria (XIe–XIIIe siècles)', *MEFR* xcvii (1985), 145–82, esp. pp. 154–61.

142 *Codice diplomatico Sulmonense*, ed. N.F. Faraglia (Lanciano 1888), p. 29 no. 20 (1098). The Walter son of Manerius, count of Valva, in *ibid.*, pp. 42–3 (1130), was probably a relation of the count Gentile in the earlier document.

143 Schwarz, *Amalfi im frühen Mittelalter*, pp. 62–8; V. von Falkenhausen, 'I Ceti dirigenti prenormanni al tempo della costituzione degli stati normanni nell'Italia meridionale', *Forma di potere e struttura sociale in Italia nel medioevo*, ed. G. Rossetti (Bologna 1977), pp. 363–8.

there, and they remained overwhelmingly Lombard. Benevento and Naples were never conquered. The duchy of Naples only finally relinquished its independence to King Roger in 1137, and by that date one may question whether southern Italy was really ·'Norman' at all. Benevento retained its independence under papal lordship, and indeed remained as a papal enclave within the south Italian kingdom right down to the Unification of 1860. Amalfi escaped from Norman rule once more in the early twelfth century, as did Bari where an independent principality under a Lombard prince, Grimoald, was established in 1118, which lasted until the time of King Roger.[144] Similarly, the Abruzzi region was never completely taken over. Thus, although nearly all of southern Italy fell into Norman hands, the conquest remained incomplete.

---

144   The date can be established from *Cod. Dipl. Barese*, v.121–2 no. 69, 123–4 no. 71.

CHAPTER IV

The conquest of Sicily

The early campaigns

Geoffrey Malaterra implied that the project for extending the Norman conquest across the Straits of Messina into Sicily was only conceived after Calabria had been completely subjugated in the spring of 1060. He alleged that:

> While he was staying at Reggio with his brother the duke, that most distinguished young man Count Roger of Calabria heard that Sicily was in the hands of the unbelievers. Seeing it from close hand, with only a short stretch of sea laying in between, he was seized by the desire to capture it, for he was always eager for conquest.[1]

However, whether Malaterra actually believed this to have been the case, or simply that he chose to emphasise Count Roger's role in the decision – as more generally in his account he stressed his role – it was clearly not the whole truth, for Guiscard had already sworn fealty to the pope as 'future Duke of Sicily' at Melfi in August 1059. Hence the reconquest of the island was already planned even before that of Calabria was finished. The recovery of the island for Christianity, after more than two centuries of Muslim rule, was something obviously likely to please the papal Curia, and make the reformers there more inclined towards a rapprochement with the Normans of south Italy. But the moment for such an enterprise was also

---

1   *Malaterra*, II.1, p. 29.

singularly well timed, for the internal situation of the island gave an attack a considerable chance of success.

Under the emirs of the Kalbite dynasty who had ruled the island from 948 onwards Sicily had enjoyed quite a long period of domestic stability and prosperity. The emirs were in theory only the representatives of the Fatimid Caliphs, the rulers of Egypt from 969 onwards. But the caliphs were far away, their overlordship little more than theoretical, and the Kalbites had become to all intents and purposes an independent, self-sufficient and hereditary ruling dynasty. By *c.* 1000 they sometimes even used the title of *malik* – 'king' – of Sicily. During this period Sicily became more obviously Islamicised. Before the Kalbites probably less than half the population was actually Muslim.[2] But though tolerated, as elsewhere in the Islamic world, Christians were still an inferior class, legally disadvantaged and subject to special taxation. Because the Muslims were a superior social group, the pressures for acculturation, albeit more unconscious than deliberate, were strong and therefore led to conversions. By 1060 probably some two-thirds of the population were Muslim, with the majority of the Christians concentrated in the north-east of the island, the mountainous Val Demone south of Messina. There were still a few at Palermo, the island's capital, but this city, growing increasingly populous and prosperous, had by the later tenth century become an overwhelmingly Islamic town. Ibn Hawkal in 977 estimated that there were about 500 mosques in the city and its suburbs, though he admitted that this number was artificially inflated by the Sicilians' propensity for private mosques solely for their own family and retainers. But he clearly found Palermo – with its five quarters within the walls, some 150 butchers' shops and 300 schoolmasters – impressive, even though he considered the learning of the latter limited, and the inhabitants' fondness for raw onions in their diet disgusting and probably harmful.[3]

However, from the early eleventh century the political consensus of Islamic Sicily began to break down. The emir Ja'far was overthrown in 1019 by a rising caused by his attempt to alter the customary system of taxation. In the same period there was considerable immigration from north Africa to Sicily, brought about by the wars which led to the rise of the Zirid dynasty in the Mahgreb and a renewed outburst of conflict there between the Sunni and Shi'a branches of Islam. Some of the latter antagonism was imported into Sicily as well, where there was tension anyway between the long-established Sicilian Muslims and the more recent arrivals from north Africa. It may be that the relatively aggressive policy pursued by Ja'far's

---

2   M. Amari, *Storia de' Musselmani in Sicilia* (above, chapter II, note 58), ii.252.
3   Amari, *BAS*, i.3–6.

brother and successor, Ahmed al-Ak'hal, who continued to raid the mainland of south Italy, and allied with the Zirids to launch naval attacks on Byzantine Greece, was an attempt to divert the attention of an increasingly divided society. If so, it was less than successful, for his increase of taxation to build up his military forces led to further revolt and to al-Ak'hal's assassination in 1037. The Byzantine expedition to Sicily in 1038 aimed to exploit these internal problems, and as we have seen was for a time successful, until itself undermined by the attack on Apulia in 1041.

The last Kalbite emir, al-Hasan, was deposed in 1052/3.[4] By then power in the island had fragmented into a number of contending principalities. The west was ruled by an emir called Abd-Allah ibn Manqut, the south and centre, including the two key centres of Agrigento and Castrogiovanni (Enna), by Ibn al-Hawwas, and the east by an emir based at Catania, Ibn Maklati. Power in Palermo increasingly rested with the civic notables, even before al-Hasan's fall. Ibn al-Hawwas was probably the most powerful of the three contending emirs, but none was in a position to dominate the whole island. The position was further complicated when a certain Ibn Timnah took over Syracuse, and then deposed and killed his neighbour at Catania, Ibn Maklati, and married the latter's widow, who was the sister of the emir of Castrogiovanni, ibn al-Hawwas. Predictably the two new brothers-in-law then fell out.

The Islamic sources for the fall of Sicily are late, and perhaps inevitably do not dwell at any length on an episode which represented a severe setback for their faith. It is perhaps hardly surprising, given his later defection, that they laid the blame for the dispute entirely on Ibn Timnah, alleging that the breach with Ibn al-Hawwas resulted from a drunken attempt to have his wife murdered, from which she was saved only by her son (presumably from her previous marriage). She fled to her brother and war resulted. After initial successes, Ibn Timnah besieged his rival in his principal stronghold at Castrogiovanni, but found it impregnable and was defeated with heavy casualties. With his support crumbling, he sailed to Calabria where he sought the help of Count Roger – offering in return to make him lord of the island.[5] However, while the accounts of Malaterra and Amatus also mention Ibn Timnah's appeal to Roger, the former suggested that this appeal came only in late February 1061. By then, not only had the Normans already decided to launch an invasion of Sicily, but in the autumn of the previous year Roger had made a brief reconnaissance in

---

4 Amari, *Storia*, ii.484.
5 Ibn al-Athir, Amari, *BAS*, i.114; An Nuwayri and Ibn Khaldun, *ibid.*, ii.181, 196 (all written in the 13th/14th centuries on the basis of older sources).

force, landing near Messina with sixty knights and inflicting a sharp defeat on a force which had sallied out from the town to attack him.[6] The Normans were almost certainly well informed as to what was going on in Sicily well before Ibn Timnah came to Reggio in search of aid. Most of the population of the north-east of the island were still Greek Christians, as was nearly all that of Calabria, and there was undoubtedly frequent contact between the two. Some emigrants still moved from Sicily to the mainland, especially at periods of tension. The family of Philaretos, who later became a monk in Calabria, crossed the Straits soon after Maniakes's army invaded Sicily in 1038.[7] Furthermore there was a Muslim colony in Reggio, whose members, so Amatus claimed, were anxious to prove their loyalty to Duke Robert, and doubtless they too were a source of intelligence as to what was going on in the island.[8] So when Ibn Timnah appeared requesting assistance, the speed with which this was forthcoming is hardly surprising. But his request did not, as the Muslim sources allege, cause the invasion; it merely enhanced its prospects of success.

The first step was a further reconnaissance in force or plundering raid early in March 1061, launched probably only a week or two after the meeting with Ibn Timnah (and clearly therefore already in preparation when he arrived). The force involved (150 knights), while still relatively small, was considerably larger than that employed the previous autumn. It landed on the north coast, plundered the area around Rometta and Milazzo, defeated a force from Messina after a hard-fought encounter, but then had some trouble withdrawing since bad weather prevented the Normans from embarking on their ships. Amatus, who adds the interesting detail that Guiscard entrusted an experienced soldier called Geoffrey Ridel (a Norman whose family came from the Pays de Caux) as joint commander with, and perhaps a restraining influence on, his brother, suggests that the whole enterprise was fraught, and that the Normans were lucky, and very relieved, to get away unscathed. However, they inflicted heavy casualties on the Muslims, and this was to have important consequences.[9] Inconclusive as these two early expeditions were, it was clearly important to probe the enemy defences, and even more so to explore the feasibility of the seaborne crossing (short as it was), since this was the first significant maritime

---

6   *Malaterra*, II.1, 3, pp. 29–30; cf. *Amatus*, V.8, pp. 229–30, who does not mention this first expedition. The generally very helpful discussion of M. Bennett, 'Norman naval activity in the Mediterranean *c.* 1060–*c.* 1108', *Anglo-Norman Studies* xv *Proceedings of the Battle Conference* (1993), 41–58, is surely wrong, at p. 51, to date this raid to February 1060 – Malaterra makes clear that Roger went into winter quarters immediately afterwards.
7   *Acta SS, April*, i.604.
8   *Amatus*, V.11, p. 234.
9   *Malaterra*, II.5–6, p. 31; *Amatus*, V.9–10, pp. 231–2.

operation that the Normans had undertaken. The importance of preventing the Normans crossing was equally clear to the Muslims, and in response to appeals from Messina a squadron was sent from Palermo, apparently by Ibn al-Hawwas who seems to have become more or less dominant in the island. Malaterra noted that the invaders' ships were more numerous, but were generally smaller than those of the Muslims, some of which at least were *dromonds*, heavy war galleys.[10] But when they launched their invasion in earnest, in May 1061, the Normans eluded the patrolling squadron by dividing their forces. Roger with an advanced guard of about 300 knights crossed at night, while Robert remained in Calabria with a much more substantial main force and most of the ships to deceive the enemy. The Muslims evacuated Messina and fled. Amatus suggested that this was triggered by the ambush of an official and his escort bringing money from Palermo to the town, whose fate disheartened the defenders, Malaterra (perhaps more plausibly?) that the earlier engagement in March had caused such casualties to the garrison that an effective defence was impossible.[11]

The capture of Messina was a crucial first step in the eventual conquest of the island. Once this was securely in Norman hands, the short sea crossing from Calabria was no longer a problem, and they always had a secure base from which to penetrate into the interior. For the Muslims, without a friendly harbour in the immediate vicinity, keeping a naval squadron at sea to interdict the narrow, stormy and unpredictable straits was hardly feasible – once Messina was captured, the Muslim ships retired 'fearing that if they remained there much longer, the sea might grow rougher and force them aground to be annihilated by their enemies'. Given the low freeboard of their galleys, the prevailing easterly current, and the particularly dangerous sea in the Straits of Messina, they were clearly wise. But other problems, such as the limited supplies of drinking water that could be carried on board ships, also ensured that henceforth the Muslims could not intercept the transfer of men and equipment from the mainland to the island.[12]

In the summer of 1061, once Messina was captured, Guiscard immediately had his main force transported across the straits. The two brothers took a week to ensure that the town was properly garrisoned and defended. Then, with a combined army numbering at the start of the campaign, according to Amatus, 1,000 knights and 1,000 infantry – though other sources

---

10 *Malaterra*, II.8, pp. 31–2. *Amatus*, V.13, pp. 234–5, said that 24 *catti*, sometimes taken to be light galleys, were dispatched, but Malaterra's passage is unambiguous. Cf. J. Pryor, *Geography, Technology and War. Studies in the Maritime History of the Mediterranean* (above, chapter I, note 66), pp. 57–70.

11 *Amatus*, V.15–18, pp. 235–7; *Malaterra*, II.8–11, pp. 32–3.

12 *Malaterra*, II.12, p. 33; Pryor, *op. cit.*, pp. 13–15, 35–8, 83–5.

suggest somewhat fewer later on – they moved along the northern side of the Monti Peloritani, and then southwards around the western side of Mount Etna, into the plain west of Catania. After a brief pause, they changed direction westwards towards Castrogiovanni (Enna).[13] The Normans appear to have been actively seeking a battle – a hazardous expedient which was unusual in medieval campaigning. Their confidence may have been derived from the relatively large size of their army compared with those deployed in many of their campaigns, or from a (probably correct) feeling that the Muslims' morale had been dented by their initial successes, or a belief that superior armour and tactics gave them the advantage – or perhaps Malaterra reinterpreted events with the light of hindsight. In any event, the Normans encountered the army of Ibn al-Hawwas on the banks of the River Dittaino to the east of Castrogiovanni, and despite being heavily outnumbered completely defeated it.[14]

Assuming this victory was as complete as Malaterra and Amatus alleged, its results were at first sight disappointing. Count Roger and a force of 300 *iuvenes* (young or unmarried knights) raided south-westwards towards Agrigento on a combined plundering and reconnaissance expedition, but Castrogiovanni proved impregnable and barred any permanent advance into the south of the island. With winter approaching, Guiscard led his army back to Messina. (Amatus indeed suggested that he allowed himself to be bought off, accepting substantial sums in tribute from Ibn al-Hawwas and other Muslim leaders.)[15] Both he and Roger then returned to the mainland, Roger remaining in Calabria while Guiscard went to Apulia. Clearly Robert could not afford to be absent from his mainland dominions for very long, and this was to be a recurrent problem for operations in Sicily. Furthermore one must remember that in the early 1060s the conquest of Byzantine Apulia was far from complete, and it was important for Guiscard not to leave this to other Normans who were actual or potential competitors. Yet viewed as a whole the 1061 campaign in Sicily had been highly successful. Not only had Messina, the essential jumping-off point for future operations, been secured, but the whole area to the north and east of Mount Etna was left in the Normans' hands. In extending their initial success at Messina, they had enjoyed two notable advantages. The Greek Christians

---

13 The town was only rechristened with its classical name by Mussolini in the 1930s. The Fascist usage was (surprisingly) continued after 1945.

14 *Malaterra*, II.17, p. 34, alleged that 700 Normans defeated 15,000 Muslims, 10,000 of whom were killed. The number of the former is entirely credible (the provision of garrisons must have diminished the original force), but that of the Muslims was surely greatly exaggerated; cf. Amari, *Storia*, iii.75.

15 *Amatus*, V.23–4, pp. 243–4.

of the Val Demone, who formed the majority of the local population, had welcomed them as liberators, and furnished them with supplies. Indeed when Count Roger returned from Calabria late in 1061, 'the Christians of these provinces were very happy to flock to him and joined him in many of his operations', and he was 'joyfully welcomed' by the Christian inhabitants of Troina, where he spent the Christmas of that year.[16] Secondly, they had a valuable local ally in Ibn Timnah, who gave them both direct military assistance and more crucially intelligence of the country and the enemy. He was, according to Amatus, 'the guide of the duke and the whole army'. When Robert returned to the mainland in the autumn, Ibn Timnah had been restored to his lordship at Catania, and this local ally was an important support to the Christian bridgehead in the north-east. Early in 1062, he helped Roger to besiege and capture Petralia, 30 km north-west of Castrogiovanni, which became an important advanced base for the Normans – and already, less than a year after the invasion proper had begun, they had advanced along the north coast more than half-way from Messina to Palermo.[17]

The Normans were thus astute enough to exploit Muslim divisions, and as earlier in Calabria they were prepared to be flexible and tolerant when it suited them, especially when it came to securing the submission of strategic strongholds. Thus when they first advanced from Messina, they accepted the surrender of the Muslim inhabitants of Rometta, the latter 'swearing fealty with oaths taken on their books of superstitious law' (i.e. the Koran).[18] Similarly at Petralia, 'the citizens, both Christians and Saracens, discussed the matter together and made peace with the count, surrendering their *castrum* and themselves to his rule'. Such tolerance was wise, for sieges of powerfully defended strongpoints were still problematic, and impossible while there was the danger of a relieving army arriving. Robert and Roger made no real effort to take either Centuripe or Castrogiovanni, both mountain towns which had been made near-impregnable through their natural position alone. They also clearly profited from the initial alarm and despondency caused by the speedy fall of Messina, and the renewed damage to Muslim morale caused by the defeat outside Castrogiovanni. Paterno (on the southern slopes of Mount Etna) was abandoned by its inhabitants, who 'melted like wax before the fire'. When Guiscard was extorting tribute from the Muslims to end his campaign in the autumn of 1061, he sent an envoy, a cleric who spoke Arabic (presumably a Greek Christian from Sicily), to

---

16 *Malaterra*, II.18, p. 35. Cf. *Amatus*, V.25, pp. 244–5.
17 *Malaterra*, II.20, p. 35. Cf. *Amatus*, V.22, p. 240 (quote).
18 *Malaterra*, II.13, p. 33.

Palermo. He reported back to the duke 'how poor morale in the city was, and that its inhabitants were like a body without any spirit'.[19]

Yet despite this promising beginning, the conquest of Sicily proved a very lengthy process. It was not finally completed until some thirty years later, some time after Robert Guiscard's death. The conquest of the Val Demone, with its mainly Christian population, proved a great deal easier than that of the rest of the island. Once the Muslims had recovered from the shock of the initial invasion, they resisted stoutly, and the problems encountered at some of the most powerful strongpoints in 1061 were repeated in future years. But there were a number of other reasons why the conquest of Sicily turned out to be a long, hard slog. Probably most significant was the rarity of the occasions when the Normans could deploy very large forces in Sicily. After 1061 Guiscard himself only came to Sicily on two further occasions, in 1064 when an abortive attempt was made to capture Palermo, and in the summer of 1071, when a second and more successful attack was made on the island's principal town. When Robert came to the island he was accompanied by a powerful army. But his concerns on the mainland – a still restive Calabria, the reduction of what remained of Byzantine Apulia, the restiveness of his fellow Normans under his rule (which from the later 1060s onwards was a significant problem) – all combined to keep him on the mainland, and to limit the reinforcements that he might dispatch to his brother. Count Roger was left to continue the pressure on the Muslims with the relatively small forces under his own command, recruited either from his own following in Calabria or from those induced to come to Sicily in the hope of immediate pay or future reward. Paid troops were an element in the Norman forces there from early on: the garrison of Petralia in 1062 was partly composed of *stipendiarii*.[20] But once the initial progress slackened and Muslim resistance stiffened, the attractions of Sicily became less alluring to those hoping for quick profits. It is notable that two of Count Roger's principal lieutenants in the earlier stages of the conquest, Geoffrey Ridel and Roussel of Bailleul, appear to have abandoned Sicily to make their careers elsewhere. Geoffrey became duke of Gaeta in 1068, as a vassal or ally of the Norman princes of Capua.[21] Roussel, who was in Sicily in 1063, entered Byzantine service in the mid- to late 1060s, and after the Byzantine defeat by the Turks at Mantzikert in 1071 had a spectacular career as an independent warlord in Asia Minor.[22]

---

19   *Amatus*, V.22, 24, pp. 240, 244.
20   *Malaterra*, II.20, p. 35.
21   Skinner, *Family Power in Southern Italy*, p. 157.
22   *Malaterra*, II.33, p. 43; Shepard, 'The uses of the Franks in eleventh-century Byzantium', pp. 299–302.

Whereas in the summer of 1061 the Normans under Duke Robert's command could dispose of up to 1,000 knights in Sicily, the forces normally available to Count Roger were a lot smaller. In November or December of that year he returned from Calabria with only 250; a year later he crossed the straits with some 300 troops, and in future years he often had considerably fewer than that, certainly for use in offensive operations. (One must remember that those fortresses in Christian hands still had to be garrisoned, even if the bulk of such garrisons might be infantry, with a small number of knights as the core.) Furthermore, as time wore on, the local assistance which had been so useful in 1061 slackened. Above all, while Roger was in Calabria in the summer of 1062, once again in dispute with his elder brother, Ibn Timnah was ambushed and killed by his co-religionists. The news of this led the garrisons at Troina and Petralia to abandon these advanced posts and retire to Messina, which was in itself a serious setback.[23] But the loss of their principal ally almost certainly led to Catania and the eastern coast below Mount Etna ceasing to be a useful aid, and perhaps even ceasing to be a Norman tributary at all and rejoining the rest of Muslim Sicily against them. Certainly Taormina, to the north of Catania, was to become a major problem in future years. In addition, the Normans' relations with the Greek Christians soon deteriorated. At least to begin with, Guiscard and Count Roger had been at pains to conciliate them and treat them well: 'both brothers treated them with the utmost kindness, promising to confer many benefits upon them if God should grant the country to them'.[24] But when Roger returned from Calabria to Sicily in the autumn of 1062 and once again garrisoned Troina, Malaterra noted that the Greeks there were less enthusiastic than before about his presence. In particular, they resented the billeting of Norman troops in their houses, apparently fearful for the virtue of their wives and daughters. (Was this Malaterra's own opinion, or an understandable albeit groundless concern, or something entirely justified because of the poor discipline of the Norman troops or the general view of soldiers through the ages of the proper function of female civilians as 'rest and recreation' for hard-working military men?).[25] Soon afterwards, while Roger was leading an expedition against Nicosia (a town some 18 km to the west), they rose in revolt, hoping to surprise the garrison whom the count had left there with his new wife, Judith of Evreux. In that they were disappointed, for the Normans were alert and held out until the count himself arrived to the rescue. But the

---

23 *Malaterra*, II.22, p. 36.
24 *Malaterra*, II.14, p. 33.
25 *Malaterra*, II.29, pp. 39–40. Cf. the story he told earlier, *ibid.*, II.12, p. 33, of the Muslim who killed his sister rather than allowing her to be captured and raped by the Normans.

situation was still desperate, for Roger found himself besieged in the upper part of Troina not only by the local Greeks but by the Muslims whom the former had called to their aid. The siege lasted for four months over a bitterly cold winter (and the mountains of southern Italy and Sicily can be almost as cold as northern Europe at that time of year). The Normans were close to starvation when Roger took advantage of his besiegers ignoring the Koranic prohibition on alcohol in an attempt to keep warm. He surprised them while they were asleep, killing many and capturing others. The Greek leaders were executed as an example to others.[26] But although the Normans had escaped, this was undoubtedly a very worrying episode, and a warning of how problematic the attempted conquest of Sicily was becoming.

A further problem for the Normans, confined as they were to the mountainous north-east of the island, was adequate supplies, and this difficulty can only have been exacerbated by the decline in relations with the Greek Christians. Hence how often, in the early years of the Sicilian conquest, Count Roger returned to Calabria to gather, not merely reinforcements, but supplies and especially fresh horses. The renewed dispute with his elder brother in 1062 undoubtedly seriously undermined the momentum of the advance in Sicily, and there was indeed a grave setback during Roger's absence. But it was crucial that he did have adequate resources in Calabria to underpin his operations in Sicily, and so Guiscard's reluctance to fulfil his earlier promises that Roger would have half of Calabria was very shortsighted. Roger's success in 1062 in forcing his brother to carry out his undertakings was necessary to the successful continuance of military operations in Sicily, given that, as we have seen, he was usually reliant on his own resources in mounting these. After finally obtaining his alloted share of Calabria, he returned to Sicily in the autumn of 1062, 'now abundantly supplied with arms, horses and the other things he needed'. In the spring of 1063 he once again went back to Calabria, leaving his wife in charge of the base at Troina, to secure replacements for the horses lost.[27] The mounted and armoured knights were the key element in the Norman army, and gave them their advantage over the Muslims in open warfare, despite their numerical inferiority. But an adequate supply of remounts was necessary if that advantage was to be maintained.

Furthermore, the Sicilian Muslims had been by no means idle during the relative lull in Norman pressure in 1062. Not only had the traitor Ibn Timnah been eliminated, but the Sicilians had also sought outside assistance from the Zirid rulers of north Africa, who had in the meanwhile

---

26 *Malaterra*, II.29–30, pp. 40–1.
27 *Malaterra*, II.29, 31–2, pp. 39, 41.

succeeded in consolidating their rather shaky authority in that region. It was very much in the interest of the Zirids to intervene, both to enhance their own reputation as warriors of the faith and since north Africa (the economy of which had been badly affected by continued instability) needed to import food from Sicily. Keeping Sicily Muslim was thus of direct benefit to their power in north Africa. The Zirid prince, al Mu'izz, had indeed already sent a fleet to Sicily in the winter of 1061, but it had been scattered by storms off Pantellaria and had never arrived. But in 1063 his son and successor Temin dispatched his two sons with substantial forces to assist the Sicilian Muslims. So as the campaigning season that year got under way, Count Roger faced (without the assistance of Robert Guiscard) a more formidable opposition than hitherto.[28]

To begin with, Roger continued an aggressive policy, raiding first around Castrogiovanni, where he lured a Muslim force into an ambush, and even pressing south as far as Butera (only 10 km from the southern coast). There may have been something of a change of tactics here – horses seem to have been as important for speed and mobility as for their shock impact in combat, while the use of ambush tactics reflected the need to husband his limited number of knights. But the arrival of the African troops, as well as the attrition of his horses during the long march to Butera in the summer heat, forced Roger back on the defensive. The two armies confronted each other near Cerami, only some 10 km west of the Norman base at Troina, probably in June of 1063 (although the approximate date can only be inferred). Malaterra's account of the battle is the only one we possess since Amatus either never dealt with the Sicilian campaigns where Guiscard was not present or, more probably, a copyist or the translator omitted this part of his account.[29] Malaterra's version was pretty tendentious, ascribing the Christian victory to divine intervention and alleging that Roger with a force of only 136 knights killed 15,000 of the enemy in the battle, and then the next day during the pursuit killed or captured some 20,000 Muslim infantry who had tried to hide in the nearby mountains. But while we may be sceptical about such figures, the Normans were almost certainly heavily outnumbered, and Malaterra's account suggests that, to begin with, Roger was reluctant to fight a pitched battle – indeed the armies faced each other for three days before engaging, and then the count needed some persuasion to launch his main attack after an initial success gained by his nephew Serlo with the advanced guard of his troops. But the result was a complete and

---

28   Ibn al-Athir, in Amari, *BAS*, i.114; Amari, *Storia*, iii.83–5, 94–7.
29   This is implied by the translator's gloss to *Amatus*, VI.23, p. 286. For the month, Amari, *Storia*, iii.100.

crucial victory. The Muslim camp was plundered, the prisoners eventually sold as slaves, and four camels which had been captured were sent to Pope Alexander II in Rome as a token of the Christian victory and of the role which St Peter was believed to have had in securing it. Malaterra added an unpleasant but convincing coda: the Normans only abandoned the battle-field when the stench of decaying corpses became overpowering.[30]

Spectacular as the victory was, the Battle of Cerami was not decisive, in the sense that it made the final conquest of Sicily possible. The Normans still held only the north-east of the island, and Count Roger's forces re-mained outnumbered and under-resourced. They were still maintained on a relatively hand-to-mouth basis. Not long after the encounter at Cerami, Roger decided to return to the mainland to co-ordinate the next steps in the campaign with Robert Guiscard. Before he left, he launched a series of plundering raids, 'to ensure that his wife and the knights remaining with her were not left without means of support [absque stipendiis]'. Booty, and such profits as those from the sale of captives into slavery, remained an essential underpinning of the Norman advance, as well as a visible testimony to their victorious progress, to encourage recruitment and (when given to churches) divine favour.[31] But after Cerami the Muslims were almost always on the defensive, and the stage was set for further and more ambitious attempts at expansion.

The capture of Palermo

It must have been obvious from the start that the key to the conquest of Sicily would be the capture of its former capital (under the Kalbite emirs) and by far its largest town, Palermo. But an attack on Palermo would only be feasible when the Normans could control the north coast of the island, and thus approach it by land. That required greater resources than Count Roger could by himself provide. He was, according to Malaterra, approached very soon after his victory at Cerami by Pisan envoys, proposing a joint attack on the city, Roger by land and the Pisan fleet from the sea. Malaterra claimed that the Pisans were too impatient and attacked before the count could join them, and thus an attempt to capture the city turned into no more than an abortive naval raid, which can be dated from Pisan sources to

30 *Malaterra*, II.33, pp. 42–5.
31 *Malaterra*, II.35, p. 45. See more generally, G.A. Loud, 'Coinage, wealth and plunder in the age of Robert Guiscard', *English Historical Review* cxiv (1999), 815–43.

18 August 1063.[32] But Roger's forces were nowhere near adequate for such an ambitious project, and it is most unlikely that as yet he contemplated a direct attack upon Palermo, even in the immediate aftermath of such a success as the battle outside Cerami. However, he was certainly probing along the north coast, for the plundering raids which he launched in the late summer of 1063 were directed against the Muslim settlements of this region, Cefalù, Collesano and Brocato – more than half-way along the coast towards Palermo from the eastern tip of the island. But to exploit his victory he needed reinforcements, and hence his trip to the mainland to consult his brother *c.* August/September 1063. The immediate result of this was the provision of an extra hundred knights, with whose help Roger conducted an ambitious *chevauchée* towards Agrigento that autumn. In 1064 Robert Guiscard himself returned to Sicily, accompanied by 500 knights, and he and Roger then did make a serious attempt to capture Palermo. They invested the city for three months, but were unable to capture it. Though their army was considerably larger than the forces normally available to Count Roger, it was probably still not big enough to launch a full-scale assault, or even to blockade the town effectively. Nor at this stage was there sufficient naval assistance, which was essential if Palermo had to be starved into surrender. So in the end nothing was achieved except for another large-scale raid into the Agrigento region as the army withdrew.[33]

We have very little information concerning events in Sicily during the next few years – which suggests either that Muslim resistance was still vigorous, or that Norman troops were only available in small numbers, or both – and thus that there were few successes to their heroes' credit for the Christian chroniclers to report. There were also, as we have seen, problems in Calabria which required Guiscard's attention, and probably Count Roger's as well. None the less, we are told that Roger maintained the pressure on the Muslims, and it would appear that the Normans were slowly advancing along the north coast towards Palermo. Petralia, which had been abandoned in 1062, was reoccupied, and its fortifications greatly enhanced, in 1066. By 1068 Count Roger was raiding close to Palermo itself, and inflicted a bloody defeat on a Muslim counter-attack at Misilmeri, which is only 12 km south-east of the city. (Malaterra added another unpleasant detail to his account: Roger announced the disaster to the Palermitans by

32 *Malaterra*, II.34, p. 45; *Gli Annales Pisani di Maragone*, ed. M. Lupo Gentile (*RIS*, Bologna 1930–6), pp. 5–6 (which claimed, *contra* Malaterra, that the Pisans captured six large ships 'filled with riches' in the harbour). *Amatus*, V.28, pp. 255–6, wrongly associates this with Duke Robert's attack on Palermo the next year.
33 *Amatus*, V.26, pp. 246–7; *Malaterra*, II.36, pp. 46–7.

attaching blood-stained parchments to the carrier pigeons which he had captured, knowing that they would return to their lofts in the city.)[34] Meanwhile Muslim unity, always precarious, was disintegrating. The troops from north Africa may have greatly strengthened the defence against the Normans, but they were still unpopular among the Sicilian Muslims. Ibn al-Hawwas resented the Zirids' take-over of Agrigento, and tried to expel them. A pitched battle resulted, in the course of which he was hit by an arrow and killed. Fighting then broke out in Palermo between the inhabitants and their erstwhile saviours, and the disorder grew to such an extent that the Zirid leader Ayûb abandoned the island as a lost cause and returned to Africa in the year 461 AH (November 1068 – October 1069).[35]

Thus when Robert Guiscard came to launch a second attack on Palermo the situation was more conducive to success than it had been in 1064. None the less, there was a considerable delay before this occurred since Guiscard was busy with the siege of Bari until April 1071, and Count Roger also took part in the later stages of that operation. But once Bari had surrendered, a major expedition to Sicily was immediately set under way. A crucial element in this was the fleet – and the blockade of Bari had considerably enhanced the Normans' expertise in naval operations. Furthermore the Bariots were themselves expected to furnish a contingent to the fleet, and some of the Greek prisoners taken at Bari were also enlisted as sailors, so in a very real sense one conquest was a stepping stone to another.[36] Before setting out, Robert also came to an agreement with Richard of Capua, partly one suspects to ensure the security of his mainland territories while he was away in Sicily, for what might well be a considerable period (though Amatus, our source for this 'alliance', did not expressly state this). But in addition Richard agreed to send a contingent of 200 knights under his son Jordan to join Guiscard's army, though in the event he later changed his mind and recalled this force before it had arrived in Sicily.[37]

Duke Robert spent June and July 1071 preparing his forces at Otranto. He dispatched Roger with an advanced force to Sicily, probably by sea, while leading the main body of his army south through Calabria. Roger's first move was to seize Catania, which surrendered four days after he arrived. (Since Taormina to the north, which blocks off the obvious land route down the coast, remained in Muslim hands until 1079, he may well have come by sea.) Malaterra suggested that this was a deliberate attempt to mislead the Muslims, making them think that it was the precursor to a

34 *Malaterra*, II.38, 41–2, pp. 47–50.
35 Amari, *BAS*, i.114, ii.181–2.
36 *W. Apulia*, III, lines 163–5, 187–8, pp. 172–4.
37 *Amatus*, VI.12–13, VII.1, pp. 275, 292.

seaborne attack on Malta. If this was the intention, then it must surely have been aimed not just at wrong-footing the Sicilian Muslims but also at diverting the attention of the Zirids. William of Apulia suggested that there were 'Africans' with the Sicilian ships at Palermo, and so it is probable that, despite their withdrawal of their army from the island a couple of years earlier, the Zirids were still furnishing naval help to the Sicilians, and the alleged threat to Malta was an attempt to persuade them to send their vessels southwards and out of the way.[38] But Catania was also a significant gain in its own right – though we have no information whether, since the death of Ibn Timnah almost a decade earlier, his emirate had remained allied with the Normans (though that seems unlikely), had stayed neutral, or been actively hostile to them. A garrison was left in the citadel – forty men was considered sufficient for this – and Roger marched overland back to Troina to rendezvous with the main force. Then – it was by now some time in August – they moved on Palermo.

The siege of Palermo lasted for five months, and reconciling the contradictions in the contemporary accounts (relatively brief, and in Amatus's case once again very confused) is by no means easy. But it is clear that the city was invested by both land and sea. Amatus said that Robert himself arrived by sea with at least fifty ships, the Bari Annals suggested fifty-eight sailed from the mainland to Sicily. William of Apulia described a major naval engagement with the Sicilian and African ships outside Palermo, although Amatus's account refers to the capture of only two vessels – so the poet's imagination may at this point have carried him away, though he admitted that most of the Sicilian ships did escape back into the harbour. William alleged that the Christians then forced an entry through the chain guarding the entrance and set most of them on fire.[39] To begin with, at least, there were sorties and sharp engagements outside the walls, but as time went on and the blockade tightened, hunger began to be a major problem for the besieged (and clearly they were not as well prepared for this as the people of Bari had been, so perhaps the attack on Catania had helped to deceive them). Amatus described how the Normans cunningly lured some of the desperate inhabitants outside the walls with loaves of bread, and then made them prisoner. By early January 1072 the Normans were ready for an assault. According to Amatus fourteen scaling-ladders had been prepared (and he cannot have been writing much more than a

---

38   *Malaterra*, II.45, p. 52; *W. Apulia*, III, lines 225–6, p. 176; *Amatus*, VI.14, p. 276. Lord Norwich, *The Normans in the South*, p. 176, is more than usually imaginative in going beyond the evidence at this point.

39   *Amatus*, VI.14, 16, pp. 277–8; *W. Apulia*, III, lines 225–54, pp. 176–8; Lupus Protospatharius, *Annales, MGH SS* v.60.

decade after the event, so such details may well be reliable). Roger attacked from the landward side while Robert and some 300 knights made a stealthy approach through the gardens outside the walls on the seaward side. The attack led by Count Roger was repulsed, but seems to have drawn in the bulk of the defenders, enabling Robert's men to scale the walls and open one of the gates. (Indeed, the way in which the city was captured was very similar to how the Crusaders took Jerusalem, twenty-seven years later, when Raymond of Toulouse's initial attack sucked in the defenders and thus allowed an assault on the other side of the city to succeed.)[40] But in contrast to what happened when Jerusalem was taken in 1099, there was no indiscriminate massacre of the inhabitants, although Amatus implied that the Normans killed quite a few of them, women as well as men, as they fought their way into the city. But in Palermo the inhabitants had one last and crucial line of defence, for the walls which had failed to protect them were those of the enlarged new town, and all those able now retreated to the original inner or 'Old City', the al-Kazar, which was itself surrounded by walls. The next morning they surrendered on terms when Robert promised that their lives would be spared and they would be allowed to continue to worship according to their own faith, 'and that [in Malaterra's words] they would not be oppressed by new and unjust laws'. Amatus suggests that it was only two days later that Robert made his formal entry into the city – presumably the al-Kazar – and processed to the main mosque which was ceremonially cleansed of all Muslim accoutrements and became the new Christian cathedral. This was probably on 10 January 1072, the date given by the Bari Annals for the capture of the city.[41]

The capture of Palermo, and the surrender of Mazzara and its surrounding district soon afterwards, marked a very clear and distinct stage in the conquest of Sicily. It was also the last active involvement of Robert Guiscard in the conquest of the island. Once measures had been taken to safeguard what had been gained – a citadel and garrison installed at Palermo,[42] a Norman called Robert appointed as its governor (with the Arabic title of emir) – and arrangements made with Count Roger and his chief lieutenants as to how those parts of the island in their hands should be divided up, Robert went back to the mainland to deal with the problems that had

---

40 J. France, *Victory in the East. A Military History of the First Crusade* (Cambridge 1994), pp. 353–5.
41 *Malaterra*, II.45, pp. 52–3; *Amatus*, VI.19, pp. 279–82; *W. Apulia*, III, lines 255–331, pp. 176–82. Date: Lupus, and the *Anon. Barensis Chron.*, *RIS* v.153.
42 The 'Anonymi Vaticani Historia Sicula', ed. J.B. Carusio, in Muratori, *RIS*, viii (Milan 1726), 765, a 13th-century text largely derived from Malaterra, suggested that Guiscard founded both the citadels that later existed in Palermo, the inland one that became part of the royal palace and the Sea Castle. That may simply have been assumption.

developed during his absence, and he never returned to Sicily again. Henceforth Count Roger, although nominally subject to his elder brother, was even more than hitherto left to govern the island and continue the conquest as he pleased: or as far as his resources, and the need sometimes to assist his brother on the mainland, permitted him to do.

In achieving the conquest of about half the island by 1072, the Normans had displayed considerable flexibility, both in exploiting Muslim divisions and in granting lenient surrender terms and toleration for Muslim worship. Admittedly at both Catania and Palermo the principal mosque was immediately converted to become a Christian church, and Norman garrisons overawed captured towns, but otherwise the conquered population appear not to have been discriminated against. At Palermo, Robert 'promised them their lives and his grace. Nobody was made an exception to this, and keeping his word, even though they were heathen, he was careful not to harm anyone. He treated all his subjects equally.'[43] The supposed foundation charter of the abbey of St Agatha at Catania later referred to Muslims who had fled for fear of the Normans, but (in its present form at least) this is of doubtful authenticity.[44] Catania remained for some time after its capture an exclusively Muslim town. Indeed, while Roger first granted it to his son-in-law, Hugh de Gercé, its governor in 1081 (after Hugh's death) was either a Muslim, or (perhaps more probably) a convert from Islam, who to judge by the Latinised form of his name *Benthumen* was a relative of the former emir and Norman ally Ibn Timnah.[45] If that family's position within the town were guaranteed, this may well explain why Catania surrendered so quickly in 1071. Given the relative numerical inferiority of the Normans, such a policy of toleration was perhaps natural – and Guiscard in 1072 must have had in mind that, even if he had a large army with him then, most of them would be returning to the mainland with him, leaving Roger to defend what had been won with at best a few hundred knights. Thus at Mazzara where 'the Saracens surrendered the town to the duke and promised him to render tribute each year', the phraseology suggests that Robert may have been prepared to allow them a degree of self-government, even if Count Roger almost immediately established a citadel there.[46]

---

43 *W. Apulia*, III, lines 327–31, p. 182.
44 Pirro, *Sicula Sacra*, i.522–3; L.-R. Ménager, 'Notes critiques sur quelques diplomes normands de l'archivio capitolare di Catania', *Bollettino del archivio paleografico italiano*, n.s. ii–iii (1956–7), 149–54, 164–5.
45 *Malaterra*, III.10, 30, pp. 61, 75. Both Amari, *Storia*, iii.164, and Chalandon, *Domination normande*, i.335, suggest that he was a convert.
46 *Amatus*, VI.21, p. 283; *Malaterra*, III.1, p. 57.

One might not be very surprised by this *Realpolitik*, for the Normans had, as we have seen, pursued a similar policy in Calabria, where they had found that a quick surrender on terms was much preferable to lengthy and drawn-out resistance. But of course in Calabria their opponents were Christians, and in the eleventh century there was not the clear separation between the two different Greek and Latin parts of Christianity that later developed. In Sicily the pragmatic policy towards non-Christians was marked. It is all the more interesting because while noting such instances as permitting Muslims to swear fealty on the Koran, and allowing them religious freedom, the chroniclers who described the conquest were at some pains to stress the religious nature of the struggle and the overtly Christian mission of the Normans. This of course reflected well on the Norman leaders, who could, here at least, be shown as following the path of virtue, not just greed. Thus William of Apulia wrote of Count Roger:

> None of his brothers, excellent though they were, entered upon so noble a war, for wishing to exalt the Holy Faith in which we all live, he fought continuously against the Sicilians, enemies of the Divine Name.[47]

But there was more to such a 'Christian' viewpoint than mere flattery, and the chroniclers repeatedly developed this theme. So Malaterra described how at Cerami Count Roger encouraged his army: 'Keep up your spirits, you brave Christian knights. We all carry the emblem of Christ, and He will not, unless He is wronged, desert us. Our God, the God of Gods, is all-powerful . . . with God going before us we shall be irresistible.' Similarly William of Apulia had Robert Guiscard exhort his men during one of the battles (or in reality perhaps skirmishes) outside Palermo: 'This city is an enemy to God, and knowing nothing of the Divine worship is ruled by demons . . . Christ makes difficult work easy. Trust in his leadership, and let's put an end to this conflict.'[48] Of course, these words were those of the writers themselves, and reflected a Christianisation of the classical rhetorical tradition, where such 'battle speeches' were a topos; even though it is not unlikely that at moments of particular crisis some similar sentiments were indeed expressed, to stiffen the sinews and enhance the morale of the Norman soldiers. But the exact words reflect how the chroniclers viewed the struggle, and both William and Geoffrey were writing at the time of (or in Malaterra's case maybe just after) the First Crusade. Malaterra indeed went on to recount how at the crisis of the Battle of Cerami there appeared

---

47   *W. Apulia*, III, lines 197–201, p. 174.
48   *Malaterra*, II.33, pp. 43–4; *W. Apulia*, III, lines 285–6, 292–3, pp. 178–80.

a knight on a white horse, with a shining cross fixed to the top of his lance, riding in front of them 'as if trying to make our men more eager for battle', before plunging into the midst of the Muslims. The Normans promptly identified him as St George. Malaterra added that some also saw a banner with a cross fixed (miraculously?) to the count's lance – an obvious allusion to the Emperor Constantine at the Milvian bridge ('in this sign you will conquer'). The idea that saintly warriors miraculously appeared fighting on the Christian side occurred also during the First Crusade, in the battle outside Antioch in June 1098 against the army of Kerbogha of Mosul (another desperate encounter against heavy odds), though here there was believed to be not just one, but a whole group of holy warriors.[49] Significantly, this vision is recounted by an author who derived from southern Italy, though whether one may therefore assume that the Antioch appearance copied what was believed to have occurred at Cerami, or, since Malaterra may not have been writing until after 1098, vice versa, cannot be certain – the actual texts must surely have been independent of each other. The Catania monk continued that after the victory of Cerami the pope sent Roger a banner, as a sign of St Peter's protection – perfectly feasible and probably true – a banner was probably used by Nicholas II to invest Guiscard with his lands in 1059, and Alexander II sent one to William the Conqueror in 1066.[50] But he also claimed that the pope granted the Norman victors 'absolution for their sins [absolutio de offensis]' provided that they were in future repentant.[51] Here we have either a remarkable anticipation of the development of the later Crusading indulgence, or a reflection of religious ideas in the wake of papally sponsored preaching in 1096.

However, while Malaterra in particular may have transferred something of the ethos of the later Crusade to Sicily, we cannot dismiss the Holy War component to the Sicilian conquest as entirely a later construct. Here the 'History' of Amatus is of crucial importance, for this was written during the lifetime of Abbot Desiderius of Montecassino, thus at the latest before 1087, and probably some years earlier, and therefore cannot anachronistically reflect the concepts of the First Crusade. Yet Amatus too saw Robert and Roger as leading an expressly religious fight. He also had Robert address his men in overtly religious terms, telling them that God would help them, that they should confess and repent their sins, and that if they believed firmly in Him they would conquer. After the capture of Palermo he described the Norman leaders processing in tears to the new cathedral, and

49   *Gesta Francorum*, ed. R. Hill (London 1962), p. 69.
50   William of Poitiers, *Gesta*, II.3, p. 154, and see below, Chapter V.
51   *Malaterra*, II.33, p. 45.

the purification of the building sanctified by angelic choirs and divine illumination. Even the defection of Ibn Timnah was seen as a sign from God.[52] This may be a monastic view, but it is also a near-contemporary one, and some of the religious manifestations described, above all the taking of the Eucharist before major battles, were clearly not just how intellectuals perceived the campaigns, but contemporary practice and (to take the crudest and most reductionist view of the Eucharist) an obvious morale stiffener, 'to fortify themselves with the Body of Christ'.[53] Yet while the Normans were conducting what was perceived, at least by their own historians, as a holy war, recovering land that was rightfully Christian (and this was a theme later taken up by Count Roger's own diplomas), in practice their policy was pragmatic. The Normans' numerical inferiority, the problems of capturing strongly fortified and populous towns and hilltop strongpoints protected by their location as well as man-made defences, and the divisions among the Muslims which were available to be exploited, meant that flexibility and a degree of tolerance coexisted with the ideology of the holy war. This was not just the case during the early part of the Sicilian conquest, for the same exigencies were to direct Count Roger's policy during the consolidation of his power on the island.

Consolidation and settlement

Before leaving Sicily in 1072, Robert Guiscard made arrangements for the future government of the island. He kept, according to Amatus, a half-share in Palermo, Messina and the Val Demone, but conceded all the rest of the island to his brother, to hold as his vassal.[54] In turn Roger granted half of what he held (or perhaps half of what was in future to be conquered) to be divided between his nephew Serlo, son of his elder brother of the same name, and his other principal lieutenant Arisgot of Pucheil, who was also a Hauteville relative. Thereafter, wrote Malaterra, 'both brothers acted separately and strove to further their own individual interests, except that when it was really necessary and one was asked by the other, each of them went to bring help to the other'.

However, the other part of the arrangement did not last long, for just as Guiscard was about to leave the island Serlo was lured into an ambush near

---

52   *Amatus*, V.9, 23, VI.19–20, pp. 231, 241–2, 282–3.
53   *W. Apulia*, III, lines 236–8, p. 176. Cf. *Amatus*, V.23, p. 242.
54   *Amatus*, VI.21, p. 283. *Malaterra*, II.45, p. 53, said that Robert retained the whole of Palermo, but gave the Val Demone to Roger. However, the duke's retention of half of Messina is confirmed by Falco of Benevento: *Falco*, p. 68, ad an. 1122.

Cerami by a Muslim called Ibrahim, with whom he was on friendly terms and who had treacherously made a pact of brotherhood with him. Serlo's death not only helped to revive Muslim morale – we are told that his severed head was placed on a spear and paraded through the towns still in Muslim hands;[55] it also removed Roger's most effective subordinate, and gave proof, if that were needed, that the Normans still faced a long, hard struggle before they could overcome the rest of Muslim Sicily. In the event, it was to be almost twenty years before the conquest of the island was complete.

There were a number of reasons for this, but probably the most important was the continued shortage of men. When Guiscard left, the majority of his army left with him. Roger was thrown back on his own resources, apart from 'the small section of the army which he persuaded to stay, partly with money, partly through promises'.[56] Furthermore, while Malaterra wrote of the two brothers helping each other, in practice after 1072 it was Roger who was summoned to the mainland to help Duke Robert, and his absences not only prevented further advances but placed the conquests which had already been made in some jeopardy. Nor were the strongholds still in Muslim hands easy to take, and in particular the great natural strength of Castrogiovanni remained as an impregnable bulwark preventing more than temporary and hazardous penetration into the south-east of the island, the Val di Noto. Indeed, in the immediate wake of Guiscard's departure and Serlo's death, the defence of existing Christian territory may have been the priority. In 1072 Roger established a fortress at Paternò in the southern foothills of Mount Etna. According to Malaterra, the purpose of this was 'to threaten Catania', which is an odd statement since Catania was already under his rule. However, given that its population was still Muslim, and the Norman garrison small, this may not have been so far from the truth, and Paternò and Catania almost certainly marked the limits of the Christian advance in eastern Sicily at this period. They continued towards the east a line of fortresses (including Cerami and Troina) protecting the territory north of the Rivers Salso and Simetto. Two years later, Roger tried to increase the pressure on Castrogiovanni, and it was clear that possession of this town was the key to the eventual completion of the conquest. 'He knew that if he could secure this place', wrote Malaterra, 'he could then use it as a flail to thrash all Sicily into obedience to him.' A direct assault on the powerful fortress seems never to have been contemplated, but instead the

55 *Malaterra*, II.46, pp. 53–4. For Arisgot of Pucheil, Ménager, 'Inventaire' [above, Ch. II, n. 76], pp. 340–1.
56 *Malaterra*, III.1, p. 57.

count built a castle on Monte Calascibetta, only 2 km north of Castro-giovanni, which not only placed the Muslim fortress under close blockade but was designed to prevent such raids northwards as the one which had led to Serlo's death – in an area which should have been under the Normans' control.[57]

However, Roger could not afford to neglect other parts of the island, nor indeed Calabria, and there was still the danger of external intervention. For while the Zirids had withdrawn their troops from the island before the capture of Palermo, they none the less remained a potential threat through their considerable fleet. In June 1074 a Zirid squadron sacked Nicotera in southern Calabria. While raids like that had no more than nuisance value, another attempt early in the next year was potentially much more danger-ous. A Zirid force made a landing at Mazara, which the Normans had conquered only three years earlier, and which was as yet an isolated en-clave on the south coast, with Trapani and the western tip of the island, which lay to the north, still untaken. The Muslims broke into the town, but were unable to capture the citadel, and the garrison held out there until the count himself could arrive with a relief force and drive the invaders back to their ships with heavy casualties.[58] Yet it had been a near-run thing, and the episode must have been a warning as to how relatively fragile was the Norman hold on Sicily, or at least their more advanced bases there. In consolidating that hold, Roger had to draw deeply on the energy and dynamism (Latin *strenuitas*) which Malaterra saw as the defining feature of his character.[59]

But at this point, when Roger was still very much needed on Sicily, events on the mainland intervened. Guiscard summoned his brother to assist him in his campaign in Calabria against their rebellious nephew Abelard, the son of their elder brother Humphrey. For much of 1075, and probably into the early months of the next year, Roger was busy besieging Abelard's base of Santa Severina in northern Calabria. He was accom-panied by at least some of his followers from Sicily.[60] Meanwhile he had left Sicily under the command of his son-in-law Hugh de Gercé, a nobleman

---

57 *Malaterra*, III.1, 7 (quote), pp. 57, 60–1.
58 *Malaterra*, III.8–9, p. 61.
59 See O. Capitani, 'Specific motivations and continuing themes in the Norman chronicles of southern Italy in the eleventh and twelfth centuries', *The Normans of Sicily and Southern Italy. Lincei Lectures 1974* (Oxford 1977), pp. 1–46, for an important examination of this theme.
60 *Malaterra*, III.4–5, p. 59. For the dating, Chalandon, *Domination normande*, i.240–1. That forces from Sicily were involved is suggested by the presence there of Rainald *de Simula*, a probable relative of the Walter *de Similia* who was killed during Roger's raid on Agrigento in 1063: *Malaterra*, II.35, p. 46. [N.B. The manuscripts of this work are all late, and variant readings of names are therefore to be expected.]

from Maine who had been given the lordship of Catania. He apparently told Hugh to remain strictly on the defensive. However, Hugh ignored his instructions and, accompanied by the count's illegitimate son Jordan, set out to attack the enemy. They were ambushed, and Hugh and many of his men were killed.[61] This was not the first setback to have occurred while Roger was absent on the mainland – one may recall the death of Ibn Timnah in 1062 – but nor was it to be the last.

The leader of the Muslim army which had defeated Hugh de Gercé was Ibn el-Werd, the emir of Syracuse, who is mentioned for the first time by Malaterra in connection with this battle.[62] For the next decade he was to be the most energetic and effective Muslim leader on the island, and one of the principal stumbling-blocks to the Norman conquest. Indeed, he was able at times to carry the war to the enemy, for he possessed at Syracuse one of the best harbours on the island and had enough ships there to launch at least one major raid on Calabria, which seems to have in particular targeted Christian churches (or perhaps churches outside the fortified towns were simply vulnerable and tempting targets).[63]

But once Roger returned to Sicily in 1076 he renewed the offensive in earnest, and the next five years saw some significant Christian gains. His first step was a punitive expedition against Ibn el-Werd's lordship in the south-east, which saw the destruction of a settlement at Judica (33 km west of Syracuse) and widespread devastation in the Val di Noto. The burning of corn at harvest-time spread famine in the Muslim areas. But the core of his strategy seems to have been to eliminate the troublesome Muslim enclaves that made much of the conquered territory still vulnerable to incursions. In 1077 he captured Trapani, and thus ensured that the west of the island was firmly under his control. Then in 1078 Castronuovo, one of the strongest Muslim fortresses in central Sicily, was betrayed to him by one of its inhabitants, a baker who (so Malaterra alleged) was seeking revenge for a flogging inflicted upon him by its emir. In late February or early March 1079 he laid siege to Taormina, the one remaining Muslim fortress north of Mount Etna, which eventually surrendered after a six-month siege. Once again the possession of a fleet was an important advantage. Both Trapani and Taormina were blockaded from the sea, and Trapani surrendered after a seaborne landing by the count's son Jordan on the peninsula which jutted out from the town into the sea took the defenders unaware and most of the animals on which they were relying for food were seized. They may also

---

61 *Malaterra*, III.10, pp. 61–2.
62 For the identification of Malaterra's *Benevert*, Amari, *Storia*, iii.151.
63 *Malaterra*, IV.1, p. 85.

have been short of water. At Taormina Roger's fleet was large enough to intimidate a Zirid squadron of fourteen vessels, which may have been trying to relieve the town, into withdrawing without a battle. To consolidate these gains he followed his usual policy of establishing citadels where these did not already exist, as he had at Mazara and as he now did at Trapani, strengthening existing fortifications and establishing adequate garrisons to overawe the Muslim population.[64]

Yet even while these advances were under way, fresh problems emerged. During the siege of Taormina, there was a revolt in western Sicily by the Muslims of Jato and the surrounding district. There were, according to Malaterra, some 13,000 Muslim families in this area, who had hitherto acknowledged Norman overlordship, paid a tax (*census*) and rendered 'service' (whatever that may mean) to the count. Jato was not much more than 20 km south-west of Palermo, and was another mountain site which nature had rendered all but impregnable:

> The mountain on which they lived was guarded on every side by a sheer drop, and the climb up was impossible except for one narrow path which had been artificially carved out to allow the citizens to enter and leave.

The problems of overcoming this stronghold were compounded by the mountainous nature of the whole region, within which the inhabitants and their animals could be hidden away and be very difficult to find, let alone attack. Roger recognised the difficulties by trying at first to persuade the Muslims to submit 'with honeyed words'. When that failed, he set out to blockade the whole district by establishing new fortresses at Partinico (to the north) and Corleone (to the south). But it was only after a long campaign and the destruction of the harvest that he forced the region's submission.[65] Roger was still keen to take advantage of divisions among the Muslims, and win some of them over to his side. We are told that he generously rewarded the man who had betrayed Castronuovo to him precisely 'to furnish a good example to others who might attempt similar schemes'. Indeed, one of his chief lieutenants at the siege of Taormina and thereafter was a converted Muslim called Elias *Cartomensis*. But while Elias remained a loyal supporter – he was later captured and put to death by his former co-religionists because he would not apostatise back to Islam – retaining the loyalty of the

---

64 *Malaterra*, III.11–12, 17–18, pp. 62–4, 66–7. For the problems of water supply at Trapani, *The Travels of Ibn Jubayr*, trans. R.J.C. Broadhurst (London 1952), p. 352.

65 *Malaterra*, III.20–1, pp. 69–70. Edrisi, the Muslim geographer at the court of Roger II, described Jato as 'strong beyond all belief': Amari, *BAS*, i.22.

subject population as a whole was by no means easy.[66] Given the hints we have that paid troops continued to play an important part in military operations in Sicily, it may be also that fiscal exploitation, though necessary, did not endear the Normans to their new subjects. Revolts remained a danger. Malaterra remarked apropos of a later episode that the Greeks of Sicily 'all hate those of our race and prefer there to be discord among us rather than peace'. This comment may of course reflect his prejudice rather than the actual views of Greek Christians, and the latter still helped in the campaigns, especially in the fleet, but it suggests that a degree of conciliation may have been necessary. Furthermore, from the siege of Salerno in 1076 onwards, Muslim troops were recruited for use in mainland campaigns; this could conceivably have been part of the *servitium* which the inhabitants of Jato rejected in that same year. They were not the only Muslims to be restive under infidel rule. Even after the conquest was finally completed, there was a Muslim rebellion at Pantalica in eastern Sicily in the autumn of 1091.[67] Yet there was little that Roger could do, at least in the short run, about his basic problem, which was that there were a great many Muslims, and only relatively few Normans. Combined with Sicilian geography, which made so many of the fortresses impossible to storm and meant that generally (unless something fortuitous occurred as at Castronuovo) they had to be reduced by hunger, it was no wonder that the conquest of Sicily was a slow business.

None the less, by 1080 the Normans were making real progress. But then, once again, events on the mainland intervened. Guiscard set off to attack the Byzantine empire, and Count Roger's presence was required on the mainland to back up his nephew, Guiscard's eldest son by his second marriage, another Roger, an inexperienced youth of no more than twenty. While he was absent Catania was betrayed to Ibn el-Werd by its governor, who was (as mentioned above) either still a Muslim or a convert from Islam. The count's son Jordan quickly recovered the town after Ibn el-Werd made the mistake of fighting a pitched battle with the Normans. But again, it had been a very dangerous episode which had come close to losing one of the most important towns on the island and greatly heartening the Muslims, who had, in Malaterra's opinion, 'rejoiced far and wide at the mockery such ignominy had brought to the Christian name'. And significantly, Jordan had been able to muster only 160 knights to retake Catania, which was doubtless why his opponent had risked a battle, knowing that the

---

66 *Malaterra*, III.12, 18, 30, pp. 64, 67, 75. On the name *Cartomensis*, which may indicate an origin from a particular Berber tribe, Amari, *Storia*, iii.158–9.

67 *Malaterra*, III.31, IV.18, pp. 76, 98; *Amatus*, VIII.13, p. 354.

Normans were heavily outnumbered.[68] When Count Roger did return to Sicily, it is interesting that one of his first moves was to strengthen the defences of Messina. While, as Malaterra noted, possession of that town was the key to Sicily, it had never since its capture twenty years earlier been threatened, and was by the early 1080s a long way behind the front line. Count Roger was either being extra careful, or was still deeply uneasy about the situation on the island. If he did feel wary, that may have been because he knew that he would once again be required on the mainland, and indeed in 1083–4, after Guiscard's return from his campaign in the Balkans, he needed Roger's aid to restore his authority on the mainland and aid the papacy against the Emperor Henry IV.[69]

Furthermore, disputes emerged among the Normans on the island, as Count Roger faced attempts by his subordinates to entrench their own authority in particular areas. The first challenge – if such it was – came from a man called Ingelmarius, a knight of relatively low status (*gregarius miles*), whom Roger had favoured and married off to his nephew Serlo's widow. He fell out with the count, probably in the early 1080s, when he began to build a castle keep at Geraci (north-central Sicily, *c.* 10 km from Petralia) without permission. More seriously, the count's illegitimate son Jordan launched, according to Malaterra, an actual rebellion in north-east Sicily while his father was on the mainland in 1083/4. Yet while Malaterra (as usual our only source) presented these as deliberate and seditious attempts to undermine the count's authority, one might suspect that they were rather attempts to consolidate lordships by those who had hitherto rendered loyal service, but not received much of an endowment – in other words the same grievance that Roger himself had earlier had against Robert Guiscard. There was the added complication in Jordan's case that, though born out of wedlock, he was the count's only healthy adult son, and probable – though not as yet designated – successor. This last circumstance was a recipe for tension in any medieval society. But what, according to Malaterra, really worried the count was the possibility that Jordan might defect to the Muslims. None the less, the trouble was quickly put down, and Jordan soon restored to favour, although the count had several of his associates blinded.[70]

Yet while it is easy to point to the various problems which hampered the completion of the conquest, it would appear that the major difficulty was simply Count Roger's absences on the mainland. Were we better informed

68 *Malaterra*, III.30, pp. 75–6.
69 *Malaterra*, III.32, 35–6, pp. 77–8.
70 *Malaterra*, III.31, 36, pp. 76, 78–9.

about the state of affairs among the Muslims, the situation might appear in a very different perspective. For when, after Robert Guiscard's death and a period spent ensuring the succession of the latter's son Roger Borsa, Count Roger was able once more to turn his attention to the island, he was able to complete the conquest of the entire island in a relatively brief period. There was one advantage that he certainly now possessed. At some stage before 1087 a peace treaty was concluded with the north African ruler Temin, which ensured that the Sicilian Muslims could no longer expect external help.[71]

The first step in the renewed offensive was a combined land and sea attack on Syracuse, launched in May 1086. The fleet, under Roger's personal command, defeated the naval forces of Ibn el-Werd, after the emir fell overboard during the battle and drowned, but the town had to be besieged for four months before it surrendered. Next spring the count moved against Agrigento, which again surrendered after a siege lasting almost four months (on 25 July 1087). Roger then mopped up the smaller settlements in the territory of Agrigento as far east as the River Salso. By now the Muslims must have been thoroughly demoralised, for even naturally defensible sites like Licata and Caltanisetta surrendered immediately. Roger was then able to secure the greatest prize of all – Castrogiovanni. He had captured the wife and children of its emir, Hamûd, at Agrigento, and he was able to use them to persuade him to surrender the fortress by leading the garrison out on a sortie where Roger (warned in advance) could ambush them. Hamûd and his family subsequently converted to Christianity.[72] By now only the extreme south-east of the island was left in Muslim hands. That this enclave received a brief stay of execution was once again due to complications on the mainland, for Roger spent the summer of 1088 in central Calabria, upholding Duke Roger Borsa against the latter's half-brother Bohemond. But in April 1089 his army and siege engines appeared round Butera. The inhabitants held out for some time, but with no prospect of relief were eventually forced to surrender. Finally Noto, the last place in Sicily in Muslim hands, surrendered voluntarily in February 1091. Here the count did not even have to move against the town: he was at Mileto, his principal residence in Calabria, when its envoys came to him to offer its surrender.[73]

---

71 *Malaterra*, IV.3, pp. 86–7.
72 *Malaterra*, IV.2, 5–6, pp. 85–8. The dates given by this author appear to be a year in arrears; see H. Houben, 'Adelaide "del Vasto" nella storia del regno normanno di Sicilia', in his *Mezzogiorno normanno-svevo Monasteri e castelli, ebrei e musulmani* (Naples 1996), pp. 84–6. I have followed the chronology of Amari, *Storia*, iii.167–80. Chalandon, *Domination normande*, i.338–9, would place the sieges of Syracuse and Agrigento both in 1086, which cannot be correct.
73 *Malaterra*, IV.12–13, 15, pp. 92–3.

But if the surrender of Noto marked the end of the military conquest, it was far from the end of the process of consolidation. Roger followed his usual practice at Agrigento and Noto and established strong citadels whose garrisons could overawe the local population. Meanwhile the former emir of Castrogiovanni, who was afraid both of his erstwhile co-religionists and that Roger would suspect him of disloyalty, had asked to be given instead lands in Calabria. Roger imitated this precedent when he took Butera, and sent its leading men to Calabria where they could do no harm. By depriving Muslim communities of their leaders, he could hope to limit their capacity to rebel. Furthermore, many Muslim aristocrats and intellectuals had already abandoned the island and gone to live in north Africa or Spain – men like the poet Ibn Hamdis who had left his native Syracuse for Seville c. 1078.[74] There had also been at least one earlier instance, in 1064, when Robert Guiscard had transferred the entire population of a captured settlement in Sicily to the mainland, to repopulate his former base at Scribla.[75] But such an expedient was very much the exception. The Muslims remained in a majority in two-thirds of the island: 'ethnic cleansing' was therefore hardly a practical proposition. The only long-term solution was either to encourage widespread conversion among the Muslim population or to induce significant immigration of Christians from the mainland. And to make either option possible, it was first necessary to create a Christian Church structure on the island, more or less de novo. In addition, even while the conquest was still under way, Roger had to administer what had been won and to reward his principal followers. If some of that reward could be a matter of promises, those could not remain unfulfilled indefinitely, as the episodes with the errant Ingelmarius and his son Jordan had shown. It would seem that lords were already being enfeoffed in at least the more northern areas of the island during the 1080s.

But, after the surrender of Noto, we are told that Roger 'thanked his knights with whose help he had been raised to this high estate very kindly, and rewarded them for their exertions, some with lands and wide possessions, and some with other sorts of recompense'.[76] This would suggest that any existing distribution of lands was greatly extended after 1091. None the less, Roger was careful to retain much of the island in his own hands, especially the centre and west. Relatively few substantial lordships were

---

74 A. Ahmed, A History of Islamic Sicily (Edinburgh 1975), pp. 76–81. Ibn al-Athir, in Amari, BAS, i.114, suggests that there were waves of exiles both when the Normans first invaded (perhaps also fleeing from internal dispute) and especially when the Zirids left the island in 1069.

75 Malaterra, II.36, p. 47.

76 Malaterra, IV.15, p. 94.

created, and these were either for close relatives of the count, or for favoured churchmen.

The creation of a new Christian Church was also already under way before the conquest was completed. When Palermo was captured, one of the first actions of Guiscard and Count Roger was to convert the principal mosque (once a church) to become the city's cathedral. The existing Greek archbishop, Nicodemos, the only prelate of episcopal rank left on the island, who had previously been carrying out his ministrations in a church outside the walls, was then installed there.[77] But for nearly a decade Palermo remained the only see on the island. It was only once the capture of Taormina in 1079 had ensured that the Val Demone was entirely in Christian hands that Roger founded a bishopric at Troina, to which he appointed a north Italian cleric called Robert. He seems to have been acting here on his own initiative, and only belatedly sought papal permission for his new bishop to receive consecration. This was reluctantly granted by Gregory VII, who clearly considered the whole business irregular, and warned Roger not to use this case as a precedent. And it was only about two years later that a proper endowment and definition of the diocesan bounds was constituted. Bishop Robert was placed in charge of a vast see stretching from Messina south to Mount Etna and as far west as Cefalù and Caltavuturo.[78] By then, even though the island was still not completely reconquered, plans were being made to develop the ecclesiastical infrastructure further. A bull of Gregory VII for the archbishop of Palermo in April 1083, which by granting him the *pallium* confirmed his status as the metropolitan of the island, envisaged the refoundation of other bishoprics which had once been known to exist there. By this stage the Greek incumbent had been replaced by a Latin archbishop called Alcherius.[79] However, the creation of further sees had to wait until the entire island had been conquered, although in the intervening period there were a number of monastic foundations, including a Greek abbey at Brolo (near the north coast about half-way between Messina and Cefalù) by 1084, and a Latin abbey on the island of Lipari, founded by 1088 and probably several years earlier.[80] Once the conquest was finally complete, Roger acted quickly, and between 1091 and 1093 four further bishoprics were established, at Catania, Syracuse, Agrigento

---

77   *Malaterra*, II.45, p. 53. His name is known only from a later papal bull of 1123, *Italia Pontificia*, x.230 no. 24.

78   *Malaterra*, III.19, pp. 68–9; Gregory, *Reg.* IX.25, p. 607; *I Diplomi della cattedrale di Messina*, ed. R. Starrabba (Documenti per servire alla storia di Sicilia, Ser. I.i, Palermo 1876–90), pp. 1–2 no. 1.

79   *Italia Pontificia*, x.229 no. 20.

80   L.T. White, *Latin Monasticism in Norman Sicily* (Cambridge, Mass., 1938), pp. 40, 77–8.

and Mazara. Unlike the creation of Troina, this was with the full agreement and sanction of the papacy. The new pope, Urban II, had visited Sicily in 1089 and had probably given verbal agreement to these developments then; certainly he confirmed the creation of the new sees at Catania and Syracuse within a few months of their foundation. At Catania he sanctioned the arrangement whereby the see was based on the cathedral-monastery of St Agatha, established (if we can believe the alleged foundation' charter) in December 1091, or perhaps slightly earlier.[81] However, he did not agree to Roger's other Benedictine monastery of Lipari also becoming the seat of a bishopric, even though it had been one in earlier centuries. The island was virtually uninhabited and far from fertile, and thus the pope considered it an unsuitable base for a diocese, and Lipari had to wait until well into the twelfth century before receiving promotion to episcopal rank.[82] Finally, in 1096, the see of Troina was transferred to Messina, a sensible enough move given that the latter was by far the more important of the two towns.[83]

Analysis of this new Church structure has been needlessly complicated by the controversies that developed in later centuries over the surviving foundation charters of the Sicilian bishoprics. The diplomatic of these documents may be questionable, surviving as they do only in later copies, as those for Agrigento and Syracuse, or at Catania in a version which is probably a thirteenth-century forgery (indeed all three alleged charters of Roger I for Catania appear to have been 'improved'). But there is no reason to doubt the gist of their contents, particularly since the contemporary, and undoubtedly genuine, papal bulls provide general confirmation for these contents. The key function of these charters was to define the diocesan boundaries, and to assign tithes from particular places to them.[84] However, the actual endowment of property varied considerably. The abbot-bishop of Catania was granted lordship over the city, including its port and a number of places in the surrounding area. Thus he effectively stepped into the shoes of the previous lay lord, Roger's late son-in-law Hugh de Gercé, and indeed of the Muslim emirs of Catania, and became one of the most important landholders of Sicily. Other sees were less well endowed, though Troina received two fortified villages (*castra*) in the Val Demone in 1082,

---

81 *Malaterra*, IV.7, 13, pp. 88–9, 92–3; *Italia Pontificia*, x.290 no. 19, 317 no. 70.

82 *Italia Pontificia*, x.359 no. 1 (June 1091). For the tangled later history of the bishopric, White, *Latin Monasticism*, pp. 88–9, 97.

83 Pirro, *Sicula Sacra*, i.382.

84 *Le Più antiche carte dell'archivio capitolare di Agrigento (1092–1282)*, ed. P. Collura (Documenti per servire alla storia di Sicilia, Ser. I.25, Palermo 1960), pp. 15–18 no. 2; *Il Tabulario di S. Maria di Malfinò*, ed. D. Ciccarelli (2 vols, Messina 1986), i.3–4 no. 1 (Syracuse); Pirro, *Sicula Sacra*, ii.842 (Mazara); Ménager, 'Notes critiques sur quelques diplomes' [above, note 44], pp. 154–9, 162–7 nos 1–3.

and perhaps a further one in 1087 (although the charter from which this is known is in its present form a forgery), while Agrigento received one village on its foundation. And although Roger's charter for Syracuse makes no mention of any landed endowment, by 1104 the bishop possessed at least three villages near the city.[85] Similarly, the abbey of Lipari received a considerable endowment of lands, churches and serfs in Sicily itself, and in the Stilo region of Calabria. This was undoubtedly necessary since a small and inhospitable volcanic island was hardly ideal for the support of a large monastic establishment. Even after its initial endowment, and having attracted a circle of benefactors among the Norman nobles of the island, the abbot still had to beg further land in northern Sicily to provide adequate pasturage for the monastery's animals, because of the aridity of Lipari itself.[86] Count Roger also had to step in to help the new bishoprics; though for them the problem was ensuring the payment of tithes from the lay nobles, arrangements for which were laid down at a meeting of the comital court at Mazara c. 1097. But the development of the Church outside the principal towns was more haphazard and piecemeal. The Mazara judgment regulated the relations between the bishops and private chapels established by landowners, and implied that providing adequate personnel to staff these was problematic.[87] There was no systematic establishment of subordinate churches and, except perhaps in the Val Demone where there were already existing Greek-rite churches, baptismal rights were almost certainly limited to the new cathedrals. Elsewhere the Christian population was too exiguous to warrant more.

The lay lordships granted by Roger I were mainly in the east and along the north coast of the island. The most important were those granted to two of his children: his illegitimate son Jordan, who was given Syracuse and extensive lands in the south-east of the island including Noto and Lentini, and another son Godfrey, almost certainly also born out of wedlock, who was given a seigneury around Ragusa (to the west of Jordan's lordship).[88] However, Jordan only enjoyed this substantial endowment for a very brief period, for he died in the autumn of 1091. Roger then granted his barony to his nephew Tancred, a younger son of his elder brother Count William of the Principate. By doing this, he repaid the debt which he owed to his

85 Pirro, *Sicula Sacra*, i.619–20; *I Diplomi della cattedrale di Messina*, 1–3 nos 1–2.
86 C.A. Garufi, 'Per la storia dei monasteri di Sicilia nel tempo normanno', *Archivio storico per la Sicilia* vi (1940), 72–3 no. 1. More generally, White, *Latin Monasticism*, pp. 81–6.
87 *Le Più antiche carte di Agrigento*, pp. 18–20 no. 4.
88 For much of what follows, S. Tramontana, 'Popolazione, distribuzione della terra e classi sociali nella Sicilia di Ruggero il Granconte', *Ruggero il Gran Conte e l'inizio dello stato normanno. Relazioni e communicazioni nelle Seconde Giornate normanno-sveve, Bari, maggio 1975* (Rome 1977), pp. 213–70, especially pp. 216–39.

long-deceased brother for the latter's support during his disputes with
Guiscard back before the invasion of Sicily had even begun.[89] In the early
twelfth century there was also a third important lordship in this south-
eastern region, based around Butera and Paternò, held by Roger's brother-
in-law Henry. But while we know that he was in Sicily from *c.* 1094 onwards,
and it may have been then that he married one of Roger's daughters by a
previous marriage, there is no direct evidence for his territorial endowment
until 1113, and it is probable that he was granted this lordship not by
Roger I, but by the latter's widow (and Henry's sister) Adelaide, during her
regency after the count's death.[90]

Another of Roger's sons, Mauger, again probably illegitimate, had lands
in the north-east of the island, though he does not seem to have been
endowed on anything like the same scale as his (half?) brothers. Two other
barons who held lands along the north coast, Robert the son of Count
William of Eu and Josbert de Luci (whose lordship was near Termini,
30 km east of Palermo), were married to daughters of Count Roger by one
or other of his first two wives, while Roger de Barneville, who held Geraci
(near Petralia) and Castronuovo (40 km south-east of Palermo), was married
to Roger's great-niece Eluisa, daughter of his nephew and lieutenant Serlo.
Roger is known to have been in Sicily by 1086, but later joined the First
Crusade, and was killed outside Antioch in June 1098, though he left a son,
another Roger, who succeeded him in Sicily.[91] Indeed, almost the only
major landowner in Sicily who was not part of the comital kin either by
blood or by marriage was Godfrey *Burellus*, who was probably the most
important baron in the north-east of the island (again he is attested as early
as 1085), and who was related to a Robert *Burellus*, an important Calabrian
landowner near Mileto.[92] The antecedents of this family are uncertain –
they might perhaps have been related to the Borell family who dominated
the Sangro Valley in the Abruzzi and squabbled with the monastery of
St Vincent on Volturno in Molise, in which case they would have been of
Lombard (or Lombardo-Frankish) descent. But this is purely conjectural. A

---

89 *Malaterra*, I.24, p. 20.
90 C.A. Garufi, 'Le donazioni del conte Enrico di Paternò al monastero di Valle Giosofat',
    Revue d'Orient Latin ix (1902), 219–20 no. 1. Cf. C.A. Garufi, 'Gli Aleramici e i normanni
    in Sicilia e nella Puglia. Documenti e ricerchi', *Centenario della nascità di Michele Amari*
    (Palermo 1910), i.47–83, esp. pp. 49–50.
91 L.-R. Ménager, 'Inventaire des familles normandes et franques emigrées en Italie
    méridionale et en Sicile (xi–xii siècles)', *Roberto il Guiscardo*, pp. 353–4.
92 For Godfrey, Tramontana, 'Popolazione, distribuzione della terra e classi sociali', pp. 229–
    31. For Robert, L.-R. Ménager, 'L'Abbaye bénédictine de la Trinité de Mileto en Calabre
    à l'epoque normande', *Bollettino dell'Archivio paleografico italiano*, iv–v (1958–9), 32–4 no. 10
    (1092), witnessed by (among others) Roger I and his son Mauger.

handful of non-Norman Frenchmen can also be identified in Sicily: Hugh de Gercé from Maine (but he died *c.* 1075), a Breton called Eviscardus who saved Count Roger's life at the cost of his own at the siege of Taormina in 1079, and an Angevin family, the Craon, found in Sicily from 1105 onwards, one of whom married a daughter of Roger de Barneville.[93] But the majority of those who profited from the conquest of Sicily were certainly genuine Normans, either relatives of Count Roger, or men who can be clearly linked with the duchy of Normandy. Josbert de Luci, for example, came from near Dieppe in the Pays de Caux. William Maulevrier, who held Galati near Capo d'Orlando (in the north-east of the island) also came from this part of Normandy.[94] So too did Robert of Eu, who was a younger son of the count of Eu, which explains why he had left Normandy to seek his fortune in Sicily. He was already established there and married to Roger's daughter Matilda (by the count's second wife, Eremburga of Mortain) by 1092, some years before his father fell out catastrophically with King William Rufus, and was blinded and mutilated after being defeated in a judicial duel. But despite that unhappy circumstance, which ought surely to have stilled any doubts he may have had as to the wisdom of his move, he appears to have returned to Normandy by 1102. Whether his wife was still alive then, we do not know.[95] The Barnevilles were another undoubtedly Norman family, who may have come from the Cotentin, although this toponym occurs in other areas of Normandy as well. Similarly Rainald Avenell, who witnessed a charter of Duke Roger Borsa on the mainland in 1092 but by 1110 had acquired a lordship near Palermo, came from the Mortain region of western Normandy. At some stage after 1110 he married, as his second wife, a granddaughter of Roger I.[96] There was also Peter of Mortain, a close adviser of Roger I who regularly witnessed his charters and who was entrusted with raising troops in Sicily for Roger's siege of Acerenza (in Lucania) in 1090. He held a lordship in the vicinity of Agrigento, though we cannot tell how substantial this was. He may perhaps have been a relative of Count Roger's second wife, Eremburga of Mortain.[97] Yet another Norman present at the comital court in the 1090s was Geoffrey de Say (from Sées: département Orne). What, if any, land he may have held is unknown, but his descendants in the later twelfth century were to

---

93   *Malaterra*, III.15–16, p. 66; *Più antiche carte di Agrigento*, pp. 35–7 no. 12; Ménager, 'Inventaire', pp. 369–70.

94   Ménager, 'Inventaire', pp. 322–7.

95   Pirro, *Sicula Sacra*, ii.1035 (1092); White, *Latin Monasticism*, pp. 245 no. 1 (1095?); Ménager, 'Inventaire', pp. 312–13 (not entirely satisfactory); *Orderic*, iv.284–5.

96   Ménager, 'Inventaire', pp. 353–4, 358–9.

97   *Les Chartes de Troia*, pp. 135–6 no. 28; *Più antiche carte di Agrigento*, pp. 3–7 no. 1; *Malaterra*, IV.16, p. 94; Ménager, 'Inventaire', pp. 330–1.

become, as counts of Gravina, one of the great aristocratic families of southern Italy.[98]

One can see how Count Roger used his numerous progeny, from his three marriages and (probably several) irregular relationships, as a means of controlling the new Sicilian establishment and binding it to himself.[99] Furthermore, most of the principal towns and fortresses (apart from Syracuse, Catania and the halves of Palermo and Messina still subject to the duke of Apulia) remained under his direct control. So too did a vast swathe of lands in the centre and west of the island; almost all of which was retained in the hands of the rulers of Sicily until late in the twelfth century – significant parts were alienated only with the foundation of the abbey of Monreale by King William II in 1176. Count Roger was also concerned to stress his dominance over his followers both by personal example and by titulature. Hence perhaps his fury with his son Jordan when the latter suggested that he, rather than his father, should command the expeditionary force which conquered Malta in 1091. The count wished to be seen as the conqueror, the man who reclaimed places for Christianity in person (though Malaterra suggested that he also displayed an entirely understandable dislike of being considered 'old').[100] But Roger also emphasised his superior status in other and more subtle ways. His role as the restorer of Christianity to a land polluted by the infidel was stressed, both in his own documents, and also in papal bulls for Sicilian recipients – though such statements also reflected Urban II's wish to maintain good relations with the man who was increasingly becoming the most powerful among the south Italian Normans.[101] From 1092 onwards he may sometimes have styled himself 'Great Count' (*magnus comes*) of Sicily and Calabria – one could be more certain about this if one could vouch for the absolute authenticity of the documents concerned.[102] If he did adopt this style (and some distinguished scholars *have* been prepared to accept the relevant documents as genuine), it was probably to differentiate himself from other counts on the mainland – Roger was after all a territorial ruler in his own right – rather than to stress his

98 Ménager, 'Inventaire', pp. 344–5.
99 For a list of all his offspring, with evidence, Houben, *Mezzogiorno normanno-svevo*, pp. 106–13.
100 *Malaterra*, IV.16, pp. 94–5.
101 E.g. the foundation charters for Troina and Agrigento [above, notes 78 and 84], and Urban's bull for Catania, *Italia Pontificia*, x.290 no. 19.
102 E.g. C.A. Garufi, *Documenti inediti dell'epoca normanna di Sicilia* (Documenti per servire alla storia di Sicilia, Ser. I.18, Palermo 1899), pp. 7–9 no. 2 (1092); White, *Latin Monasticism*, pp. 246–7 no. 3 (1098). For a sceptical view, H. Enzensberger, 'Cancelleria e documentazione sotto Ruggero I', *Ruggero il Gran Conte e l'inizio dello stato normanno* [above, note 88], pp. 19–20.

superior status over his vassals, for one of the most marked features of the new establishment in Sicily was that there were no other counts on the island until shortly before his son Roger II accepted a royal crown in 1130. Admittedly in Calabria his nephew Rodulf (younger brother of Count Robert I of Loritello) may have used a comital style, as count of Catanzaro, from *c.* 1088 – certainly his descendants did. But he was a vassal of the duke of Apulia, not of Roger I.[103] By contrast, Roger refused to allow any of his subordinates in Sicily, even his sons or his nephew Tancred, to call themselves counts. In his charters Godfrey of Ragusa and Mauger were styled only as 'Godfrey/Mauger the count's son', while even after Roger's death, the lord of Syracuse was only 'Tancred, son of Count William'.[104] Similarly, when Countess Adelaide installed her brother in his lordship in south-east Sicily, for some years – indeed as late as 1122 – charters refer to him only as 'Henry, son of the Margrave Manfred'. It was only later, perhaps after Roger II's acquisition of the duchy of Apulia, that Henry was styled 'Count of Paternò'.[105] Only in some later forgeries do we find counts in Sicily before 1130 (the ruler of the island apart), and the use of such a comital title in a purportedly pre-1130 Sicilian charter must be deemed *ipso facto* a sign of forgery or later interpolation. Neither Roger I, nor later his widow on behalf of her infant sons, wanted any of the new Sicilian barons, however closely they might be related, to have any claims to independent authority or to a rank which challenged that of the island's ruler.

None the less, this was not the most pressing problem which faced Count Roger after 1091. Far more significant was the demographic balance in what was a 'classic' medieval colonial society. The count, his barons and their Norman and French followers formed a small, and potentially vulnerable, ruling group over a virtually entirely alien subject population. Admittedly there was as yet no unbridgeable gulf between Greek and Latin Christians, for there was still only one Church, recognised by both Greeks and Latins. Yet, given the barriers of language and culture, and the problems which had sometimes arisen during the conquest, the fact that what Christian population there was on Sicily was almost entirely Greek cannot have been entirely satisfactory to the Norman rulers. Furthermore, only in the

---

103 *Malaterra*, IV.11, pp. 91–2; E.M. Jamison, 'Note e documenti per la storia dei conti normanni di Catanzaro', *Archivio storico per la Calabria e la Lucania*, i (1931), 451–70.

104 S. Cusa, *I Diplomi greci ed arabi di Sicilia* (Palermo 1860), p. 551 (1102); Pirro, *Sicula Sacra*, i.619–20 (1104); Tramontana, 'Populazione, distribuzione della terra e classi sociali', pp. 217, 220.

105 C.A. Garufi, 'Le donazioni del conte Enrico' [above, note 90], 219–20 no. 1 (1113), 223–4 no. 3 (1122); while *ibid.* no. 2, in which he is called count, is a forgery. For his later title, *Alexandrini Telesini Abbatis Ystoria Rogerii Regis Sicilie, Calabrie atque Apulie*, ed. L. de Nava (FSI, Rome 1991), lib. II *c.* 1, p. 24.

north-east of the island were these Christians in the majority, and even in that region there were still some Muslims. Messina and Troina apart, the Muslims were almost certainly in the majority (in most cases the overwhelming majority) in the towns. The situation that resulted could be precarious. The thirteenth-century history of the bishops of Agrigento recorded that the first bishop:

> built his cathedral and court building, which he completed within six years, next to the citadel for fear of the countless Saracens living in Agrigento, for there were few Christians there before the death of King William II [i.e. 1189].[106]

Not surprisingly, considerable efforts were made to attract Christian settlers to Sicily. After his capture of Malta Count Roger offered the prisoners whom he had found there the opportunity to settle in Sicily as free tenants in a new village which he would provide for them at his own expense, 'which he would exempt from all tribute and servile exaction in perpetuity'.[107] Similarly Abbot Ambrose of Lipari in 1095 also offered land on generous terms, free from all servile exactions and labour services and subject only to tithes, to settlers on the Aeolian islands, with full ownership and right of free alienation thereafter if they were prepared to stay there for a minimum of only three years.[108] These especially generous conditions may have been a consequence of the uninviting nature of Lipari and the neighbouring islands, but though the abbot offered somewhat less favourable terms for settlers on his estates on the Sicilian mainland around Patti (and, significantly, they were expected to provide military service in defence of the church), the key element of personal freedom remained. Here, however, land was offered specifically to 'men of the Latin language': thus this was a deliberate attempt at social planning, not simply an economic measure.[109] Such Christian immigrants from the Italian mainland might generally expect generous terms in Sicily, and efforts to attract them continued throughout the twelfth century, in a slow but eventually successful attempt to change the population structure of the island. By contrast, indigenous Greek and Muslim peasants, and sometimes even Greek immigrants from Calabria, were tied more closely to the soil, and generally reduced to the

---

106 *Più antiche carte di Agrigento*, p. 307.
107 *Malaterra*, IV.16, pp. 95–6.
108 C.A. Garufi, 'Memoratoria, chartae et instrumenta divisae in Sicilia nei secoli xi a xv', *BISIME* xxxii (1912), 119 no. 1.
109 Known from a charter of Roger II of January 1133, *Rogerii II Regis Diplomata Latina* (Codex Diplomaticus Regni Siciliae, Ser. I.2(i), Cologne 1987), pp. 63–6 no. 23; White, *Latin Monasticism*, pp. 84–5.

status of villeins, not least to try to prevent the sort of disruption in the wake of the conquest that would leave fields abandoned and uncultivated, and lords without income. From very soon after the final victory of 1091, both the count and also other Sicilian landowners had *plateae* drawn up recording the names of the serfs on their estates.[110] The superior status of Latin Christian immigrants remained for a long time. When in the mid-twelfth century a French baron who had been granted a lordship in Sicily tried to impose new levies on Latin Christian tenants on his lands, the latter 'asserted the liberties of the citizens and townsmen of Sicily', and protested that 'it was only those Muslims and Greeks who were classified as villeins who had to pay tithes and an annual money rent'.[111]

Yet despite such inducements, the attraction of new settlers to Sicily only very gradually changed the make-up of the island's population. Probably the most significant group of new immigrants were the north Italians who settled on the lands of their compatriot Henry of Paternò. By the mid-twelfth century they formed a sizeable (and still distinct) group among the island's population.[112] But since Henry may well not have even acquired his lordship until after 1101, this source of immigrants can only later have become significant. In the long run it was important in creating a Christian majority in the south-east, as well as in the north-east, of the island, and ultimately in displacing most of the Muslims in this region. But even then, the west of the island remained predominantly Muslim, and places such as Alcamo (*c*. 38 km south-west of Palermo) continued to have an entirely Muslim population even as late as the 1180s.[113] Above all, the great tract of territory in the centre-west of Sicily which was part of the comital (and later royal) demesne until its donation to Monreale, was still even in the early thirteenth century almost exclusively Muslim – only some 3 per cent of those named in the late twelfth-century *plateae* listing Monreale serfs were Christians.[114] Given such circumstances, it was not therefore surprising that strongpoints in predominantly Muslim areas, such as Noto, remained

110 V. D'Alessandro, 'Servi e liberi', *Uomo e ambiente nel Mezzogiorno normanno-svevo. Atti delle ottave giornate normanno-sveve, Bari, ottobre 1987* (Bari 1989), pp. 309–13. Cf. I. Peri, *Uomini, città e campagne in Sicilia dall'XI al XIII secolo* (Bari 1978), pp. 33–40.

111 *The History of the Tyrants of Sicily by 'Hugo Falcandus' 1154–69*, trans. G.A. Loud and T.E.J. Wiedemann (Manchester 1998), p. 197.

112 *The History of the Tyrants of Sicily*, p. 208, claimed that the Lombard (i.e. north Italian) towns of south-east Sicily could provide 20,000 fighting men in 1168, though this figure is surely an exaggeration.

113 *The Travels of Ibn Jubayr*, p. 350.

114 H. Bercher, A. Courteaux and J. Mouton, 'Une abbaye latine dans la société musulmane: Monreale au XIIe siècle', *Annales, Economies, Sociétés, Civilisations* xxxiv (1979), 525–47, especially pp. 531–4.

heavily garrisoned right through until the later twelfth century. However, the control of the Muslim population was assisted by the fact that, especially in western Sicily, most of the rural cultivators lived after the conquest in open, undefended villages in the valleys – a settlement pattern dictated more by the water supplies than directly by the conquerors.[115] Where conversion to Christianity did take place, largely in the eastern parts of the island, it was overwhelmingly to the Greek rite rather than the Latin – perhaps reflecting the imperfect nature of the conversion of the indigenous inhabitants from Greek Christianity to Islam in the preceding centuries.[116] Furthermore, in the early years after the conquest Greek immigrants from Calabria were probably more numerous than Lombards or others of the Latin rite, although the extent and causes of such immigration have been disputed by modern scholars.[117]

This demographic balance was reflected in how Sicily was governed. The early governors of Palermo may have been Normans: the knight Robert appointed by Guiscard in 1072 and the Peter Bidone (i.e. son of Guy?) attested in 1086. Normans or Frenchmen were also employed as castellans, as for example a certain Robert at Agrigento in 1112.[118] But most of the other officials in the service of the count of Sicily were Greeks and Arabs, albeit the latter were often Christian converts. (For the comital, and later royal, officials conversion *was* a significant factor, but these were numerically few in relation to the overall population.) Existing Arabic land divisions continued in use. For example, if we can assume that the surviving charter, which appears to have been tampered with, is based on a genuine original, Roger I gave a village to the see of Troina in 1087, with its bounds defined 'according to the ancient Saracen divisions'. A similar practice was almost certainly followed in later documents from Lipari, in 1133–4, where boundary clauses in Arabic were added to texts in Greek.[119] It is probable that not only registers of land divisions, but those of the rights and services pertaining to property, continued in use, just as similar cadastral surveys from the Byzantine period were used in Calabria, though we only find the term *dafatir* (Latin: *deftarii / quaterniones*), which was used to describe these, after the

---

115   *Ibid.*, pp. 530–1. For Noto, *The History of the Tyrants of Sicily*, pp. 67–8.

116   J. Johns, 'The Greek Church and the conversion of Muslims in Norman Sicily', *Byzantinische Forschungen* xxi (1995), 133–57.

117   L.-R. Ménager, 'La Byzantination religieuse de l'Italie méridionale (IXe–XIIe siècles) et la politique écclésiastique des normands en Italie', *Revue d'Histoire Ecclésiastique* liv (1959), 5–40; criticised by A. Guillou, 'Inchiesta sulla popolazione greca della Sicilia e della Calabria nel medio evo', *Rivista storica italiana* lxxv (1963), 53–68.

118   Ménager, *Recueil*, pp. 181–4 nos 52–3; *Più antiche carte di Agrigento*, pp. 29–33 no. 10 (which von Falkenhausen considers authentic, despite the editor's suspicions).

119   *Diplomi della cattedrale di Messina*, pp. 2–3 no. 2; Cusa, *Diplomi greci ed arabi*, pp. 515–17.

considerable reorganisation of the Sicilian administration undertaken *c.* 1145. The lists of serfs (*plateae*: Arabic *jarida*) continued to be written in Arabic (or in bilingual documents including Arabic) right through the twelfth century, while all but a very few comital charters before Roger II's take-over of the duchy of Apulia in 1127 were written in Greek – which was of course the language of almost all the inhabitants of those parts of Calabria he ruled, as well as that of the majority of Christians in Sicily. The head of Roger I's writing office was a Greek called Nicholas, while the chief minister of the young Roger II as count of Sicily after 1112 was also a Greek, Christodoulous. Indeed some Greeks from Calabria were recruited as notaries, or for other positions in the comital administration, in Sicily.[120] Meanwhile Muslim troops were an important component of the count's army on the mainland. They were employed as early as the siege of Salerno in 1076, in the march on Rome in 1084, and in most of his campaigns in support of his nephew Roger Borsa in the 1090s. Eadmer of Canterbury, who saw these Muslim troops during the siege of Capua in 1098, alleged that the count forbade their conversion to Christianity. We might be sceptical about his claims that but for this the influence of St Anselm would have converted many of these soldiers – however, preserving their cohesion and *esprit de corps* may well have dictated such a prohibition.[121]

A further reflection of the population structure of Sicily came in the religious patronage of Roger I. Between *c.* 1084 and his death in 1101 the count founded three Latin monasteries, at Lipari, Catania and Patti, and one nunnery, St Mary of Messina. The first two in particular were very generously endowed. But in the same period at least twenty Greek monasteries were founded in the north-east of the island, some fourteen of them by Roger himself. This was an obvious (but none the less effective) means of making his rule more acceptable to those who were in the overwhelming majority among the Christian population. But we should not necessarily assume that his motives for such foundations were entirely pragmatic or political. The prayers of Greek monks were just as efficacious as those of Latin ones, for they were still all part of one Church, and the recruitment of monks for such monasteries provided for the spiritual needs of the existing

---

120 See especially V. von Falkenhausen, 'I Ceti dirigenti' [above, Ch. III, note 143], pp. 346–56, and her 'Il Popolamento: etniè, fedi, insediamenti', in *Terra e uomini nel Mezzogiorno normanno-svevo. Atti delle settime giornate normanno-sveve, Bari, ottobre 1985* (Bari 1987), pp. 39–73; Enzensberger, 'Cancelleria e documentazione' [above, note 102], pp. 15–23; H. Takayama, *The Administration of the Norman Kingdom of Sicily* (Leiden 1993), pp. 25–56, 81–8, 133–5.

121 *The Life of St. Anselm, Archbishop of Canterbury, by Eadmer,* ed. R.W. Southern (London 1962), pp. 111–12. Cf. *Amatus,* VIII.14, p. 354; Landulf, *Historia Mediolensis,* III.33, *MGH SS* viii.100; *Malaterra,* IV.17, 22, 26, pp. 96, 100, 104.

Christian population. By contrast, monks for the Latin abbeys had to be brought in from the mainland. Hence Roger's religious policy largely followed the demographic structure of his dominions.[122]

Thus while a Norman count ruled the whole of the island of Sicily after 1091, changes on the island were limited. The count relied heavily on indigenous officials and practices in the exercise of his government. Similarly, while a group of predominantly Norman landowners was installed there, alterations to the overall balance of population were slow, and only really began to have an effect on the social structure in the mid-twelfth century. The Normans were after all an even smaller ruling minority on Sicily than they were on the mainland.

---

122 White, *Latin Monasticism*, pp. 39–45. M. Scaduto, *Il Monachismo basiliano nella Sicilia medievale, rinascita e decadenza, sec. XI–XV* (Rome 1947), pp. 80–143, discusses the evidence in detail and adds two further pre-1101 foundations to those listed by White.

CHAPTER V

The Normans, the papacy and the two empires

The investiture of 1059

The recognition of Richard Quarrel as Prince of Capua in the spring of 1059 and of Robert Guiscard as Duke of Apulia a few months later meant a complete reversal of papal policy towards the Normans of southern Italy over the previous decade. Furthermore, when Nicholas II invested Guiscard as duke at the synod of Melfi in August 1059, he also potentially infringed the western empire's claims to overlordship over southern Italy. These imperial rights were hardly a dead letter, for they had been exercised as recently as 1047 by Henry III. That the pope was in 1059 drawing on imperial precedent was made clear by his use of a banner to invest Guiscard with his lands, for this symbol was the insignia generally used by the emperors in the eleventh century when granting fiefs to their principal subjects: Conrad II had for example used a banner to invest Guaimar IV with the principality of Capua, and Rainulf I with the county of Aversa, in 1038.[1] The consequences of this agreement between the pope and the Norman leaders were to be profound and long-lasting. From the Normans being considered – as a contemporary set of Roman annals described them – the *Agareni* (children of Hagar [cf. Genesis, xxi.9–21] – 'untouchables'/'pagans' – the same word was often used to describe Muslims), they became among the principal allies and supporters of the Gregorian reform papacy in the dispute which developed with the Emperor Henry IV. So intertwined did

---

1   *Amatus*, II.6, pp. 63–4. The main source for the use of the banner in 1059 is the Amalfi Chronicle, Schwarz, *Amalfi im frühen Mittelalter*, p. 212, copied by *Romuald*, p. 185. Important discussion by Deér, *Papsttum und Normannen*, pp. 13–36.

the interests of the two become that when Abbot Desiderius of Montecassino was elected as pope in 1086–7 imperial supporters perceived him as simply a creature of the Normans.[2]

Yet it would be quite wrong to assume that in 1059 Nicholas II and his advisers were deliberately seeking to extend papal authority, or to challenge the prerogatives of the western empire. As has already been suggested, the reasons for the papal volte-face towards the south Italian Normans were pragmatic: a reflection of the very difficult situation which faced the reform party in Rome in 1058–9. In addition, the sanction of the Normans' leaders as legitimate rulers was an acknowledgement of reality: that their take-over of southern Italy was irreversible, and that the interests of the Church, and of the Christian people of southern Italy, therefore required them to be accepted as part of the political community of Christendom. The alliance with the Normans in 1059 was not directed against the empire. Indeed, the problem for the reformers at Rome in the late 1050s was rather the weakness of imperial authority, not its strength. The military aid of Richard of Capua [see above, p. 129], and the assistance which the pope hoped would be forthcoming in the future from Robert Guiscard, was necessary because, after the death of Henry III in 1056, those who governed Germany in the name of his young son were unable, because of problems at home, to help the reformers whom the emperor had installed at Rome in the first place.

When Stephen IX (Frederick of Lorraine) had died at Florence on 29 March 1058, the noble families of Rome had taken the opportunity to reassert their traditional control over the Church, by arranging the election of a candidate drawn from their ranks, John Mincio, cardinal bishop of Velletri, as Pope Benedict X. The reformers, most of whom were outsiders who had been brought to Rome by Leo IX and his successors, refused to accept this and after some delay elected their own candidate, Bishop Gerard of Florence, as Pope Nicholas II. But the reformers' problem was that they had very little support in Rome itself or in its immediate hinterland. At first they looked to Godfrey of Lorraine, who as margrave of Tuscany (in right of his wife Beatrice) was the most powerful territorial ruler of northern Italy, and who was the elder brother of the previous pope, Stephen. But though Godfrey helped to install Nicholas at Rome, he then left for the north with the rival pope still at liberty and his supporters undefeated and in possession of the lands immediately to the south and east of Rome. It was this predicament that led the reformers to seek the aid of Richard of Capua,

---

2 *Liber Pontificalis*, ii.335 G.A. Loud, 'Abbot Desiderius of Montecassino and the Gregorian Papacy', *Journal of Ecclesiastical History* xxx (1979), 323.

and it was the latter's knights who were responsible for the capture of Benedict X and the submission of his supporters in the early months of 1059. Nicholas then sought to safeguard the reform party's control of the papacy by promulgating new rules for the conduct of subsequent papal elections, entrusting these to the cardinal bishops (whom the pope himself appointed) rather than, as had formerly been the case, 'the clergy and people of Rome' in general – which in practice had usually meant the leading Roman families.[3]

However, to consolidate this victory, a longer-term agreement with the Normans was needed, and not just with Richard of Capua, invaluable as his assistance had been, but with Robert Guiscard. Hence in the summer of 1059 Nicholas set off for the south, travelling first to Montecassino, whose new abbot, Desiderius, had almost certainly been a key intermediary in the negotiations with Prince Richard. In late August he went on to Melfi to hold a synod, attended by many of the leading churchmen of the south, and by both Richard of Capua and Robert Guiscard. The latter, claimed William of Apulia, summarily abandoned the military operations he had been conducting in Calabria in order to meet the pope.[4] But the meeting was unlikely to have been as unpremeditated as William implied (and his chronology is anyway unreliable, for he places this soon after the death of Robert's brother Humphrey, actually two years earlier). Melfi was after all one of Guiscard's principal possessions in Apulia, and the holding of a papal council there must surely have been arranged in advance and with his agreement. At this meeting Robert swore fealty to the pope, and in return received investiture of his lands as a vassal of the Holy See and the title of duke.

By far the best guide to the purpose behind the pope's actions is the terms of the oath itself (which is here given in full)

> I Robert, by the grace of God and St Peter Duke of Apulia and Calabria, and in future with the help of both of Sicily, from this hour and henceforth shall be faithful to the Holy Roman Church and the Apostolic See, and to you my lord Pope Nicholas. I shall do nothing by word or deed whereby you lose life or limb or be taken captive unlawfully. I shall not knowingly betray, to your injury, information which you have entrusted to me instructing me not to share it. I shall everywhere help the Holy Roman Church to hold and secure the rights [regalia] of St Peter and his property, to the best of my ability, against all men. And I shall help you to hold the

---

3 Detailed discussion in T. Schmid, *Alexander II. und die römische Reformgruppe seiner Zeit* (Stuttgart 1977), pp. 68–80; P. Partner, *The Lands of St. Peter. The Papal State in the Middle Ages and the Early Renaissance* (London 1972), pp. 115–26; Cowdrey, *The Age of Abbot Desiderius* [above, Ch. III, note 98], pp. 111–17.

4 *W. Apulia*, II, lines 384–6, p. 152.

Roman papacy securely and honourably. I shall seek neither to invade nor acquire the land of St Peter and the Principality, nor shall I presume to plunder them either without the clear permission of you or your successors who shall enter into the honour of St Peter, with the exception of what you grant to me, or your successors shall grant. I shall endeavour in good faith to see that the Holy Roman Church receives annually the tribute [*pensio*] which has been agreed from the land of St Peter which I hold or shall hold. All churches which lie under my lordship, with their possessions, I transfer into your power, and I shall defend them in fealty to the Holy Roman Church, and I shall swear fealty to no one except with the reservation of my fealty to the Holy Roman Church. And if you or your successors should leave this life before me, I shall, in accordance with the instructions that I am given by the better cardinals, Roman clergy and laymen, assist in the election and ordination of a pope to the honour of St Peter. I shall observe all the above in good faith to you and the Holy Roman Church, and I shall observe this fealty to your successors who are appointed to the honour of St Peter and who shall have confirmed to me the investiture which you have granted to me. So help me God.[5]

It can be seen from this that while there was a defensive element, that Robert would respect papal territory, the real stress in the oath was the military help that he would in future render to his overlord; helping the pope 'to hold the Roman papacy securely', and ensuring that after his death he would, if required, help the reformers at Rome (for this is what 'the better cardinals, Roman clergy and laymen' meant) to elect a pope of their choosing. Such a provision was directed against the Roman nobility, who were still, despite their defeat in 1058–9, a very real threat to the position of the reformers, given the very limited support the latter had at Rome.[6] This issue was of crucial importance to the very survival of the reformed papacy, and was far more significant to them than any powers that the popes might seek to exercise over southern Italy, of which there is little or no mention in the oath, although in recognition of his new status Robert also promised to pay an annual *census* (i.e. a financial tribute) to the pope from those lands he held directly in his own hands.[7] This was, apart from anything else, a very useful augmentation of papal finances – for the reformers lacked the family links which had enabled previous popes to control and to exploit the territory round Rome, and hence the papacy now had to subsist on a greatly reduced income from its property in this area.

---

5   *Le Liber Censuum de l'Eglise Romaine*, ed. P. Fabre and L. Duchesne (3 vols, Paris 1889–1952), i.422.
6   Schmid, *Alexander II*, pp. 76, 115, suggests that only in the Trastevere district west of the Tiber was there any support for the reformers.
7   *Liber Censuum*, i.421.

However, while there was no express mention of the emperor – and in 1059 there was no emperor since the nine-year-old Henry IV had not received imperial coronation nor was likely to for some years to come – a recognition of imperial claims over southern Italy was not entirely ruled out. Robert was not prohibited from swearing fealty to the emperor in future, provided that the rights of the papacy were expressly recognised in any future oath (and what other third party except the emperor can have been envisaged in this clause?). Similarly, in the papal election decree of Lent 1059 which was directed against the Roman nobility, the emperor's right to receive formal notification of any papal election was preserved.[8] Indeed, a number of historians have argued that in dealing with the south Italian Normans in 1059 Pope Nicholas saw himself as representing the emperor's interests, in the way that Leo IX had done with regard to Benevento in the early 1050s.[9] This may be going too far, but certainly the agreement was not in any sense a deliberate challenge to imperial rights (nor indeed was the papal election decree). Both these measures were rather a response to the specific problems of the reformed papacy in 1059.

Although cast in the form of a vassalic oath between subject and over-lord, the emphasis in this agreement was on a political alliance, in which Robert Guiscard would provide the military muscle that the reformed papacy lacked. The oath therefore embodied a far more equal relationship than was often the case between lord and vassal. Useful as papal recognition of his status was in bolstering Guiscard's position in southern Italy, he was already master of most of the region. The papacy needed him far more than he needed it. What papal recognition gave him was respectability, and the support of the Church. This last was by no means a negligible factor, but his power hardly depended upon it. This reality was reflected in the contemporary narrative sources. For of the three principal authors concerned with Robert Guiscard, only William of Apulia actually mentioned his investiture at the synod of Melfi. Both Amatus and Malaterra briefly mentioned his assumption of the ducal title, but connected this with his capture of Reggio in 1060, and made no mention of any papal role.[10] One might of course ascribe Malaterra's account to the wish of a Norman propagandist, writing about forty years later, to downgrade the significance of any papal investiture, assuming that he was aware of it at all. But Amatus was writing earlier, and was not unsympathetic to the reformed papacy:

---

8   D. Jasper, *Das Papstwahldekret von 1059. Überlieferung und Textgestalt* (1986), especially pp. 3–9, which summarises the voluminous literature on this issue.

9   Deér, *Papsttum und Normannen*, pp. 87–90; I.S. Robinson, *The Papacy 1073–1198. Continuity and Innovation* (Cambridge 1990), pp. 376–7.

10 *Amatus*, IV.3, p. 184; *Malaterra*, I.35, pp. 23–4.

indeed the other work apart from his 'History' which survives from his pen, 'The Deeds of the Apostles Peter and Paul' (written *c.* 1078) was a vigorous manifesto in support of the papal primacy and the reform of the Church.[11] His 'History' is disorganised, and in its present form almost certainly incomplete, and we cannot entirely rule out the omission of a relevant passage. But it appears unlikely that he considered the papal investiture as particularly significant.

However, while the preservation and defence of the reformed papacy at Rome was of primary importance, other considerations also played their part in persuading Nicholas II to conclude his agreement with Robert Guiscard. As has been suggested, the reality of Norman power in the south was such that it was in the Church's interests to accommodate it. It is noteworthy that Abbot Desiderius of Montecassino, whom Nicholas appointed as a cardinal in March 1059 and (if we are to believe the Montecassino chronicle) also as his legate for south Italian affairs, was already on friendly terms with both Richard of Capua and Robert Guiscard. He had come to an arrangement with Richard to protect his monastery's property even before the latter had captured Capua and before his own election as abbot – while he was provost of the Cassinese cell in Capua. Guiscard had helped him when he was in Apulia in the spring of 1058, about to embark on papal business for Constantinople. The death of Pope Stephen had aborted this mission, and he needed to return as speedily as possible to Montecassino to ensure his own election as abbot – a position to which he had already been designated by the pope, who was his predecessor as abbot. Guiscard had supplied horses and a safe-conduct to do this. One of his first actions as abbot had been to welcome Richard as a visitor to Montecassino with all the ceremony due to a reigning Capuan prince (even before his formal recognition as such by the papacy) [above, p. 127]. Thus Desiderius, the abbot of the richest and most prestigious monastery in southern Italy, was already an ally of the Normans, as well as of the reform party at Rome, several of whose most influential members had been present at his election, and he had the requisite contacts with the Norman leaders to facilitate an agreement.[12]

But peace between the papacy and the Normans benefited the south Italian Church as a whole, not just Montecassino. This consideration undoubtedly influenced Pope Nicholas, for one should not forget that the papacy was a religious institution, not a political one, however much it was

---

11   *Il Poema di Amato su S. Pietro Apostolo*, ed. A. Lentini (Miscellanea Cassinese 30–1, 1958–9). Brief discussion by Loud, *Church and Society in the Norman Principality of Capua*, pp. 66–7.
12   *Chron. Cas.* III.8–9, pp. 369–72. Frederick had retained the abbacy after his election as pope.

forced by circumstance to involve itself in political issues. An agreement with the Normans would enable the reformers at Rome to extend their programme to the churches of south Italy far more effectively than had hitherto been the case. And in this respect William of Apulia's account of the synod of Melfi is extremely interesting, for his main stress was on the pope's attempts there to enforce celibacy on the local clergy, while Guiscard's investiture was mentioned almost as an afterthought.[13] During his visit to southern Italy, and most probably during the Melfi council, Nicholas dismissed several unsatisfactory local bishops and replaced them with monks from Montecassino, a precedent which his successor Alexander II followed when he held a council in southern Italy in 1067.[14] One should also take into consideration the clause in Guiscard's oath in which he swore to transfer the churches under his lordship to papal ownership. This was an issue of great importance to the papacy, for it particularly concerned the bishoprics in the areas which had been, or in 1059 still were, under Byzantine rule. The papacy had long been concerned to reassert its historic claims to the obedience of these sees, which since the Iconoclast dispute in the eighth century had been subjected to the patriarch of Constantinople. The Byzantine authorities had made some concessions in the 1020s, recognising papal jurisdiction over the archbishopric of Bari and some of the other sees in northern Apulia. But the papacy wished to assert its direct authority over the whole of southern Italy, including those sees in the Terra d'Otranto and Calabria where the population and clergy were overwhelmingly or exclusively Greek. By 1059 Guiscard had captured all but the extreme south of Calabria, and hence his co-operation was essential to secure this desirable end. Furthermore, as has been suggested above [pp. 37–9], the tensions created by the Ottonians' involvement in southern Italy had led to a period of ecclesiastical competition in which both Rome and Constantinople had been creating new bishoprics and raising existing sees to archiepiscopal rank. This had resulted in overlapping jurisdictions, conflicting claims and a chaotic provincial organisation – insofar as it existed at all, given a number of autocephalous sees in the former Byzantine region. From the time of Leo IX's first visit to the south in 1050, the papacy had begun to reorganise the south Italian Church in an attempt to remedy this unsatisfactory situation. But without the co-operation of the lay rulers – and by 1059 this meant the Normans – there could be little chance of success: indeed early efforts, such as Leo IX's confirmation of the extravagant claims of the archbishopric of Salerno over dioceses in northern Calabria in 1051, had probably made

13 *W. Apulia*, II, lines 388–405, pp. 152–4.
14 *Chron. Cas.* III.14, 24, pp. 376–7, 391.

matters worse.[15] The reorganisation of the diocesan structure in southern Italy was to be an important part of papal policy towards the region over the next forty years. It was a long and slow process, not completed until the pontificate of Paschal II in the early twelfth century. Nor were Norman efforts always helpful, for they sometimes encouraged the pretensions of churches under their control to the detriment of the rights of other churches which were not – as with the dispute, which the Normans largely created, between the archbishopric of Salerno and its erstwhile suffragan at Conza, which led the latter also eventually to be deemed an archbishopric [below, p. 262]. But the alliance between the Norman leaders and the papacy made reform, both to the Church's structure and to the morals of its clergy, possible.[16] Continued hostility would not. Finally, the agreement of 1059 described Guiscard as future duke of Sicily. The recovery of the island for Christianity was a major potential benefit to come from the new situation, and the possibility of securing this was another important reason for Pope Nicholas to recognise Robert as the legitimate ruler of Apulia and Calabria and the papacy's ally.

One problem which remains with regard to the events of 1059 concerns the possible investiture of Richard of Capua, who had already rendered the pope such signal assistance. We know that he too was present at the synod of Melfi, for while he was there, and acting on the pope's advice, he granted a monastery on the Gargano peninsula (an area over which, it will be remembered, his family had claims) to Montecassino.[17] Yet we do not know whether he too was invested with his principality by Nicholas II. For although an oath of fealty sworn by him to the papacy was also preserved in the papal archives, and like that of Guiscard it was copied at the end of the twelfth century into the *Liber Censuum* (the official record of the rights, privileges and income of the Roman Church), it dated not from 1059 but from his expedition to Rome in October 1061.[18] However, he had already sworn fealty to the papacy earlier in the year, albeit to the Roman archdeacon

---

15   L. Pennacchini, *Pergamene Salernitane (1008–1784)* (Salerno 1941), pp. 27–9 no. 2.

16   See N. Kamp, 'Vescovi e diocesi nel passagio dalla dominazione bizantina allo stato normanno', in *Forme di potere e struttura sociale in Italia nel medioevo*, ed. G. Rosseti (Bologna 1977), 379–97; C.D. Fonseca, 'L'Organizzazione ecclesiastica dell'Italia normanna tra l'XI e il XII secolo. I nuovi assetti istituzionali', in *Le Istituzioni ecclesiastiche della 'Societas Christiana' dei secoli XI e XII* (Miscellanea del centro di studi medievali 8, Milan 1977), pp. 327–52; H. Houben, 'Il Papato, i normanni e la nuova organizzazione ecclesiastica della Puglia e della Basilicata', in H. Houben, *Tra Roma e Palermo. Aspetti e momenti del Mezzogiorno medioevale* (Galatina 1989), pp. 121–35.

17   T. Leccisotti, *Le Colonie Cassinesi in Capitanata* ii *Il Gargano* (Miscellanea Cassinese 15, 1938), 59–60 no. 15 [= Loud, 'Calendar', no. 3].

18   *Liber Censuum*, ii.93–4.

Hildebrand as Nicholas's representative rather than to the pope in person.[19] Probably this was deemed sufficient, even if the text of that oath no longer survives. One assumes that, by the time the *Liber Censuum* was compiled, or perhaps when the earlier sources on which it drew were written, an oath taken to an actual pope was deemed to carry more weight as a precedent, and hence the text of the 1061 oath was recorded for posterity as an exemplar of the fealty owed for the principality.[20]

The papacy and southern Italy 1060–80

Richard was in Rome in 1061 because the reform papacy's need for military assistance had not disappeared, despite the defeat of the antipope's supporters in 1059. On the death of Pope Nicholas in July 1061 there was further dispute. The cardinals (and one assumes that in accordance with Nicholas's election decree the lead was taken by the seven cardinal bishops) elected another reformer, Bishop Anselm of Lucca, who took the pontifical name of Alexander II. But the Roman nobility remained hostile, and Alexander was only formally enthroned in Rome on 30 September 1061 with the aid of Richard and his Capuan Normans. Two days later Richard swore fealty to the pope in the Lateran palace, and in return was presumably once more invested with his principality as the pope's vassal. But, as in 1059, his support was far more important to the pope than vice versa. This was made abundantly clear a few weeks later when a council of north Italian bishops, supported both by the German court and by the Roman nobles, elected a rival pope: Bishop Cadulus of Parma (as Honorius II).

The Church remained in schism until 1064, and it was only when the imperial court (whose involvement in the dispute had always been rather half-hearted) withdrew its support from Cadulus that his challenge was abandoned. He led two expeditions to Rome to displace Alexander, and while the principal role in defending the latter's cause was played by Godfrey of Lorraine – it was he who forced Cadulus to withdraw from Rome in 1062 – throughout this period Richard's Norman knights also helped Alexander to maintain his hold there. Cadulus's partisan, Bishop Benzo of Alba, gave a vivid picture of these Normans, so he claimed, 'rushing madly into the squares, chanting at the tops of their voices "war, war" '. Indeed, he

---

19 *Liber Pontificalis*, ii.335.
20 Richard's 1061 oath was recorded *c.* 1086 in the canonical collection of Cardinal Deusdedit, which in turn drew on Alexander's now lost register: Schmidt, *Alexander II*, pp. 222–3.

alleged that the German princes described Alexander as 'the idol [*simulacrum*] of the Normans'.[21] We may well take these comments with some scepticism – they were written more than twenty years later at a time when the pope, Gregory VII, and his Norman allies were at war with the German court, and Benzo felt that Gregory's links with the (to him) barbarous Normans were something that laid him particularly open to criticism. Indeed, he denounced the Normans, whom he said might better be described as 'the no-men [*nullimani*]', in the crudest scatological terms.[22] Yet the very fact that he should bother to do this, in the specific context of the Cadulan schism, suggests that Norman support for Alexander remained by no means negligible, even if Prince Richard himself was preoccupied with the con-solidation of his rule over his own principality. Certainly, the Normans of Capua had played a crucial part in Alexander securing his position in Rome in the first place, as was recognised by other imperialist authors.[23] But, despite his oath in 1059, Guiscard played no part in these events, and as we have seen spent the early 1060s largely in Calabria and Sicily [above, p. 132].

At this stage, therefore, supporting the papacy was hardly a high priority for him. One should, however, note there was still amicable contact during this period, for Count Roger sent notification of his victory at Cerami, and some of the spoils, to the pope.[24] But that the relationship only mattered to the Norman leaders when it suited them was shown clearly in 1066, when Richard of Capua's troops invaded the Roman Campagna. The prince was rumoured to want the Roman patriciate (to be the temporal ruler of the City therefore). So alarmed was Pope Alexander by this that he summoned his ally Godfrey of Lorraine to drive the Normans back. It was even ru-moured that the German king was going to intervene to protect the papacy, although in the end this imperial expedition never took place. Godfrey's army marched south into the north of the principality, and for eighteen days his forces and Richard's troops faced each other across the River Gari near Montecassino. Eventually Godfrey, whose army was running short of food, was persuaded to withdraw by a substantial bribe.[25] But the Normans' territorial ambitions were far from satisfied, and a year later Richard's troops were penetrating into Marsia [above, p. 142]. The attempts of the Normans to extend their power northwards into the Campagna and the Abruzzi remained a problem for the papacy until well into the pontificate of Gregory VII (1073–85). Although the popes were never able to rule the

---

21 *Ad Heinricum IV Imperatorem*, II.18, III.21, *MGH SS* xi.620, 630.
22 *Ibid.*, III.1, p. 622.
23 E.g. Cardinal Beno, *Gesta Romanae Ecclesiae*, *MGH Libelli de Lite*, ii.380.
24 *Malaterra*, II.33, pp. 44–5 [above, p. 157].
25 *Chron. Cas.* III.23, pp. 389–90; *Amatus*, VI.9–10, pp. 270–2.

Abruzzi effectively, they certainly had claims there, and they were also keen to protect churches in this region from attacks on their property; such depredations were an inevitable concomitant of the Norman penetration.

None the less, despite the problems with Richard of Capua in 1066, relations remained for the most part good up until the accession of Gregory VII in 1073. In the summer of 1067 Alexander II made a long visit to the south, from July through to October, and held another important reforming council at Siponto. He was still perturbed by Norman alienations of church property – he excommunicated Guiscard's brother William for his thefts from the archbishopric of Salerno, and at Siponto he threatened a knight called Paganus of Biccari with excommunication if he did not restore property taken from the bishopric of Troia.[26] But since he visited both Robert's Apulian base at Melfi and Capua he was clearly on good terms with the principal Norman leaders. This in turn enabled him to exercise his authority over the south Italian Church. This papal leadership, and his continued good relations with the Normans, was shown in October 1071 when Alexander consecrated the new abbey church of Montecassino, in the presence of Richard of Capua and his family, as well as the Lombard princes of Benevento and Salerno, the duke of Naples, a number of Lombard nobles from the Abruzzi, and 'other powerful and noble men, whether our people or Normans, from the surrounding lands'. (Guiscard's absence was explicable: he was busy besieging Palermo at the time.) Ten archbishops and more than thirty bishops were also present.[27] Montecassino was closely allied with, and had been much favoured by, Richard of Capua.

During these years Alexander took steps to ensure that his authority was recognised by local churchmen, and that the right sort of ecclesiastics were appointed to south Italian sees. Archbishop John of Trani, an important ally of the patriarch of Constantinople, was deposed at his Lateran synod of 1063.[28] He appointed Gerard, a learned German monk of Montecassino, to the archbishopric of Siponto in 1064. During his visit to the south in 1067, probably at his council at Siponto, he dismissed three unsatisfactory bishops, two of whom were guilty of simony. And at the same time he drew on south Italian clerics to staff the Roman Church, notably a former notary of Prince Richard, Aldemarius, who had become a monk at Montecassino, and whom he appointed as a cardinal and abbot of S. Lorenzo fuori le Mure.[29]

---

26 *Italia Pontificia*, viii.351–2 nos 23–5.

27 *Chron. Cas.* III.29, pp. 398–400. Cf. Leo Marsicanus, 'Narratio de Consecratione et Dedicatione Ecclesiae Casinensis', *MPL* clxxiii.997–1002; Bloch, *Montecassino in the Middle Ages*, i.118–21.

28 Schmidt, *Alexander II*, pp. 187–95.

29 *Chron. Cas.* III.24, p. 391; *Italia Pontificia*, ix.148 no. 1, 157 no. 6, 204 no. 4.

It is probable that he at least confirmed (as canonically he should have done), even if he did not appoint, the Latin (and probably Norman) arch-bishops who were installed at Taranto and Otranto soon after the capture of these towns. Hugh of Otranto replaced a sitting Greek archbishop who is known to have attended a patriarchal synod in Constantinople in 1066; hence his appointment was not just that of a Frenchman but of someone who recognised the pope's authority in place of someone who did not. Alexander II may also have confirmed the choice of Bishop Baldwin of Melfi, to judge by his name perhaps a Fleming, who was found in office from 1067: this see was later deemed to be directly dependent on the pope, and it may have been so already. And although, because the conquest was still going on, structural reorganisation was as yet difficult, a new archbishopric was installed at Acerenza, which had up to then been a (at least theoretical) suffragan of Salerno, in 1068.[30] We are not just dealing, therefore, with a political relationship, but with ecclesiastical changes which that political relationship made possible.

Yet within a few months from the accession of the Roman archdeacon Hildebrand as Gregory VII in April 1073 the relationship between the papacy and Robert Guiscard had broken down. The two remained in dispute for some seven years, during most of which Guiscard was excom-municated. However, while Gregory took a stronger line on most issues than the relatively pacific Alexander – and the death the previous year of Cardinal Peter Damian had also removed a significant influence for mod-eration at the Curia – it was not just the change of pontiff which led to the breach. Indeed, that was probably not the main cause of the dispute. To begin with, the pope's attitude appears to have been emollient. Soon after his enthronement Guiscard was taken seriously ill, and a rumour reached the pope that he had actually died. Gregory wrote to Sichelgaita to console her for Robert's death and to offer her eldest son investiture with his father's lands.[31] Given that the duke had only just completed the suppres-sion of a serious rebellion in Apulia, and that Roger Borsa was only thirteen, the latter's succession was by no means assured – or, at the least, likely to be unopposed. Papal investiture was in such circumstances of real value, and the offer was a generous one, even if Gregory also desired the continuance of ducal obligations towards him. We need not therefore see this letter, as one modern commentator has done, as 'profoundly hypocritical'.[32] But when, after hearing of his recovery, Gregory travelled to the south to meet Guiscard, everything went wrong. Why this happened is a good question, for Amatus

---

30 *Italia Pontificia*, ix.409, 435, 456–7 no. 6, 497.
31 *Amatus*, VII.8, p. 298.
32 Norwich, *The Normans in the South*, p. 198.

– our principal source for what occurred – never expressly explained the cause. The root of the problem was surely the continued incursions into territory under papal overlordship. And here there was in the summer of 1073 one very significant development. When Gregory arrived in Benevento in early August, Prince Landulf VI surrendered the town and its immediate territory – all that was now left from his principality – to the pope, and received it back from him as a papal vassal.[33] Attacks on Benevento and its exiguous *contado* would henceforth be attacks on papal property. In addition, Norman pressure was by now making serious inroads into the Abruzzi, and having an extremely damaging effect on church property in that region [above, p. 142]. Guiscard may not have been directly involved, but since the Normans' most important leader in this region, Count Robert of Loritello, was his nephew, the pope doubtless felt that the duke could, if he chose, have exercised a strong restraining influence. But he had not done this. Gregory had been receiving complaints about Norman depredations from local churchmen, and in that same year responded by appointing to the vacant abbacy of Casauria a brother of the count of Marsia, who had therefore excellent local connections, and who as abbot of the monastery on the Tremiti islands had already shown his determination to enforce his authority by all possible means, however brutal. (Hildebrand, as he then was, had commended his actions at Tremiti, but Desiderius of Montecassino had been profoundly shocked by them.) The pope then personally consecrated the new abbot, Transmund, as bishop of Valva in plurality.[34] He clearly hoped that a man of such uncompromising character might defend these churches effectively.

Meanwhile, attempts by the abbot of Montecassino to arrange a face-to-face meeting between Guiscard and the pope proved a fiasco. The duke was unwilling, or perhaps unable, to meet Gregory on the Montecassino lands (which were after all within the principality of Capua), and flatly refused to enter Benevento to meet him there. Given what the Normans had already inflicted on its inhabitants, it was hardly likely that he would now entrust his life to their mercy. 'And immediately discord grew between them, and ill-will and great anger.'[35] The pope's response was to go to Capua, where on 14 September 1073 Prince Richard swore fealty to Gregory, as he had twelve years before to his predecessor. Amatus suggests

---

33 Gregory, *Reg.* I.18, *MGH Ep. Selectae*, ii.30–1.
34 *Chron. Casauriense*, cols, 864–5; Gregory, *Reg.* I.85a, p. 123. Abbot Transmund had had three mutinous Tremiti monks blinded, and one of them also deprived of his tongue: *Chron. Cas.* III.25, p. 392. For complaints by Abruzzi churchmen, see also the *Liber Querulus de Miseriis Ecclesiae Pennensis*, *MGH SS* xxx(2).1461–7, especially 1465–7.
35 *Amatus*, VII.9, p. 299.

that Gregory was deliberately trying to take advantage of the poor relations that prevailed between the prince and Guiscard. That in turn Robert took a jaundiced view of the prince was hardly surprising, given that Richard had not only reneged on his promise to assist in the attack on Palermo but had also lent his support to the rebellion which had broken out in Apulia in 1072. In a letter written from Capua to his Milanese ally Erlembald, the leader of the pro-papal Pataria movement in that city, Gregory himself admitted that he was relieved that the Normans were no longer acting in concert, and that he wanted them to make peace between themselves only with his agreement.[36]

Over the winter of 1073–4 Gregory went a good bit further than this. He wrote to a number of north Italian and southern French princes whom he thought sympathetic, asking them to take part in, or furnish troops for, a military expedition which would in the first instance go to southern Italy to be directed against Guiscard. One of those to whom he wrote was the count of St Gilles, whom the pope noted was the father-in-law of Richard of Capua. This is the only indication we have that the latter's first wife, Guiscard's sister Fressenda, had died and that the prince had married again. The dissolution of this personal link may have contributed towards the hostility between the two Norman leaders, or at least removed one of the factors inhibiting it. Then, at his Lenten synod in March 1074 Gregory excommunicated the duke and his supporters. His attempts to raise troops in France appear to have been unsuccessful, despite (or was it because of?) his proposal that once the Normans had been 'pacified' his army would then go on to help the Byzantine empire against the Muslims who were attacking it. But by the summer of 1074 he had raised a force from northern Italy, with the help of his most reliable allies in that region, Beatrice of Tuscany (Godfrey of Lorraine's widow) and her daughter Matilda. However, it broke up in disorder before even reaching Rome. Amatus, ever ready to accuse Gisulf of Salerno of anything, blamed him for this fiasco, both for his failure to provide adequate money for the army and because the Pisan contingent's dislike for him led to their withdrawal. But we have no corroborative evidence for this, although another source mentioned the tumult and sedition that suddenly arose among the Lombard vassals of Beatrice and Matilda as the reason why the expedition dispersed.[37] And since Gisulf had already lost much of his principality to the Normans he was not necessarily in a position to provide large subsidies to the pope.

36 Gregory, *Reg.* I.25, p. 42. *Amatus*, VII.1–2, 4–5, 10, pp. 292–3, 295–7, 300.
37 *Amatus*, VII.12–14, pp. 303–7; Bonizo of Sutri, *Liber ad Amicum, MGH Libelli de Lite*, i.604; Gregory, *Reg.* I.46, 49, 85a, pp. 70–1, 75–6, 123 [English trans. of the first two letters in E. Emerton, *The Correspondence of Gregory VII* (Columbia 1932), pp. 22–3, 25–6].

Furthermore it is clear that Gregory had been disappointed by the response to his appeal. In April 1074 he wrote angrily to Godfrey IV of Lorraine (son of the papacy's defender in the 1060s by his first marriage, and also Matilda's husband): 'Where is the help which you pledged? Where are the knights whom you promised that you would lead to us for the honour and assistance of St Peter?' But the duke of Lorraine did not appear, hardly surprisingly since he was by this time bitterly estranged from his wife and unlikely to support any enterprise in which she was involved.[38] It may in fact be that the forces raised for the pope were not that numerous, and in consequence by no means enthusiastic to confront the formidable army which was, by 1074, available to Guiscard.

On the other hand Robert Guiscard appears to have been, at least for a time, keen to come to an agreement with the pope. Amatus stressed his humility in wishing to clear himself of any charges made against him. His account undoubtedly protests Robert's virtue too much; but in another letter to Beatrice and Matilda in October 1074 Gregory mentioned that the duke had sent several offers of fealty to him, although he had not as yet decided what his response should be.[39] By Lent 1075 he had made up his mind, doubtless influenced by the continued infiltration into the Abruzzi. He excommunicated Guiscard for the second time, and extended the sentence to include Robert of Loritello as well.[40] Yet this had no discernible effect on Guiscard, who continued his campaign against his rebellious nephew Abelard in Calabria and the frontier squabbles with the prince of Capua.

However, one should not view papal relations with the Normans of southern Italy in a vacuum. During this period Gregory was becoming increasingly preoccupied with affairs in Germany and northern Italy and his relationship with their ruler, Henry IV. In the early part of his pontificate he was, although sometimes critical of the king, not unfavourably disposed towards him. He wrote, for example, to the duke of Swabia in September 1073, from Capua, that 'we have no ill will towards King Henry' and expressed the hope that 'the empire and the priesthood should be bound together in harmonious union'. In Richard of Capua's oath of fealty to him, sworn only a few days later, it was expressly envisaged that the prince would at some point in the future also swear fealty to Henry IV, provided that the interests of the Roman Church were protected. In December 1074 the pope wrote to Henry himself, outlining a revival of his plans to help the

38 Gregory, *Reg.* I.72, pp. 103–4. Godfrey III, 'the Bearded', had died in 1069. Godfrey IV was his son by his first marriage; Beatrice his second wife whom he had married in 1054, and Matilda (born *c.* 1045) her daughter by her previous marriage to Boniface of Tuscany.
39 *Amatus*, VII.14, p. 306; Gregory, *Reg.* II.9, p. 139 [Emerton, *op. cit.*, pp. 45–6].
40 *Reg.* II.52a, p. 197.

beleaguered empire of Constantinople (this time there was no mention of any preliminary expedition against the Normans), and raising the possibility that an expedition under his personal command might then press onwards to recover the Holy Sepulchre for Christendom. In such an event, he would leave the king to guard the interests of the Church in his absence.[41] But such harmony was short-lived. In his Lenten synod of 1075 he not only excommunicated Guiscard and his nephew: he laid the same penalty on five of King Henry's household who had been involved in simony, suspended the archbishop of Bremen for disobedience and three other German prelates as well, and also suspended two bishops from northern Italy and deposed a third. Despite these provocative actions, relations improved once more for a time in the summer of 1075, and Henry's military success against the rebellious Saxons, which greatly strengthened his internal position in Germany, gave Gregory pause for thought and made his attitude to the king temporarily more emollient. But by the end of 1075 he was once more scolding Henry for disobedience, and in particular for his interference in the disputed archiepiscopal election in Milan.[42] Henry, who by this time had had enough, summoned a council of bishops which declared Gregory deposed; the pope retaliated by excommunicating the king and suspending him from office, and by the spring of 1076 the papacy and empire were in open conflict.

We cannot be certain of how much of this Robert Guiscard was aware. But, given his close and amicable relations with Desiderius of Montecassino and the latter's contacts in Rome, he was probably well informed of the increasingly difficult situation in which Gregory was placed. For his part, Desiderius was active in 1075–6 in trying to broker a peace agreement between Guiscard and Richard of Capua, and it is most unlikely that he was here functioning as Gregory's agent. As the pope had noted two years earlier [above, p. 199], it was not in his interest for the Normans to make peace without his direct involvement. By contrast, for Montecassino, whose lands and far-flung network of churches were vulnerable in times of disorder, domestic peace within southern Italy was desirable whatever the interests of the papacy. Furthermore, when negotiations between the two leaders broke down, at Apice near Benevento, in the summer or autumn of 1075, the stumbling-block was Richard's insistence that any written treaty should have a clause reserving his fealty to the pope.[43] If these negotiations

---

41 *Reg.* I.19, I.21a, II.31, pp. 31–2, 35–6, 165–8 [Emerton, *Correspondence*, pp. 15–16, 56–8].

42 *Reg.* III.3, 7, 10, pp. 246–7, 256–9, 263–7 [Emerton, *Correspondence*, pp. 80–1, 83–90].

43 *Amatus*, VII.17, pp. 309–10. Cf. generally, Cowdrey, *The Age of Abbot Desiderius*, pp. 126–31.

had been initiated on papal orders, such a reservation would surely have been a matter of course.

However, his conflict with the empire, and the internal problems in Rome which emerged at the same time, led Gregory to soften his attitude towards Robert Guiscard and the Apulian Normans. As early as March 1076, only a month after his excommunication of the German king, he began to make overtures to them. His approach was subtle and indirect. Interestingly, his intermediary was not Abbot Desiderius (was he considered too closely tied to the Normans and insufficiently loyal to papal interests?) but Archbishop Arnold of Acerenza. Gregory's letter to Arnold suggests that Count Roger of Sicily had already been making overtures to him, and perhaps Guiscard had as well. The archbishop was instructed to absolve Roger and the knights who were fighting with him against the Muslims in Sicily, provided that they were penitent and obedient. (It is not quite clear from the letter whether this absolution was from their sins in general, or from excommunication – though Roger and his men might well have been deemed to share the penalty laid on Guiscard's supporters in 1074.) The pope continued:

> Furthermore, if he should give you any message from his brother Duke Robert, you are to reply to him that the Roman Church leaves the doorway to mercy open to anybody at all who led on by love of penitence abandons their notorious offences and desires to tread firmly on the path of righteousness. If therefore Duke Robert is ready to behave as a son should to the Roman Church, then I am ready to receive him with paternal love, to grant justice to him with its advice, to free him as a penitent from the bond of excommunication and to number him among the Divine flock.[44]

In other words, the door to reconciliation was open – all the Normans had to do was to walk through it. And for a time at least, Gregory had good hopes that they would. In April he told one of his Milanese supporters:

> the Normans have communicated to us their desire to make peace. They would most willingly have done this already, and made satisfaction to St Peter . . . if we had been willing to accede to their wishes over certain matters. With the help of God we hope to accomplish this in the near future, not to the detriment of the Roman Church but to its advantage, and to recall them firmly and securely to their fealty to St Peter.[45]

---

44   Gregory, *Reg.* III.11, pp. 271–2.
45   *Reg.* III.15, pp. 276–7 [Emerton, *Correspondence*, p. 91].

The reasons for this new-found flexibility are obvious. Gregory might well need the Normans' military aid, and he could not risk them allying with the German ruler. That was a real danger, not just a theoretical possibility. During the spring or early summer of 1076 Henry sent an embassy to Robert Guiscard inviting him to hold his lands as an imperial vassal, and (if we can believe Bonizo of Sutri) expressly asking him to join him in military action against Gregory. Robert refused, albeit politely, and according to Amatus protested his loyalty to the pope and St Peter, from whom he held his lands. Obviously he had no wish to saddle himself with a further overlord, or any obligations to the emperor, though according to Amatus he added that he might be willing to be Henry's vassal for some new territory that the latter might grant him.[46] This loyalty from one with whom he was at odds must have been gratifying to Gregory (and we can assume that he was informed about what had happened). But it must have been clear to the pope that a settlement with the Norman leader was desirable.

On the other hand, while Robert was giving the appearance of similarly seeking a settlement, and protesting his loyalty to the papacy when it suited him to do so, he had other and more immediate interests. The pope's letter to Wifredus of Milan had mentioned the Normans' desire for him to grant their wishes in 'certain matters'; no doubt the chief of these was the legitim- isation of their continuing territorial acquisitions. Even as Gregory was expressing his optimism that a settlement was possible, Duke Robert and Prince Richard were finally making peace, but with the intention of extend- ing their conquests through the seizure of Salerno and Naples. (Once again Desiderius of Montecassino acted as the middleman.)[47] In May 1076 Robert's army began the siege of Salerno. Later on in the summer of 1076 he helped the prince of Capua in his ultimately fruitless incursion into the Roman Campagna, and either then, or more probably in 1077 after the capture of Salerno, he sent a substantial reinforcement of 500 knights to help his nephew Robert of Loritello's invasion of the county of Chieti [above, pp. 142–3]. Gisulf of Salerno was a papal ally: he had been one of the people whom Gregory had notified of his election on the day after it had occurred (Abbot Desiderius was another), and had supported him in his proposed expedition of 1074. Amatus indeed claimed that 'the pope loved Gisulf above all other lords'. Gregory commissioned Desiderius to try to protect him, perhaps by persuading him to make further concessions to buy peace from Guiscard, but this proved fruitless. (The pro-Norman sources

46 *Amatus*, VII.27, pp. 320–1; *Liber ad Amicum, MGH Libelli de Lite* i.604. It is possible that these refer to two separate embassies.
47 *Amatus*, VII.28–9, pp. 322–3.

203

suggest that it was Gisulf who refused to give ground, but one may suspect that actually it was Robert who had no wish to be bought off.)[48] And once Salerno had been captured, and Gisulf eventually released, he may well have taken refuge in Rome – certainly he later became one of Gregory's trusted agents and, most unusually for a layman, acted as one of his legates in France in 1081.[49]

In these circumstances, and even though his relations with the German empire were at crisis point, it was hardly surprising that Gregory's attitude to the south Italian Normans hardened. At the end of October 1076 he told his allies in Milan that 'the Normans who have repeatedly perjured themselves are trying to steal the Church's property', but that he trusted in the Lord to humble their pride; 'however, we shall never share in the sacrilege of their invasion by consenting to it'. Had some attempt been made to persuade him to acquiese in the invasion of the Campagna, perhaps by granting what had been conquered in fief to the Normans?[50] But although the Montecassino chronicle implied that his immediate response to this attack was to excommunicate the prince and the duke (in the latter's case for the third time), there is no clear evidence that he did so at this time. Gregory himself was very much preoccupied with the crisis in Germany, and spent the winter and spring of 1076–7 in northern Italy. He did not return to Rome until September 1077. By then, his position with regard to the German king was much stronger – Henry IV had submitted to him at Canossa in January, and was now facing a rival claimant to his throne, elected by a council of German rebels. But this in turn placed Gregory in a difficult position, for it was his priestly duty to arbitrate impartially between the two factions. In the summer of 1077 he proposed to go to Germany in person to resolve the dispute, and even early in the next year he was still trying to arrange a meeting between the two parties which could find a just and generally acceptable solution.[51] In such circumstances he was probably reluctant to make further difficulties for himself by making a solution to the problem of the south Italian Normans even more difficult, however much he disapproved of their behaviour. But the territorial pressure continued, and in the end, by attacking Benevento, Guiscard left him no choice. At his Lenten synod at the end of February 1078 Gregory excommunicated all the Norman invaders of the land of St Peter: both those who were invading

---

48   *Amatus*, VIII.7, 13, pp. 348, 353; *Chron. Cas.* III.45, p. 422; Gregory, *Reg.* I.1–2, pp. 3–4.
49   *Reg.* VIII.23, p. 566.
50   *Reg.* IV.7, p. 305.
51   *Reg.* IV.23–4, V.15, pp. 334–8, 374–6 [Emerton, *Correspondence*, pp. 121–3, 129–30].
      See I.S. Robinson, 'Pope Gregory VII, the princes and the *pactum*, 1077–1080', *English Historical Review* xciv (1979), 721–56.

the Campagna and the Abruzzi, and the army besieging Benevento. In addition he threatened any bishop or priest who dared to ignore his ban and minister to them with deprivation of their priestly status. That this sentence included Richard of Capua is clear, for as he lay on his deathbed a month later the prince was absolved by the bishop of Aversa.[52]

Even before his father's death his son Jordan had sought to be reconciled with the Church, and had gone to Rome to receive absolution. His accession as prince therefore brought Capua back once more into obedience with the papacy, and destroyed the united front which the Normans had presented to Gregory for the previous two years. Jordan also frustrated Guiscard's siege of Benevento [above, pp. 141–2]. In the summer of 1078 Gregory himself made a brief visit to Capua. Montecassino also enjoyed closer relations with the pope than it had had for some years – something explicable on the abbey's part by Prince Jordan's change of heart, but on Gregory's side perhaps showing his wish to use Desiderius once more to persuade those south Italian Normans who were still recalcitrant to come to their senses.[53]

Yet this strategy – if such it was – proved ultimately fruitless, for two good reasons. First, the new prince of Capua was far more concerned with his own interests than those of the papacy, and showed himself a singularly unreliable ally. His submission in 1078 had probably been motivated only by a desire to act independently from his father. By the end of 1078 Gregory was complaining about Norman attacks on Montecassino (which Jordan should have been in a position to stop), and in April 1079 he was reproving the prince for a whole series of misdeeds, including the removal of some treasure from Montecassino. (Desiderius as usual was trying to appease the Normans, and the pope for a time laid an interdict on the abbey.) By the end of the year Jordan had made peace with Guiscard, and the south Italian Normans were once more united and excommunicate.[54] Secondly, all attempts to find a peaceful solution in Germany failed, and given the intransigence of the two rival kings and their supporters it was inevitable that they would, although Gregory cast the blame on Henry's side. In March 1080 he excommunicated him for the second time and declared him definitively deposed. Faced with such an open confrontation with the empire and the ruler whom most of his subjects still supported, a deal with the Normans became a necessity, for their military aid might soon be once

52 Gregory, *Reg.* V.14a, p. 371; *Amatus*, VIII.36, p. 374.
53 *Amatus*, VIII.33, pp. 372–3.
54 Loud, 'Abbot Desiderius of Montecassino and the Gregorian papacy', pp. 312–15; Cowdrey, *The Age of Abbot Desiderius*, pp. 133–6. The key letter is Gregory, *Reg.* VI.37, pp. 453–4.

more urgently needed. Although he repeated his excommunication of the Norman invaders of papal property in the same synod in which he excommunicated Henry IV, he softened his sentence by a notable piece of equivocation: if any Norman had a legitimate claim against the inhabitants of these territories he should seek justice from the properly constituted authorities there. If they should deny him, he could recover his property, though not in the manner of a plunderer. In other words, you can take what you want, provided you do it nicely![55] In June Gregory met Guiscard and Prince Jordan for a conference at Ceprano, on the border between the principality of Capua and the Roman Campagna. Guiscard, who was already preparing an expedition against the Byzantine empire, may now have been almost equally as anxious for a settlement. The Norman leaders formally submitted to the pope and were freed from excommunication. Guiscard swore fealty to the papacy once again, and was again invested with his lands. (We have no record of Jordan being similarly invested, but he may already have received this investiture from Gregory in 1078. Generally each pope performed such a ceremony to a particular ruler only once. But Jordan did once more swear fealty.)[56] However, satisfying as these ceremonies may have been to the pope, he had to make one humiliating concession. When he invested Robert with the lands that he had held from popes Nicholas and Alexander, he added:

> With regard to that land which you hold unjustly, that is Salerno, Amalfi and part of the March of Fermo, I shall be patient with you, trusting in God Almighty and your goodness, that you will in future act to the honour of God and St Peter, as it is right that you should (and for me to accept), without danger to your soul or mine.[57]

Guiscard could therefore keep what he had taken in defiance of the pope, who would hope that at some stage in the future his conscience would trouble him enough to hand it back to its rightful owners. But, while waiting for that singularly unlikely event to occur, pope and duke would once more be firm friends and allies.

It will be seen from this account that the relationship between the papacy and the Normans of southern Italy was an essentially practical one, in which one side offered legitimacy and the other provided political and military support (when it felt like it), and otherwise paid very little attention to papal

---

55 *Reg.* VII.14a, p. 481.
56 Deusdedit, *Collectio Canonum*, ed. V. Wolf von Glanvell (Paderborn 1905), p. 396.
57 *Ibid.*, p. 395 = Gregory, *Reg.* VIII.1b, pp. 515–16.

fulminations. It will be noticed too how much influence external events had on the course of the relationship, and in particular how they caused Gregory VII to display more flexibility than his reputation for intransigence, both among contemporaries and among modern historians, might at first suggest. But two further aspects of this relationship, both of them the subject of somewhat questionable theories by modern scholars, need discussion.

First, it has been suggested that the popes pursued a deliberate policy of 'divide and rule' towards the Normans of southern Italy, in particular playing off the principality of Capua against the duchy of Apulia.[58] But although, as we have seen, Gregory VII had no wish for the prince to ally with Guiscard while the latter remained excommunicate and disobedient to papal commands, there is no evidence that this was in any sense a long-term papal policy. What the papacy wanted from the Normans was their military and political support. If they were to be able to help the papacy effectively, then peace and co-operation between them was desirable. Soon after the meeting at Ceprano, Gregory dispatched a general letter to loyal bishops and others faithful to St Peter seeking recruits for a military expedition against the imperialist stronghold of Ravenna. In it he stressed how both Robert and Jordan had promised *unanimiter* to come to the defence of the Church.[59] Even when Guiscard had been (from Gregory's point of view) disloyal, what the pope had sought was not to encourage dispute in southern Italy but to bring peace to the region. When he sought recruits for his expedition in 1074 he stressed that: 'we are not trying to bring this force of fighting men together for the sacrifice of Christian blood, but in order that our enemies . . . may fear to join battle and be more easily won over to the right side'. Once peace had been made with the Normans, then the army could progress onwards to help the embattled Christians at Constantinople.[60] Furthermore, peace and co-operation were also necessary if the Church in southern Italy was to enjoy the benefits of reform. This policy was to be shown clearly after Guiscard's death when Urban II and his successors were active in promoting domestic peace and supporting the lay powers in southern Italy.

Secondly, it has also been argued that much of the tension between the papacy and the south Italian Normans stemmed from their very different concepts of the nature of the link between them. While the Normans viewed their lands as unequivocally their own, held direct from God, and papal investiture as having no more than a declarative function, the popes saw

58 Cowdrey, *Age of Abbot Desiderius*, pp. 120–1, 125; Robinson, *Papacy*, p. 368.
59 Gregory, *Reg.* VIII.7, pp. 524–5 [Emerton, *Correspondence*, p. 163].
60 *Reg.* I.46, pp. 70–1 [Emerton, *Correspondence*, p. 23].

their tenure of their dominions as papal fiefs as essentially precarious, dependent on their good behaviour and obedience, and having to be validated anew each time there was a new pope or Norman prince. Hence papal investiture with their lands had a real constitutive function. It was, it is alleged, to emphasise this element that Gregory VII altered the wording of the oath of fealty sworn by the Norman leaders. Thus the last sentence of the oath sworn by Richard I of Capua in 1073 reads:

> I shall observe in good faith all the above to you and to the Holy Roman Church, and I shall maintain this fealty to your successors who have been ordained to the honour of St Peter, [and] who shall choose to confirm to me the investiture which you have granted to me.

Guiscard's oath sworn in 1080 used the same phraseology, with the addition that this future investiture would be granted him, 'if my guilt [*culpa*] shall not remain' (was this a reference to the papal territory he held illegally?). The oath of 1073 remained the model for later ones sworn by Norman rulers in southern Italy, and these two opposing concepts of the status of the south Italian lands remained a source of friction right down to the mid-twelfth century, after Roger II of Sicily had created a unified kingdom comprising both mainland south Italy and the island of Sicily.[61]

But ingenious as this theory is, it has some serious flaws. To begin with, the additional clause in the 1073 oath might be double-edged. If a pope did not choose to confirm his predecessors' investiture, then any obligation of fealty and assistance would also be dissolved – which was hardly in the papacy's interests since it needed that support. Then, although investiture was repeated, this was because fealty was a personal bond, not necessarily because popes wished to retain the right to deny investiture. Nor was there always any great urgency in repeating the ceremony, nor much publicity given to it. The only evidence for Guiscard swearing fealty to or being invested by Alexander II is the remark by Gregory in 1080 that Robert had previously been granted his lands by both his predecessors Nicholas and Alexander. But assuming this to have been true, it can only have happened during the pope's visit to south Italy in 1067 – for there would appear to have been no other occasion when he and Guiscard can possibly have met. Yet Alexander had already been pope for six years, so clearly neither he nor Robert saw such a ceremony as having a very high priority. Similarly Robert only swore fealty to Gregory and received investiture in 1080, again seven years after the latter had become pope. Of course, this was explicable

---

61   *Reg.* I.21a, VIII.1a, pp. 36, 515; Deér, *Papsttum und Normannen*, especially pp. 107–63; Robinson, *Papacy*, pp. 368–73, who accepts Deér's arguments rather uncritically.

because of Guiscard's excommunication, and had they actually met in 1073, as was intended, then the ceremony of fealty and investiture would probably have taken place then, soon after the start of Gregory's pontificate. But although Guiscard had not received investiture from him, and had also been cast out from the Church's communion, Gregory still considered his title valid. It may be understandable that when Gregory wrote to the archbishop of Acerenza in 1076, he hoped that 'Duke Robert' would be penitent – he was after all making a peace offer. But when Guiscard was excommunicated in 1074 and 1075, the sentences still referred to him as 'Duke Robert of Apulia', even though Gregory himself had not then formally invested him with this title. Nor did Gregory at any time suggest that because of his excommunication Robert's right to rule was invalidated: he sought simply that he should return to his proper loyalty to St Peter. This was a striking contrast to the pope's attitude to Henry IV of Germany. When he was suspended from office in 1076 and then definitively deposed in 1080 Gregory considered that his subjects were absolved from their fealty and that his right to rule disappeared. 'Every people formerly subject to him is absolved from the bond of the oath which has been sworn to him.' King Henry was unworthy to rule, and as a hardened and unrepentant excommunicate *could not* by definition rule over a Christian people.[62] Why Guiscard's excommunication was somehow qualitatively different from King Henry's is a moot point. Gregory hoped for his repentance, but then in 1076 at least (if not in 1080) he hoped that Henry too might be brought to penitence. He needed the Normans, and thus did not wish to exacerbate the dispute in the way that he did with the king of Germany by attempting to undermine his secular authority. Such an attitude may have been inconsistent. But it also unequivocally demonstrates that not only did Robert Guiscard consider his right to rule to be independent of papal investiture, but once he had been recognised in 1059, subsequent popes took the same view.

Robert Guiscard's attack on Byzantium

Even as Guiscard made peace with Gregory VII in the summer of 1080, another important concern was emerging which was to dominate the last

---

62 Gregory, *Reg.* IV.3, p. 298 (September 1076, quote), and especially *Reg.* VIII.21, pp. 544–63 (March 1081, to Bishop Hermann of Metz) [Emerton, *Correspondence*, pp. 105–7, 166–75]. The modern literature on this topic is vast, but Robinson, *Papacy*, pp. 295–8, 403–11, provides a succinct summary. Cf. his *Authority and Resistance in the Investiture Contest* (Manchester 1978).

five years of his life and complicate his renewed alliance with the papacy. A month after Robert had sworn fealty to him, and while he was still in the extreme south of papal territory near the Capuan frontier, Gregory wrote two circular letters in quick succession to the bishops of southern Italy. The first of these denounced the recent election of the imperialist antipope Guibert of Ravenna and sought their support against him. But the second was devoted to an entirely different issue. Here the pope condemned the deposition of the Byzantine Emperor Michael VII – it was, he wrote, done 'neither justly nor rationally, but rather unworthily and maliciously'. He then recorded how the emperor had come to southern Italy to seek Guiscard's aid – in this he was, as we shall see, the victim of a piece of cynical deception. Finally, he ordered the bishops to urge all those who were about to take part in the duke's expedition to help Michael to do so in a proper spirit of penitence and true faith; showing by this phraseology that he regarded the expedition as a Just War, within the terms defined long ago by St Augustine.[63]

To understand the context of this letter, and of the forthcoming expedition to which it referred, we need briefly to regress – to examine both the plight of the Byzantine empire in general and its relations with the Normans in the period of nearly a decade since the surrender of Bari in 1071. For by 1080 the empire was on the verge of complete dissolution, and the deposition of the Emperor Michael appeared to offer Guiscard the opportunity for the most spectacular conquest of his career.

The loss of its south Italian provinces was only part of a much greater crisis for Byzantium. As we have already noted, the attacks on the empire by the Turks in Asia Minor and by the Pecheneg nomads in Thrace had prevented significant aid being sent to the embattled Italian possessions and greatly facilitated the conquests of the Normans. So menacing were Turkish incursions becoming that the Emperor Romanus IV, a general whose elevation to the throne was itself a symptom of the deepening crisis, determined to put an end to them once and for all [see above, p. 135]. But his counter-attack ended in a catastrophic defeat at Mantzikert in Armenia in August 1071, in which the emperor himself was captured. What made this so disastrous was not simply the military loss but the internal collapse that it precipitated. As the Byzantine ruling class squabbled among themselves, Turkoman nomads penetrated ever deeper into the empire's heartland in Asia Minor, meeting little or no resistance. By 1080 only a few enclaves on the north coast were left in Byzantine hands. Furthermore the loss of its

---

63 Gregory, *Reg.* VIII. 5–6, pp. 521–4 [the first only translated by Emerton, *Correspondence*, pp. 161–3].

wealthiest provinces exacerbated the grave financial and economic problems from which the empire had already been suffering, even while its
frontiers were still relatively intact. Michael Psellus, the ablest of contemporary Byzantine historians, blamed the disastrous imperial finances on the
personal irresponsibility of the emperors – and significantly he thought that
these difficulties had already reached crisis point in the 1050s. Modern
historians prefer to see the root cause of the problem in long-term structural
deficiencies in the government, and especially the taxation system of the
empire, combined with the over-extension of its frontiers under the later
emperors of the Macedonian dynasty (*c.* 963–1028). But few would disagree
with Psellus that by *c.* 1050 there were already serious problems.[64] The
subsequent loss of Asia Minor, which deprived the government of its principal source both of tax revenue and of recruits for its army, made matters
much worse. Between 1040 and 1081 the hitherto stable currency was
devalued to a third of its former fineness. These financial difficulties had
grave political and military consequences, particularly since the defence of
the remaining parts of the empire was now largely dependent on foreign
mercenaries. Thus in 1074 Romanus's successor Michael VII tried to recruit an army from the Caucusus to combat the renegade Norman, Roussel
of Bailleul, who was trying to carve out an independent lordship in Asia
Minor. But he was unable to pay them, and they promptly went home
again.[65] In such circumstances the ease with which the Turks took over the
Asian provinces after 1071, largely by infiltration and without having to
fight major battles, was hardly surprising.

The situation of the empire was so grave that its rulers were desperate
for allies and military aid. Hence, despite the conquest of Bari, they made
overtures to the south Italian Normans; and, to judge by Gregory VII's proposed expedition in 1074, also to the papacy – despite the breach of 1054
[for which see above, p. 120]. The first step was taken by Romanus IV,
probably about the time that Bari finally surrendered in April 1071. He
sent envoys who proposed a marriage between one of his sons and one of
Guiscard's daughters. Mantzikert put paid to that idea, but a year or two
later Michael VII renewed the offer. This time the bridegroom was to be
his younger brother, still only a child. Robert, however, refused. Indeed he
remained outwardly unimpressed even when a second offer was made,
although Amatus recorded that in fact he was very pleased, but was deliberately holding out for better terms. Finally a third embassy was sent from
Constantinople in March 1074; this time proposing a marriage between

---

64   *Michael Psellus: Fourteen Byzantine Rulers* [above, Ch. III note 12], p. 311.
65   *Nicephori Bryennii Historiarum Libri Quattuor*, ed. P. Gautier (Brussels 1975), II.19, pp. 182–3.

Michael's baby son Constantine and one of Robert's daughters. In return for this the duke was offered the Byzantine court rank of *nobilissimus*, the highest that could be held by someone not of imperial blood, one of his sons the only slightly lower rank of *curopalates*, and a number of other dignities were to be distributed among his followers, all of which carried substantial annual pensions. In total, Robert and his men stood to gain annual payments equalling about 200 lb of gold. The bribe was considerable, but also, since he was still in the process of suppressing rebellion among his nobles, the availability of substantial sums for distribution to his men would be politically useful. This time Robert accepted, and the agreement was ratified in a formal treaty in August 1074 (the text of which was written by Michael Psellus). This recorded that in return for these gifts, the girl would be treated with all honour as a reigning empress-consort, lodged in the palace and with a magnificent suite. Robert meanwhile would be expected not to threaten the empire's frontiers, and to aid in driving away its other enemies (which presumably meant that he would facilitate the recruitment of Norman mercenaries, rather than providing help in person, which held far too many dangers).[66] Finally, in 1076 Robert's daughter actually arrived at Constantinople. In the same year the emperor granted a substantial additional grant to the abbey of Montecassino, whose monks had almost certainly acted as intermediaries during these diplomatic contacts. (Abbot Desiderius had been for some time sending envoys to Constantinople to recruit skilled workmen for his new basilica, and to buy icons and other precious objects for its decoration – he had the contacts therefore to facilitate negotiations.)[67]

Quite how this money was raised, and whether such payments were made in full or even in part, is a very good question, given the parlous shape of the imperial finances and the desperate expedients to which Michael and his ministers resorted to raise funds. The latter indeed played a major part in his eventual downfall. But for the time being it suited both sides. The Byzantines were freed from one potential threat and could continue to recruit valuable mercenaries, while connection with the imperial house boosted Robert's prestige, doubtless very usefully in his dealings with Gregory VII and Henry IV in the mid-1070s, with his Greek subjects, and probably too with his fellow Normans. No doubt too the money for salaries, if it was actually paid, helped to reinforce the latter's loyalty, although the only one

---

66 H. Bibicou, 'Une page d'histoire diplomatique de Byzance au XIe siècle: Michel VII Doukas, Robert Guiscard et la pension de dignitaires', *Byzantion* xxix/xxx (1959–60), 43–75 [text of treaty at pp. 44–7]; *Amatus*, VII.26, pp. 318–20.
67 Lupus Protospatharius, *Annales, MGH SS* v.60; *Chron. Cas.* III.32, 39, pp. 403–4, 415–16.

of his followers to whom we know that one of these dignities was granted was an official, Maurelianus the Catepan (governor) of Bari, who was given the senior rank of *proedros*.[68] But although Guiscard was in the dominant position, and could thus afford to wait for the most favourable possible terms, the agreement helped to stabilise his regime in other ways too. The Byzantines had after all already helped to stir up one revolt against him, in 1067–8, and might try to do so again if opportunity arose. They had also given a refuge to dissidents such as Joscelin of Molfetta [above, p. 134]. They had furthermore recently received his tiresome brother-in-law Gisulf of Salerno when the latter had stopped off at Constantinople on his way to Jerusalem on pilgrimage, and furnished him with a substantial subsidy. Indeed Amatus (whose account was predictably hostile to the prince) alleged that Gisulf actively solicited Byzantine aid against the Normans.[69] Given the empire's problems after Mantzikert, it was unlikely that Byzantine hostility would have had more than nuisance value. But the empire had until very recently still been a great power, and the extent of its decline may not have been quite so speedily apparent to contemporaries as it is to us, with the light of hindsight. Meanwhile Guiscard was still imposing his authority over his fellow Normans, and in 1074 he was in dispute with both the papacy and Richard of Capua and had not yet conquered Salerno. An alliance with Byzantium suited him at this time more than risking even the nuisance value of Byzantine agents stirring up disaffection among his subjects.

But by 1080 the situation was very different. Most obviously Michael VII had been overthrown by a military coup (in March 1078). The new emperor, Nikephoros III Botaniates, had no intention of allowing the marriage to go ahead, and Guiscard's daughter (whom the Greeks had rechristened Helena) was no longer the future empress but a prisoner – in effect a hostage – at Constantinople. Any subsidy from Byzantium had undoubtedly stopped too. But, in addition, Salerno had been captured, renewed revolt in southern Italy had been stamped out, and the pope was seeking an alliance once again. Indeed, an expedition to aid the legitimate emperor seemed (as we saw above) just and right to Gregory VII, and was another reason for the restoration of the latter's favour to Guiscard. And the weakness of the empire must by now have been much more readily apparent. By 1080 the Turks had taken over nearly all of Asia Minor, and the Balkan

68 Ménager, *Recueil*, pp. 144, 150, nos 44–5; *Cod. Dipl. Barese*, v.23–4 no. 12.
69 *Amatus*, IV.36–8, pp. 207–11. *When* this visit took place is unclear, so disorganised is the 'History' of Amatus. It has usually been dated *c.* 1062, but Bibicou, *art. cit.*, p. 53, places it as late as 1073.

principalities formerly obedient to the empire had abandoned it. Meanwhile Botaniates faced a series of revolts at home, and his hold upon the imperial throne was at best precarious.

Furthermore, Guiscard had a most useful pretext for his intervention, for early in 1080 a man appeared in southern Italy who claimed that he was the former emperor Michael. He sought Robert's help to restore him to his throne and rescue his own captive daughter. There is no doubt that this man was an impostor. The real Michael VII had become a monk at the great monastery of St John Studios in Constantinople, and was to end his life as archbishop of Ephesos. But while even the pro-Norman sources agreed that the refugee in Italy was a fraud, they differed as to whether he was acting on his own initiative or was from the first a stooge set up by Guiscard. The Byzantine historian Anna Comnena reported both versions of the story, though she favoured the second, which she considered all the more likely because of Robert's natural cunning. Malaterra, naturally disposed to make excuses for the duke, reported that he had some doubts about the pretender's identity, but suppressed them, particularly when some of his entourage who had been to Constantinople claimed to recognise the former emperor.[70] It undoubtedly suited him to do so, not least in enlisting Pope Gregory behind the enterprise.

In March 1081 Robert sent a fleet under the command of his son Bohemond to attack the island of Corfu in the Adriatic, and if possible to secure bases on the Albanian mainland. Over the next two months he gathered his main force at Otranto and Taranto – we know that he himself was at Taranto in early May. Malaterra claimed that he had mustered 1,300 knights for the expedition. But by then the situation was already changing. Pope Gregory, who had initially supported this enterprise, was coming to realise that the agreement in the previous year might not benefit the papacy nearly as much as he had hoped. In February he had written to Abbot Desiderius, asking whether Robert would come in person to assist his planned military operations against Henry IV's supporters after Easter, or at least send a substantial force to aid him (which suggests that Robert was keeping the pope well and truly in the dark about the imminence of his embarkation). He also complained once more about the continued territorial incursions of Robert of Loritello, whom he wanted Robert to control. In May he wrote again, prompted by Henry IV's appearance in northern Italy and by rumours which had reached him of the German king's attempts to win Guiscard's support. He was worried not so much by any

---

70   *The Alexiad of Anna Comnena*, trans. E.R.A. Sewter (Harmondsworth 1969), pp. 58–60 [Bk I.12]; *Malaterra*, III.13, p. 65.

danger of Guiscard defecting as by the likely harm that Robert's failure to assist him would do to his wavering support in Rome.[71] Probably very soon after this letter was sent, Robert himself reported Henry's approaches. But he refused to deflect his expedition:

> he assured him that he would never have set this expedition in motion if he had foreseen the enemy's attack, but he said that since the preparations were so far advanced it would be impossible to abandon the enterprise.[72]

He then set off across the Adriatic, first to Corfu, where the main town on the island surrendered on 21 May, and then to Butrinto nearby on the Albanian mainland, and northwards along the coast to Valona. If we can believe Anna Comnena, somewhere north of Corfu the fleet was badly battered by a summer storm, and Robert's own ship damaged.[73] By 17 June his army had laid siege to Durazzo, the principal town of the region. The attack on Byzantium was now well and truly under way.

But while his expedition was gathering, the situation had also changed at Byzantium. In April 1081 the usurper Botaniates was himself deposed in a military coup and replaced by a young general, Alexius Comnenus (nephew of the former emperor Isaac, 1057–9). Alexius was supported by the former imperial family, the Ducae, to one of whom he was married. He was a man of ability, both as a soldier and, even more so, as a politician, whose attempts to stabilise his rule were helped by the wide-ranging marital connections of his prolific kin. William of Apulia, who was remarkably well informed on affairs at Byzantium, had a high opinion of him – as opposed to his notably poor one of the elderly Botaniates.[74] But at the time his seizure of the throne probably seemed no more than another symptom of the Byzantine collapse (he was after all the seventh emperor in twenty-five years, and only one of his six predecessors had remained undisturbed on the throne until his death). If we are to believe the later testimony of his daughter, the situation was desperate:

> Alexius knew that the empire was almost at its last gasp . . . the Romans [i.e. Byzantines] had no worthwhile forces . . . in the imperial treasury there were no reserves of money.[75]

---

71 Gregory, *Reg.* IX.4, 11, pp. 577–9, 588–9 [Emerton, *Correspondence*, pp. 181–4]; *Malaterra*, III.24, p. 71; Ménager, *Recueil*, pp. 122–4 no. 39. The dates in this and subsequent pragraphs are drawn mainly from Lupus Protospatharius and the *Anon. Barensis Chron.*
72 *W. Apulia*, IV, lines 181–4, p. 214.
73 *Alexiad*, p. 132 [Bk III.12].
74 *W. Apulia*, IV, lines 77–121, 142–58, pp. 208–12.
75 *Alexiad*, p. 124 [Bk III.0].

Anna Comnena was not of course disposed to minimise the problems – the greater the danger, the more the empire owed to the indomitable courage of her admired father. But since, immediately after his accession, Alexius was forced to the desperate expedient of seizing church treasures to pay his troops – despite the risks of alienating churchmen and pious laity when he was as yet hardly secure on the throne – her estimate may well have been valid.[76]

This in turn raises the question of what Robert's intentions were. The conquest of the empire as a whole, even in its truncated form in 1081, might seem to have been so ambitious a project as to be unrealistic – despite Anna's express testimony that this was indeed Guiscard's aim. But Amatus, writing at about the time the expedition left, may support her view, for he thought that Michael VII had sought a marriage alliance 'to avoid being driven from his lordship over the empire'. Was this just hyperbole, or a reflection of what was intended in 1081? And Anna suggested, realistically enough, that Robert intended to use his Albanian campaign as a springboard – if he was successful there, then he would aim more ambitiously thereafter. There was also a recent precedent for aiming to take over the empire from the Durazzo region, for in 1077–8 the governor of that province, Nicephoros Bryennios, had revolted and come very close to seizing the empire from this base.[77] Since most of the territory that was left to Byzantium was in Greece and Thrace, Durazzo was no longer the peripheral province that it had been in the days when the empire's centre of gravity was in Asia Minor. Furthermore the Via Egnatia connected it directly to Thessalonica, and hence Constantinople. In addition, there had been for a considerable period close connections, both trading and cultural, between the eastern coast of the Adriatic and northern Apulia. Slavs from the Balkans had settled in Bari and the Capitanata. Some of these were servants or even slaves, but at Devia, on the Gargano peninsula, for example, there was a free Slav colony. Guiscard was thus well informed about affairs on the eastern side of the Adriatic, and had useful connections and potential allies there. Sailors from Ragusa (Dubrovnik) and the other towns of the Dalmatian coast formed part of his fleet in 1081.[78]

---

76 *Alexiad*, pp. 156–8 [Bk V.1–2].
77 *Alexiad*, pp. 38, 136 [Bks I.4, IV.1]. Cf. *Amatus*, VII.26, p. 318.
78 *W. Apulia*, IV, lines 302–3, p. 220; Martin, *Pouille*, pp. 437–8, 504–9. N.B. the connections between Ragusa and the monastery of Tremiti, and the Slav *zupan* who witnessed two charters at Devia in 1053, *Cod. Dipl. Tremiti*, ii.27–30 no. 9 (1023), 150–6 nos 47–8. Indeed Greeks formed only a small proportion of the population of the Durazzo province: A. Ducellier, *La Facade Maritime de l'Albanie au Moyen Age. Durazzo et Valona du XIe au XVe Siècle* (Thessaloniki 1981), p. 45.

Robert may also have had another, albeit subsidiary aim, although this can only be inferred since none of the sources actually mentions it. But before leaving Italy, he had formally designated his eldest son by his second wife, Roger Borsa, as his successor.[79] Roger then remained behind in Apulia. By contrast Bohemond, his son by his first wife, commanded the advance force of the expedition and played a prominent role throughout its subsequent history. Did Guiscard intend, at the very least, to create a principality in the Balkans for his eldest son, to compensate him for being denied the succession to the duchy of Apulia (and Bohemond had as yet little or no landed endowment in southern Italy)? It is at least possible. But if so, this would be no more than a by-product, or a consolation prize, of the expedition. So parlous did the empire's position appear to be in 1081, and so helpless had it been earlier in resisting the Turks, that a complete conquest must have appeared a quite feasible proposition.

Admittedly, Malaterra considered that the duke's army, for all its 1,300 knights (a substantial figure compared with his forces on earlier occasions), was hardly large enough for the task in hand, and was very much dependent upon his own confidence and leadership; 'for the duke was extraordinarily bold and determined in military matters'. But from the Byzantine side the situation looked very different. 'Alexius saw the magnitude of the task and was afraid. He knew that his own forces were vastly outnumbered by the Latins.'[80] Needless to say, we cannot judge between these two views, and no doubt both sides were prone to exaggerate the other's strength. But no more favourable moment for an attack could have presented itself; for politically, financially and militarily the Byzantine empire was at its lowest ebb. Yet the enterprise was still clearly fraught with danger, and Robert's recruiting efforts were unpopular. Even William of Apulia admitted that some had to be coerced to join in.[81] Nor can many of the 'counts' to whom the sources refer on this expedition be identified. It is indeed easier to find out who remained behind in southern Italy, and some of the most influential nobles did. Apart from Gerard of Buonalbergo and Robert of Loritello, who were associated with young Roger in the government of Apulia, these also included such former rebels as counts Peter of Andria, Henry of Monte Sant'Angelo and Geoffrey of Conversano (one of Guiscard's nephews), and his other rebellious nephew Abelard. That Robert took hostages with him from those

---

79   *W. Apulia*, IV, lines 186–92, p. 214.
80   *Alexiad*, p. 137 [Bk IV.2]; cf. *Malaterra*, III.24, p. 71. *Orderic*, iv.16–17, estimated Robert's army to be in all 10,000 strong, but added that 'it was not by numbers, but by the courage of his men that he struck terror into the hearts of his adversaries'.
81   *W. Apulia*, IV, lines 128–32, p. 210; *Alexiad*, pp. 65–6 [Bk I.14].

who stayed, as Anna alleged, is entirely credible.[82] By contrast, apart from his sons Bohemond and Guy, another nephew Richard the Seneschal, and Count Amicus of Molfetta (assuming him to be the Count 'Amiketas' to whom Anna refers), the few others who can be identified as taking part in the expedition are minor figures, sometimes otherwise unknown.[83]

The siege of Durazzo lasted from June 1081 until February 1082. Alexius did everything in his power to lift it. He dispatched one of his most trusted associates, his brother-in-law Giorgios Paleologos, who had played an important part in the coup which had brought him to power, to command the defence.[84] He secured naval aid from Venice with the promise of extensive commercial privileges within the empire. In August he left Constantinople himself at the head of a relieving army, though its progress seems to have been slowed by the need to wait for fresh drafts of troops. But by October he was ready, and while his Venetian allies attacked by sea, Alexius moved to engage Robert's army on land. However, it was difficult to co-ordinate such an ambitious operation, and the Venetians had already been defeated, albeit with some difficulty, before the Byzantine army appeared. None the less battle was joined, and on 18 October 1081 Robert secured a complete victory. The decisive moment came when an initial attack by the Varangian Guard (many of whom were Anglo-Saxons who had left England after the Norman take-over) resulted in their becoming isolated from the rest of the Byzantine army. The Varangians took refuge in a church where they were massacred. Alexius and the remains of his army retreated in disorder, leaving their camp to be plundered by the victors. But even then it took four more months to capture Durazzo, and in the end the city was betrayed by a Venetian called Domenico, not stormed.[85]

Mid-winter in the Balkans was not the best time to exploit such a success, and Alexius had had the chance to regroup his forces after his defeat. The emperor's plan seems to have been to block the Via Egnatia at Ochrid, encourage disaffection in the enemy's forces, and undertake a diplomatic offensive in Italy. Robert meanwhile sought to outflank him by advancing up

---

82 *Alexiad*, p. 69 [Bk I.16]. Peter: *Cod. Dipl. Tremiti*, iii.250–3 no. 84. Henry: F. Carabellese, *L'Apulia ed il suo comune nell'alto medioevo* (Bari 1905), pp. 297–8 [from Cava, *Arm. Mag.* B.25]. Geoffrey: *Cod. dipl. pugliese* xx.104–5 no. 45. Abelard: see below, p. 247. At least two more important lords remained at home, Humphrey of Montescaglioso and Count Richard of Sarno, although the latter was still a minor.

83 *Alexiad*, pp. 146–8 [Bk IV.6]. Guy: Ménager, *Recueil*, p. 128 no. 40. Richard: B. Figliuolo, 'Ancora sui normanni d'Italia alla prima crociata', *Archivio storico per le provincie napoletane*, civ (1986), 14–16 [from Cava, *Arca* cxv.11].

84 *Alexiad*, pp. 97–100, 125–6 [Bks II.10–11, III.9].

85 *Malaterra*, III.26–8, pp. 72–5; *W. Apulia*, IV, lines 270–505, pp. 218–30. On the Venetian and Amalfitan settlement at Durazzo, Ducellier, *Façade Maritime*, pp. 70–5.

the Devoli river valley to the south and capturing Kastoria; perhaps hoping to advance from there down the Vistritsa Valley towards Thessalonica. But no sooner had he done this than disquieting news arrived from Italy. Henry IV's army was approaching Rome, and renewed revolt had broken out in Apulia, probably stirred up by Byzantine agents. Pope Gregory had already greeted the news of his victory in the autumn with an urgent request for help against the German king. Robert had ignored that plea, but now the situation in Italy required his presence. He left Bohemond and his constable Briennus in charge of the army, and in April crossed back to Apulia, with only two ships.[86]

Robert's return to Italy did not end the campaign in the Balkans, and for some eighteen months after his departure Bohemond prosecuted operations with vigour. About a month after his father's departure he defeated a counter-attack by Alexius near Ioannina. He then tried to attack along the Via Egnatia, but although he defeated Alexius in another battle and captured the town of Ochrid, he was unable to take the citadel there, and was thus checked. Early in 1083 Bohemond launched a renewed offensive, this time considerably further to the south with the intention of conquering Thessaly and opening up southern Greece to potential attack. This would have the effect of depriving Alexius of a region which was one of his principal sources of revenue, for it was one of the few areas where the imperial administration was still functioning. Bohemond forced the passes and captured Trikkala, but was held up by a long siege of Larissa. Alexius had decided by this stage to avoid pitched battles, in which the Normans' armoured knights gave them too much of an advantage; rather he harassed his enemy through guerrilla tactics. By the autumn, with supplies running short and disaffection growing among his troops – energetically fostered by the Byzantines – Bohemond was forced to retreat. And while he had been engaged in northern Greece a *coup de main* by the Venetians retook Durazzo. Some of the Norman forces retreated with him to his other coastal base at Valona, others surrendered and enlisted in Byzantine service. Towards the end of 1083 Alexius also succeeded in retaking Kastoria, at which point Bohemond abandoned the enterprise and returned to Italy.[87]

Guiscard meanwhile had his hands full in Apulia. One cannot be certain, from the exiguous sources available, quite how extensive was the revolt that had broken out in his absence. We do know that the ringleaders were once again the duke's nephew Abelard and his half-brother Herman,

---

86   *W. Apulia*, IV, lines 506–26, pp. 230–2; *Malaterra*, III.33, p. 77; Gregory, *Reg.* IX.17, p. 597 [Emerton, *Correspondence*, pp. 185–6].

87   *W. Apulia*, V, lines 1–106, pp. 236–40; *Alexiad*, pp. 162–73, 181–3 [Bks V.4–7, VI.1]. Best secondary discussion, Angold, *Byzantine Empire 1025–1204*, pp. 106–9.

and his other nephew Geoffrey of Conversano. In addition there had been insurrections at Troia and Ascoli in the Capitanata, and probably at Bari as well. When Guiscard landed at Otranto in April 1082, his first task was to relieve Oria, then under siege by Geoffrey of Conversano. The revolt would seem to have been serious, both because of the Byzantine subsidies that were being sent to Abelard, who took refuge at Constantinople once the rebellion had failed, and because of the time it took to suppress. Since Roger Borsa appears to have put down the rising at Troia (a key town the duke could ill afford to lose) without Robert's help, it is probable that the latter moved first against the count of Conversano in southern Apulia before dealing with the problems further north. He then moved on to Bari, where he imposed a substantial fine on the citizens, and in May 1083 he laid siege to Herman's base at Canne, which he stormed on 10 July. But the suppression of the rebellion had taken him in all fifteen months.[88]

Furthermore, while this was happening, Henry IV and his imperial army had in the early months of 1082 established themselves in the hills to the south of Rome and had blockaded the City. The German ruler was joined by Jordan of Capua, who abandoned his fealty to the pope and recognised the German king (still not crowned emperor) as his overlord. The Montecassino chronicle suggested that Henry's presence destabilised the principality of Capua by encouraging its Lombard inhabitants to plot insurrection, and it was this which forced the prince and his Norman followers to submit to the emperor, to protect their own position. This may or may not have been true (this section of the chronicle continuation was written some time later and its author may have been reading back from the rebellions after Jordan I's death in 1090). But Prince Jordan had always gone his own way, and changed sides as he saw fit. He may have wished to avoid hostilities with an imperial army that he could not match – William of Apulia said bluntly that he was afraid of losing his principality. But he may also have reckoned that with Henry's support he could redress the balance of power in southern Italy, which by the 1080s was heavily weighted in favour of Guiscard and the duchy of Apulia. Certainly both he and Desiderius of Montecassino were at Henry's court at Albano at Easter 1082 – though the chronicle account did its best to disguise quite how far Desiderius compromised himself in acknowledging Henry.[89] Pope Gregory

88 W. Apulia, IV, lines 506–35, pp. 230–2; Malaterra, III.34, pp. 77–8; Anon. Barensis Chron, RIS v.154; Lupus Protospatharius, Annales, MGH SS v.61.
89 Chron. Cas. III.50, pp. 430–3; W. Apulia, V, lines 110–17, p. 242. Cf. G.A. Loud, 'Abbot Desiderius of Montecassino and the Gregorian papacy', Journal of Ecclesiastical History xxx (1979), 305–26; Cowdrey, Age of Abbot Desiderius, pp. 154–65 (with a rather different interpretation). On the authorship of this section of the chronicle, ibid., pp. 239–44.

responded by excommunicating Jordan, and probably Desiderius as well. During the summer of 1082 he wrote both to the archbishop of Capua and the other bishops of the principality to enforce spiritual sanctions upon it, and to the archbishop of Naples to prevent the ruler of that city helping Jordan. In the first of these letters he said that anyone who was unable to stand up to 'the pressure of the impious' should flee to 'the glorious duke' (Robert).[90] Yet we have no record that he wrote directly to Robert asking for help at this time: though since the last book of his register is disorganised and clearly incomplete we should perhaps not rule out such communication entirely.

The rebellion in Apulia had taken time to suppress, and once Canne had been captured Robert's next step was to launch a campaign against Prince Jordan of Capua. He did during 1083 send a substantial sum of money to Rome which was used to persuade the citizens to remain loyal to Gregory. But it was only after he had made his nephew submit to him that, early in 1084, he moved in person to provide military help for Gregory in Rome – two years after his return to southern Italy from Albania. When he did finally act, the pope's situation was desperate, for in March 1084 Henry IV had finally forced his way into Rome. Gregory was besieged in the Castel Sant'Angelo, while Henry reiterated his deposition, arranged the coronation of the antipope Guibert (Clement III) in St Peter's and then his own imperial coronation at Clement's hands. Only then did Guiscard march to Gregory's rescue – even if he may well have been gathering his forces before Henry entered the City. By the time he arrived, in late May 1084, the emperor had withdrawn. Robert's army was clearly substantial; it included forces from Sicily under Count Roger, and even some Muslim troops. Guiscard in turn forced his way into Rome, but though he rescued the pope his troops became embroiled in a pitched battle with the citizens, and much of the town was burned down as a result. Gregory's position was now untenable, and he was forced to leave with Guiscard's army and withdraw to the south. There he remained, first at Benevento and then at Robert's embryo capital at Salerno, where he died in May 1085.[91]

Thus, whatever his own difficulties in southern Italy, Robert was remarkably leisurely in bringing aid to his beleaguered papal ally (and nominal

---

90   Gregory, *Reg.* IX.26–7, pp. 609–11. Archbishop Hervé of Capua seems to have been a key figure; Alexius Comnenus had earlier written to him as part of his diplomatic offensive against Guiscard: *Alexiad*, p. 126 [Bk III.10].

91   *Malaterra*, III.37, pp. 79–80 (the best contemporary account); Cowdrey, *The Age of Abbot Desiderius*, pp. 170–4. W. *Apulia*, IV, lines 564–6, p. 234, claimed that this was the largest army Guiscard ever mustered, numbering (so he alleged) 6,000 knights and 30,000 infantry. For Muslim troops, see above, p. 184.

overlord). Nor indeed, once Gregory had withdrawn from Rome, did he do more than provide him with a refuge. The papal alliance was very much secondary to his own interests, and he made no move to help Gregory until all his affairs in southern Italy were satisfactorily resolved and the pope's situation was desperate. Nor did he try to re-establish Gregory in Rome when he did finally go to his rescue. The behaviour of his troops had indeed made Gregory's position there impossible. Robert was in any case far more interested in resuming his attack upon Byzantium. Despite the advanced season, he crossed the Adriatic once more in October 1084.[92]

Guiscard may have been anxious to recommence his attack on Byzantium as soon as possible so as not to allow Alexius Comnenus any more time to cement his hold upon the throne, and strengthen his military position. He was also anxious to relieve the garrison which Bohemond had left holding out in Corfu. Alexius was certainly not without problems: he faced vocal criticism from churchmen for his seizure of their treasures, and Anna referred to 'a whispering campaign' against him in Constantinople, and a conspiracy among the aristocracy (though she tactfully avoided naming many names). There were also difficulties with Paulician heretics who had earlier been settled in the Balkans, and with the Pechenegs on the Danube frontier.[93] None the less, his position was probably stronger than in 1081 and Robert had missed his best chance.

His second expedition was fraught from the start. Bad weather prevented operations for two months after his return to Albania, then Robert faced a determined naval attack by a combined Byzantine–Venetian naval squadron, which was routed only after a desperate battle, in which his son Roger was wounded, in January 1085. When – not before time – his fleet was laid up for the winter, and his troops went into winter quarters at Vonitsa, the cold (and probably shortage of supplies as well in a country which had already been plundered back and forth for several years) helped to trigger an epidemic. (No doubt ignorance of the most elementary hygiene precautions played its part too, as so often with medieval armies.) William of Apulia claimed that 500 knights died, and Bohemond was ill enough to have to return to Salerno for treatment.[94] When spring came Robert refloated his ships: both William and Anna noted his ingenuity in doing this, damming the River Glykys to raise the water level. He then sent his advance force under his son Roger south to Cephalonia, the island which commands the

---

92 *Anon. Barensis Chron.*, *RIS* v.154.
93 *Alexiad*, pp. 183–4 [Bk VI.2–4].
94 *W. Apulia*, V, lines 143–228, pp. 244–8 (for Bohemond, lines 223–8, confirmed by *Orderic*, IV.28). On the naval battle, *Alexiad*, pp. 188–9 [Bk VI.5], which alleged that Robert behaved with extreme cruelty to the Venetian prisoners.

entrance to the Gulf of Patras – it may be therefore that he was thinking of an attack on the Peloponnese rather than renewing the conflict in the mountains of Albania. But disease was probably still present among his men. When Robert himself sailed south he was taken desperately ill with fever, with what William of Apulia called 'the burning flux'. He reached Cephalonia where his wife and son were waiting for him, but died there on 17 July 1085. Thus, concluded William of Apulia, 'the man who had never allowed his men to show fear in his presence and who had been accustomed to raise the spirits of others now rendered up his own spirit'.[95]

Robert's death brought an abrupt halt to what had been very much a personal expedition, and one where, to judge by the hints in the sources, he had had to exercise a great deal of pressure to persuade many who were reluctant to take part. William of Apulia wrote of the fear which enveloped his troops once they knew of his death, and their hasty and panic-stricken embarkation. But there was another good reason why the expedition was promptly abandoned. Roger Borsa had to hurry back to Italy to assure his succession as duke, and the need for haste was all the more pressing since his elder half-brother, and potential rival, Bohemond had already returned there. After 1085 the Normans of southern Italy were preoccupied with their own affairs, and no longer threatened the Byzantine empire. It was to be more than twenty years before Bohemond took up his father's ambitions once again (in 1107–8), and by then Alexius Comnenus was firmly in the saddle of a revived Byzantine empire. The opportunity for a further, and most ambitious, conquest had been fleeting, and soon disappeared.

The papacy and southern Italy after 1085

The deaths of Gregory VII and Robert Guiscard left the reformed papacy in a parlous position. The sack of Rome and the excesses committed by Guiscard's troops had made the City untenable, even though some Gregorian supporters still remained there. The reformers themselves were in disarray. Many of the cardinals, and most of the papal officials, had deserted Gregory in 1084 and gone over to his rival Guibert of Ravenna (Clement III). So divided were those who had remained loyal to Gregory that after his death there was a year's interregnum before the election of a new pope.

95 Date confirmed by numerous sources, see H. Houben, *Il Libro del capitolo del monastero della SS. Trinità di Venosa (Cod. Casin. 334): una testimonianza del Mezzogiorno normanno* (Galatina 1984), p. 132. W. *Apulia*, V, lines 284–336, pp. 252–4, gives a long and rhetorical account of his deathbed (quote lines 334–6).

When the reformers finally decided upon a candidate, Abbot Desiderius of Montecassino, he was reluctant to accept the post, and the best part of another year passed before he at last consented to his election (as Pope Victor III) in March 1087. By then he was a sick man, and although he was able to hold a council at Benevento in August, he died a month later (on 16 September 1087). A further six months passed before the Gregorians elected Urban II at Terracina, on the southern border of the papal Campagna, in March 1088. In the meantime the rival, imperially sponsored pope, Clement III, had widespread support within Christendom as a whole, above all in northern Italy and Germany. The council held by his legates at Mainz in May 1085 (at the time of Gregory's death) showed just how strongly he was now entrenched as the 'legitimate' pope – even if the German Church, and secular society in that country, remained divided against itself. Nor was Clement idle in seeking to extend his authority: he was in contact with most European rulers, and while he had little whole-hearted support, a number of these princes remained neutral, and for some years were reluctant to recognise Gregory's successors.[96]

In these circumstances, the support and protection of the Normans of southern Italy was vitally important for the reformers. The relationship between the reform papacy and the Normans was indeed closer and more stable after 1085 than before. Admittedly it has been suggested that one of the reasons for Desiderius's initial reluctance to accept the papal throne was due to problems with Duke Roger of Apulia and his mother Sichelgaita – he was unwilling to take office without the whole-hearted and united support of the south Italian Normans (and Roger cannot have been overjoyed by involvement in Gregorian councils of his deposed uncle, Gisulf of Salerno, whose principality he was now ruling). But Jordan of Capua was always one of those pressing him to receive the papacy, and once the Normans had settled their differences, the situation was resolved. It was indeed the combined persuasion of Duke Roger and Prince Jordan which made Desiderius finally accept his election, at a council held at Capua, in March 1087. And it was the escort of Jordan of Capua's troops that enabled Desiderius to enter Rome and receive consecration as pope in May 1087.[97]

If Desiderius was generally perceived, especially by the imperialists, as 'the pope of the Normans', the situation did not significantly change under Urban II, even if his election was less open to charges of Norman interference than was that of Victor III. But although the Gregorians retained

96 J. Ziese, *Wibert von Ravenna. Der Gegenpast Clemens III (1084–1100)* (Stuttgart 1982), pp. 95–177.
97 *Chron. Cas.* III.65–8, pp. 447–50; Cowdrey, *The Age of Abbot Desiderius*, pp. 193–206.

some supporters in Rome, especially in the Trastevere region to the west of the Tiber (which had escaped the sack of 1084), much of the City still preferred Clement III. The latter was in Rome in the summer of 1087, again in the spring of 1089 when he held a synod, and he remained in residence there for a year from February 1091 onwards. Even after Clement left the City for the last time in the spring of 1092 he still had supporters in Rome. Frenchmen on their way to the First Crusade found St Peter's held by his partisans in 1096, and it was only in 1098 that the Gregorians finally regained possession of the Castel Sant'Angelo. Furthermore much of the area immediately around Rome was also in the hands of Clement's supporters during the early years of Urban's pontificate. Urban himself spent only about a third of his pontificate actually in Rome, a third in either northern Italy or France (above all in 1095–6 when he preached the First Crusade), and the other third in southern Italy.[98] His presence in that region was particularly marked in the early years of his pontificate, up to the end of 1093, during which he made three extended visits to Norman Italy, spending a total of almost thirty-three months there. During this period he held councils at Melfi in September 1089, at Benevento in February 1091, and at Troia in February 1093. He travelled widely through mainland south Italy, but his most frequent stopping point was Benevento, to which he made seven separate visits during the course of his pontificate.[99] This town was itself papal property – as a result of its surrender to Gregory VII by its last prince in 1073. But his presence there, and indeed in southern Italy as a whole, would have been impossible without the agreement of the Normans. Nor indeed did this situation change overmuch under Paschal II (1099–1118), who also made repeated stays at Benevento, and who held four of the twelve recorded synods of his pontificate in southern Italy.[100]

Urban needed the assistance of the Normans to such an extent that he was prepared to sanction, or at least to turn a blind eye to, Jordan of Capua taking over the southern part of the papal Campagna. By 1089 Jordan would seem to have been the *de facto* ruler of that area, achieving therefore what had been a recurring ambition of his father, and he died in November 1090 at Priverno, within papal territory. The continuator of the Montecassino chronicle wrote of Jordan 'taking almost all of the Campagna away from the jurisdiction of the Apostolic See', but in fact pope and prince remained

---

98   A. Becker, *Papst Urban II. (1088–1099)* (2 vols, Stuttgart 1964–88), i.98–113, 121–2;
     Partner, *Lands of St. Peter*, pp. 138–47; Robinson, *Papacy*, p. 374.
99   H. Houben, 'Urbano II e i normanni', in his *Mezzogiorno normanno-svevo* (Naples 1996),
     pp. 115–43, especially pp. 134–43 (containing maps of Urban's journeys); Vehse,
     'Benevent als Territorium des Kirchenstaates' [above, Ch. III, note 135], p. 110.
100 Robinson, *Papacy*, p. 127.

on good terms. The pope was prepared to acquiesce in this extension of Jordan's authority rather than to allow his territory to fall into the power of those who supported the rival pontiff.[101] Urban had no great illusions about his Norman allies; his own opinion of them was by no means flattering. He also realised that, as a result of the horrors of 1084, they were greatly disliked in Rome. When he returned to the City in 1089 he was at pains to stress to his supporters there that he had come without a Norman army to assist him.[102] But he still needed the support and protection of the south Italian Normans, as indeed did his successor. In 1108–9 Jordan's son, Prince Robert I of Capua, intervened in the Campagna to help Paschal II to reassert his authority, and when in 1111 the Emperor Henry V marched on Rome and arrested Pope Paschal the reformers once again sought military aid from the Normans of Capua, even if the latter were, in the event, too few to provide an effective counter to the powerful imperial army.[103]

That the Capuan Normans should try to assist the papacy in time of trouble suggests that the obligation in the traditional oath of fealty remained a live issue, and therefore that the princes probably continued to swear fealty to successive popes, and in return to receive investiture with their principalities. We have, however, no direct evidence for any such ceremony from after the time of Jordan I until 1128, when Prince Robert II swore fealty to Pope Honorius II. But such a supposition seems far more plausible than assuming, as some historians have done, that Jordan's fealty to Henry IV in 1082 meant that Capua remained thereafter an imperial vassal, or that because Richard II of Capua became the vassal of the duke of Apulia in 1098 this cancelled out any link with the pope (and one should note that Urban II was actually present with the prince and duke in 1098). Such legalistic assumptions misunderstand the significance of these oaths, the taking of which were often the product of short-term circumstances, and in the case of those sworn to the popes, which were important over a longer term, they marked rather a mutually supporting alliance than the 'legal dependence' of the lay ruler on the pontiff. Oaths and ceremonies were symbolic, not constitutive.[104]

The dukes of Apulia certainly continued to swear fealty to the papacy. Roger Borsa took an oath to Urban II at the council of Melfi in 1089, and

---

101   *Chron. Cas.* IV.10, p. 474; Loud, *Church and Society*, pp. 86–7, 95–7.
102   P.F. Kehr, 'Due documenti pontifici illustranti la storia di Roma negli ultimi anni del secolo xi', *Archivio della reale società romana di storia patria* xxiii (1900), 277–80.
103   *Chron. Cas.* IV.39, pp. 506–7; Loud, *Church and Society*, pp. 99–100.
104   A notable example of such a legalistic interpretation is H. Hoffmann, 'Langobarden, Normannen und Päpste. Zum Legitimätsproblem in Unteritalien', *QFIAB* lviii (1978), 137–80, here especially at pp. 167–73. For 1128: *Falco* p. 90.

to Paschal II at S. Trophimena, near Amalfi, in about 1100. His son Duke William swore fealty to Paschal at the council of Ceprano in October 1114. In this last case we are told expressly that the pope invested the duke with his principality and handed him the insignia of office – almost certainly a banner. But in none of these cases does the text of what was sworn survive (the *Liber Censuum* had no need to record further texts once the precedent had been established with Robert Guiscard and Richard I). The references to such ceremonies in the contemporary sources are sufficiently incidental to make the lack of such mentions with regard to the Capuan princes (for whom we have relatively little evidence after 1090) quite explicable.[105] In this case omissions in the sources are not necessarily evidence that something did not happen.

Nor should we be surprised that the princes of Capua provided more direct help to the papacy than the dukes; their dominions did after all border directly on papal territory. But on one occasion Duke Roger did provide important military assistance. In 1101 he besieged and forced the surrender of Benevento, not because he was attempting, as his father had in 1077, to conquer it for himself, but to compel the increasingly restive citizens to acknowledge the rule of their rightful overlord Pope Paschal.[106] The dukes were also assiduous attenders of papal councils held within their dominions. But here the papacy was assisting them rather than vice versa. For at Melfi in 1089 and at Troia in 1093, and again in later papal councils at Troia in 1115 and 1120, popes proclaimed the Truce of God. This was an innovation not previously seen in southern Italy. That the popes now felt that it was necessary reflected the decline in effective ducal authority after Guiscard's death, in particular within Apulia itself: partly a consequence of the later dukes basing their rule primarily in the principality of Salerno. However, Melfi and Troia, where these councils were held, were still ducal towns, and the duke was himself present at each of these four councils, and also at Urban's council at Bari in 1098. By proclaiming the Truce in his company, and on his property, successive popes were trying to bolster his flagging rule, as well as benefiting from his help in enforcing the Truce, and thereby fulfilling their spiritual duty of fostering peace among Christians. But perhaps the most notable instance of the alliance between the papacy and the Norman rulers, and of the popes lending their prestige to aid the secular princes, was the presence of Urban II with the army of Duke Roger as he and his uncle the count of Sicily besieged Capua in the summer of

---

105   R. Somerville, *Pope Urban II, the Collectio Britannica and the Council of Melfi (1089)* (Oxford 1996), pp. 228, 258; *Romuald*, pp. 199, 207; *Chron. Cas.* IV.49, p. 516.

106   *Annales Beneventani*, ed. Bertolini, p. 151; Vehse, 'Benevent als Territorium des Kirchenstaates', pp. 111–15.

1098, as they sought (successfully) to restore Prince Richard II to his capital, from which he had been driven by an insurrection some years earlier. Urban tried to secure a peaceful solution, but when the Capuans refused to accept their prince back he gave his blessing to the besieging army.[107] There was therefore no question of the popes trying in any sense to limit the power and authority of the Norman rulers in the period after 1085 – rather they were trying to enhance it.

The frequent visits of Urban II and Paschal II to southern Italy were also important to the Church in a more narrowly ecclesiastical sense. The large number of bishops who attended their councils – it was claimed that there were no less than 185 at Bari in 1098 – were a significant reminder to Christendom as a whole that they were the legitimate pontiffs, as opposed to the wretched pretenders whom the emperor supported (even if such figures were artificially boosted by the unusually large number of sees in southern Italy). But Urban and Paschal also used their presence in the south to work for the improvement and renewal of the local Church much more effectively than had been possible for previous popes. They promoted the appointment of reforming prelates, developed new cult centres, dedic-ated new and rebuilt churches, granted privileges to monasteries which were centres for the dissemination of reforming ideals such as Montecassino and Cava, and continued the structural changes in the diocesan system which their predecessors had begun. Urban's pontificate was particularly important for this last aspect. For example, in 1089 he brought an end to the long-running dispute between the archbishoprics of Bari and Trani, confirming that there would be in future two separate archiepiscopal prov-inces. In 1091 he approved the transfer of the see of Oria to Brindisi (though here he was reluctant to recognise archiepiscopal pretensions). At about the same time he also confirmed Taranto as a metropolitan see with its own province, and in 1098 he arranged a solution to another long-standing dispute, between the archbishoprics of Salerno and Conza, again confirm-ing the existence of two separate provinces. By such actions he played a decisive part in giving the south Italian Church the structure it was to retain for the rest of the Middle Ages.[108] At Bari Urban promoted the new church of St Nicholas, built to house the bones of the saint which had been stolen from Myra in Asia Minor in 1087, as a centre for reforming ideals, and in 1089 he consecrated its founder, Abbot Elias, as archbishop of Bari.[109] A

---

107 *Malaterra*, IV.27, p. 106; *Italia Pontificia*, viii.23–4, 29–31, nos 72, 76, 101, 113, for full references to the Truce of God.

108 See Fonseca, 'L'Organizzazione ecclesiastica', and Houben, 'Il Papato, i normanni e la nuova organizzazione ecclesiastica della Puglia e della Basilicata' [above, note 16].

109 *Cod. Dipl. Barese*, i.61–3 no. 33; Lupus, *Annales, MGH SS* v.62.

year or so later he also attempted to install another monastic reformer, Bruno, the founder of the Carthusian order, as archbishop of Reggio; and when he refused the promotion Urban then appointed a cardinal, Rangerius, a former monk of Marmoutier in Touraine, to that see.[110] But we should not assume that such intervention was an assertion of papal authority riding roughshod over that of the lay rulers. Elias of Bari claimed that he had been unanimously elected by the people of that town, with the consent of Duke Roger, and that Urban II had been invited to dedicate his new church by Bohemond, who by then was Bari's direct ruler. Since Duke Roger made a donation to his church after Elias's election as archbishop but before his consecration, we may indeed conclude that this choice was one he had approved. Similarly in 1092 Roger himself chose a new bishop at Troia, but in the presence of a papal legate and, we are told, with the assent of the clergy and people.[111] Urban II was thus working with, and not against, the lay rulers in the ecclesiastical as well as the political sphere.

Such co-operation also enabled the pope to assert his jurisdiction over those dioceses in Calabria and the Terra d'Otranto which at the time of the Norman conquest had been ruled by Greek bishops. Some of these sees were converted to the Latin rite – although the presence of a Latin bishop did not necessarily mean that all his subordinate clergy were therefore Latin as well. It has been argued that the Normans and the papacy collaborated in a deliberate programme of Latinisation, but there is little evidence of this being true. Conversion to the Latin rite did not follow automatically on the Norman take-over – indeed how could it when the Normans were relatively few in number and in central and southern Calabria the population remained overwhelmingly Greek? Even where Latin bishops were installed, this might be up to a generation after the actual conquest, as for example at Tropea and Squillace, where Latin bishops were only appointed in the 1090s. There was still only one Church, and to the papacy the key factor was not the language in which services were conducted, nor even uniformity of practice over such matters as the use of unleavened bread at the Eucharist and clerical celibacy (though naturally the popes would have preferred Roman customs to be followed). The crucial issue was the recognition of papal authority, and provided that the Greek prelates of southern Italy were prepared to do this then Urban II and his successors were happy to confirm them in office. The Greek archbishop of Reggio, who had been elected in exile at Constantinople, recorded with horror that his colleagues at Rossano and S. Severina had formally recognised the papal primacy at

---

110   *Italia Pontificia*, x.21–2.
111   *Cod. Dipl. Barese*, i.64–5 no. 34; v.27–9 no. 14; *Les Chartes de Troia*, pp. 134–5 no. 27.

the council of Melfi, and by doing so had retained their offices. Both these archbishoprics, and five other sees in Calabria and Gallipoli in the Terra d'Otranto, were still ruled by Greek prelates as late as 1200.[112] When the Greek archbishop of Rossano confirmed at the Melfi council died in 1093, Duke Roger Borsa did indeed try to substitute a Latin successor, but faced with a revolt by his brother-in-law, William de Grandmesnil, who had tried to seize Rossano, he rapidly changed his mind and placated the inhabitants by allowing them to elect a Greek instead. (The new archbishop was probably Nicholas Maleinos, scion of a family of Greek landowners who remained important after the conquest: he is known to have been in office in 1105, and also to have received a privilege from Duke Roger.)[113] Clearly it was not in the duke's interest needlessly to antagonise his Greek subjects.

Nor was it in the papacy's interest, for one of Urban's dearest wishes was to reunite the sundered Church. Soon after he became pope negotiations began for a formal reconciliation between the 'reforming' papacy and Constantinople. Even though that was never quite achieved, without this renewed contact it is unlikely that a crusade would have been called in 1095. (The issue was also important to Urban because he had to forestall any possible agreement between the Greeks and his imperialist rival Clement.) At an early stage during these negotiations, Urban visited Sicily specifically to consult Count Roger about his relations with the Greeks. That he should do this shows how important southern Italy was to the papal Curia. But it was also a sensible move since the southern part of Calabria, which was ruled by the count, was overwhelmingly Greek (as were the majority of the Christian inhabitants of Sicily). Who could therefore advise him better on Graeco-Latin relations, and quite probably also provide translators and Greek-speaking clerical diplomats? Roger urged the pope to accept the Byzantine emperor's invitation to come to Constantinople, although in the end this visit proved impractical.[114] But southern Italy continued to play an important part in relations between the two sections of the Church, and these diplomatic negotiations were another reason for the large proportion

---

112 For detailed discussion, G.A. Loud, 'Byzantine Italy and the Normans', in *Byzantium and the West. Proceedings of the XVIII Spring Symposium of Byzantine Studies, Oxford 1984*, ed. J.D. Howard-Johnston (Amsterdam 1988), pp. 227–33 [reprinted in *Conquerors and Churchmen*], *contra* especially L.-R. Ménager, 'La "Byzantination" religieuse de l'Italie méridionale (IXe-XIIe siècles) et la politique monastique des Normands en Italie', *Revue d'histoire ecclésiastique* liv (1959), 5–40. Basil of Reggio's letter: W. Holtzmann, 'Die Unionsverhandlungen zwischen Kaiser Alexios I und Papst Urban II im Jahr 1089', *Byzantinische Zeitschrift* xxviii (1928), 66–7.
113 *Malaterra*, IV.22, p. 100; *Italia Pontificia*, x.100.
114 *Malaterra*, IV.13, pp. 92–3. Exhaustive discussion, Becker, *Papst Urban II*, ii.108–77.

of the early part of his pontificate that Urban spent in the south. The issue was discussed once again at the council over which he presided at Bari in October 1098, and at which both Greek prelates from southern Italy and Byzantine envoys from Constantinople were present, as well as Duke Roger of Apulia.[115]

Unlike the duke of Apulia and the prince of Capua, Count Roger of Sicily was not a papal vassal. He was still in theory a subordinate of his nephew the duke, although in practice they were more like equals, and Roger Borsa increasingly needed the count's military assistance to enforce his authority in northern Calabria and against his brother Bohemond. But Count Roger and the papacy co-operated with each other just as much as did the duke and pope. Roger required papal sanction for his creation of new bishoprics in Sicily [above, pp. 174–5], but this was hardly something that the pope could, or would wish to, refuse since it forwarded the restoration of Christianity to a hitherto Muslim island. As the soldier who had brought Christ back to Sicily, Roger was a valued and greatly respected papal ally, and if we are to believe Malaterra 'extraordinarily zealous and devout in dealing with matters ecclesiastical', as well as the senior in terms of age and experience, if not in status, among the Norman leaders of south Italy. His high standing with Pope Urban was shown when in 1095 the latter encouraged a marriage between Roger's daughter Maximilla and Conrad, the eldest son of the Emperor Henry IV, who had two years earlier abandoned his father and made his peace with the reformed papacy.[116] The one hitch in the relationship came when Urban, in 1097 or early in 1098, appointed Bishop Robert of Troina as his legate in Sicily without securing the count's prior approval. Canonically Urban was well within his rights, but it was a tactless and unnecessary gesture, although his choice of legate was in itself perfectly acceptable – Robert was one of the count's closest advisers, not least concerning the advisability of the marriage with young Conrad. None the less, Roger was sufficiently angry to have the bishop and some of his household arrested. The quarrel was soon resolved when the count and pope met face to face at the siege of Capua in June 1098. Roger acknowledged his fault in seizing the bishop and his entourage, and issued a charter confirming the liberty of the church of Troina/ Messina. In return a month later Urban granted a bull to the count, and to his heirs, in which he pledged not to appoint legates to his lands without his prior consent, to entrust the count himself with the oversight of churches

---

115   Eadmer, *Historia Novorum*, ed. M. Rule (London: Rolls Series, 1884), pp. 104–6; Becker, *Papst Urban II*, pp. 190–8.

116   *Malaterra*, IV.23, p. 101 (quote *ibid.*, c. 29, p. 107); Becker, *Papst Urban II*, i.133–7.

instead of a legate when he felt this was appropriate, and giving him the right to veto the attendance of his bishops at papal councils.[117]

This privilege was to be exploited for centuries to come by the kings of Sicily to justify their control over the Church in their dominions. As a result it remained the focus of controversy right down to the eighteenth century, to such an extent that later papal propagandists sometimes denounced it as a forgery.[118] But it should be stressed that although the immediate cause of its issue was a dispute, generally Count Roger was a close ally of the pope, and not only Malaterra (from whom, in a work dedicated to the count, we might expect this) but also Pope Urban stressed his devotion and obedience to the Church, and his place as its 'special and most dear son'. Nor indeed did it give him *carte blanche* to trample over ecclesiastical liberties: he was to act instead of a legate 'on occasions when we shall send word to you from our side'. Roger was indeed already exercising considerable authority over the Sicilian Church, but this was inevitable since he had founded and endowed its bishoprics and most of its monasteries. What the privilege of 1098 did was to sanction in theory powers that he already exercised in practice.[119] His successors may have exploited it to the hilt, and far beyond any reasonable interpretation of its phraseology. As early as 1117 his son Roger II was rebuked for exceeding his authority and acting on his own initiative, whereas the 1098 privilege stressed the count's role as the pope's agent, albeit one marked out by unusual rights for a lay ruler.[120] But the original grant was the product of specific circumstances, and needs to be examined within its contemporary context. While later popes, even during the twelfth century, came to regret the privilege, they recognised its validity, at least insofar as it applied to the island of Sicily rather than the mainland dominions of the kings, and until the renegotiation of its terms with King Tancred in 1192. But what was significant in the more general context of papal relations with the south Italian Normans in the later eleventh century was not so much what was granted, but the fact that the privilege was given to Count Roger, his eldest son Simon (who died in 1105) and his other legitimate heirs. If the Gregorian papacy was prepared to allow some, albeit limited, rights over the Church in their dominions to the counts of Sicily on an hereditary basis, it is surely perverse to argue, as some scholars have

---

117 *Malaterra*, IV.29, pp. 106–8; *Italia Pontificia*, x.338 no. 20.
118 A.D. Wright, '"Medievalism" in Counter-Reformation Sicily', in *Church and Chronicle in the Middle Ages. Essays Presented to John Taylor* [above, Ch. III, note 56], pp. 233–49.
119 The classic examination of E. Jordan, 'La politique ecclésiastique de Roger I et les origines de la "legation sicilienne"', *Moyen Age* xxxii (1922), 237–73; *ibid.*, xxxiv (1923), 32–65, retains its value.
120 *Liber Censuum*, ii.125–6.

done, that the investiture by the popes of the Normans' lands was viewed as conditional and revocable. They were after all the popes' principal allies, and the 1098 privilege was an important sign of the mutually beneficial symbiosis that linked the two together.

CHAPTER VI

Government and society in Norman Italy

Robert Guiscard and the aristocracy

The Hauteville brothers' leadership was never entirely accepted by their
fellow Normans. Drogo's succession to William the Iron Arm had been
challenged by Count Peter son of Amicus in 1045/6, and William of Apulia
suggested that Peter's lordship in the coastal plain of northern Apulia around
(but not yet including) Trani was actually wealthier than were the possessions of Drogo and his brother Humphrey at that time.[1] Nor did his defeat
then remove Count Peter's ambitions, for soon after Guiscard had succeeded his half-brother Humphrey as leader of the Apulian Normans and
while he was busy extending his conquests in Calabria, Peter seized Melfi,
the Normans' first conquest in Apulia, and very much the centre (and
probably the symbol) of the Hautevilles' lordship: 'the most outstanding of
all the towns of the county and its premier seat' (it was there, a few months
later, that Guiscard was to marry Sichelgaita). Amatus indeed recorded that
Count Peter 'had great envy of Robert and tried to damage him in any way
he could'. Guiscard moved quickly to blockade Melfi, soon drove his rival
out and forced him to sue for peace.[2] But Count Peter and his powerful
family remained a major obstacle to the consolidation of Robert's rule in
Apulia.

This initial challenge to Robert's rule may also have been linked to the
circumstances of his accession, for when Humphrey died early in 1057 he

---

1   *W. Apulia*, II, lines 20–37, pp. 132–4.
2   *Amatus*, IV.5, p. 186. On the marriage, *Malaterra*, I.37, p. 22.

had left a young son, Abelard, whom he probably intended as his successor. However, Robert had ignored any claims the boy may have had, and taken the title of Count of Apulia and the *de facto* leadership of the Normans for himself.[3] Count Peter was unlikely to have had much concern for Abelard's claims (and the latter was too young to challenge his uncle's coup). But Peter may well have felt that they weakened Robert's chances of securing the loyalty of other Normans. If so, he clearly underestimated the speed and ruthlessness of his opponent.

None the less, Robert's transition from warlord to territorial ruler was to be slow and fraught with difficulty, and during his rule he faced a whole series of revolts, not primarily from among the conquered Lombards and Greeks but from his fellow Normans, and in some instances from his own family. There were major insurrections in Apulia in 1067–8, 1072–3, 1079–80 and 1082–3; this last breaking out while he and his army were fighting the Byzantines in Albania. His nephew Abelard was probably the most determined and embittered of his opponents, but the powerful 'sons of Amicus' kin-group, and especially Count Peter II of Andria and his cousin Count Amicus of Molfetta, played a major part in most of these outbreaks. (The Hautevilles' original rival, Count Peter I, had died at some time before 1064.)[4] A number of other Norman lords were also involved, including another of the duke's nephews, Count Geoffrey of Conversano – one of the most powerful territorial lords in southern Apulia, and perhaps the strongest in that region. He was one of the moving spirits in three of the four rebellions, although he seems to have remained loyal to his uncle during the 1072–3 outbreak. Furthermore, behind much of the trouble of the 1070s lay the princes of Capua, for, perhaps conscious that Guiscard's power was outstripping their own, both Richard I, and later his son Jordan (yet another of Robert's nephews, for his mother was Guiscard's sister), sought to destabilise ducal rule. The princes also had a family interest in the region, for the counts of Monte Sant'Angelo, who took part in the 1072–3 and 1079–80 revolts, were the sons of Richard's younger brother Robert.[5] Yet Richard of Capua was not without similar problems within his own principality and family, facing rebellions from his son-in-law William of Montreuil and later from his son Jordan and the latter's principal ally, his uncle and Richard's youngest brother, Count Rainulf of Caiazzo. Guiscard did indeed provide help to Richard against William of Montreuil *c.* 1071,

3 *Romuald*, p. 183; 'Chronicon Amalphitanum', in Schwarz, *Amalfi im frühen Mittelalter*, pp. 208–9.
4 Houben, *Die Abtei Venosa*, p. 245 no. 12; Jahn, *Untersuchungen zur normannische Herrschaft*, p. 205. See Table VI for this family.
5 For this family, Jahn, *Untersuchungen zur normannische Herrschaft*, pp. 322–30.

reckoning 'to rein in William's pride, lest his own knights follow his example'. But any gratitude the prince felt was short-lived, although it was in response to Robert's help that he offered to assist him in the attack on Palermo.[6]

There were a number of reasons why Guiscard's rule was so often challenged. The chroniclers tended to ascribe the revolts simply to jealousy at his success and power: 'Robert's glory, which had been so greatly increased, began to invite not a little envy, where there should instead have been praise. His virtues were envied by those elected counts by the people, who numbered twice six.'[7] Certainly, as William of Apulia hinted rather obliquely when he referred to the original twelve counts of 1042, memories of the territorial share-out that had then been agreed may have played their part, for the Hautevilles (at that stage William and Drogo) had been only two among the twelve, and their subsequent conquests and pre-eminent position were no doubt resented by some of those whom they had outstripped. Abelard, of course, had a real grievance, for Robert had usurped his own position. Family relationship was anyway no guarantee of loyalty – competition within the kin-group was often intense, as Duke William of Normandy had discovered to his cost in the 1040s and 1050s [above, pp. 87–8], and thanks to the extraordinary fecundity of Tancred de Hauteville and his wives, and the number of his sons who had settled in Italy, the subsequent kin-group was an extensive one which developed into several separate dynasties, each with their own interests. External interference played a part as well: Byzantine agents and subsidies stirred up the rebels in 1067 and again in 1082, and the prince of Capua aided the revolts of 1072 and 1079. But the key issue for most of the discontented barons was probably Robert's efforts not merely to reign but actually to rule, to give real meaning to his papally sanctioned title and to exercise his authority as duke of Apulia by exacting his rights as their overlord.

From the earliest years of his reign Robert had done his best to emphasise his prescriptive right to rule: through his marriage with Sichelgaita at Melfi in 1058, his investiture with the ducal title by Nicholas II in 1059 (once again at Melfi), and with the acclamation by his army as duke after the capture of Reggio in 1060. His marriage, celebrated in great state – Robert was 'dressed as though he were an emperor' – was almost certainly the first by a Norman leader to a *legitimate* daughter of a Lombard prince, as opposed to an illegitimate child or collateral female relative [above, p. 128]. Guiscard was also at pains to ensure the full attendance of the Apulian

6 *Amatus*, VI.12, p. 275. William had earlier been at the ducal court at Troia in July 1067. Ménager, *Recueil*, pp. 76–9 no. 18.
7 *W. Apulia*, II, lines 444–8, p. 156.

nobility even the reluctant Count Peter son of Amicus was coerced into attending.[8] The assumption of the ducal title was a clear indication that Robert viewed his status as superior to the other Norman leaders, not merely as 'first among equals' with those other Normans who had assumed or inherited a comital title. He was also at pains to have it accepted by his followers; hence the formal acclamation by his men at Reggio – which would seem to be how the chroniclers' accounts of this episode should be interpreted – one should note too Malaterra's emphasis on how Robert 'profusely thanked his brother and the rest of the army with whose help he had attained such a high honour, and rewarded the deserving'. The significance of this event is shown by its mention by both Amatus and Malaterra as (in their opinion) the occasion when he assumed the ducal title, for as has already been noted [p. 190 above] neither of them discussed the papal investiture.[9]

That a showdown with the more recalcitrant, or independent, among his fellow Normans was delayed as long as it was, until the autumn of 1067, was to a considerable extent due to Robert's commitments elsewhere, and to the desire of the leaders in Apulia to mop up what remained of Byzantine territory there. However, Malaterra suggests that when Guiscard returned to Apulia in the autumn of 1060, after the capture of Reggio, 'he found that nearly everyone had been plundering his property, which was [in consequence] in great disorder'. The winter of 1060–1 was spent in recovering and restoring his possessions.[10] Absence therefore posed problems. While we have no indications that something similar happened later on, except during actual rebellions, Guiscard's preoccupations in Calabria and Sicily during the early to mid-1060s allowed the other Norman nobles to make independent conquests of Byzantine territory, notably the capture of Taranto by Count Peter's son Godfrey in 1063, and Robert of Montescaglioso's seizure of Matera in 1064 [above, p. 132]. Thus when Duke Robert was free to concentrate his attention on the completion of the conquest of Apulia in 1067, he was faced with some very powerful nobles who had up to then been largely outside his control, and had no intention of submitting to any more intensive rule than the loose rein to which they had hitherto been subject. At the head of the revolt, which broke out in the autumn of 1067, were the duke's nephews Abelard and Geoffrey of Conversano, Joscelin of Molfetta, the latter's son-in-law Amicus (from the powerful kin-group of that name), and Roger Toutebouve (probably the

---

8 *Amatus*, IV.20, p. 196.
9 *Malaterra*, I.35, pp. 23–4: 'After receiving the city, Robert Guiscard put into effect a long-standing desire of his and was gloriously and triumphantly created duke'. Cf. *Amatus*, IV.3, p. 184.
10 *Malaterra*, II.2, p. 30.

lord of Monopoli, which had been granted to his namesake/father? in 1042). The confused and defective account in the surviving text of Amatus stressed the importance of Byzantine subsidies to the rebels of 1067, and the particular links of Joscelin of Molfetta with the Byzantine *dux* Perenos.[11] But Malaterra gave a very interesting alternative explanation for the adherence of one of Guiscard's own relatives to the rebel cause:

> Robert attempted to make Geoffrey of Conversano (his sister's son) render service to him for Montepeloso, and for the many other *castra* which he held from him; even though Geoffrey had not received either it or the others from him, but had gained them from his enemies through his own energy [*strenuitas*], and without help from the duke. When he refused to do this, the duke set off with his army and went to besiege this *castrum*.[12]

With the decisive attack on Bari in preparation, it was hardly surprising that Guiscard was anxious to secure military contingents from the Apulian nobles. But as this passage suggests, they would not necessarily welcome such an extension of ducal authority.

One further, albeit more speculative, factor may be suggested. During the late summer of 1067 Pope Alexander II made a lengthy visit to southern Italy, holding councils at Siponto and Melfi (the latter at the beginning of August) and going on to visit Salerno. That he should have made this journey is another indication as to the dating of the revolt, for one may assume that he would not have travelled into a region in the grip of civil war. He certainly met Guiscard during his visit to the principality of Salerno, one of the purposes of which was to persuade Robert's younger brother William to hand back Church property which he had seized – no doubt Robert was asked to use his influence to persuade the sinner to repent – and given that Melfi was a ducal town – indeed the nearest thing to a capital that Robert possessed – quite possibly the two met there as well. It was almost certainly during this visit that Alexander renewed his predecessor's investiture of Robert as duke [above, p. 208].[13] This renewed legitimisation of his position no doubt appeared helpful to Guiscard as he attempted to

---

11   *Amatus*, V.4, pp. 224–7. *W. Apulia*, II, lines 451–3, p. 156, named the leaders of the rebellion as Geoffrey, Abelard and Joscelin. Most authors have followed Chalandon, *Domination Normande*, i.177–9, in dating the beginnings of this revolt to 1064, and suggesting therefore that there was a protracted campaign, lasting some four years until its suppression early in 1068. However, Jahn, *Untersuchungen zur normannische Herrschaft*, pp. 101–5, argues very convincingly for a much shorter duration, beginning after September 1067. [See also note 14 below.]

12   *Malaterra*, II.39, p. 48.

13   *Italia Pontificia*, viii.14 nos 23–5, 351–2 nos 22–5, especially no. 23. The pope was at Capua on his way home by 12 October.

get a grip on the situation in Apulia, a region which he had for some years rather neglected. But it is possible that such a ceremony, with its reminder of his superior status, had an adverse effect on some of the Apulian nobles who resented any attempt to curb their independence. Could it conceivably have contributed towards the outbreak of the revolt which began even as the pope was making his way northwards back to Rome?

Robert was in Calabria when the revolt occurred (probably in October or November 1067, certainly no earlier). Amatus stressed the speed with which he moved to suppress it, and we know that he began the siege of Montepeloso on 16 February 1068, although he was delayed there for some time before the town was betrayed to him. The remaining rebels surrendered soon afterwards, except for Joscelin and Roger Toutebouve who fled to Byzantium. The suppression cannot have taken very long since Robert was able to commence the siege of Bari in August, and some time was surely needed for preparations before that city was invested.[14] The rebels' property was confiscated, except for Geoffrey who lost Montepeloso but otherwise escaped unscathed (protected by his family relationship with Guiscard), while Abelard and Amicus were allowed to join the ducal household and offered the possibility of either recovering at least some of their possessions or being given other new property as an incentive towards future loyalty. By October 1069, although he was still in the ducal entourage, Amicus had been granted the lordship of Spinazzola (in the Murge region of inland Apulia, 22 km east of Venosa).[15] Abelard was given land in Calabria, which to judge by later events included the town of Santa Severina (midway down the eastern side of the Calabrian peninsula, *c.* 20 km inland from Crotone).

If the rebellion of 1067/8 was, in part at least, a reaction to the strengthening of ducal authority, so too was that of 1072. The details of what happened are far from clear: Amatus maintained that the revolt began (with the connivance of the prince of Capua) while Robert was still in Sicily, while William of Apulia suggested that it was only after he had returned and held a council at Melfi that hostilities began. Reconciling the two accounts is therefore by no means easy, although both agree that the ringleader of the rebellion was Count Peter II of Andria, that most of the

---

14 *Amatus*, V.4, p. 226; Lupus, *Annales, MGH SS* v.59. For the siege of Montepeloso, cf. *W. Apulia*, II, lines 459–77, pp. 156–8, an account stressing Robert's astuteness and subtlety. The dating of these events has been confused by the *Anon. Barensis Chron., RIS* v.152, which claimed that Joscelin fled in 1064, but this is palpably in error since he was still in Molfetta in June 1066 when he and his son-in-law Amicus made a donation to the monastery of Venosa: Houben, *Die Abtei Venosa*, pp. 246–8 no. 13.

15 Ménager, *Recueil*, pp. 80–2 no. 20 = Houben, *Die Abtei Venosa*, pp. 248–50 no. 14. He still retained this up to 1079: *W. Apulia*, III, lines 642–3, pp. 198–200.

fighting centred around his lordship in northern Apulia, and that the decisive steps in Robert's victory were first the surrender of Trani (known to have taken place on 2 February 1073) and then a little while later the capture of Count Peter himself in a skirmish outside Andria. Both accounts also agree that a key role in the duke's victory was played by a Lombard, his brother-in-law Guido, and it was he who actually captured Count Peter. But whether or not there was already trouble brewing before the council at Melfi, William's account certainly suggests that Guiscard himself was responsible for driving Count Peter into open rebellion, and that once again the issue which had provoked the breach was the provision of military service. 'The duke did not trust Peter since he had previously refused to send help to him in Sicily.' His response was to demand that the count hand over Taranto, which he had been ruling on behalf of his juvenile nephew, Richard (whose father Godfrey had conquered it from the Byzantines back in 1063). Not surprisingly Peter refused and prepared for war.[16] He was not, however, alone: he was allied with his cousin Amicus and Abelard (neither of them therefore won over by the relatively generous treatment they had received after the previous rebellion), Abelard's half-brother Herman, a Calabrian baron called Robert (or possibly Roger) Areng (once again the text of Amatus is defective), and Count Richard of Monte Sant'Angelo, who was supported by his uncle the prince of Capua. Against this formidable coalition the duke's principal supporters were his nephew Robert of Loritello, his brother-in-law Guido, and Geoffrey Ridel, the duke of Gaeta from the west coast – whom one might have expected to have been allied with his neighbour the prince of Capua, but who had earlier been one of Guiscard's lieutenants in Sicily [above, p. 149].[17] Once again Robert's speed of response seems to have been a decisive factor, catching the rebels before they were ready or united, and with the capture of Count Peter and Herman, and then the capture of and change of sides by Richard of Monte Sant'Angelo, the revolt fizzled out.[18] Once more the treatment of the rebels was relatively mild, although Robert confiscated Trani from Count Peter and Giovenazzo from Amicus. Taranto, however, seems to have been left in Peter's hands – perhaps because, despite his earlier demand, it was really the property of the infant – and therefore guiltless – Count Richard, and there was therefore no real excuse for its confiscation. Amicus

---

16   *W. Apulia*, III, lines 348–71, pp. 182–4. Peter made a donation to a monastery at Taranto 'with the consent of his most dear nephew and lord Richard' in May 1072, in a document dated by the regnal years of the Byzantine emperor: *Cod. Dipl. Cavensis*, ix.366–9 no. 125.

17   Geoffrey had been duke of Gaeta since February 1068 or earlier: *Cod. Dipl. Caiet.*, ii.86 no. 235.

18   *Amatus*, VII.2–6, pp. 292–7.

seems to have retained the rest of his lordship apart from Giovenazzo: certainly by September 1073 he was still in possession of Terlizzi (10 km inland from Molfetta).[19]

The suppression of the 1072/3 rebellion had therefore seen a considerable accretion of Robert's resources at the expense of the 'son of Amicus' kin-group. Of the rebels only Abelard remained irreconcilable, and he was the only one of the Apulian nobility not to swear fealty to Roger Borsa as Guiscard's heir when the duke fell dangerously ill in the summer of 1073. He remained defiant for some years in his Calabrian stronghold of Santa Severina, and as a result his brother Herman remained in custody as a bargaining chip. Santa Severina only finally surrendered during the winter of 1075–6.[20] Even then Abelard remained a problem, taking refuge in the strongly fortified town of Sant'Agata di Puglia (on the border with the principality of Salerno, about 50 km east of Benevento), which had once again to be besieged, and it was only in the early months of 1078 that he finally gave in.[21]

Only a few months later there was a further, and very serious, rebellion. Once more Guiscard himself helped to provoke it. He used the occasion of the marriage of one of his daughters to the son of the north Italian Margrave Azzo of Este, celebrated at Troia, probably in the summer of 1078, to demand an 'aid' (Latin: *auxilium*) from the nobles who attended the ceremony, to augment his daughter's marriage portion. This was one of the usual prerogatives of overlordship, but it was clearly an innovation for the duke to seek this from his men. William of Apulia recorded that Robert had not asked for such a subsidy when his other daughter had been sent to Byzantium to marry the emperor's son, and that this was much resented by his leading men: 'the Norman counts frequently complained among themselves about such bad and infuriating behaviour of the duke towards them, but for a long time they kept their anger and disloyalty concealed'.[22] Those involved in the subsequent conspiracy included the usual malcontents: Abelard, Count Peter II of Andria and his cousin Count Amicus. But what made this rebellion especially dangerous was the number of others involved. Geoffrey of Conversano and his brother Count Robert of

---

19 *Cod. Dipl. Barese*, iii.27–8 no. 16. Robert's rule was acknowledged at Trani for the first recorded time in April 1074, and again in April 1075: *Cod. Dipl. Barese* ix.13–15 no. 7; Prologo, *Carte di Trani*, pp. 60–1 no. 19.

20 *Amatus*, VII.20–1, pp. 312–14; *Malaterra*, III.5–6, pp. 59–60.

21 *Amatus*, VIII.34, pp. 373–4; *Malaterra*, III.6, p. 60. The chronology of neither account is very clear, and that of Amatus telescopes events which took place over several years, but it places his submission at about the time of the death of Richard I of Capua (i.e. *c.* April 1078).

22 *W. Apulia*, III, lines 486–51, pp. 190–2 (quote, lines 509–10).

Montescaglioso dominated south-central Apulia. Jordan of Capua, who was already at loggerheads with Guiscard, came out in support of the rebels, along with his cousin Count Henry of Monte Sant'Angelo (who had succeeded his elder brother Richard, another of the rebels of 1072–3). Furthermore Abelard exploited important connections within the towns of coastal Apulia. He arranged to marry the daughter of Argyritzus, the Bari notable who had been instrumental in surrendering the city to Guiscard in 1071 [above, p. 136], having already married off his sister to a man called Gradilon, who to judge by his name was a man of Slav origins, presumably of high status, an immigrant (or descendant of immigrants) from Dalmatia, of whom there were many in northern Apulia.[23]

The rebellion broke out in the early days of 1079 when Count Peter seized Trani, his former possession of which he had been deprived in 1073. On 3 February 1079 Bari was betrayed to Abelard, who a little while later captured Ascoli. The rebels were assisted by the urban militias of most of the northern Apulian towns (although since such places as Andria and Corato were still subject to Count Peter we should not be too surprised at this). But what made the rebellion especially threatening was that the Apulian revolt seems to have been accompanied by disturbances in other areas as well: when it broke out, Guiscard was marching into Calabria to quell an insurrection at Cosenza, and it was only once he had solved the problems there – seemingly by concessions rather than repression – that he was free to turn his attention to Apulia. But when he did march north, with a relatively small force of some 460 knights, even though he was outnumbered by his opponents, his response was as usual speedy and decisive. Abelard was wounded in a battle outside Bari, the town of Giovenazzo, which had remained loyal to the duke, was reinforced, the rebel strongholds in inland Apulia were picked off one by one, and perhaps most importantly, in the autumn of 1079 Robert came to an agreement with Prince Jordan, brokered by Desiderius of Montecassino, which removed his enemies' principal hopes of external aid. Count Amicus submitted to him, and soon afterwards his nephews Geoffrey of Conversano and Robert of Montescaglioso changed sides. Bari surrendered to him early in 1080, and Taranto in April, after which Count Peter, the last of his enemies left in the field, also submitted and surrendered Trani.[24]

---

23 The conspirators were listed by *W. Apulia*, II, lines 515–38, pp. 192–4. Slavs: Martin, *Pouille*, pp. 504–9. There were Slav colonies in the Gargano region, and Count Amicus had led an expedition into Dalmatia in 1074/5. Cf. *W. Apulia*, commentary on p. 303.

24 *W. Apulia*, III, lines 539–687, pp. 194–202, is the principal account of this revolt, but some further details may be gleaned from *Chron. Cas.* III.45, p. 423; Lupus, *Annales, MGH SS* v.60.

The rebellion had been sufficiently serious to take fifteen months finally to suppress, and represented something of a watershed in terms of Guiscard's response to the opposition he had faced. The Norman rebels who submitted remained personally inviolate, even Abelard who witnessed a ducal diploma in June 1080. But such mercy did not extend to Gradilon, who was savagely mutilated after his capture at Trevico in June(?) 1079.[25] Non-Norman outsiders risked the loss of far more than just some, or even all, of their lands. But retribution, albeit less brutal, also overtook some of the Norman rebels. In the wake of this insurrection Robert undertook a considerable territorial reorganisation in Apulia, installing loyal followers in lordships confiscated from his opponents. Even before the rebellion had been finally suppressed, he had granted Amicus's possession of Spinazzola to a former vassal of that count, Godfrey, who had stayed faithful to him.[26] Not only did he retain control of Trani, but this time he did confiscate Taranto, and also nearby Castellaneta, from Count Peter. Any rights of the latter's nephew Richard were summarily disregarded. Robert retained Taranto in his own hands, but Castellaneta and Mottola were given to another of his nephews, Richard, the illegitimate son of his long-dead brother Drogo, who in return for this grant later accompanied him on his expedition against Byzantium.[27] Abelard's former possession of S. Agata di Puglia was entrusted to a Breton called Rainulf, whose son was later (under Roger Borsa) to be the ducal constable, and may be considered therefore a proven loyalist.[28] When another of the rebels, the duke's nephew Robert of Montescaglioso, died in July 1080 his extensive lordship was split up. His brother Geoffrey (of Conversano) was allowed to inherit Matera, but Montescaglioso itself was granted to a man called Humphrey, from an entirely different family, and Robert himself took over Tricarico.[29] Furthermore, to strengthen his hold on Bari, Robert secured from Gregory VII, at their meeting at Ceprano in June 1080, the translation of one of his trusted clerical *familiares*, Bishop Ursus of Rapolla, to the archbishopric of that city.[30]

---

25 Abelard: Ménager, *Recueil*, pp. 101–4 no. 31. Gradilon: *W. Apulia*, III, lines 611–14, p. 198. This occurred before Robert went to Salerno, where we know him to have been in June 1079: Ménager, *Recueil*, pp. 95–7 no. 27.

26 *Reg. Neap. Arch. Mon.* v.89–90 no. 430.

27 Houben, *Die Abtei Venosa*, pp. 269–70 no. 37. The titular former lord of Taranto was still alive, and in August 1080 residing with his uncle in Andria: Houben, *ibid.*, pp. 264–6 no. 32.

28 Ménager, *Recueil*, pp. 187–91 no. 55; *Cod. Dipl. Aversa*, pp. 10–11 no. 6.

29 Lupus, *Annales*, *MGH SS* v.60; Jahn, *Untersuchungen zur normannische Herrschaft*, pp. 286–9 (again, a helpful guide to some very dubious charter evidence).

30 F. Babudri, 'Le Note autobiografiche di Giovanni, arcidiacono barese e la cronologia dell'arcivescovato di Ursone a Bari', *Archivio storico pugliese*, ii (1949), 134–46. According to the *Anonymi Barensis Chron.*, *RIS* v.153, Ursus actually entered Bari on 4 August 1080.

We are less well informed about the last revolt against Guiscard, in 1082–3. It would appear that Abelard, who had abandoned southern Italy and fled to the court of Alexius Comnenus, returned, once more well supplied with Byzantine money, to stir up trouble while Robert was busy in Epiros. He was joined by his half-brother Herman, the lord of Canne. At the same time there were revolts against Norman rule at Troia and Ascoli in the Capitanata, the former suppressed with uncharacteristic savagery by the duke's son Roger Borsa, and in southern Apulia Geoffrey of Conversano attempted to seize Oria. Guiscard landed at Otranto in April 1082 and moved immediately to raise the siege of Oria. But while Malaterra, who tells us of this episode, implied that the rebellion was thereafter very rapidly suppressed, in fact Canne, the final rebel stronghold, only surrendered in June 1083. Hence, as with the 1079/80 revolt, it took Robert fifteen months to quell this insurrection, which suggests that it was a good bit more serious than the chroniclers imply. The substantial fine which Robert levied from the citizens of Bari suggests that they too were involved.[31] Abelard fled once more to Constantinople, where he died soon afterwards, but it seems that the other rebel leaders got off fairly lightly. Once again Geoffrey's relationship with his uncle, or perhaps a speedy submission, or possibly his connections with other powerful nobles (his wife was the daughter of the count of Boiano) protected him, and he appears not to have lost any of his extensive territories. By September 1083 he was acknowledging Guiscard's rule in his charters, and he appears to have accompanied (or been made to accompany) Robert on his second and last expedition against Byzantium in 1084/ 5.[32] Similarly, despite the sack of Canne by Robert's army, Herman later recovered his lordship over the town, which he retained until his departure on the First Crusade in 1096.[33]

However, while there were recurrent revolts in Apulia, and a hard core of persistent rebels who were ready to take part in anti-ducal conspiracies, one must not exaggerate the extent of the disaffection among the nobility. Other Norman counts such as Robert of Loritello and Gerard of Buonalbergo – who were associated with Roger Borsa in ruling the duchy during Guiscard's absence in 1081 – remained consistently loyal. Gerard was one

31 *Malaterra*, III.34, pp. 77–8; *W. Apulia*, IV, lines 506–36, pp. 230–2, and 309; Lupus, *Annales, MGH SS* v.61; *Anonymi Barensis Chron.* (as above); *The Alexiad of Anna Comnena*, p. 127 (the evidence for Abelard's return).
32 Jahn, *Untersuchungen zur normannische Herrschaft*, pp. 244–5, 372–4 no. 5; *Orderic*, IV.32.
33 Jahn, *Untersuchungen zur normannische Herrschaft*, pp. 148–9; E.M. Jamison, 'Some notes on the *Anonymi Gesta Francorum*, with special reference to the Norman contingent from south Italy and Sicily', *Studies in French Language and Literature Presented to Professor Mildred K. Pope* (Manchester 1939), pp. 199–200.

of the leaders of the ducal army fighting against Richard of Capua in 1073.[34] A number of other prominent men were entirely ignored by the chroniclers, and we may therefore assume either remained uninvolved or assisted Guiscard – the chroniclers are much less specific concerning those who supported him than about his enemies. Perhaps the most interesting of these figures was Count Peter of Lesina – for although his brother Amicus and his cousin Peter were two of the most inveterate rebels we have no hint that he was ever involved in the insurrections. In December 1081, at a time when the last rebellion may already have been in preparation, Peter of Lesina was in the company of Robert of Loritello, witnessing the renunciation by Abbot Desiderius (another long-term ally of Guiscard) of Montecassino's claims over the monastery of Tremiti. After Guiscard's death he accompanied Roger Borsa on his visit to Sicily in the summer of 1086, and he witnessed a further ducal charter in 1092.[35] It would seem therefore that he did not share his relations' hostility to the duke (although it should be pointed out that there is no evidence that they were involved in the last of the rebellions against Guiscard, nor that they opposed Roger Borsa after 1085). It may be that ruling a lordship in a peripheral area in the north of Apulia, Count Peter of Lesina was sufficiently far from the main centres of ducal power not to have felt threatened by Guiscard's efforts to strengthen his authority over his nobles. For in three of the four rebellions, whatever other grievances might have existed, Guiscard's own actions contributed to the outbreak, and in 1079 quite probably caused it. Furthermore, in the other instance, it is at least possible that in 1082–3 his efforts to recruit participants and money for his expedition against Byzantium, which was far from popular [above, p. 217], may have been a factor in rousing resentment. The rebellion in Troia was caused, we are told, by opposition to the tribute he demanded. But in 1081 Robert took one prudent precaution – for his old opponent Count Amicus accompanied him on the expedition.[36]

The most obvious consequence of the revolts was the great extension of ducal lordship. By the 1080s most of the larger towns in Apulia – Bari, Trani, Brindisi, Taranto, and Otranto on the coast, as well as (probably smaller, but still important) inland settlements such as Troia, Melfi, Venosa and Acerenza – were under the direct dominion of the duke. When one adds to this Salerno (probably the largest town in mainland south Italy at this period), the overlordship of Amalfi, extensive property in northern Calabria, and Palermo and half of Messina in Sicily, the scale of Guiscard's

---

34 *Amatus*, VII.22, p. 314.
35 *Cod. Dipl. Tremiti*, ii.250–3 no. 84; Ménager, *Recueil*, pp. 181–6 nos 52–4, 212–14 no. 60; *Les Chartes de Troia*, pp. 134–5 no. 27.
36 *W. Apulia*, IV, lines 506–7, p. 231; *The Alexiad of Anna Comnena*, pp. 146–7.

resources becomes apparent. Tribute from the towns, rents from ducal lands, and a substantial share of the booty from successful warfare in Sicily, and in the 1080s against Byzantium (at the battle outside Durazzo in 1081 the emperor's tent was reserved for the duke), meant that by the later stages of his rule he was extremely wealthy. The scale of his cash resources and treasure can be seen from the long account of his benefactions to Montecassino given by the abbey chronicle. Most of these gifts came from the 1070s onwards, and his first major donation of real property to that monastery only in June 1080, after the suppression of the third rebellion – the gift of a monastery and other revenues in Taranto, a town which had only very recently been confiscated.[37] Similarly his financing of the rebuilding of Salerno cathedral took place after 1077 [see above, p. 140]. By 1085 the scale of ducal resources and power was very different from what it had been when Guiscard assumed the title in 1059.

The aristocracy and ducal government after 1085

By the time of Robert's death southern Italy was dominated by a small group of interconnected Norman families, or more properly kin-groups (for we should be thinking in terms of extended groupings with several distinct branches rather than nuclear families or *lignages*). Foremost among these were the duke's own relatives. In addition to Roger of Sicily, ruling the southern half of Calabria as well as the island of Sicily, Guiscard's son Bohemond was given much of the ducal property in southern Apulia by his half-brother Duke Roger in 1088 [see below, p. 257]. But by the later eleventh century there were four further comital dynasties descended from Robert's siblings. His brother William's son Count Robert of the Principate (fl. 1080–99) was probably the wealthiest and most powerful aristocrat in the principality of Salerno after the duke; his massive seigneury stretched from the mouth of the River Sele on the western coastal plain south of Salerno eastwards to Ascoli and Candela on the border of southern Apulia. This eastward extension of their interests led him and his family to be generous patrons of the southern Apulian abbey of Venosa, where his elder brothers were buried, as well as of the leading Salernitan monastery of

---

37   Ménager, *Recueil*, pp. 101–4 no. 31; *Chron. Cas.* III.58, pp. 438–40. The emperor's tent: *Malaterra*, III.27, p. 74. For the wider context, G.A. Loud, 'Coinage, wealth and plunder in the age of Robert Guiscard', *English Historical Review* cxiv (1999), 815–43.

Cava.[38] Count Robert's younger brother Tancred became an important landowner in Sicily in the early 1090s [above, p. 176]. Another of Guiscard's nephews, Count Robert of Loritello (d. *c.* 1096), was the major figure in the northern Capitanata, whose interests stretched, as we have seen, up into the Abruzzi [above, pp. 142–3]. Meanwhile the latter's younger brother Rodulf was established as count of Catanzaro in Calabria from *c.* 1088, with the agreement of Roger of Sicily, although he remained a ducal vassal [above, p. 180] – his descendants also retained some property in the Capitanata.[39] Despite his involvement in the rebellions against his uncle, Geoffrey of Conversano (d. 1100) remained very influential in southern Apulia, holding Conversano, Monopoli and Noicattaro (all south of Bari), Matera (inland and further south on the Murge ridge), and Satriano on the border between Apulia and the principality of Salerno. Fairly soon after Guiscard's death – certainly before 1089 – he acquired the important port of Brindisi, possession of which confirmed his dominance of the coastal region of southern Apulia, and he also gained Nardo in the Terra d'Otranto, probably before 1092. Indeed he and his sons were among the major profiteers from the disputes which developed in Apulia under Roger Borsa.[40] In addition, yet another of Guiscard's nephews, Richard the Seneschal, was lord of Mottola and Castellanata, near Taranto, from 1080/1 [above, p. 243], although he appears never to have used, or been granted, a comital title. He remained a close ally of his cousin the duke, but his lordship disappeared after he died childless *c.* 1117/18.[41]

A number of separate comital lineages also developed among the extended family of Prince Richard I of Capua. His younger brother Rainulf became established as count of Caiazzo (about 15 km upstream from Capua on the River Volturno), probably after 1078 during the reign of his nephew Jordan, to whom he was close [above, p. 235]. He brought a whole series of former Lombard counties under his control (notably Caiazzo, Alife, Telese and Sant'Agata dei Goti), and his descendants dominated the region between Capua and Benevento. His son Robert, who succeeded him in 1087/8,

38 E. Cuozzo, *Normanni, nobilità e cavalleria* (Salerno 1995), pp. 97–100; Houben, *Die Abtei von Venosa*, pp. 267 no. 34 (1080), 277–9 no. 47 (1085), 287 no. 55 (1088), 303–5 nos 73–4 (1096, 1097), 307–9 no. 76 (1097), 313–15 no. 80 (1101), 316–17 no. 82 (1103), 318–19 nos 84–5 (1105), 322–3 no. 89 (1112).
39 For the latter, *Cod. Vat. Lat.* 4939 [the chartulary of St Sophia, Benevento], fols 207v–208r (June 1118); Benevento, Museo del Sannio, Fondo S. Sofia, vol. 10 no. 26, *Les Chartes de Troia*, pp. 168–71 no. 43 (both November 1120).
40 Jahn, *Untersuchungen zur normannische Herrschaft*, pp. 241–54; Martin, *Pouille*, pp. 737–9.
41 E. Cuozzo, 'La Contea normanna di Mottola e Castellaneta', *Archivio storico per le provincie napoletane* cx (1992), 7–46, which is also a very helpful guide to the problems of Richard's charters.

acted as guardian for Richard II of Capua until the latter came of age in 1093, and a charter of his still acknowledged Prince Richard's overlordship in 1105 (although this may have been because it suited him to do so at a time when both were allies in a campaign in the north of the principality).[42] But thereafter Robert and his son Rainulf II, who succeeded him *c.* 1116, became increasingly independent, and their interests turned eastwards towards Benevento and away from Capua. Their pretensions towards independence were shown too by their charters, which omitted the regnal years of the princes while imitating the outward style and phraseology of the princely *scriptorium*.[43] Jordan I of Capua created another county for his younger brother Jonathan, the centre of which was at Carinola (20 km north-west of Capua). After Jonathan's death in 1094 this passed to a third brother Bartholomew and his descendants, with whom it remained until the German conquest of the kingdom of Sicily in 1194. For some years in the early twelfth century, from *c.* 1112 until 1134, the counts of Carinola also ruled the duchy of Gaeta.[44] But in addition the princes' lands and claims in the Gargano region, derived from their ancestor Rainulf of Aversa's share of the division of Apulia among the Norman leaders in 1042, fell to another brother of Richard of Capua, Robert, and his sons, who became known as the counts of Monte Sant'Angelo. Their possessions included Lucera on the Capitanata plain, and Lacedonia in central Apulia, and their vassals included a number of other Capitanata barons, such as William of Nonant, lord of Fiorentino. The counts of Monte Sant'Angelo retained their links with the principality of Capua through their patronage of Montecassino: shortly before 1100 Count Henry established a hospital (*xenodochium*) which was subordinated to Montecassino outside the town of Sant'Angelo. Count Robert had married Drogo de Hauteville's widow Gaitelgrima, one of Guaimar IV of Salerno's daughters, and her brother John, who had been driven from Salerno by Guiscard in 1077, eventually became the abbot in charge of his nephew's hospital. The counts of Monte

---

42 *Regesto di S. Angelo in Formis*, ed. M. Inguanez (Montecassino 1925), pp. 84–6 no. 28 [Loud, 'Calendar of the diplomas of the Norman princes of Capua', no. 46]; E. Gattula, *Accessiones ad Historiam Abbatiae Casinensis* (Venice 1734), pp. 222–3, and cf. the princely charter confirming this grant, *ibid.*, pp. 223–4. For the context, *Chron. Cas.* IV.25, p. 491. More generally, G. Tescione, 'Roberto, conte normanno di Alife, Caiazzo e S. Agata dei Goti', *Archivio storico di Terra di Lavoro* iv (1975), 1–52.

43 G.A. Loud, 'The Norman Counts of Caiazzo and the abbey of Montecassino', *Monastica* i *Scritti raccolti in memoria del xv centenario della nascità di S. Benedetto* (Miscellanea Cassinese 44, 1981), 199–217, at pp. 201–3.

44 Hoffmann, 'Die Anfänge der Normannen' [above, Ch. II, n. 10], 106–9; W. Schütz, *Catalogus Comitum. Versuch einer Territorialgliederung Kampaniens unter den Normannen von 1000 bis 1140 von Benevent bis Salerno* (Frankfurt 1993), pp. 372–5.

Sant'Angelo were the principal obstacle to Robert of Loritello's pre-eminence in the Capitanata region, and it is possible (though unprovable) that their role in two of the revolts against Guiscard had as much to do with rivalry towards the latter's nephew and loyal supporter as with any intrinsic dislike of the duke. However, this branch of the Capuan princely family died out *c.* 1105.[45]

The third extended kin-group among the Norman aristocracy was that of the sons of Amicus, who had for a considerable period been the Hautevilles' principal rivals in Apulia. By 1085 their participation in the insurrections against Guiscard had cost them dearly, and the family was nowhere near as powerful as it had been only a generation earlier, having lost Trani, Giovinazzo, Spinazzola, and Taranto and its surrounding lordship. None the less when Guiscard died Count Peter II still held Andria, and his cousins Peter and Amicus retained the counties of Lesina and Molfetta. The family therefore remained a significant power both in the coastal region north of Bari and in the northern Capitanata. They also retained links across the Adriatic with Dalmatia. Amicus's son Godfrey was returning from there when he visited the monastery on the Tremiti islands in 1092/3. But the charter which he granted as a result of that visit is revealing, for it suggests that he may have been in exile or have taken refuge in Dalmatia, and that his restoration of property in the Campomarino area in the northern Capitanata to Tremiti in August 1093 was a thank-offering because God had 'restored him to his power'.[46] Godfrey was still in control of Molfetta in 1100, and even extended his power to acquire Canne – profiting from the departure of its previous lord Herman on the First Crusade, from which he did not return.[47] However, in the longer term his branch of the family continued to decline. In 1111 the two *castella* Godfrey had restored to the abbey of Tremiti in 1093 were granted to the abbey as if *de novo* by Count Robert II of Loritello, who seems by this date to have taken control of Campomarino. The 'sons of Amicus' may also have lost Molfetta. Roger 'son and heir of Count Godfrey' (fl. 1120–9) did retain his inland lordship at Terlizzi, but significantly no longer employed the comital title.[48] However, while the loss of Campomarino was undoubted, it is possible

---

45   Jahn, *Untersuchungen zur normannische Herrschaft*, pp. 322–30. For the *xenodochium*, *Le Colonie Cassinese in Capitanata* ii *Gargano*, ed. T. Leccisotti (Miscellanea Cassinese 15, 1938), pp. 29–37 nos 1–3. For John, *Amatus* VIII.28, p. 369.

46   *Cod. Dipl. Tremiti*, iii.255–7 no. 86.

47   *Cod. Dipl. Barese*, iii.48–9 no. 32; *Cod. Dipl. Barese* vii *Le Carte di Molfetta (1076–1309)*, ed. F. Carabellese (Bari 1912), 8–9 no. 4; *Cod. Dipl. Barese* viii *Le Pergamene di Barletta, Archivio Capitolare (897–1285)*, ed. F. Nitti di Vito (Bari 1914), 48–9 no. 26; Ughelli, *Italia Sacra*, viii.790–3; Jahn, *Untersuchungen zur normannische Herrschaft*, pp. 221–2.

48   *Cod. Dipl. Tremiti*, iii.262–4 no. 90; *Cod. Dipl. Barese*, iii.58 no. 41, 62–3 no. 45.

that what was taking place elsewhere was rather the continued division of the family's holdings – if the Count William of Canne attested in 1117 was another son of Count Godfrey.[49] Similarly the Lesina branch of this kin-group may have divided their lands, giving rise to a new county of Civitate from *c.* 1120, or perhaps a little earlier.[50] The evidence is exiguous, and we cannot be entirely certain that these later counts of Canne and Civitate were related to the 'sons of Amicus' family – it is possible, although less likely, that other nobles were whittling away at their possessions and adopting the comital style. [However, see below, p. 253] But whatever the case with regard to Canne and Civitate, the family retained the county of Andria until dispossessed by King Roger in 1132, and that of Lesina until 1155/6.

Two further comital dynasties ruled over important seigneuries in the mountainous centre of the peninsula. The counts of Ariano were descended from Gerard of Buonalbergo, Guiscard's long-time ally and nephew of his first wife Alberada. Gerard, who died in 1086, his son Herbert (fl. 1088–1100) and grandson Jordan (d. 1127) ruled over a lordship which dominated Irpinia, the region east of Benevento on the border of Apulia proper. The *caput* of this county became established in the hilltop town of Ariano, some 25 km east of Benevento. This seigneury may indeed have been one of the earliest established by the Normans in Italy – Gerard appears to have had a predecessor, or possibly a local competitor, a certain Count Hubert, from whom one undated charter survives, and who was present at the Battle of Civitate – but since Gerard had already established himself in this region by *c.* 1047 he is unlikely to have been Hubert's direct successor, even if he later confirmed the grant that the latter made in his one and only surviving charter.[51] It is possible that Gerard was another relation of Guiscard, perhaps through the latter's mother [above, pp. 113–14]. The counts of Ariano were much involved with affairs in and around Benevento, and were major patrons of the town's wealthiest and most prestigious monastery, St Sophia. From 1119 onwards Count Jordan became embroiled in a bitter dispute for supremacy in this area with Rainulf II of Caiazzo.[52]

To the north of Benevento, and stretching from the Monti del Matese northwards as far as the valley of the River Sangro, lies the region known

---

49 *Cod. Dipl. Barese*, viii.56 no. 33.
50 Dating and evidence: Martin, *Pouille*, pp. 719–20; the interpretation is mine.
51 *W. Apulia*, II, line 132, p. 138. The views criticised are those of E. Cuozzo, 'Intorno alla prima contea normanna nell'Italia meridionale', *Cavalieri alla conquista del Sud. Studi sull'Italia normanna in memoria di Léon-Robert Ménager*, ed. E. Cuozzo and J.-M. Martin (Bari 1998), pp. 171–93.
52 *Falco*, pp. 42–6, 52–4, 60–2.

from the twelfth century onwards as Molise. This derived its name from a family from Moulins-la-Marche on the southern border of Normandy (modern dépt. Orne), whose ancestor Guimund had fallen foul of William the Conqueror and been driven from Normandy in the early 1050s [above, p. 89]. His son Radulfus or Raoul had probably already made his way to Italy, for William of Apulia described him as count of Boiano as early as 1053. Possibly this reference to his comital title was retrospective, but by the time of his death, between 1092 and 1095, he had established a massive and virtually independent lordship in this mountainous inland region, taking over a number of former Lombard counties which had been based in the small towns of Venafro, Isernia, Boiano, Trivento and Larino. Like the counts of Ariano, Radulfus and his descendants were also benefactors of St Sophia, Benevento, but their attempts to extend their lordship were not directed south towards Benevento but rather north into the Abruzzi and eastwards down the Biferno and Trigno valleys towards the Adriatic. They also retained links with the principality of Capua, within which the western part of their lordship was in theory situated – although after 1090 the princes rarely if ever intervened in this inland region. The counts were benefactors of Montecassino, perhaps hardly surprising since this was relatively close (only c. 20 km) to Venafro in the south-west of their lands; and in the 1090s they still recognised Capuan princely overlordship, although after 1100 any overt subordination seems to have disappeared. None the less they remained patrons of Montecassino, to which Count Hugh (I) gave the *castrum* of Vitecuso (8 km north-west of Venafro) in 1105, and where his son Simon was buried after his death in an earthquake at Isernia in 1117.[53] Although their lordship was situated in a relatively poor upland area, the counts of Boiano (or counts of Molise as they became known after 1140) were militarily formidable – in the mid-twelfth century their lands (by then somewhat reduced from what they had held at the beginning of the century) contained some 250 knights' fees, and with the emergency levy (the *augmentum*) they could muster (at least in theory) a force of 486 knights.[54]

A number of Count Radulfus's brothers also emigrated to southern Italy in the wake of the family's ruin in Normandy. One of these, Guimund, made his career in the principality of Salerno quite separately from the

---

53 Cf. Gattula, *Accessiones*, p. 207 (March 1092), and *Reg. S. Angelo in Formis*, pp. 47–50 no. 17 (February 1097), both of which acknowledge Prince Richard II, with Gattula, *Accessiones*, pp. 224–5 (the Vitecuso charter), which does not. For Simon: *Chron. Cas.* IV.62, p. 525. More generally, A. de Francesco, 'Origini e sviluppo del feudalismo nel Molise fino alla caduta della dominazione normanna', *Archivio storico per le provincie napoletane* xxxv (1910), 70–98, especially pp. 78–85; Ménager, 'Inventaire des familles normands', pp. 332–6.

54 E.M. Jamison, 'The administration of the county of Molise in the twelfth and thirteenth centuries', *English Historical Review* xliv (1929), 536.

main branch of the family. There he was closely associated with Robert Guiscard's brother, Count William of the Principate – being excommunicated along with the count by Alexander II for his depredations at the expense of Salerno cathedral in 1067, and present at William's deathbed in 1080. He held land in the valley of S. Severino to the north of Salerno, and married Emma, the heiress to Eboli (although the later lords of Eboli seem to have been descended from her first husband Radulfus Trincanocte rather than Guimund). Guimund was, however, dead by 1083, by which stage his widow was ruling over his lordship in the name of her under-age grandson.[55]

These five kin-groups therefore provided not merely the overall rulers of Norman Italy, but the most powerful aristocratic lineages therein. There were of course a number of other families which were also important, if not quite to the same degree. In the principality of Salerno there were, for example, the counts of Sarno, descended from a certain Count Affredus who married Gaitelgrima, the daughter of Prince Guaimar IV who had previously been married to two other prominent Normans, Count Drogo of Apulia and Count Robert of Monte Sant'Angelo. From 1081, by which time she had been widowed for a third time, she was ruling this lordship on the northern border of the principality in the name of her son Richard.[56] (When one takes into account also the active role played by Guiscard's wife Sichelgaita, the principality of Salerno had more than its fair share of vigorous dowagers in the 1080s.) Yet the counts of Sarno, who continued to rule this seigneury until they either died out or were driven out by King Roger c. 1138/9, were unusual in that they were styled as counts although they had a relatively restricted lordship, were not directly related to either the princely or ducal dynasties, nor descended from the 'counts' who shared out Apulia in 1042, or (as was the case with the counts of Ariano and Boiano) from counts established by the time of the Battle of Civitate in 1053. Apart from the junior branches of the ruling dynasties of Capua and Apulia, and the counts of Sarno, we rarely if ever find noble families in Norman Italy adopting a comital title after c. 1060. Where charters ascribe the title of count to members of other Norman families/kin-groups (apart from the six discussed above), these are almost always later forgeries, or

---

55 *Italia Pontificia*, viii.351–2 nos 23–5; Houben, *Die Abtei Venosa*, p. 267 no. 34; *Amatus*, VIII.12, pp. 352–3; *Le Pergamene di S. Nicola Gallucanta (Secc. IX–XII)*, ed. P. Cherubini (Altavilla Silentina 1991), pp. 255–60 nos 100–1 (1083), 279–80 no. 110 (1089); Cava, *Arca* xvi.36 (1095). Radulfus Trincanocte may have been Count Rainulf II of Aversa; *Chron. Cas.* II.66, p. 301.

56 Cava, *Arm Mag.* B.17, B.24 (May 1082); Schütz, *Catalogus Comitum*, pp. 528–34. Genealogical chart: G.A. Loud, 'Continuity and change in Norman Italy: the Campania in the eleventh and twelfth centuries', *Journal of Medieval History* xxii (1996), 327 [reprinted *Conquerors and Churchmen*].

interpolated documents, or sometimes careless transcriptions or interpretations by sixteenth- and seventeenth-century antiquaries – as in a number of the fragmentary copies which are almost all that survives of the once rich archive of the Hautevilles' house monastery of Holy Trinity, Venosa.[57] Other cases are few. A count of Calvi, in the principality of Capua, attested only in 1089–92, was a direct replacement for a dispossessed Lombard count. The counts of Civitate and Manopello, who appeared *c.* 1100 on the northern frontier of Norman settlement, probably came from collateral branches of an existing comital family; most likely that of the counts of Lesina. Richard, the first count of Manopello, may have been one of the sons of Count Peter II of Lesina, or just possibly related to the counts of Loritello.[58] But whatever the truth about his origin, apart from in this peripheral region there were no new counts in Norman Italy in the late eleventh century.

However, although a comital title was prestigious, it conveyed no special powers that were not enjoyed by other territorial lords who lacked such a distinction. They exercised exactly the same judicial and financial rights over their lordships as did counts, and while some counts like those of Monte Sant'Angelo and Loritello had a number of other seigneurs as their vassals, there were other *domini* or *seniores* (the contemporary terms most normally employed for such lords) who if they acknowledged any dependence at all did so only to the duke.[59] Thus in southern Apulia, neither the descendants of Humphrey of Montescaglioso, installed by Guiscard in 1080, nor those of Aitard of Lecce, one of whose sons held Lecce and another Gravina from about the same date, were counts. (The only documents which refer to them as such are forgeries – and the Montescaglioso documents in particular are something of a minefield.)[60] Nor indeed was Richard the

---

57 E.g. the attribution of a comital title to Arnulf of Lavello (possible, but no other evidence), and to Rainald Malcovenant of Marsico (unlikely, not used by his son): Houben, *Die Abtei Venosa*, pp. 252–3 no. 18, 259–61 nos 25, 27, p. 296 no. 63.
58 Calvi: *Cod. Dipl. Caiet.*, ii.142–3 no. 262; *Cod. Dipl. Aversa*, pp. 401–2 no. 54. Manopello: Biblioteca apostolica vaticana, Archivio di S. Pietro, Pergamene Caps LXXII.53(i) [the chartulary of S. Salvatore di Maiella], fol. 27r (1098), has Count Richard as the son of Count Peter (of Lesina?); Rivera, 'Le Conquiste dei primi normanni in Teate, Penne, Apruzzo e Valva' [above, Ch. III, n. 138], p. 116. A charter of Richard of L'Aigle described him as count of Pico (in the north of the principality of Capua) in 1091, but a later charter of his (1107) did not use the comital title, nor did the Montecassino chronicle accord it to him. Was this an unsuccessful claim, or transcription error? *Cod. Dipl. Caiet.*, ii.143–5, 178–80 nos 263, 282; *Chron. Cas.* IV.7, 12, pp. 471, 481.
59 Martin, *Pouille*, p. 717.
60 Jahn, *Untersuchungen zur normannische Herrschaft*, pp. 286–311; G. Antonucci, 'Goffredo, conte di Lecce e di Montescaglioso', *Archivio storico per la Calabria e la Lucania* iii (1933), 449–59; E. Cuozzo, 'La Contea di Montescaglioso nei secoli XI–XIII', *Archivio storico per le provincie napoletane* ciii (1985), 7–37; Martin, *Pouille*, pp. 736, 741–3.

Seneschal a count, although he was a Hauteville, and unlike some of his relatives a close ally of both Guiscard and Roger Borsa. Yet these men were in no sense inferior in authority to those who were counts. Roger of Sicily married one of his daughters by his first wife to Count Henry of Monte Sant'Angelo, but was some years later prepared to give another as wife to Rodulf 'Machabeus', son and successor to Humphrey of Montescaglioso.[61] Similarly in the principality of Salerno, alongside the counts of the Principate and of Sarno, there were other powerful territorial lords who did not enjoy a comital title: but Roger son of Turgisius, lord of S. Severino in the north of the region, and a major landowner also in the Cilento region in the south of the principality (fl. 1081–1125), and the brothers Roger and Robert, successively lords of Eboli (attested 1089–1121), enjoyed just as much authority and status. When Count William II of the Principate swore to protect the property of the abbey of Cava in April 1116 his oath was witnessed and guaranteed by Prince Robert I of Capua, Hoel lord of S. Agata di Puglia, the ducal constable, and Robert of Eboli. The last two barons were clearly the count's social equals, even if neither of them possessed such an extensive seigneury. Similar oaths to respect Cava's property were sworn a few years earlier by Roger of S. Severino and Jordan, lord of Nocera (the younger brother of Prince Robert I of Capua). Roger's was guaranteed by Prince Robert, his brother Jordan and Robert of Eboli, while among the witnesses to Jordan's oath was the count of Sarno.[62] Nor do the marriage connections of those families which possessed a comital title mark them off from those who did not. If William I of the Principate married a niece of Prince Guaimar IV, and the counts of Sarno were descended from one of his daughters, Roger of S. Severino married his granddaughter, while his great-niece Mabilia was married to Robert of Eboli, and after his death in 1121 she wed another Norman baron, Simon of Théville.[63] Thus in the early twelfth-century principality of Salerno, and indeed the duchy of Apulia as well, possession of a comital title, however prestigious this may have been, did not make its possessors any different from other powerful territorial lords. This was shown some years later, after the creation of the unified kingdom of Sicily, when as part of his reorganisation of the mainland nobility King Roger granted comital titles c. 1150 to the grandson of Roger of S.

---

61 Houben, *Mezzogiorno normanno-svevo* [above, Ch. IV, n. 72], pp. 108–9.
62 Cava, *Arm Mag.* E.21 (September 1111), E.34 (March 1114), E.47, edited Loud, 'The abbey of Cava' [above, Ch. III, note 126], 176–7. Cf. G. Portanova, 'I Sanseverino dalle origini al 1125', *Benedictina* xxii (1976), 105–49.
63 Cava, *Arm Mag.* E.43 (March 1118), F.21 (February 1122), *Arca* xxi.21 (July 1119). For Roger's wife, *Arm Mag.* F.18 (June 1121); Loud, 'Continuity and change', pp. 329–31.

Severino (as count of Caserta) and to a descendant, probably the great-great-grandson, of Aitard of Lecce (as count of Montescaglioso).[64]

The two most significant changes which affected the nobility after Guiscard's death were the growing independence of some of the Apulian lords, and the creation of a new and extensive seigneury for Robert's eldest son Bohemond, whom his father had excluded from the ducal succession. As ducal rule became less effective in Apulia, so Guiscard's successors, his son Roger Borsa (duke 1085–1111) and grandson William (1111–27) concentrated their attention more on the principality of Salerno than on the duchy of Apulia proper (and especially the coast and the south of that region). One symptom of this change of focus was that whereas Guiscard was buried at Venosa, the Apulian abbey founded by his brother Drogo to which Robert had moved his elder brothers' remains in 1069, his successors chose to be interred in Salerno cathedral.[65] However, William of Apulia claimed that Robert Guiscard himself had decided, towards the end of his life, to make Salerno his principal residence in southern Italy. To that end Robert not only had the citadel overlooking the town strengthened but also had a new palace built within the walls.[66]

One must, however, ask whether this concentration on the west coast was the cause, or an effect, of the decline of ducal authority on the Adriatic side of the peninsula. Nor can one simply ascribe the problems which occurred in Apulia after 1085 to the character defects of Robert's successors compared with their formidable predecessor. Admittedly the (probably contemporary) obituary notices of dukes Roger and William contained within the chronicle attributed to Romuald of Salerno suggest why they might have had problems dealing with fractious underlings. Duke Roger was prone to 'pardoning those sentenced to death by him . . . a lover of peace, merciful to sinners, kind to his own men, peaceful to foreigners, amiable to all' who 'tried to win the love rather than the fear of both his own people and foreigners'. But while acknowledging that these and the very similar qualities displayed by his son contributed to their popularity, the author also recorded: 'although Duke William was much loved by his barons and men, he was however held to some extent in contempt by them for his kindness and patience'. Similarly, while extolling the many good qualities of Duke Roger, Geoffrey Malaterra noted that 'the influence of his

---

64   E. Cuozzo, *Catalogus Baronum. Commentario* (Rome 1984), pp. 271–5, 'La Contea di Montescaglioso', 30–2; Martin, *Pouille*, pp. 778–9.

65   Houben, *Die Abtei Venosa*, pp. 139–40, 145; *Romuald*, pp. 205, 214.

66   *W. Apulia*, V, lines 280–1, p. 250; cf. *ibid.*, III.465–9, pp. 188–90. The lower palace/castle was that later known as the Terracena palace.

piety made him a little remiss in the rigour of his justice'.[67] But there are other explanations for the problems in Apulia after 1085. Guiscard had after all faced a series of revolts from a group of persistent rebels. Nor had he made any provision for Bohemond, who apart from being some years older than Roger Borsa was also an experienced commander, and as a son born within marriage (albeit to a wife who had been repudiated) had good cause to resent his exclusion from the ducal succession in favour of a younger half-brother. If Robert *had* intended to provide for him out of his Balkan conquests, this enterprise had come to naught. Furthermore, after the death of Jordan I in 1090 the principality of Capua began to have similar problems: the princes' authority became limited to the region immediately round Capua itself, and the nobles of the north and east of the principality grew increasingly independent. The difficulties facing the dukes of Apulia after 1085 were a product of aristocratic particularism, not ducal incompetence. Furthermore, like his father, Roger faced opposition from within his own kin-group.

Nor did the challenge to Roger Borsa's authority follow immediately on his accession. Bohemond attended his court and witnessed several of his charters in the spring of 1086, if not thereafter. But so too did a number of the leading magnates from Apulia. Bohemond, Richard the Seneschal and Rodulf, the younger brother of Robert of Loritello, were with the duke at Salerno in May 1086.[68] Count Peter of Lesina accompanied him when he visited Sicily in August of that year.[69] The former rebels Herman of Canne and Amicus of Molfetta were with him in Calabria in May 1087.[70] It was only late in 1087 or early in 1088 that Bohemond, 'led by his ambition for the ducal honour', rebelled against him, although if we are to believe Orderic Vitalis the former may already have taken refuge with his cousin, Jordan of Capua. (However, Orderic was writing this section of his 'History' more than forty years later and a long way away, and should therefore be treated with some caution.) Roger defeated his brother in a skirmish near Benevento, but was unable to prevent him seizing Oria and causing chaos in southern Apulia and northern Calabria. Malaterra claimed that Duke Roger found it difficult to deal with this insurrection because of his financial problems, which in turn suggests that the ducal administration was already in difficulties. But even so he still retained the loyalty of powerful Apulian nobles such as Count Herbert of Ariano and those two former rebels, Peter of Andria and Henry of Monte Sant'Angelo, who witnessed a grant of his to

---

67 *Romuald*, pp. 205–6, 214; *Malaterra*, IV.4, p. 87.
68 Ménager, *Recueil*, pp. 178–80 no. 51. Bohemond also witnessed *ibid.*, nos 47, 49 and 57.
69 Ménager, *Recueil*, pp. 181–6 nos 52–4.
70 Ménager, *Recueil*, pp. 212–15 no. 60.

Venosa in August 1088. In the end Roger found it easier to buy his brother off, letting him keep Oria and granting him also Taranto, and Otranto and Gallipoli on the Salentine peninsula, as well as overlordship over his cousin Count Geoffrey of Conversano. This last was quite a shrewd move, because it necessarily embroiled Bohemond with a powerful and independently minded noble who had no wish to be subjected to him. A year or so later, after renewed trouble with Bohemond in northern Calabria, Duke Roger bought him off once more, with the cession of Bari and Giovinazzo, in return for his brother giving Cosenza (which he had seized) back to him.[71]

Roger and Bohemond had made peace by May 1090, but the latter remained a destabilising factor. In 1093, when Roger fell dangerously ill and was rumoured to have died, his brother took the opportunity to seize a number of places in Calabria, acting ostensibly in the name of the duke's infant son but acting in fact in his own interest. He was aided by one of the more important barons in northern Calabria, the duke's brother-in-law William de Grandmesnil. However, the duke's recovery and swift action by Roger of Sicily restored the situation. Nor was the duke quite as merciful as the opinions quoted above suggest. The lands of one of Bohemond's principal allies in Calabria were confiscated in 1088 and divided between Roger of Sicily and Rodulf of Loritello, the new count of Catanzaro. In 1093 William de Grandmesnil was forced into exile at Constantinople and his lands confiscated, although he was eventually able to redeem most of them in return for a substantial bribe.[72] While the proclamation of the Truce of God by Urban II at Melfi in September 1089 and again at Troia in March 1093 showed that law and order had deteriorated [above, p. 227], not all the Apulian nobles had deserted Duke Roger. In November 1093 he was at Melfi, along with counts Henry of Monte Sant'Angelo, Geoffrey of Conversano, Richard of Andria and Robert of Loritello.[73] After 1093 Bohemond became more amenable, taking part in the duke's expedition to reconquer Amalfi in 1096 – although he abandoned this to set off on the First Crusade.[74] And from 1096 he was absent from southern Italy for almost ten years, returning only in 1105 and then preoccupied with his expedition against Byzantium.

The support of his uncle Roger of Sicily was clearly very important to Duke Roger, even if it came at a price – part of the lands confiscated from

71 *Orderic*, IV.168; *Malaterra*, IV.4, 9–10, pp. 87 (quote), 90–1; Houben, *Die Abtei Venosa*, pp. 284–7 no. 54, 293–4 no. 60.
72 *Malaterra*, IV.11, 20–2, pp. 91–2, 99–101.
73 Ughelli, *Italia Sacra*, i.923.
74 *Malaterra*, IV.24, p. 102; *Gesta Francorum* [above, Ch. IV, note 49], p. 7.

Hugh Falloc's son in 1088, and a half-share in Cosenza in 1090. Another who remained consistently loyal to the duke was Richard the Seneschal. He continued to witness ducal charters; the last time he did this was for a document of Duke William as late as 1115. His own charters showed his continued attachment to his ducal cousins, for in various of his pious bene-factions he specifically mentioned the souls of Robert Guiscard and Roger Borsa (though also Bohemond). Richard had of course been given his lord-ship by Guiscard at the expense of a rebel, and his provision for Robert's soul suggests that he remained properly grateful for that. He also continued to hold some property in the principality of Salerno, which provided an-other incentive for loyalty.[75] Furthermore while Roger Borsa was forced to hand over the important towns of Bari and Taranto to Bohemond, he retained the ducal possessions in inland Apulia, above all Melfi and Troia. Barons from this region (like Rainulf and his son Hoel, the lords of S. Agata di Puglia) witnessed his charters, and were sometimes to be found at Salerno. Hoel became the duke's constable.[76] Furthermore, in his last years Duke Roger took advantage of the death of counts Henry and William of Monte Sant'Angelo to reassert his authority in the Capitanata, capturing Monte Sant'Angelo itself in the autumn of 1105 and Lucera in August 1107. Nor were these simply short-term gains. He granted Lucera as a new lordship for his illegitimate son William, and both there and at Monte Sant'Angelo ducal rule continued to be acknowledged throughout his (legitimate) son's reign as duke.[77] Roger Borsa was thus by no means as ineffectual as the chroniclers seem to imply.

None the less, by the early twelfth century most of the Apulian coast, the south of that province, and the distant frontier region north of Monte

---

75 Ducal charters which he witnessed: L. von Heinemann, *Normannische Herzogs- und Königsurkunden aus Unteritalien und Sizilien* (Tübingen 1899), pp. 11–12 no. 5 (March 1089); *Les Chartes de Troia*, pp. 133–5 no. 27 (March 1092); *Reg. Neap. Arch. Mon.*, v.275–6 no. 508 (April 1102); Leccisotti, *Le Colonie cassinesi in Capitanata* ii *Gargano*, 49–50 no. 9 (November 1110); Ughelli, *Italia Sacra*, ix.192–3 (February 1113); Pirro, *Sicula Sacra*, i.457 (May 1115). He was also listed as a witness in Cava forgeries of '1086' and '1090'. Richard's charters: *Cod. Dipl. Barese*, v.91–3 no. 50 (April 1108), 102–3 no. 57 (April 1111); Cava, *Arm Mag.* E.39 (1115).

76 Rainulf: Ménager, *Recueil*, pp. 187–91 no. 55 (1086); von Heinemann, *Herzogs- und Königsurkunden*, pp. 11–12 no. 5 (1089), 17–18 no. 8 (1092). Hoel: Ughelli, *Italia Sacra*, i.923–4 (1096); T. Leccisotti, *Le Colonie cassinesi in Capitanata*, iv *Troia* (Miscellanea Cassinese 29, 1957), 85–7 no. 23 (1114); Cava, *Arm Mag.* E.47 (1116); von Heinemann, *Herzogs- und Königsurkunden*, pp. 25–8 nos 14–15 (1116, 1117).

77 *Romuald*, pp. 203–4; Cava, *Arm Mag.* E.40 (April 1115). Duke's regnal years in dating clauses of charters at Lucera, Cava, *Arca* xix.8 (May 1110), 28 (January 1111), xxi.101 (February 1124); at Monte Sant'Angelo, *Les Actes de l'Abbaye de Cava concernant le Gargano (1086–1370)*, ed. J.-M. Martin (*Codice Diplomatico Pugliese* xxxii, Bari 1994), pp. 56–102 nos 5–26 (1111 to 1125/6).

Gargano had escaped from effective ducal authority. The counts of Loritello, for example, might not be hostile and would very occasionally attend the ducal court. (Their family's possession of lands in the Capitanata close to the ducal town at Troia doubtless encouraged them to remain on good terms with him.) But their activities and those of their relatives further north were entirely outwith ducal control, they actively sought to increase their territory at the expense of their neighbours (they as well as the duke profited from the disappearance of the counts of Monte Sant'Angelo), and their proud style of 'count of counts' expressed their independence. The youth of Duke William, who was at most fourteen when he succeeded his father in 1111, and the long minority of Bohemond II, who was only three when his father died two weeks after Roger Borsa, gave further impetus to the breakdown of authority in Apulia. Bohemond's widow Constance was unable to prevent the partial dismemberment of his lordship. The rivalry with the counts of Conversano, already present in her husband's time, degenerated into open warfare, and the citizens of Bari took advantage of this to throw off her rule. After a period of internal factional dispute, one of the town patricians, Grimoald Alfarenites, took over and proclaimed himself 'Prince of Bari' in 1118. Such incidents as the murder of Archbishop Riso of Bari, ambushed as he rode from Bari to Canosa in 1117, make it hardly surprising that once again papal councils proclaimed the Truce of God in the region, especially since the peace of the Benevento region was also breaking down at this period.[78] Yet Duke William was still (albeit somewhat precariously) in control of inland Apulia – Melfi and Troia remained ducal possessions – and he remained the secure and undisputed ruler of the principality of Salerno. Just as in the late Lombard period a century earlier, the Salernitan region remained an island of stability on the increasingly fragmented mainland.

The problems which faced his successors show the limitations of Guiscard's state-building. He had been able to complete the conquest of Apulia and to overcome repeated challenges from his fellow Normans. But despite his build-up of ducal property there, his insertion of loyal supporters into the power structure, and the resources brought to him by the conquest of Calabria and the principality of Salerno, he had been unable to consolidate his rule in Apulia sufficiently firmly to resist the split among his sons after his death. There was no ducal administration outside those lordships which they themselves possessed, which they ruled in just the same way, and with the same officials, as did other lords. There was no 'ducal law' over and

---

78 *Romuald*, p. 206; *Falco*, p. 34; *Anon. Barensis Chron., RIS* v.155–6; *Cod. Dipl. Barese*, v.121–2 no. 69, 123–4 no. 71.

above the authority of territorial lords. Above all the duke was unable to control aristocrats' resort to *guerra*, private warfare among themselves, which became increasingly common after 1085. At best he might take sides in such disputes, as Duke William did when he supported Constance and Bohemond II in their long-running dispute against Count Alexander of Conversano in 1120. In the 1120s Duke William was forced to beg money and military support from his cousin Roger II of Sicily, at the price of surrendering ducal Calabria and what the dukes had retained in Sicily.[79] Centralised authority in Apulia was only imposed after the conquest of the region by Guiscard's nephew Roger II of Sicily in the 1130s. And the bitter opposition to his take-over by the leading Apulian nobles, some of them the grandsons of those who had opposed Guiscard, showed how much they valued their independence.

The Church

If the Norman conquest of southern Italy led to fundamental changes in lay society, with the creation of new principalities and the imposition of a Normanno-French aristocracy and military class, the eleventh century also saw equally significant developments within the south Italian Church. There were major alterations to the confused and inchoate diocesan structure, with the foundation of new bishoprics, and the creation of new metropolitan provinces and the reorganisation of those that already existed *c.* 1000. In Sicily a Church structure had to be created virtually from scratch and Latin clergy brought in from outside. Both in the island, and to a much greater extent on the mainland, there were new monastic foundations; quite a few of those on the mainland were eventually incorporated into the extensive congregations which developed around the most important and successful monasteries such as Montecassino, Cava and Venosa. Many private churches and extensive donations of land were also given by their owners to these wealthy abbeys. In Calabria and the Terra d'Otranto bishoprics and other churches were converted from the Greek to the Latin rite, although this was a halting and incomplete movement; and in southern Calabria, where the population remained overwhelmingly Greek-speaking down to the late Middle Ages, it had barely begun by 1100. From 1050 onwards the papacy took an increasing interest in the south Italian Church, seeking to impose its own authority and new and stricter standards of

---

79 *Falco*, p. 68.

behaviour for the clergy, and attempting to reorganise the Church's structure and arbitrate between contending claims among rival bishoprics and other churches.

By no means all of these developments were peculiar to southern Italy. There was a general expansion of monasticism and widespread foundation of new churches all over Christendom from *c*. 1000 onwards: 'the world cladding itself in a white mantle of churches', according to the Burgundian chronicler Radulf Glaber, writing in the 1030s.[80] Monastic congregations were hardly confined to southern Italy: those of Cluny, Gorze and Hirsau spring to mind from north of the Alps. Pressure for ecclesiastical reform grew, both from Rome, from the pontificate of Leo IX onwards, and also from provincial foci such as Cluny, Vallambrosa and the Pataria at Milan, and from local Church leaders like archbishops Hugh of Lyons and Lanfranc of Canterbury. Indeed the revival and reform of monasticism was already under way in Normandy a generation before Bruno of Toul became Pope Leo. None the less, the Church in Norman Italy was unusual in a number of respects. The changes in ecclesiastical organisation on the mainland were far more drastic than in other regions that had long been Christian. The presence of substantial numbers of Greek Christians who were brought under the authority of the papacy and of secular rulers who worshipped according to the Latin rite was also unprecedented. And important as monasticism was throughout the western Church, in few if any other areas did monasteries play quite such a dominant role *vis-à-vis* the secular Church as they did in southern Italy.

One must also enquire as to what role the Normans invaders played in creating or promoting these ecclesiastical changes, how far there was any discernible 'Normanisation' of the south Italian Church, and what impact the patronage of the new Norman rulers and aristocracy had upon that Church. To what extent was the Church used or manipulated by the Normans, and how far did local churchmen use the Normans for their own ends?

First and foremost the organisation of the south Italian Church underwent wide-ranging changes. The ravages of the early Middle Ages and the late tenth-century disputes between Rome and Constantinople had left the southern third of the peninsula with a chaotic and poorly rooted diocesan structure. In the early eleventh century there was, for example, only one other bishop in the principality of Salerno, that of Paestum, in addition to the archbishop in the capital city. The Church in the principality was remarkably disorganised, with what direction there was coming from the

---

80 *Radulfus Glaber Opera* [above, Ch. II, n. 8], p. 116.

prince, the archbishop little more than a figurehead, individual churches enjoying complete independence from him, if not from their lay owners, and some churches having only an ephemeral existence.[81] By contrast, there is at least some, albeit limited, evidence for active archiepiscopal government in the principality of Capua, which had an established diocesan structure with a province of seven bishoprics, and networks of rural *pievi* or baptismal churches probably already in existence under the last Lombard princes. Only two extra sees were founded in the Capuan principality during the course of the eleventh century: for the Normans' new town of Aversa, to which the first bishop was consecrated by Leo IX *c.* 1050, and before 1098 at Acerra, on the principality's south-eastern border (which had formerly been part of the duchy of Naples and remained ecclesiastically subject to its archbishop).[82] By contrast four new suffragan sees for the archbishopric of Salerno were founded, three of them in the 1050s, and despite objections from Salerno a new archbishopric was created at Conza, which by 1100 had half a dozen suffragans along the inland frontier of the principality. At the same time much more extensive provision was made at a lower level, with a network of baptismal churches ruled over by archpriests developing.[83] In Apulia, where the foundation of new sees began in the later tenth century and continued into the early twelfth, the contrast was even starker. In 900 there had been only eight bishoprics in the region: by the twelfth century there were forty-six, many of which were very small and very poor, and, especially in the region inland from Bari where almost every small town had its cathedral, often cheek by jowl one with another. By the early twelfth century the reorganisation by the papacy of these dioceses into provinces had largely been completed [cf. above, p. 228], although the consequent structure was not entirely satisfactory: the province of Benevento, which included most of the Capitanata dioceses, had twenty-two suffragan sees, that of Bari twelve, Acerenza six, Otranto five, but Taranto and Trani only two apiece, and Brindisi one. Several other bishoprics, notably those of the ducal towns of Melfi and Troia, were made directly subject to the papacy, outside the jurisdiction of any archbishop. Furthermore the organisation of the subordinate churches within the diocese remained rudimentary, *pievi* with a network of dependent chapels were found

---

81   V. Ramseyer, 'Ecclesiastical reorganization in the province of Salerno in the later Lombard and early Norman periods', *Anglo-Norman Studies* xvii *Proceedings of the Battle Conference 1994* (1995), 203–22.

82   *Italia Pontificia*, viii.280–1, 476. For the early eleventh century, see especially Archbishop Atenulf's charter for the bishopric of Suessa: Ughelli, *Italia Sacra*, vi.535–7 (1032).

83   Fonseca, 'L'Organizzazione ecclesiastica dall'Italia normanna' [above, Ch. V, note 16], pp. 341–2; Ramseyer, *art. cit.*, pp. 205–12.

only in the area immediately surrounding Bari, and the development of a proper parochial system was to be even slower in Apulia than elsewhere in southern Italy.[84]

The Normans did not initiate these changes; the creation of new sees in Apulia began in the late tenth century and most of the new towns founded by Basil Boiannes in the Capitanata had acquired bishops before the invasion of 1041–2. But they played some part in continuing the process. Where towns did not already possess a bishopric their new Norman lords were often responsible for its foundation, as was Roger of Sicily at his Calabrian base at Mileto (1080), Humphrey son of Aitard at Gravina (1092) and Richard the Seneschal at Mottola (1081) and Castellaneta (before 1111). However, such actions required papal sanction, and often had the encouragement of archbishops who sought suffragans to boost their own authority. Nor did the actions of individual Norman lords always contribute towards the solution of ecclesiastical problems. The archiepiscopal pretensions of Conza, which created a long-running dispute with the existing archbishopric at Salerno, were encouraged by the counts of the Principate, and the rivalry between Bohemond and the counts of Conversano fuelled the rival claims of the churches of Oria and Brindisi to be the seat of the archbishopric in that region.[85]

Local lords were just as prominent as the territorial rulers in the foundation of new sees, and at least in Apulia it is unlikely that the dukes ever controlled, or appointed the incumbents of, more than a minority of bishoprics – although by 1080, with most of the important towns under his rule, Guiscard did control several archiepiscopal seats. Nor is there any evidence that he himself was responsible for any new sees, although Roger Borsa persuaded Victor III to authorise the foundation of the diocese of Ravello, on the Amalfitan peninsula, in 1086.[86] However, Roger of Sicily was extremely active, not just at Mileto but above all in the creation of a Church hierarchy from scratch on Sicily [above, pp. 174–5]. He worked closely with the papacy, once peace between the Norman rulers and Rome had been restored in 1080, although Gregory VII was unhappy about the count's failure to consult him before setting up bishoprics at Mileto and Troina. (Nevertheless Gregory retrospectively confirmed his actions.) Urban II subsequently united to Mileto two defunct Calabrian sees the origins of

84 Fonseca, *art. cit.* pp. 337–8, 341; Martin, *Pouille*, pp. 563–77, 631–41.
85 Gravina: *Codice diplomatico del regno di Carlo II d'Angio*, ed. G. del Giudice, i (Naples 1863), appendix pp. xxxii–iv. Mottola: Cava, *Arm Mag.* B.15 [ed. P. Guillaume, *Essai Historique sur l'Abbaye de Cava* (Cava 1877), appendix pp. xi–xii]. Kamp, 'Vescovi e diocesi' [above, Ch. V, n. 16], pp. 383–5; Martin, *Pouille*, pp. 573, 576–7.
86 Ughelli, *Italia Sacra*, i.1182–3.

which dated back to the late Roman period, and thus provided historical antecedents for the new diocese.[87] The rulers were also important in providing economic support for some (generally the more important) sees which were under their direct control. Both Guiscard and Roger Borsa made grants of land to the archbishopric of Salerno (already well endowed by the last Lombard princes), Guiscard financed the reconstruction of the cathedral, and Roger donated the city's Jewry to the archbishop in 1090.[88] Other favoured sees which possessed less landed property than that of Salerno received a tithe of ducal income from their diocese. Guiscard granted this valuable privilege to the sees of Troia and Bari, and Roger Borsa to the archbishopric of Amalfi. In this last instance the share of revenue conceded included that from dues on trade, which at Amalfi would have been especially lucrative. (Similarly in 1103 Roger added a tithe of his port revenues at Salerno to his previous generosity to that see.)[89] Guiscard made a grant of property from his fisc to the archbishop of Bari in 1084, Duke Roger and his mother also gave the Jewry at Bari to the archbishop in 1086, and he similarly gave the Jews of Melfi, as well as a landed endowment, to its bishopric in 1093.[90] But only a few dioceses enjoyed such grants, and in both Apulia and Calabria many bishoprics lacked an adequate endowment, a problem which was to persist right through the Middle Ages. Only seven of the forty-six Apulian dioceses possessed any sort of territorial lordship, that is authority over whole villages or extensive tracts of land, with some fiscal and judicial rights.[91] One should also note the political motivations that lay behind such ducal grants as have been cited above. The favours granted to the archbishoprics of Salerno and Bari helped to consolidate ducal rule in recently conquered towns where there were very few Norman settlers. Patronage of Salerno cathedral, as well as of the monastery of Cava, worked to legitimise the take-over of the principality, since by doing this the Norman dukes were imitating (and improving upon) the actions of their Lombard predecessors, patronising churches that had been favoured by the earlier princes. Similarly Roger Borsa's grant to the archbishop of Amalfi came immediately after that duchy had once again submitted to

87 Gregory VII, *Reg.* IX.25, p. 607; *Italia Pontificia*, x.138–9.
88 Ménager, *Recueil*, pp. 108–10 no. 34; L.A. Muratori, *Antiquitates Italicae Medii Aevi* i (Milan 1738), 221–2, 899–900. The scale of its landed property is shown by Robert's confirmation charter of October 1080: Ménager, *Recueil*, pp. 110–13 no. 35.
89 Ménager, *Recueil*, pp. 120–2 no. 38 (1081), 129–33 no. 41 (1082); Ughelli, *Italia Sacra*, vii.200–1; A. Balducci, *Archivio della curia arcivescovile di Salerno* i *Regesto delle pergamene (945–1727)* (Salerno 1945), 16 nos 35–6.
90 Ménager, *Recueil*, pp. 171–2 no. 47; Ughelli, *Italia Sacra*, i.923.
91 Martin, *Pouille*, p. 600.

his authority after a lengthy rebellion. But we cannot, however, entirely exclude religious motivation. Roger Borsa had a reputation for piety, and when he confirmed his father's grant of a share of ducal revenues to the bishop of Troia in 1097 (from rents, servile renders and market dues) he did so in return for his name being inscribed in the *Liber Vitae* of the cathedral, so that ever after the canons would pray for him.[92]

The incumbents of those sees favoured by the Norman rulers were usually men they themselves had chosen. Ursus of Bari (archbishop 1080–9) was a ducal *familiaris* transferred from his previous see of Rapolla to Bari precisely to have a trustworthy man presiding over the city's cathedral. His archdeacon, John, noted disapprovingly that his neglect of his spiritual duties was the consequence of his preoccupation with secular matters, and his frequent exhaustion because of his service to the duke.[93] Archbishop Hugh of Lyons alleged that Roger Borsa demanded Desiderius of Montecassino's agreement to confirm the appointment of Alfanus II as archbishop of Salerno in 1087 in return for his support for Desiderius as pope, and disparaged the archbishop-elect's character. While such charges reek of disappointment and *Schadenfreude* – Hugh would dearly have liked to be pope himself – we may well believe that the duke wanted his own man filling the see.[94] Bishop Gerard of Troia (1090–7) was certainly Duke Roger's choice, albeit with some obeisance towards the canonical norms in that the clergy and people of the town gave their assent, in the presence of a papal legate (Troia being one of the sees directly subject to the Roman Church). The see in turn benefited: Roger granted the bishop two entire villages and their inhabitants, and in December 1095 Gerard sought him out in Calabria and begged the gift of the ducal levy on sheep (the *herbaticum*: literally 'grass tax') in the territory of one of these.[95] But such favoured prelates were not necessarily Normans. To judge by their names Ursus and Alfanus were both local Lombards; before his promotion Alfanus had been the cleric in charge of the church of St Massimo in Salerno. Gerard of Troia was a north Italian, as were several other Apulian prelates at the end of the eleventh century: for example Archbishop Albert of Siponto (1100–16). Where Frenchmen were chosen as bishops, they were not necessarily from Normandy. Of the three other bishops of Troia to hold office between 1059 and 1101, one was a Norman, another a *Francigenus* (from the Ile-de-France therefore?) and the third from Maine. Similarly of the bishops

---

92 *Les Chartes de Troia*, pp. 142–4 no. 32.
93 Babudri, 'Le Note autobiografiche' [above, note 30], p. 144.
94 Hugh of Flavigny, *Chronicon*, *MGH SS* viii.467–8. Alfanus was archbishop 1087–1121.
95 *Les Chartes de Troia*, pp. 134–6 nos 27–8, 141–2 no. 31.

appointed to Roger I's new Sicilian sees after 1090, Stephen of Mazara was a Norman from Rouen, but the bishops of Agrigento, Catania and Syracuse were from, respectively, Burgundy, Brittany and Provence.[96] Overall, only a minority of prelates were Norman or French; to judge by their names – which in most cases is all the evidence we have to go on – less than a third of the thirty-six south Italian bishops and archbishops who attended the dedication of the new church of Montecassino in 1071 can have been Frenchmen. The proportion may have grown somewhat over the next few years, and there were some regions where during the late eleventh and early twelfth centuries Norman/French bishops predominated, notably the southern part of the principality of Capua and the Terra d'Otranto. Similarly in those towns which were actually Norman foundations (above all Aversa and Mileto), there were Norman bishops; as for example Guimund, a former monk of Le-Croix-Saint-Leufroi in Normandy, bishop of Aversa 1088–94, whose brother Robert had previously been the abbot of the monastery of St Lawrence in that town. But elsewhere, for example in the principality of Salerno and in the north of the principality of Capua, native prelates remained the norm. This also tended to be the case in the larger towns which were relatively late in falling into Norman hands.[97] At Salerno all three of the long-lived prelates who held the archbishopric between 1058 and 1136 were local men. At Bari Archbishop Ursus, himself a Lombard although an outsider to the town, was succeeded by a local cleric, Elias, abbot of the new monastic church of St Nicholas, built to house the relics of the saint translated from Myra in Asia Minor to Bari in 1087. Duke Roger consented to his election, but (or so the new archbishop claimed) he had been freely elected 'with one voice' by the people. Given the popularity of the new cult, it would have been difficult for the duke, even if he had been so minded, to oppose this choice, and similarly Bohemond when he acquired the town soon afterwards, before Elias had received consecration. But there is no evidence that Elias was unacceptable to the Norman rulers, and Duke Roger was already a benefactor of the church of St Nicholas.[98] By contrast, although Guimund of Aversa was a Norman with a personal

96 *Malaterra*, IV.7, p. 89; Ughelli, *Italia Sacra*, vii.392; *Italia Pontificia*, ix.205 no. 8.
97 N. Kamp, 'Vescovi e diocesi', and 'Soziale Herkunft und Geistlicher Bildungsweg der unteritalienische Bishöfe in normannisch-staufischer Zeit', *Le Istituzioni ecclesiastiche della 'Societas Christiana' dei secoli XI e XII* (Miscellanea del centro di studi medievali 8, Milan 1977), pp. 89–116, are fundamental studies. See also G.A. Loud, 'Churches and churchmen in an age of conquest: southern Italy 1030–1130', *The Haskins Society Journal* iv (1992), 37–53 [reprinted *Conquerors and Churchmen*], and for 1071, Bloch, *Montecassino in the Middle Ages*, i.118–21.
98 *Cod. Dipl. Barese*, i.64–5 no. 34; v.22 no. 11, 27–9 no. 14.

connection with the town, he was apparently a papal appointment, not the choice of Prince Jordan of Capua, and he had earlier been critical of the election of Jordan's ally Desiderius as pope.[99]

It has, however, been argued that the dukes did have a deliberate policy towards Church appointments in Calabria and the Terra d'Otranto, seeking to install if not Norman, at least Latin-rite bishops instead of Greeks, and also to forward the growth of Latin monasticism at the expense of Greek monasteries which were often made subject to Latin ones, either to the new foundations in the region or as part of the congregations of powerful houses from other areas such as Cava. The effect of this was to encourage the emigration of Calabrian Greeks, many of whom were the descendants of refugees from Sicily. These returned to the island, thus strengthening the Christian population there and further promoting the Latinisation of Calabria – or certainly of the northern and central parts of that province – even if the population of the Sila Grande and Aspromonte mountains in the south remained resolutely Greek.[100] However, this interpretation should be treated with caution. While a number of sees were converted to the Latin rite – notably Tursi in Lucania by 1065, Otranto by 1067 [above, p. 133], and Reggio Calabria in 1079 – this was a slow and uncertain process. In the Otranto region in the extreme south of Apulia the installation of Latin prelates, generally French, took place before the conquest was complete, and may have been more for reasons of security than from the deliberate intention to Latinise their churches on religious grounds. Once the Norman conquest was firmly established in this area a Greek bishop reappeared for a time at Lecce (Theodore 1092–1101); and at Gallipoli, although there was briefly a Latin bishop in the early twelfth century, thereafter the see remained under the rule of Greek-rite bishops until as late as 1513. In Calabria the sees of Tropea and Squillace received Latin bishops for the first time in the 1090s, and Roger Borsa attempted to install a Latin when the Greek archbishop of Rossano died in 1093. But he backed down in the face of the Greek populace's resistance.[101] At least nine sees in Calabria still had Greek bishops in 1100. Furthermore, even if a Latin bishop had been installed, there were still Greek clergy in almost every

---

99   Loud, *Church and Society in the Norman Principality of Capua*, pp. 87, 96.
100   L.-R. Ménager, 'La "Byzantinisation" religieuse de l'Italie méridionale (IXe–XIIe siècles) et la politique monastique des Normands d'Italie' [Part II], *Revue d'histoire ecclésiastique* liv (1959), 5–40.
101   *Malaterra*, IV.22, p. 100; Kamp, 'Vescovi e diocesi', pp. 386–7, and more generally Loud, 'Byzantine Italy and the Normans' [above, Ch. V, note 112], pp. 215–33, especially pp. 227–33.

diocese, including ones like Malvito and Cosenza in the north where the population had never been exclusively Greek and in which Latin bishops had presided since the conquest of the 1050s.[102]

Guiscard himself cannot be construed as in principle hostile to Greek bishops: in 1066 he confirmed the rights and property of the see of Tropea for its newly elected Greek bishop, Kalokyros.[103] Nor was Latinisation deliberately promoted by the papacy. There was still only one Church in the eleventh century. The popes expected to be recognised as its head, by Greeks as well as Latins; but provided such recognition was conceded, they were not opposed to Greek bishops and clergy [cf. above, pp. 229–30]. Such a consideration particularly applied to Urban II, who from the beginning of his pontificate was actively seeking better relations with Constantinople. At the council of Melfi in 1089 he confirmed the Greek archbishops of Rossano and Santa Severina in office, once they had acknowledged the Roman primacy. A number of Greek prelates were exiled from their sees and took refuge at Constantinople: John of Trani in 1063, Hypatios of Otranto a few years later, and Basil of Reggio in 1079, and they regarded themselves as victims of Latin oppression.[104] But others were prepared to coexist with the papacy and with their new Norman masters. Among the five bishops who assisted Archbishop Alcherius of Palermo at the dedication of Roger I's new eremitical monastery of St Maria della Torre in 1094 was a Greek, Theodore of Squillace, in whose diocese the new foundation lay and who had already been involved in setting it up.[105]

Guiscard and his brother founded a number of Latin monasteries in Calabria. Robert was responsible for the Benedictine houses of St Euphemia, in the valley of Nicastro in central Calabria, c. 1061/2, St Maria of Mattina, some 70 km to the north in the Val di Crati, which was dedicated in 1065, and the nearby St Maria of Camigliano, about which little is known but which appears to have been founded before 1080.[106] Roger's principal foundations in southern Calabria were the Benedictine monastery of Sant'Angelo (later the Holy Trinity) at Mileto, dedicated in 1080, a house of canons at Bagnara, on the coast 25 km north of Reggio (1085) and the eremitic

---

102 NB the references to Greek clergy in Ménager, *Recueil*, pp. 220–1 no. 63 (1086/7); Ughelli, *Italia Sacra*, ix.192–3 (1113).

103 Ménager, *Recueil*, pp. 73–5 no. 17.

104 D. Stiernon, 'Basile de Reggio, le dernier métropolite grec de Calabre', *Rivista di storia della chiesa in Italia* xviii (1964), 189–226, especially pp. 199–203, 223–6.

105 Ughelli, *Italia Sacra*, IX.425.

106 Ménager, *Recueil*, pp. 38–47 no. 11, 65–8 no. 15; V. von Falkenhausen, 'Una ignota pergamena greca del monastero calabrese di S. Maria di Camigliano', *Rivista storica calabrese* n.s. i (1980), 253–60. Cf. L.-R. Ménager, 'Les fondations monastiques de Robert Guiscard', *QFIAB* xxxix (1959), 1–116, especially pp. 4–20.

community of St Maria in the mountains near Stilo (in existence by 1092, even if its church was not consecrated until 1094). Most of these abbeys were exempted from episcopal control and placed directly subject to papal authority. A number of Greek monasteries were made subject to these Latin foundations. One, St Nicholas de Donnoso, on the northern border of Calabria, was given to Mattina at its foundation. Mileto had at least fourteen cells in Calabria by 1100, the majority of which had been in origin Greek, as well as three Greek monasteries in north-eastern Sicily granted to it by Count Roger at, or very soon after, its foundation.[107] But one cannot therefore assume that these new abbeys were part of a coherent policy to change the Calabrian Church. Two of them were the result of fortuitous external stimuli. St Euphemia was founded to provide a home for a group of *émigré* Norman monks headed by the exiled Abbot of St Evroul, Robert de Grandmesnil, whose sister very soon afterwards became Roger of Sicily's first wife. Given his connections with the Hautevilles – he himself later took part in Guiscard's campaign against Richard of Capua in 1073/4, and the expedition against Byzantium in 1081, as did his nephew William who married Guiscard's daughter Mabel – it is hardly surprising that the monastery was favoured. Monks from St Euphemia were sent to take over Venosa, probably about the time that Robert decided to make it his family's mausoleum (*c.* 1069), and colonised the new foundations of Mileto and the cathedral monastery of Catania.[108] Twenty years later St Maria near Stilo was set up by Roger I for Bruno of Rheims, the founder of the Chartreuse, who after a brief spell at the court of his former pupil Urban II had gone to Calabria with a few companions to resume their lives as hermits. Bruno was offered the vacant archbishopric of Reggio, but declined the position; he and his followers 'despising the vanity of worldly glory, chose to fight alone for God', as Roger's foundation charter proclaimed. Such an eremitic community was actually much closer to Byzantine ideas of monasticism than the conventual Benedictine model; we need not therefore be surprised that the Greek bishop in whose diocese the community was, Theodore of Squillace, confirmed the foundation and surrendered his authority over it, 'freely and unforced', although 'on the prayers of Count Roger and on the advice of various of his barons'.[109] Far from being excluded, the Greek bishop was

---

107 Ménager, 'Byzantinisation [II]', p. 34.
108 *Orderic*, II.100–4, IV.16, 22, 32, 168; *Amatus*, VII.11, pp. 302–3; Houben, *Die Abtei Venosa*, pp. 139–42.
109 Trinchera, *Syllabus*, pp. 69–71 no. 53. For Roger's foundation charter and subsequent ducal confirmations, L.-R. Ménager, 'Lanfranco, notaio pontificio (1091–1093), la diplomatica ducale italo-normanno e la certosa di S. Stefano del Bosco', *Studi storici meridionali* iii (1983), 3–37 (quote from p. 26).

intimately involved in creating this Latin monastery. Nor should we assume that because he was persuaded to agree to its exemption, which was confirmed soon afterwards by Urban II, this was somehow an anti-Greek measure. Mattina had also been exempted soon after its foundation, and its diocesan (the bishop of Malvito) was a Latin. Similarly the monastery at Mileto was exempted by Urban II, at Roger I's request, in 1098: here the bishopric had been founded as a Latin see.[110]

Other factors ought also to be taken into consideration. Robert's monastic foundations during his early years as duke were concentrated in Calabria because that was where he was the undisputed ruler in the 1060s and where the bulk of his property was. In Apulia by contrast, at this stage he lacked the property to endow abbeys, and what resources he had for pious benefactions were directed towards his brother's foundation of Venosa. But the foundation and endowment of monasteries was something expected of a ruler, not just that he would wish to make provision for his soul – and there is nothing to indicate that Robert was other than conventionally pious – but also as a necessary part of his *bella figura*, a mark of his status, and to record his memory for posterity. There is no need therefore to assume that the foundation of Benedictine or (later) other sorts of Latin monasteries was the product of anti-Greek prejudice. Similarly, when after his take-over of Taranto in 1080 Robert donated the Greek monastery of St Peter *Imperialis* there to Montecassino, this was more probably in recompense for Abbot Desiderius's role in helping to negotiate an agreement with the papacy than because of any wish to 'Latinise' what was and remained a town of mixed Lombard/Greek population. St Peter *Imperialis* remained for some years as a Greek monastery while under Cassinese rule; it was only a generation later, from *c.* 1116 onwards, that it was governed by Latin provosts, and even then its charters were still redacted in Greek. Another monastery at Taranto, also dedicated to St Peter, remained attached to the Greek rite at least to 1131, and its final conversion to the Benedictine Rule may have been as late as 1188.[111]

St Peter *Imperialis* was an active institution when given to Montecassino. But not all erstwhile Greek monasteries were so fortunate. Many of them were very small. St Nicholas de Donnoso, which was part of the original endowment of Mattina, never had more than about five monks. Such communities often had a limited life-span, collapsing of their own accord, especially after the death of the founder or of his family. Cava was given a

---

110   *Italia Pontificia*, x.91 no. 2, 145 no. 1. In 1086/7 Duke Roger confirmed all the rights of the bishop of Malvito except over Mattina and the property of St Euphemia and Venosa: Ménager, *Recueil*, pp. 220–1 no. 63.

111   Ménager, *Recueil*, pp. 101–4 no. 31; C.D. Fonseca, 'La Chiesa di Taranto tra il primo e il secondo millenio', *BISIME* lxxxi (1969), 109–12.

deserted Greek monastery in the Val di Sinni in 1053, and it is probable that many of the Greek churches in Calabria and Lucania donated to Latin monasteries were in much the same situation. In 1089 the abbot of St Nicodemus de Kellarana approached Count Roger, pleading his house's poverty, and requesting that it be exempted from various dues and services. Within a decade it was subject to Mileto.[112] But where there was still a viable community, then (as at Taranto) incorporation within the congregation of a Latin monastery did not necessarily mean the immediate conversion of the house to the Benedictine observance. St Nicholas Gallucanta was a Greek monastery in Lombard territory, at Vietri just outside Salerno, part-ownership of which was given to Cava in 1087, but its abbot, Theophylact, who had already ruled the house for thirty years, remained in office until at least 1100, presumably until his death.[113] In Lucania St Maria of Kyrozosimi was also donated to Cava, in 1088, but the first reference to a Latin prior in charge comes only in 1112. Another Greek monastery in Lucania, St Maria of Pertosa, was given to Cava by a Norman/French lord in 1121. But his family had made a number of earlier donations to this house, so clearly they regarded it favourably even though it was Greek. The first evidence for a Latin prior comes only in 1161, and even then in a charter written in Greek. And despite its alleged poverty and its subjection to Mileto in the 1090s, St Nicodemus of Kellarana remained a Greek house until the end of the Middle Ages.[114] Furthermore, the French family of Clermont (Chiaromonte) who gave Kyrozosimi to Cava not only continued to benefit it but also were generous patrons of Carbone, the most important Greek monastery in Lucania, which remained firmly Greek throughout the Norman period and beyond. Carbone's benefactors also included Richard the Seneschal, and it was much favoured by Bohemond and by his son Bohemond II during the short period when he ruled the lordship of Taranto (1123–6).[115] Similarly various members of the Hauteville family favoured the Greek monastery of the Patiron of Rossano, established by Bartholomew of Simeri in the early years of the twelfth century. In August 1122 Robert

---

112 *Saint-Nicholas de Donnoso (1031–1060/1)*, ed. A. Guillou (Corpus des Actes Grecs de l'Italie du Sud et de Sicile 1, Vatican City 1967), p. 13; *Cod. Dipl. Cavensis*, vii.193–5 no. 1175; Ménager, 'L'Abbaye bénédictine de la Trinité de Mileto' [above, Ch. IV, note 92], pp. 24–6 no. 6.

113 *Le Pergamene di S. Nicola Gallucanta* [above, note 55], pp. 36–7, 264–5 no. 104 (donation to Cava), 308–9 no. 125 (last reference to Theophylact).

114 L. Mattei-Cerasoli, 'La Badia di Cava e i monasteri greci della Calabria superiore', *Archivio storico per la Calabria e la Lucania*, viii (1938), 275–6 no. 1; Trinchera, *Syllabus*, pp. 96–7 no. 74, 118–19 no. 90, 214–15 no. 162; Ménager, 'L'Abbaye bénédictine de la Trinité de Mileto', pp. 90–1.

115 Ughelli, *Italia Sacra*, vii.74–5; Robinson, 'The history and chartulary of . . . Carbone' [above, Ch. III, note 19], pp. 246–61 nos 26–8.

Guiscard's daughter Mabel and her son William (II) de Grandmesnil made a donation to it 'seeing their spiritual father Bartholomew . . . is a just man of studious life'.[116]

The foundation of Latin monasteries in Calabria cannot therefore be seen as a deliberate assault upon their Greek counterparts, nor were the Norman rulers and other lords intrinsically hostile to Greek-rite churches and monks. Count Roger was also a generous benefactor of Greek monasteries in Sicily [above, p. 184], something continued after his death by his widow. The abbey of St Philip of Fragala, founded by her husband *c.* 1090, was a particular favourite of hers.[117]

Robert Guiscard's monastic patronage cannot be fully examined, given how much of the documentation has been lost. From his Calabrian foundations we have only a handful of early documents from Mattina, several in rather suspect texts, and one single document, the foundation charter, for St Euphemia. If rather more survives from Venosa, the copies we have are late and incomplete, and several of the Guiscardian documents are later forgeries, or at best heavily interpolated.[118] But from 1069 onwards, when Robert handed Venosa over to the Norman monks from St Euphemia and had the bodies of his elder brothers re-interred there, it was one of the principal recipients of his religious favour. Orderic Vitalis claimed that when Abbot Berengar took over at Venosa:

> the little flock of twenty monks entrusted to his care was entirely given up to worldly vanities and neglectful of divine worship; but by the grace of God he increased their number to a hundred and reformed their morals so thoroughly that they provided several bishops and abbots to govern Holy Church.[119]

Whatever the problems of the documentation, it is clear that Guiscard was a significant benefactor of Venosa, and the community may well have approached the size that Orderic suggested by the end of Berengar fitz Heugon's abbacy in 1094: the enlarged (and never completed) abbey church was about the same size as the contemporary cathedral at Salerno and about twice that of the Desiderian basilica at Montecassino. The abbey attracted a wide range of benefactors from the Apulian nobility, and also

---

116 Ughelli, *Italia Sacra*, ix.292.
117 Cusa, *I Diplomi greci ed arabi di Sicilia* [above, Ch. IV, note 104], pp. 393–402, 405–8, nos 5–9, 12–13.
118 H. Houben, 'Falsi diplomatici nell'Italia meridionale: l'esempio di Venosa', in his *Medioevo monastico meridionale* (Naples 1987), pp. 129–49.
119 *Orderic*, II.102.

the counts of the Principate, the first of whom, Guiscard's younger brother William, chose it as his place of burial. Like the Calabrian foundations, Venosa was directly dependent on the papacy.[120]

However, in his later years both the scale and the direction of Robert's benefactions changed. The two principal monastic recipients of his generosity were the abbeys of St Benedict at Montecassino and Holy Trinity, Cava. This reflected the growing scale both of his ambitions and of what he now had to give, for both houses received property in places recently brought under direct ducal rule in Apulia. At Cava he took over from the Lombard princes of Salerno as the principal benefactor of what was effectively the princes' house monastery. His gifts to Montecassino were a consequence, not just of that house's pre-eminence within southern Italy, as the oldest, the wealthiest and the most prestigious monastic house in the region, but of the significance of Abbot Desiderius as an intermediary in Robert's relations with both the princes of Capua and Gregory VII. The extraordinary scale of his benefactions to that monastery is revealed by his obituary notice in the continuation of Leo Marsicanus's abbey chronicle. Many of these gifts were of cash or precious commodities, gold and silver dishes, textiles, even a carpet, as well as Saracen slaves, presumably captives from the Sicilian campaign. It has been calculated that the value of the gifts in gold alone was the equivalent of about eighteen times the annual census that the duke agreed to pay the papacy in 1059: testimony to the scale of the wealth that Robert had at his disposal in his later years. For while by no means all of these donations can be dated (and the list appears not to be in strict chronological order), it is probable that most of these gifts were given to Montecassino after the mid-1070s.[121] Although Robert had established friendly relations with Desiderius as far back as 1058, when he had given him horses and a safe-conduct to return from Bari to Montecassino to secure his own election as abbot, there can have been little further contact between the two until Robert's invasion of the principality of Capua in 1073/4, and the duke visited the abbey for the first time in 1076, when he showered the monks with gifts. There was of course a strongly political motive for such favour: Desiderius had negotiated an agreement between Robert and Richard of Capua, he was the obvious go-between with the papacy, and Montecassino was a major territorial power in the north of the principality of Capua, whose goodwill was worth cultivating in itself. The monks, however, chose to perceive this favour as religiously motivated

---

120 Houben, *Die Abtei Venosa*, especially pp. 127–9, 179–80, 195–8.
121 *Chron. Cas.* III.58, pp. 438–40. English translation in Loud, 'Coinage, wealth and plunder' [above, note 37], p. 822. V. von Falkenhausen, 'Aspetti storico-economici nell'età di Roberto il Guiscardo', *Roberto il Guiscardo*, p. 132.

(or perhaps one should say that there was *also* a religious motivation). Hence Amatus's description of the 1076 visit:

> He [Robert] entered the chapter house to speak with the brothers, and humbly and gently he gave much gold, because the brothers prayed to God that He pardon his sins. And as a father with the brothers he went around the monastery, visited the infirmary, and provided in abundance everything that they needed. He asked each of them that he pray to God for him.

Indeed, Amatus continued: 'the duke so loved Abbot Desiderius that he held him in reverence like St Benedict'. Robert and Sichelgaita 'chose him for their father, and for the protection and safety of their souls'.[122] No doubt calculation did not exclude piety, and the scale of his generosity to Montecassino was certainly impressive. But while Robert gave substantial gifts in cash and specie to Montecassino from the mid-1070s, and perhaps earlier, his first donation of real property came only in June 1080 when, probably at the Ceprano conference, he gave it the monastery of St Peter *Imperialis* at Taranto. Subsequently he gave Montecassino two monasteries and several churches at or around Troia (October 1080), a church and various property, including a warehouse, at Amalfi (October 1082), and two monasteries in northern Calabria (date uncertain). Sichelgaita added the port of Cetraro in the same area, which was part of her dower, in 1086.[123] Similarly, and hardly surprisingly, his benefactions to Cava began only after the conquest of the principality of Salerno – his first donation came in July 1079. While most of the gifts of Duke Robert, and later his son, to Cava were of property and rights within the principality, there was also that of the monastery of St Benedict at Taranto (May 1081, just before his departure for the Balkans) and Roger Borsa's of a monastery in Bari and of a church outside its walls in August 1086.[124]

Two substantive points emerge from this list. First, one is reminded of Malaterra's remark that Robert was, in the early 1060s, 'generous with money, but stingy in giving out the smallest portion of land'. As was suggested above [p. 124], this may have stemmed not from natural miserliness but from his relatively limited resources in the earliest years of his rule.

---

122 *Amatus*, VIII.22, 36, pp. 362, 375. For the earlier contacts, *Chron. Cas.* III.9, p. 371; *Amatus*, VII.10, p. 302.

123 Ménager, *Recueil*, pp. 101–4, 113–20, 133–6, 150–60, 173–5, nos 31, 36–7, 42, 48, deperdita nos xii–xiii. Cf. H.M. Willard, *Abbot Desiderius and the Ties between Montecassino and Amalfi in the XIth Century* (Miscellanea Cassinese 37, 1973).

124 Ménager, *Recueil*, pp. 122–4 no. 39, 181–4 nos 52–3.

His relations with Montecassino back this up: donations of real property followed after those of money and portable wealth, although he continued also to be generous with cash until his death. And while he had annexed Troia soon after he became duke, his other donations of churches and property were at places acquired considerably later, and occurred after he had consolidated his position in Apulia in the wake of the 1079–80 revolt. Secondly, one should consider the impact of these gifts upon the beneficiaries. Montecassino had held property at a number of places in Apulia in the early Middle Ages, but most of this had subsequently been lost. Cava, a much more recent foundation (*c.* 1011–20), had no Apulian possessions before 1079. These ducal gifts began (in the case of Cava) and played a major part in (in that of Montecassino) the extension of their ecclesiastical and territorial empire away from their existing bases and over southern Italy as a whole. There were of course other benefactors who also played their part in this process. Count Henry of Monte Sant'Angelo made important gifts to both monasteries, and was responsible for the extension of their interests into the Gargano region. Richard the Seneschal and the lords of Sant'Agata di Puglia were generous to Cava (but they owed their lordships to Guiscard and remained loyal to the dukes after 1085). Ducal gifts and ducal favour therefore played a crucial role in developing the interests of these two great monasteries. They also profited from an absence of competition, for there were few existing monastic houses in northern and central Apulia to compete for pious benefactions. The dukes benefited other Campanian monastic houses, although to a much more limited extent. Guiscard gave a church at Taranto to St Lawrence, Aversa, and there were small benefactions to St Sophia, Benevento, although this abbey benefited more indirectly from ducal protection than from significant gifts, and the major extension of its property came after Robert's death.[125]

The acquisition of churches in Apulia and northern Calabria – and in the case of St Sophia also in Molise – was part of a massive extension of the ecclesiastical congregation and the secular property of these abbeys. Montecassino acquired several *castella* (fortified villages) from Richard I of Capua, largely confiscated from Lombard aristocrats reluctant to accept his rule, and also property from these same nobles, who preferred to endow churches rather than have their lands seized by the Normans. The result was a significant expansion of the *Terra Sancti Benedicti*, the block of territory

---

125 Loud, 'The abbey of Cava, its property and benefactors' [above, Ch. III, note 126], pp. 148–57. For a more extensive examination, G. Vitolo, *Insediamenti cavensi in Puglia* (Galatina 1984). Ménager, *Recueil*, pp. 124–9 no. 40; G.A. Loud, 'A Lombard abbey in a Norman world: St Sophia, Benevento, 1050–1200', *Anglo-Norman Studies* xix *Proceedings of the Battle Conference 1996* (1997), 273–306, especially pp. 286–9.

that lay around the monastery itself.[126] Desiderius and his successors also purchased property on a large scale and bought out claims. Cava's purchases were less individually spectacular. It was, to begin with at least, less wealthy than Montecassino, and landholding was more fragmented in the principality of Salerno than in the north of the principality of Capua. But Cava too began to purchase land regularly. All these monasteries received many donations of churches, and sometimes of other monasteries which themselves possessed small networks of subordinate churches and chapels. A case study comes with the network of monastic houses founded in the Abruzzi by the early eleventh-century reformer Dominic of Sora (d. 1032). Most of these ended up becoming absorbed into the Cassinese congregation as the families which had patronised them, the counts of Marsia and Sangro, switched their benefactions towards the abbey of St Benedict. Not only this, but younger sons from these families became monks at Montecassino, and used this as a springboard to high office within the Church. Desiderius's successor as abbot, Oderisius I, was a son of Count Oderisius II of Marsia, as was Transmund, successively abbot of Tremiti, of St Clement of Casauria and bishop of Valva [for whom above, p. 198]. The abbey's chronicler Leo, who died c. 1115 as cardinal bishop of Ostia, came from this family, as did Gerard, abbot of Montecassino 1111–23. Abbot Oderisius II (1123–6) came from the comital family of Sangro.[127] But important as these Abruzzese connections were to Montecassino, they were only part of a much wider process by which this and the other great Benedictine abbeys of southern (and indeed central) Italy, like modern-day conglomerates swallowing family businesses, took over 'local' monasteries and acquired pievi and chapels. The Gregorian reformers' stress on the sinfulness of lay possession of churches was an underlying factor, although one should note that it was only occasionally mentioned in charters, and these monastic congregations were already expanding fast before such express allusion to this motivation can be attested. One of the earliest such examples comes in a donation charter to Montecassino from a vassal of Count Rainulf I of Caiazzo in 1089: here the person warning him of how wrong it was for a layman to own churches was Urban II himself, on his way to the synod of Melfi. But already, under the abbacy of Desiderius (1058–87), Montecassino had received some ninety-three churches, the overwhelming majority from laymen, and although the pace slackened somewhat

---

126 Cowdrey, *The Age of Abbot Desiderius*, pp. 2–12; Loud, *Church and Society in the Norman Principality of Capua*, pp. 50–1, 82–3; L. Fabiani, *La Terra di S. Benedetto* (2 vols, Miscellanea Cassinese 33–4, 1968), i.84–100.

127 J. Howe, *Church Reform and Social Change in Eleventh-Century Italy. Dominic of Sora and his Patrons* (Philadelphia 1997), pp. 123–48.

thereafter, it gained a further fifty-five before 1126.[128] If such acquisitions by Cava were fewer and less widespread, then that abbey's empire was still substantial. A papal bull confirming its possessions in 1100 named eleven dependent monasteries and thirty-eight churches, and this list was clearly incomplete, omitting subordinate churches of the dependencies. A similar, but more exhaustive, bull a year later for St Sophia, Benevento, listed eight dependent monasteries and some 120 churches and chapels.[129]

Not all of these acquisitions were the result of gifts by Normans. Montecassino's links with the Lombard nobility of the Abruzzi have already been noted, and the build-up of its ecclesiastical empire was already under way in the 1040s, in the early stages of the conquest. But many of the churches donated to monastic houses did come from Normans. The expansion of Montecassino and Cava into Apulia was almost entirely the consequence of Norman benefactions, as was that of St Sophia, Benevento, into Irpinia, the Capitanata and Molise. The most important of this abbey's patrons were the Norman counts of Ariano and Boiano, even though Benevento was never captured by the Normans, and from the death of its last prince in 1077 onwards it remained an independent town under papal rule.[130] Indeed, none of these three great monasteries was in any sense a 'Norman' house or a Norman foundation. Montecassino had been refounded on its original site in 950, and St Sophia converted from a nunnery to a male monastery *c.* 940. Cava was founded before 1020, was favoured by Gisulf II, and had already acquired property, peasant colonists and subordinate cells in Cilento (in the south of the principality) before Guiscard's conquest. A legal case heard in the presence of Duchess Sichelgaita in 1083 revealed that Cava had eight dependent cells and 212 unfree peasants in that region by 1076.[131] Monasteries which were Norman foundations were also favoured. The monastery of St Lawrence and the nunnery of St Blaise at Aversa benefited greatly from the princes of Capua and their nobles, Venosa (as we have seen) from Guiscard and his family and much of the new Norman 'establishment' of Apulia, Mileto from Count Roger. Yet among the greatest beneficiaries of the Norman conquest were monastic houses which were in no senses Norman. The overwhelming majority of monks named in the surviving late eleventh- and twelfth-century necrologies

128 H. Dormeier, *Montecassino und die Laien im 11. und 12. Jahrhunderts* (Stuttgart 1979), p. 56 (donations are listed pp. 28–52); H. Hoffmann, 'Chronik und Urkunden in Montecassino', *QFIAB* li (1971), 201–5, Anhang II.

129 J. von Pflugk-Harttung, *Acta Pontificum Romanorum Inedita* (3 vols, Leipzig 1880–6), ii.169–71 no. 206; *Cod. Vat. Lat.* 4939 fols 147v–150v.

130 Loud, 'A Lombard abbey in a Norman world', pp. 282–3, 287–8.

131 Ménager, *Recueil*, pp. 136–41 no. 43.

from Montecassino had Lombard names, and almost all its abbots came from the Lombard nobility which remained in the Abruzzi and the north of the principality of Capua. There were admittedly good practical reasons why the first Norman princes of Capua were generous to it: Montecassino was a valuable ally in controlling the principality, and the abbey in turn benefited from the princes' protection against its immediate neighbours, especially the (Lombard) counts of Aquino. But even after princely power declined and the north of their principality slipped from their control, the later princes were generous to the Cassinese dependency of St Angelo in Formis outside Capua – itself a substantial institution which had forty or more monks by the time of Desiderius's death.[132] Cava too remained a primarily Lombard house. It was much favoured by the dukes of Apulia, the counts of the Principate, the lords of S. Severino and other Norman families, but surviving Lombard nobles, some of them descended from cadet branches of the old princely family [above, p. 139], were also among its benefactors. Indeed the patronage network of Cava after 1085 suggests that once the actual conquest was over the fusion between Lombard and Norman was relatively rapid.

Native and Norman

By the death of Roger I in 1101 the conquest of southern Italy had, insofar as it was ever fully accomplished, been completed. How far, and for how long, the Normans and other Frenchmen who had settled in the south remained a distinct and separate group is one of the most difficult questions to arise out of the conquest. Nor is it easy to assess how far the settlement of a new governing class created social changes which affected the mass of indigenous south Italian society. This is particularly the case with regard to the 'Lombard' areas (the Campania, northern and central Apulia, the Abruzzi borderland) where religiously, culturally and even linguistically there was more affinity between the immigrants and the natives than in the predominantly Greek Calabria and the Terra d'Otranto, or in Graeco-Arabic Sicily, especially since on the island the Normans were an even smaller minority than they were elsewhere.

The question of numbers is imponderable: we shall never know how many Normans/Frenchmen settled in southern Italy and what proportion

---

132   Loud, *Church and Society in the Norman Principality of Capua*, pp. 127–8; *Chron. Cas.* III.37, p. 414.

of the total population they were (although one scholar has suggested that there may have been some 2,000–2,500 noble and knightly settlers).[133] Such an estimate is no more than guesswork; but the slowness, and the incompleteness, of the conquest imply that the newcomers were few. The Norman take-over of southern Italy was for quite a long time infiltration rather than conquest, and never assumed the character of a *Volkwanderung* like the Germanic invasions of the Roman empire (and recent historians have even tended to play down the scale of genuine migrations there). The Norman take-over of southern Italy was never universal – certainly not as complete as their compatriots' conquest of England. Even after 1100, the aristocracy was never exclusively Norman. In the northern frontier regions Lombard nobles like the counts of Aquino, Sangro and Marsia remained entrenched. But there were other areas where a native upper class remained significant too, as in the principality of Salerno. Here the early twelfth-century lords of Giffoni (to the east of Salerno) and Capaccio (in the south) were direct descendants of the Lombard Prince Guaimar III (d. 1027). If the Giffoni family eventually disappeared after 1114 this was not due to expulsion or conflict, but simple failure of heirs. Other Lombard families, if of less exalted descent, remained among the lesser nobility of the principality, and could play a prominent role in its affairs in the twelfth century. Many of the vassals of the most powerful Norman feudatory in the region, the count of the Principate, were Lombards. An excellent example might be Lampus, lord of Fasanella, son of a certain Count Guaiferius, who in December 1128 was one of the witnesses when Count Nicholas of the Principate fulfilled a deathbed bequest to the abbey of Cava by his father Count William II. Then, in October 1134 Lampus himself gave a proprietary church to Cava. Lampus was undoubtedly a Lombard. His wife Emma (notice the adoption of a French name) was from the family of the lords of Capaccio, and was in fact the great-granddaughter of Guaimar III. His lordship, based around a *castrum* in the hills between the coastal plain of Paestum and the inland Vallo di Diano may have been small: Fasanella itself was a fief of only two knights in the mid-twelfth century, though Lampus held three knights' fees elsewhere in the principality and he also had at least one other knight as his vassal. But by 1142 he was a royal justiciar, one of the key local officials of the new Sicilian kingdom, and in the 'Catalogue of the Barons' – the register of military service drawn up *c.* 1150 – Lampus was in charge of a constabulary comprising much of the principality of Salerno and thus of a force totalling at least eighty knights and 273 sergeants (and this figure, given in the 'Catalogue', is almost certainly

---

133 von Falkenhausen, 'I Ceti dirigenti prenormanni' [above, Ch. III, note 143], p. 327.

an underestimate).[134] Another example from the same period is Romuald Guarna, archbishop of Salerno from 1153 to 1181, and the author (or alleged author) of the chronicle which is one of our chief sources for post-1100 southern Italy. Romuald's family were prominent within Salerno itself, both in the Church and in civil government. [See genealogical chart VIII.] His grandfather was a certain Count Romuald *Grassus* ('the fat'), who died before 1109. (In Lombard Salerno a comital title was a mark of aristocratic status, and did not signify a territorial lordship.) His cousin John (d. 1133) was archdeacon of Salerno cathedral, and the latter's father, also John (the archbishop's great-uncle), had been a city judge. The archbishop's father Peter was a notary who was appointed *strategotus* (governor or mayor) of Salerno by Duke William *c.* 1125. Three of his brothers were landowners with their own lordships, two within the principality, one at Castellamare di Stabia near Naples. His cousin Lucas became a royal justiciar.[135] The archbishop's family may have been upwardly mobile – from town dignitaries to minor nobility, but they exemplify the Lombard families who were still well represented within the lower ranks of the Salernitan nobility in the twelfth century.

There were also areas where Greek landowners continued to hold property and wield influence, as around Bisignano and Rossano in central Calabria, and Stilo further to the south. In Rossano the Maleinoi, a family already prominent in the tenth century, continued to be so in the early twelfth, when one of their number became the archbishop. His relatives were benefactors of both the Greek monastery of St John Theristes, near Stilo, and the Latin hermits established by St Bruno.[136] Were the documentation for Calabria better we might indeed lay more stress on the significance of such Greek families, although since much of Calabria was mountainous and thinly populated it cannot have supported a very numerous class of non-working landowners. But the circumstances of the conquest, with so many of its small towns surrendering by negotiation, suggest that any disturbances to the existing structure were limited and slow. The Latin monasteries founded by Roger I were well endowed, and places such as Mileto were centres of Norman/French settlement, but the population that surrounded them was still very largely Greek.

---

134 Cava, *Arm Mag.* G.14, *Arca* xxv.3; *Catalogus Baronum*, ed. E.M. Jamison (Fonti per la storia d'Italia, Rome 1972), pp. 85–6, 92, arts 462, 487. For his vassal Alferius of Monte Marrano, Cava, *Arca* xxiv.45 (1138). More generally, Loud, 'Continuity and change', pp. 324–6.

135 *Romuald*, introduction pp. v–x. For his father, Cava, *Arca* xx.19 (1116), xxii.4 (1125), and for his brothers, *Catalogus Baronum*, pp. 82–3, 98, arts 446, 450, 525.

136 *Italia Pontificia*, x.100; von Falkenhausen, 'I Ceti dirigenti prenormanni', p. 355.

In Calabria, and also in Sicily, Greek officials played a key role in carrying out 'Norman' rule. Some Greek administrators may have emigrated from Calabria to Sicily in the early Norman period. One of the most important officials at Roger I's court in his last years was a Greek called Nicholas de Mesa, who was described as 'protonotary and chamberlain', that is head of the writing office and also a financial officer. The logothete Leo was, if both Byzantine precedent and later evidence be taken into account, the master of ceremonies and supervisor of the court. A third Greek officer, the Emir Eugenios, found from 1092 onwards, was the ancestor of a dynasty of officials who served the kings of Sicily right down to the German conquest of 1194. All three of these officers were associated with Count Roger and his wife in the building and endowment of the (Greek) monastery of St Philip of Fragala. During the Countess Adelaide's regency after Roger's death, another Greek, the Emir Christodoulos, became increasingly prominent. At this stage Greeks were far more important in the comital administration than the Muslim converts who became prominent after the foundation of the monarchy in 1130, although lower-level Muslim/ Arabic Christian officers were undoubtedly employed. Not surprisingly these indigenous officials continued to use existing administrative practices such as the compilation of lists of serfs (Greek: πλατεια; Arabic: *jarida*) [above, p. 181], and probably that of land registers according to existing territorial subdivisions (*defetir*). Certainly existing pre-conquest registers were used. Furthermore most comital charters were written in Greek, even when the recipients were Latin churches, and only after Roger II had inherited the duchy of Apulia in 1127 did it become necessary to organise a separate Latin branch of the *scriptorium*.[137]

However, the use of indigenous officials was just as prevalent in other areas. The entourage of Richard I of Capua included a number of Lombards, notably Pandulf son of Guala (attested from 1063 to 1078), his brother Atenulf, Landulf son of Auloaldus (whose father was a judge at Capua), as well as two sons of the former ruler of Amalfi Sergius (presumably Sergius III, exiled from Amalfi in 1028). Another probable Lombard was the *viceprinceps* Cedrus who devoted much of the substantial fortune he acquired to the endowment of Montecassino and eventually became a monk

---

137   E.M. Jamison, *Admiral Eugenius of Sicily. His Life and Work* (London 1957), pp. 33–40; H. Takayama, *The Administration of the Norman Kingdom of Sicily* (Leiden 1993), pp. 31–5, 43–6; V. von Falkenhausen, 'Il Popolamento: etniè, fedi, insediamenti', *Terra e uomini nel Mezzogiorno normanno-svevo* (Atti delle settime giornate normanno-sveve 1985, Bari 1987), pp. 47–8; C.-R. Brühl, *Urkunden und Kanzeli König Rogers II von Sizilien* (Cologne 1978), pp. 21–3.

there.[138] Such Lombard officials were rather less prominent during the reign of Jordan I, and disappeared entirely after the revolt of Capua against its Norman rulers in 1091. During the 1090s Richard II was mainly based in Aversa and his entourage was for a time exclusively Norman. One of his charters recorded the confiscation of the property of a Lombard *ministerialis* 'who left our fealty and adhered to our enemies'. But Lombard officials soon reappeared: notably Grimoald, count of the Palace, who witnessed a charter of Count Hugh of Boiano in 1097, and the same man or his son of the same name who was active in 1114–15. In this last year Prince Robert I made a grant to the abbey of St Angelo in Formis at his request.[139] Another officer who from his name was a Lombard was Sico, *vicecomes* of Maddaloni, in 1112, and a Lombard *fidelis* called Manso and his brother appeared in princely charters of the 1120s. Most significant was Odoaldus the chamberlain, who appeared as petitioner or witness in no less than seventeen princely charters between 1107 and 1132. Although nomenclature is the only guide to ancestry in these references, since it was not the practice (so far as one can see, ever) for the male children of Normans/ Frenchmen to receive Lombard names (daughters occasionally did so), we may safely assume that these people were indeed Lombards.[140]

Men of Lombard descent were similarly active in the ducal administration. Guiscard's charters were written by a number of people, but more survive from a notary with the typically Lombard name of Urso than any other. Most of Roger Borsa's charters were written by another notary with a characteristically Lombard name, Grimoald, who was active from 1086 until 1102.[141] But though their function was important, notaries were not necessarily persons of consequence. The pre-eminent role of Lombard administrators can, however, be demonstrated within the principality of Salerno. Two of these officers, Peter the chamberlain and Romuald the duke's *vicecomes*, were among the witnesses to a division of property between Gregory, lord of Capaccio (grandson of the Lombard prince Guaimar III) and the abbey of Cava which was agreed at the ducal palace in Salerno in November 1103. What was especially interesting about this transaction was that

138 Loud, 'Calendar', nos 2, 4–6, 8–10, 12–14, 16, 21; *Chron. Cas.* IV.13, p. 482 (trans. Loud, 'Coinage, wealth and plunder', p. 840); Schwarz, *Amalfi im frühen Mittelalter*, pp. 46–7, 202.
139 *Cod. Dipl. Aversa*, pp. 403–7 no. 56 [Loud, 'Calendar', no. 62]; *Reg. S. Angelo in Formis*, pp. 47–55 nos 17–18, 119–20 no. 41 [Loud, 'Calendar', no. 105]. Grimoald's widowed daughter-in-law made a donation to Cava in December 1114: Cava, *Arm. Mag.* E.38.
140 Sico: Loud, 'Calendar', no. 101. Manso: *ibid.*, nos 112, 128, 131, 133. Odoaldus first appeared in *ibid.*, no. 90, last no. 145. His daughter married another Lombard, Landenulf: *Le Pergamene di Capua*, ed. J. Mazzoleni (Naples 1957–60), i.74–8 no. 31 (1152).
141 H. Enzensberger, 'Bemerkungen zur Kanzlei und Diplomen Robert Guiskards', *Roberto il Guiscardo*, pp. 107–13.

Cava's share of this land had previously (in 1091) been given to Peter and his brother, identified as sons of Sergius (certainly not Norman therefore), by Duke Roger Borsa, who described them as 'his beloved *fideles*'. Ten years later the brothers had donated the land to Cava, in return for the souls of their parents, and of Robert Guiscard and Duchess Sichelgaita. This faithfulness was indeed further rewarded, for between 1106 and 1110 Peter son of Sergius was the duke's master chamberlain, i.e. his chief financial officer.[142]

His successor as master chamberlain was another Lombard, Alferius Guarna, from the prominent civic family we have already encountered. He was the son of the judge John Guarna and brother of the archdeacon Peter. When Alferius died in December 1125, the witnesses who attested his will were his cousin the *Strategotus* Peter and Landulf son of Oderisius, the duke's *manescalcus* (marshal?). (The cousins were closely associated – when Alferius, not yet a chamberlain, gave a church he owned to Cava in 1116 the charter was written by Peter.) Another ducal chamberlain in 1125, Alferius's deputy, or one of them, was a certain Hugh Mansellus. We know nothing about his origins, or whether he was a Frenchman or a Lombard, except that he was married to the sister of an undoubted Lombard called Atenulf, whose grandfather was a certain 'Count' Ursus.[143] Atenulf was also probably an official, because after the creation of the kingdom of Sicily in 1130 he, like his brother-in-law, became a prominent figure in the royal administration. Hugh was a royal chamberlain in 1139, active in the southern part of the principality of Capua, while Atenulf was similarly a royal chamberlain in the principality of Salerno in 1144–6, and later became a chamberlain in the royal palace at Palermo and a figure of consequence at the royal court, where he was murdered in 1161.[144] Similarly Alferius Guarna's son Lucas became a senior royal official, one of the king's local justiciars from 1172 until 1189. His son Philip was raised to comital rank by the Emperor Henry VI in 1195.[145] Thus not only were Lombard officials the mainstay of the ducal administration in the Salerno principality in the early twelfth century, and especially of the ducal finances, but members of these two family groups continued to play an important part in the royal administration throughout the period of the Norman kings.

---

142 Cava, *Arca* xvii.13, 84, 114, 115.
143 Cava, *Arca* xx.19, xxix.99 (1157, giving the text of the will), *Arm Mag.* F.34; Salerno, Archivio diocesano, Mensa Archiepiscopalis, I.53.
144 *The History of the Tyrants of Sicily by 'Hugo Falcandus' 1154–69*, trans. G.A. Loud and T.E.J. Wiedemann (Manchester 1998), pp. 96–7, 102–3, 123–4.
145 Takayama, *Administration*, p. 158. His career can be traced in the following documents unknown to that author: Cava, *Arca* xxxiv.15, 76, xxxix.25, xlii.35, 37. Philip: Ughelli, *Italia Sacra*, vii.504.

The role of these Lombard officers in the ducal administration under Guiscard's son and grandson raises important questions as to the interaction of Lombard and Norman, and to what extent, and for how long, the distinction between the two continued to matter after 1100. Some modern scholars have argued that this distinction was significant, and continued to be so for some considerable time. An interesting recent study has suggested that a perception of separate ethnic identity remained alive within the principality of Salerno until about 1180, while another scholar has also suggested, albeit rather unconvincingly, that a sense of Lombard solidarity helped motivate the rebels against King William I of Sicily in this same region in 1161.[146] However, the evidence that there was any Lombard/Norman split into the second half of the twelfth century is slight.

The contemporary chronicles might suggest that there was not only a real sense of separate identity, but also some continued hostility, into at least the early years of that century. The Montecassino chronicle alleged that during Henry IV's Roman expedition of the 1080s: 'on hearing this nearly all the men of these parts conspired together with one heart and mind against the Normans, that when the emperor came from Rome they would all rise up together as one against them'. No doubt this was an exaggeration, but the author clearly did not consider it wholly implausible. This section of the continuation may be derived from a tract written as early as the 1090s, but the final redaction was made c. 1120, and should probably be taken as a view of that date.[147] Writing during this same period 1090–1120 – more precise dating is impossible – the author of another monastic chronicle, that of St Vincent on Volturno, blamed the Normans, 'acting without king and without law', for the alienation of his abbey's property and the decline in its fortunes after c. 1040. Similarly the Casauria chronicle waxed eloquent about the greed and wickedness of the Normans who afflicted that abbey (and while this was completed in the 1170s it draws on contemporary memory, perhaps even contemporary written texts). The early part of Falco of Benevento's chronicle, probably written during the 1120s, also had some sharp remarks about the Normans who harassed his native city, alleging, for example, that the counts of Caiazzo and Ariano 'were convulsed with envy and hatred of the Lombards'. Meanwhile, from

146 J. Drell, 'Cultural syncretism and ethnic identity: the Norman "conquest" of Southern Italy and Sicily', *Journal of Medieval History* xxv (1999), 187–202; E. Cuozzo, 'A propos de la coexistance entre Normands et Lombards dans le royaume de Sicile. La révolte féodale de 1160–1162', *Peuples du Moyen Age. Problèmes d'Identification*, ed. C. Carozzi and H. Taviani-Carozzi (Aix-en-Provence 1996), pp. 45–56 [= Cuozzo, *Normanni, nobilità e cavellaria*, pp. 144–59].
147 *Chron. Cas.* III.50, p. 430; Cowdrey, *Age of Abbot Desiderius*, pp. 239–44.

the Norman side, Malaterra was both hostile to, and contemptuous of, both Lombards and Greeks, criticising the former for their untrustworthiness and the latter for their cowardice.[148]

Yet while this evidence might appear convincing, some qualifications must be made. Both Volturno and Casauria were monasteries which had been successful and prestigious in the period before the Normans came but, situated as they were in unstable frontier areas, were exceptions to the general tendency for monasticism to profit from the era of conquest. Their historians clearly resented this decline. Nor in fact were the Normans the sole, or even the primary, agents of their problems – both houses suffered just as much from the predatory attentions of the indigenous nobility in regions where the Normans never fully displaced the existing landholders. The principal profiteers from Volturno's decline were the Borell counts of Sangro. Casauria suffered because, while the Normans who infiltrated the Abruzzi did make benefactions to local monasteries, they preferred to patronise smaller and less well-endowed houses rather than the rich and powerful abbey of St Clement.[149] [Cf. above, p. 143] These writers' hostility to the Normans therefore not only was unfair, but reflected the peculiar circumstances of the places where they were writing. The same could be said for Falco: Benevento had after all escaped the Normans' grasp, and if one could expect a sense of continued Lombard identity it would be the obvious place to find it. Even so, his comments cannot be taken at face value – the counts of Ariano whom he claimed so disliked the Lombards were patrons of the overwhelmingly Lombard abbey of St Sophia. These remarks may tell us something about Falco – they do not say anything about the attitude of the Normans. But more importantly such hostile comments only occur in the early section of the chronicle. Later on Falco was very critical about King Roger, whom he saw as a threat to Benevento's independence. But he never characterised him as a Norman; indeed after c. 1115 the word 'Norman' disappeared entirely from Falco's account (which was written in several stages, generally not too long after the events in question). It would seem that Lombard identity or solidarity was far less important to Falco than being a citizen of Benevento. The later part of his chronicle had fulsome praise for some of Norman descent – provided they opposed Roger II.[150]

---

148 *Chron. Vult.* i.231; *Chron. Casauriense*, cols 863, 868–9; *Falco*, p. 10; *Malaterra*, I.6, 13, III.13, pp. 10, 14, 64.

149 Loud, 'Churches and Churchmen' [above, note 97], pp. 37–9; Feller, 'Casaux et *castra* dans les Abruzzes' [above, Ch. III, n. 141], pp. 150–61.

150 Cf. G.A. Loud, 'The genesis and context of the chronicle of Falco of Benevento', *Anglo-Norman Studies* xv *Proceedings of the Battle Conference 1992* (1993), 177–98.

The evidence for division or hostility between Norman and Lombard is therefore weak, after *c.* 1100 when Malaterra was writing. Admittedly the revolts of the towns of Capua and Gaeta against their rulers in the 1090s may have had an anti-Norman element. But they may also have been motivated by a sense of urban solidarity against an exploitative outside ruler. And as we have seen there were also Lombards who were quite prepared to collaborate with the newcomers, and even in the principality of Capua any interruption to their participation in the Norman regime was of brief duration.

There *were* factors which might encourage a continued sense of separate identity, the most important of which was the use of distinct legal systems. Lombard law remained dominant in non-Greek southern Italy, and Roman law in the Graecophone areas. There were significant differences between Lombard law and Normanno-French customary law, especially with regard to marriage and inheritance. Lombard women were, for example, always treated as minors legally, who could only act in legal cases or property transactions with the consent of their *mundoalds* or legal guardians. Yet while law might be a factor in perpetuating separate ethnic identities it was not necessarily one which enhanced division. Amalfitans within the principality of Salerno had been subject to Roman law, not the Lombard codes, for a long time before the Norman conquest, and they continued to be so after it. Yet this did not prevent the closest economic, social and familial relationships with native Salernitans.[151]

The key factor breaking down any such divisions was intermarriage. While it was not entirely unknown for Norman women to come to Italy, most of the immigrants to the south were male. Roger I's first and second wives both came from Normandy, but one might suspect that this was more likely at a higher social level than for the rank and file of the conquerors. Even at the top level intermarriage between Norman men and Lombard women was common. At least four of the Hauteville clan, and several other undoubtedly Norman aristocrats, like Roger of San Severino and Robert of Eboli, married women from the old princely family of Salerno. Jordan I of Capua married Guaimar IV's youngest daughter. Malaterra blamed Roger Borsa for being soft on Lombards because of his Lombard mother, but as we have seen [above, p. 141] this also made him more acceptable as a ruler to them. There were also a few examples of intermarriage the other way, of Norman/French women, or at least daughters of Norman/French fathers, who married Lombard men. Sometimes the consequence of such a union was acculturation, but it was not necessarily always towards the husband's identity or law. An interesting example comes with the 'de Mannia' family,

---

151   Taviani-Carozzi, *Principauté lombarde de Salerne*, ii.800–37.

descended in the male line from the lords of Capaccio, and hence the Lombard princes of Salerno, but who through marriage adopted the name, and most likely took over the property, of a Norman, William de Mannia [from Magny (Calvados) or Magny-le-Désert (Orne)], and adopted Norman lineal inheritance rather than the partible inheritance that Lombard law espoused.[152] Nor were the Normans necessarily hostile to Lombard law; they were quite prepared to use it when it suited them. The princes of Capua justified the confiscation of property from rebels 'according to the law of the Lombards'. In 1089 Count Geoffrey of Conversano (or at least his notary) cited clause eighteen of the laws of King Liutprand to justify his possession of property abandoned for more than three years. In 1104 Robert of Eboli gave one of his men an orchard and received in return a *launegilt* (counter-gift) 'as is ordered by a law of the Lombard kings', although this appears to be a justification for what was actually a sale – the reciprocal 'gift' was a valuable ox.[153] Obviously we cannot assume that the wording of a charter reflects the precise instructions of the donor: such documents were drawn up by professional notaries, nearly all of whom were Lombards (or in Calabria and Sicily, Greeks). Yet one presumes that the finished document was read out and formally approved by the person in whose name it was written, and that the content was acceptable to them.

All this suggests therefore that the effective integration of Normans and Lombards was already under way during the early years of the twelfth century. By then many of those whom we might continue to think of as 'Normans' were actually of mixed Norman/Lombard parentage. That of course would not necessarily prevent a sense of identity – of belonging to one group or the other – and that would usually be the father's group, especially since the majority of mixed marriages were probably of Norman men to Lombard women. But here the way in which people described themselves is illuminating, for in the years around 1100 personal identification began to change. Until the early years of the twelfth century men still referred to themselves as, for example, 'Donebaldus son of Herbert, sprung from the race of the Normans', and 'Lambert from the Norman race' (these two both from Salernitan charters of 1096). Similarly in 1109 a legal deposition recorded the deathbed wishes of one 'Adelmus the Norman'. (However, in this last case, one should note that one of the witnesses who testified was the deceased's Lombard brother-in-law Landulf, yet another of the sons of the ubiquitous 'Count' Romuald Grassus, the forefather of the

---

152 Loud, 'Continuity and change', pp. 324–5.
153 Gattula, *Accessiones*, pp. 164–5 (1065); *Reg. S. Angelo in Formis*, pp. 86–9 no. 29 (1095); *Cod. dipl. pugliese*, xx.113–15 no. 49; Cava, *Arm Mag.* D.50.

Guarna clan.)[154] But from soon after 1100 the descriptions started subtly to change; thus we have 'Robert and William, sons of Angerius who was born in the province of Brittany' (1104), 'Adam son of Gilbert the Norman' (1115 and 1118), 'Herbert the son of Herbert the Norman, called Ass's Head [*Caput asini*]' (1118), and 'Gerard de Marcia, son of the late Rao the Norman' (1122) – he was a vassal of the count of Ariano from Irpinia; and 'Hugh the Seneschal of Count Nicholas, son of Gilbert the Norman' (1128).[155] These men described themselves as the sons of Normans (or Bretons); and in one other case we have 'Castellana the daughter of William the Norman' (1120); but they did not refer to themselves as Normans. Furthermore they were very much intermingled with Lombard society: the daughter of the unfortunately named Herbert *Caput asini* was married to one of the Lombard lords of Capaccio.[156] As time went on, so even the sons of Normans became increasingly rare in the sources, but then as immigration ceased (as it did after the early 1100s) and the effects of intermarriage became more pronounced it surely became less and less important whether or not one was a Norman or the son of a Norman.

Our examination of this issue concludes with a 'snapshot' of one particular moment, midway through the twelfth century, by which time ethnic identity was for all practical purposes irrelevant, at least in what had once been Lombard south Italy – the question was of course very different where clear linguistic and religious divisions existed, in Calabria and Sicily. Our scene is set in the principality of Salerno, probably (although the relevant document does not make this explicit) at Capaccio in the south, where the abbot of a local church leased some land to the widow of a judge, in April 1146. The abbot, Lando, was probably a Lombard. But for some unknown reason this seemingly routine transaction took place before a remarkably cosmopolitan gathering of notables. Archbishop William of Salerno was a north Italian from Ravenna, a foreigner imported by King Roger, as was the royal chancellor Robert (an Englishman from Selby in Yorkshire). The bishop of Paestum, about whom nothing is known, was there. So too were four local notables. Two of them were of Norman origin, at least on the paternal side, the brothers Simon and Fulk *de Tivilla* (Théville, dept Manche). Simon was either the man who twenty-five years earlier had married a woman from the former Lombard princely family, or possibly the brothers were the children of that union [above, p. 254]. The other two witnesses

---

154 Cava, *Arca* xxi.5 (a later transcript), xvi.59, xviii.71.
155 Cava, *Arca* xviii.14, xx.33, 113, xxi.1; Biblioteca apostolica vaticana, Pergamene Aldobrandini, Cart. I no. 51; Cava, *Arm Mag.* F.44.
156 Cava, *Arca* xxi.28; Loud, 'Continuity and change', p. 331.

were both Lombards already well known to us, the royal justiciar Lampus of Fasanella and Atenulf the chamberlain [above, pp. 279, 283]. There is no indication in this gathering that the ethnic origins of these four men were the least bit significant, let alone that those of Norman descent were superior to men of Lombard origin – it was the two latter who were the royal officials, and in the document their names precede those of the Théville brothers.[157] By 1146 the distinction between Lombard and Norman had become irrelevant. By the mid-twelfth century the political distinction which mattered was between *regnicoli* and the *transmontani* like Archbishop William and Robert the chancellor whom the kings were recruiting to their court.

The small numbers of the conquerors, the blending together of Norman and Lombard into one society, if not within one generation then at most within a couple once the conquest was completed, and the political fragmentation of Norman Italy after 1085–90, had other consequences. Such innovations as the fief, vassalage, and homage (which last made only a belated appearance after 1110), though sometimes found in southern Italy, never spread universally. Vassals, in the sense of men who served another, were present, but often the word 'vassal' was used of unfree peasants, not knightly clients. Freeholds were always more common than fiefs, and many so-called *feuda* were in fact peasant tenements held for rent, not the holdings of knights who owed military service. Before the foundation of the monarchy in 1130 fixed arrangements about knight service, though not entirely unknown, were extremely rare.[158] Some men of Lombard origin owed personal service because of their status, not in return for any property they held from a lord (indeed, examples of these can be found even in the later twelfth century). Churches were only occasionally subject to military obligation in the early twelfth century, although some of them, like Montecassino, had a considerable military capacity. Furthermore paid military service was probably common: as when Roger I installed a garrison of *stipendiarii* at Petralia in Sicily in 1062. It was only with the creation of a unified kingdom after 1130 that an organised system of military obligation emerged, and this was imposed from above by Roger II to provide the most effective defence for his embattled kingship rather than developing organically out of existing institutions.[159]

---

157 Cava, *Arca* xxvi.45.

158 E.g. the bishop of Chieti (a Norman) agreed to provide one knight's service for forty days from a *castellum* he had purchased (1087 x 1101): Ughelli, *Italia Sacra*, vii.700.

159 C. Cahen, *Le Régime Féodale de l'Italie Normande* (Paris 1940), remains fundamental. Paid troops: *Malaterra*, II.20, p. 35; Loud, 'Coinage, wealth and plunder', p. 841.

Lordship over localities certainly strengthened in the late eleventh and early twelfth centuries: powerful landowners exploited their rights over tolls, mills, ovens, wine and olive presses, water and pasture, and peasants became subject not merely to dues for their use, but also to customary renders and cash imposts at the major church festivals. Many free peasants lost that freedom, as lords forced them into dependency. The long lists of serfs given to the Hautevilles' Calabrian monastic foundations are indicative of these developments, in an area where in the Byzantine period most of the population were free peasants. In the Capitanata and southern Apulia seigneurial demesnes were constituted, and in the former region labour services imposed on peasants to work them, although these were never as heavy as in parts of northern Europe. Thus in 1100 the peasants of S. Lorenzo in Carminiano owed their lord, the bishop of Troia, sixteen days' work a year, divided between the times of sowing, harvest and threshing, and in 1116 those of S. Severino owed the abbot of Torremaggiore up to twelve days at sowing and harvest.[160] But over much of the mainland (Sicily and Calabria may have been different), it is by no means clear that this strengthening of seigneurial lordship was a direct consequence of the Norman conquest. Much the same was happening elsewhere in Europe; the exploitation of bannal rights and resources like mills was the norm all over France. In southern Italy ecclesiastical landlords, many of them Lombards, were pursuing similar policies to laymen – the development of the abbey of Cava's seigneury, both in the vicinity of the monastery and in Cilento, is a case in point, and the origins of this antedate the Normans' conquest of Salerno.[161] Other factors were at work too, above all the growth in population which took place in southern Italy as elsewhere in eleventh- and twelfth-century Christendom. This led to the settlement and development of hitherto neglected and thinly populated areas like the Capitanata and Cilento. Much work remains to be done before the extent and ramifications of these developments can be fully elucidated. Were this a different book, perhaps one entitled 'Social Change in Norman Italy', vastly more space would be devoted to such problems. As it is, all one can do here is to draw them to the reader's attention.

---

160   *Les Chartes de Troia*, pp. 144–5 no. 33; M. Fuiano, *Città e borghi in Puglia nel medio evo* i *Capitanata* (Naples, 1972), pp. 155–7 no. 1.
161   Important discussions in V. Ramseyer, 'Ecclesiastical Power and the Restructuring of Society in Eleventh-Century Salerno' (University of Chicago, Ph.D. 1996), pp. 558–609; Martin, *Pouille*, pp. 318–24, also J.-M. Martin, *Italies Normandes, XIe–XIIe siècles* (Paris 1994), pp. 181–8.

CONCLUSION

The Norman conquest changed southern Italy for ever. The Normans expelled the Byzantines from mainland south Italy and the Muslim rulers
(and some of the upper class) from Sicily, although the great mass of the
Greek and Muslim population remained where they were under the rule of
their new masters. From being a frontier between Greek east and Latin
west, and Christian north and Muslim south, southern Italy and Sicily
became unequivocally part of the Christian west. The ports of Apulia became the embarkation points for Crusaders and pilgrims to the Holy Land,
south Italian foodstuffs helped to feed the growing populations of the north
Italian towns, and sometimes those of the new Crusader states as well.
Messina in particular became one of the great commercial entrepôts of the
twelfth- and thirteenth-century Mediterranean.[1] New political structures
were created, which in 1130 were combined together to form a new kingdom, comprising the whole of the southern part of the peninsula and Sicily.
Despite initial hostility, especially from the German emperors who still
claimed overlordship over southern Italy, this kingdom was to endure for
more than 700 years. Meanwhile a long-term process of acculturation,
and the immigration into Sicily of Latin Christians, both from the mainland
south and from northern Italy, first attenuated and then swamped the
surviving Greek and Muslim populations. By 1250 Sicily was an overwhelmingly Latin island. Greek Calabria retained its identity longer, but the
Greek zone was slowly attenuated in the late Middle Ages, and eventually
dwindled away. None of this would have happened without the Norman
conquest.

Yet, as this study has shown, there are many qualifications that must be
made when assessing the role of the Normans themselves. The conquest
was for many years a slow and uncertain process; indeed up to the 1040s
there barely was a conquest – no more than slow infiltration by a relatively
small number of mercenaries. From the invasion of Apulia in 1041 the

---

1   D.S.H. Abulafia, 'The merchants of Messina: Levant trade and domestic economy', *PBSR*
    liv (1986), 196–212.

Normans did indeed begin to take over, but even then they were at first only a part of a rebellion against Byzantine rule, and it took some years before they were in control of more than limited areas of the peninsula. Southern Italy was divided, authority was weak – even Salerno, the most stable and prosperous of the Lombard principalities, was beginning to fragment by the 1040s, while the other native south Italian states were well on the way to dissolution even without the Normans' help. The Byzantine empire was too distracted by internal problems and external threats to its heartland to mount a sustained defence of its peripheral Italian provinces. Similarly Arabic Sicily was divided, and the Normans' establishment on the island was aided both by the Greek Christian fifth column and even by Muslim collaborators. However, despite these weaknesses, the conquest of southern Italy still took about ninety years from the first coming of the Normans until the final surrender of Islamic Sicily. The numerical weakness of the newcomers was undoubtedly the principal reason for the length of this process, and it also did much to shape the nature of the society which emerged out of the conquest. That society was shaped by a paradox. The larger proportion of those whom the south Italians described as *normanni* were from the duchy of Normandy, although their ranks were swelled by others from Brittany, Maine, Flanders, and other French principalities. But because they were always a small elite, and because there was no mass migration, or even such a significant settlement as occurred in post-1066 England, the conquest was never quite completed. Some of the principal towns were never conquered (Benevento and Naples), others remained nominally subject to Norman rulers but largely free from their influence, as Amalfi, Gaeta and (to a considerable extent) Bari. Even Salerno, the *de facto* capital of one of the new Norman principalities, remained an overwhelmingly Lombard town. The Normans never formed a closed elite; they relied on native allies and collaborators, never formed more than a minority among the upper ranks of the Church, and the native aristocracy was subsumed, but not entirely replaced. Most, but not all, of the great aristocrats of post-1100 southern Italy were Normans, drawn from a close-knit and relatively small set of kin-groups, and dominated by the descendants of Tancred de Hauteville and Richard Quarrel. But many of the indigenous lesser nobility remained, and as Frenchmen and Lombards intermarried, the barriers swiftly broke down. It is a good question when being Norman ceased to matter in 'Norman' Italy: a more extended investigation than there has been space for here is certainly needed, but the evidence would seem to suggest that it was not much more than a generation after the death of Roger I in 1101.

The most prominent figure in the conquest was Robert Guiscard. This book has attempted to place him in the wider context of the political and social evolution of southern Italy, but his spectacular career, from younger son of a numerous family in Normandy to Calabrian freebooter, and then from warlord to a major territorial ruler, the ally (when it suited him) of popes, and the equal of kings and emperors, inevitably draws the eye. The vainglorious epitaph on his tomb at Venosa [above, p. 4] was not far short of the truth, for he *had* taken on and beaten the two great rulers of eleventh-century Christendom, the Salian emperor of Germany and the βασιλευς of Constantinople. This was echoed two centuries later in the time of another French conqueror of southern Italy, Charles of Anjou, when the author of a (generally very derivative) history of the region described Robert as:

> That best of dukes, the glory of the Norman race,
> A worthy knight of knights, an example of honour,
> Guiscard, more courageous than all, and second
> To none, whom alone the whole world feared
> Above all else. Mars himself was amazed by his daring,
> Minerva by his wisdom, Mercury by his eloquence.[2]

However, we must be wary at accepting such hyperbole at face value. It was not just that Guiscard was far from being the chivalric hero portrayed here, although it is unlikely that those he crossed such as his nephew Abelard, his brother-in-law Gisulf, the 'sons of Amicus' kin-group, or even Gregory VII, would have deemed him 'an example of honour'. But, important as he was in forwarding the Norman conquest, it was not his work alone. The Normans were already well established when he came to Italy in 1046/7, and the conquest was still going on, in Sicily and the Abruzzi, when he died. Nor was he ever the undisputed leader of the south Italian Normans. The counts of Aversa (or princes of Capua as they became) worked inde-pendently, and up to the 1070s it was they, not Guiscard, who were the effective supporters of the reformed papacy. Guiscard's power and resources later outstripped those of the princes, and he was able to force Jordan I of Capua into submission in 1083/4, but ironically it was Roger Borsa, normally seen as but a pale shadow of his father, who secured the prince's fealty in 1098 – not Guiscard. But while Duke Roger was probably a more assertive and effective ruler than some historians (both medieval and mod-ern) have portrayed him, he was unable to prevent Apulia from fragment-ing after 1085. Yet this was a reflection of his father's rule, for Guiscard had faced a whole series of revolts, largely by his fellow Normans, many of them

---

2 'Anonymi Vaticani Historia Sicula', *RIS* viii.754.

his own family. He had defeated them all, but had not eradicated the underlying problem. Furthermore, the key figure undermining Roger Borsa's rule was his half-brother Bohemond, whom Robert had excluded from the succession, made no direct provision for, but treated as his lieutenant during the expedition against Byzantium. Perhaps, had that expedition succeeded, Bohemond's destiny might have lain elsewhere, and Roger Borsa's rule stood a better chance of success. As it was, by the time Bohemond left on Crusade in 1096, ducal power in Apulia proper was already on the wane. But Guiscard's success against Byzantium was only momentary, de-spite catching the empire at almost the weakest point in its history, with its finances in ruins, its governing class fighting among itself, and Asia Minor falling to the Turks. Revolt at home, and the problems of his papal ally, deprived him of the opportunity either to conquer the empire, or at least to create a new principality in the Balkans. But Guiscard's inability firmly to consolidate his rule in Apulia cost more than his chance of success in 1081/2. It led his successors to concentrate their attention on the west coast principality of Salerno, and prevented the unification of southern Italy for another half a century. When Roger II did create his kingdom, he faced a long, hard struggle to overcome the ingrained particularism of the nobles and towns of Apulia. But Roger II had the advantage of a secure base in Sicily and undisputed control of Calabria. This might suggest that his father's state-building had been more effective than that of Guiscard. But Roger I had the advantage that, unlike his brother, he did not face powerful nobles already entrenched before he had begun to rule.

Thus, for all his victories, in political terms Guiscard's career was some-thing of a dead end. The pattern of short-term success but which miscarried in the longer term was repeated in other spheres. If he had moved to the pope's rescue in 1084, he failed to secure the latter's position in Rome. While Robert could defy Gregory VII in the 1070s, and secure what was a more or less complete triumph in the settlement of 1080, Urban II and his successors had to prop up the rule of the later dukes through the proclama-tion of the Truce of God.

It was therefore not perhaps surprising that as time went by Robert Guiscard's reputation faded somewhat. His name never disappeared. But the creation of an enduring political and institutional legacy of the Norman conquest of the south was the work of his nephew, and the emergence of the kingdom of Sicily had changed the outlook of those who lived thereafter, for whom his career became rather the stuff of legend than a significant contribution to creating the world in which they lived. Romance literature subsumed Guiscard's conquests in those ascribed to Charlemagne. The English writer Roger of Howden, who had actually visited the Sicilian *regno*, at least knew of him, and that he was a great conqueror, although he thought that he was a contemporary of Henry I (actually half a century his junior) and was mainly interested in the legend that Sichelgaita had poisoned him.[3] But by the late twelfth century Guiscard was an increasingly distant memory even at the abbey of Venosa, which he had endowed and chosen as his and his brothers' mausoleum. The abbey's chronicle reported a series of visions, from the time of Abbot Aegidius (1167–81), in which Robert appeared. In one he reproved a sick brother who had thoughtlessly gone to sleep on his tomb. Another implied that while he served the monks, they did not do enough to serve him. In a third vision he chided the custodians of his tomb who had allowed a knife, which he had presented to the monastery as a symbol to confirm his donations 'as is the custom of the Normans', to grow rusty through neglect. As they had failed to care for that, so they had neglected his memory and the endowments he had given them.[4] Perhaps these fanciful tales encapsulate the enigma of Robert Guiscard: he was still a powerful presence a century after his death, but by then his legacy could seem irrelevant even to those who above all others might have been expected to cherish it.

---

3   *Gesta Regis Henrici Secundi*, ed. W. Stubbs (Rolls Series, London 1867), ii.200–1. For his posthumous reputation more generally, Taviani-Carozzi, *La Terreur du Monde*, pp. 487–500.
4   Houben, *Die Abtei Venosa*, pp. 441–2.

GENEALOGICAL TABLES

Table I   The Hauteville kin

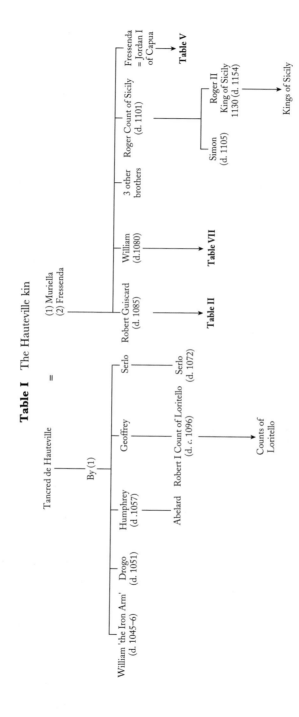

Table II The descendants of Robert Guiscard

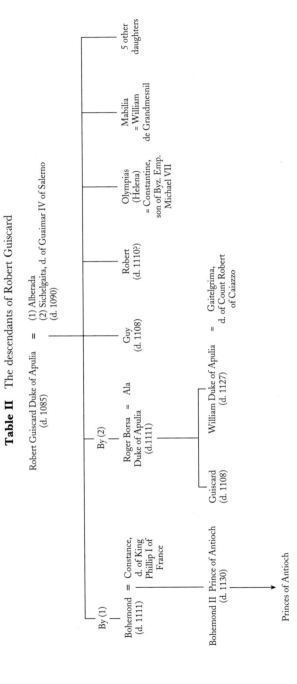

Table III   The Lombard princes of Capua and Benevento

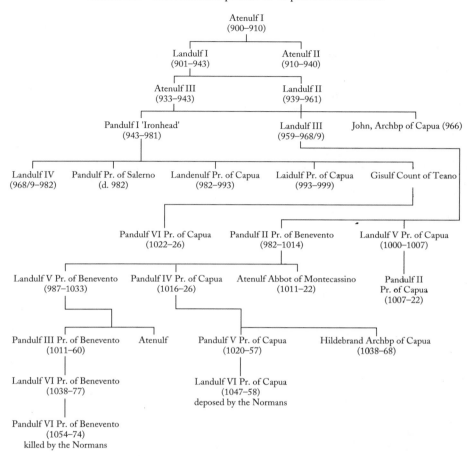

Up to 982 princes ruled jointly in both principalities. Regnal years given are those in which they were styled prince, even though at first in association with a father, brother or cousin.

Table IV The family of the Lombard princes of Salerno

Gregory, Consul and Duke of the Romans

Pandulf = Theodora

John (983–999) = Sichelgaita

Guaimar III = Gaitelgrima (999–1027)

John (d. 1018)

Guaimar IV = Gemma (1027–52)

Guido

Maria = Count William of the Principate

Guaimar I of Giffoni (d. pre–1096)

Guaimar II of Giffoni (d. 1116)

Counts of the Prinipate

Landulf

Guido (d. 1075)

John

Guaimar

Gisulf II (d. pre–1091) (1052–77)

Sichelgaita = Robert Guiscard

Dukes of Apulia

Gaitelgrima (1) Drogo (2) Count Robert of Monte Sant' Angelo (3) Count Affredus of Sarno

Gaitelgrima (2) = Prince Jorden I of Capua

Prince of Capua

Guaimar of Capaccio

Sichelgaita = Ascittinus of Sicignano

Guaimar = Sybilla (d.1137)

Guaimar

Counts of Monte Sant' Angelo and Sarno

Gregory of Capaccio (fl. 1092)

William of Trentenaria

Robert of Trentenaria (d.1156)

John of Capaccio

Jordan, lord of Corneto

Emma = Lampus of Fasanella

Pandulf

Gisulf

Emma

William de Mannia = Altruda

Gisulf

William

Table V The Norman counts of Aversa and princes of Capua

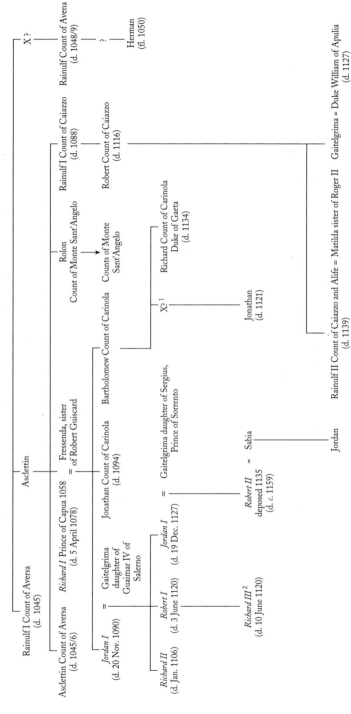

1. See H. Hoffmann, 'Die Anfänge der Normannen in Süditaliem', *Quellen und Forschungen* xlix (1969), 108–9.
2. I have preferred the precise dates of the *Annales Cavenses*, ad an. 1120, for the deaths of Robert I and Richard III rather than the vaguer testimony of Falco, who dates their deaths to May.

Table VI The descendants of Amicus

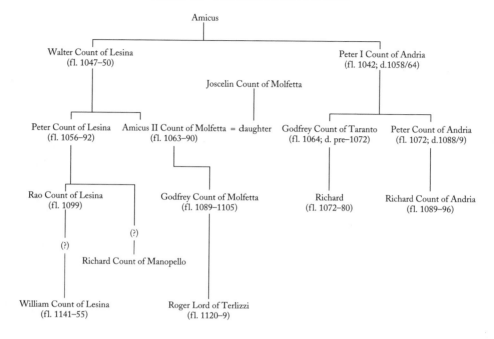

Table VII The counts of the Principate

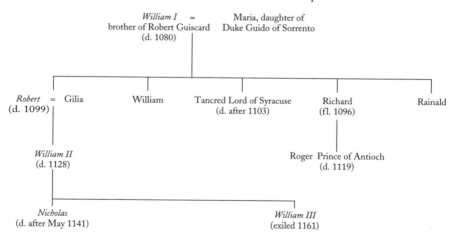

Table VIII The Guarna family of Salerno

- Count Romuald *Grassus* (d. before 1109)
  - John Guarna judge (d. pre–1115)
    - Alferius ducal chamberlain = Gemma (d. 1125)
      - Lucas Justiciar 1172–89 = Dofa
        - Phillip Count of Marsico 1195
      - Matthew
    - John archdeacon (d. 1133)
  - Landulf (fl. 1109)
  - Peter Guarna Strategotus = Elena 1125 (d. 1157)
    - Phillip Lord of Castelmagno (d. 1147)
    - Romuald (II) archbishop 1153–81
    - Lucas Lord of Castelmandra
    - Robert archdeacon (d. 1180)
    - James Lord of Castellamare (d. 1187)

MAPS

Map I Southern Italy

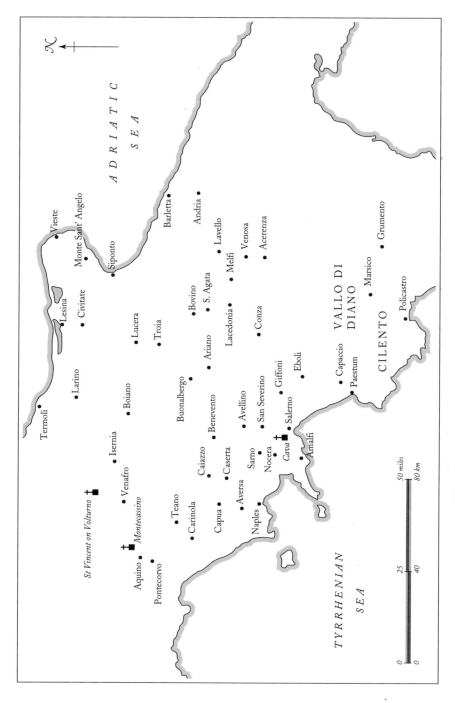

Map II The Capitanata, Molise, Campania and the Basilicata

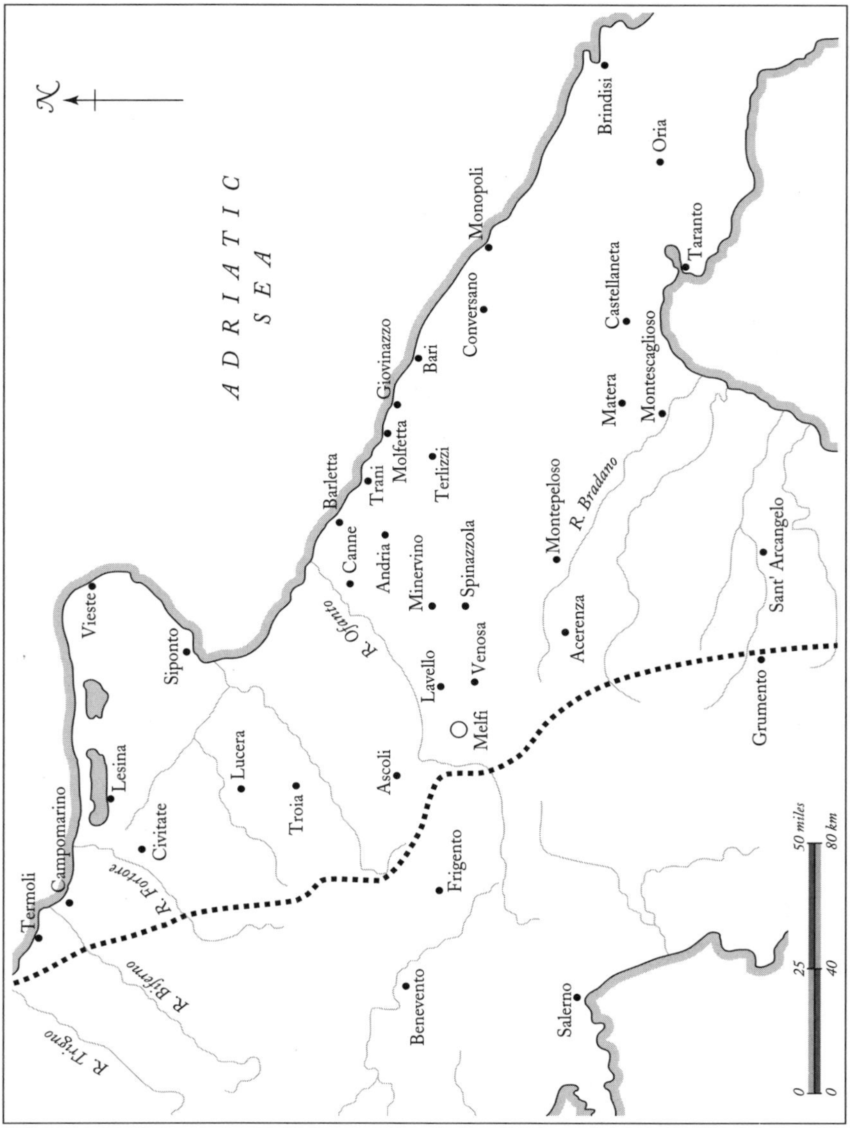

Map III Apulia

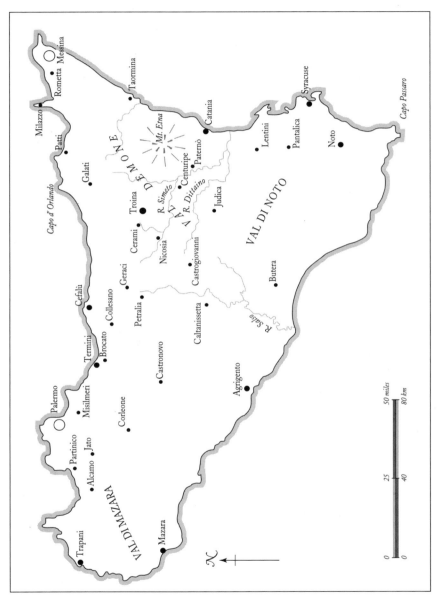

Map IV Sicily

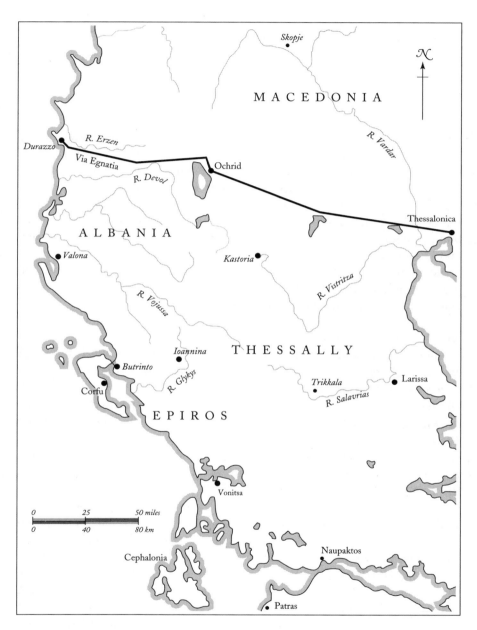

Map V Robert Guiscard's campaigns against Byzantium, 1081–5

A BRIEF GUIDE TO FURTHER READING

Despite the intrinsic interest of the subject, the available literature for Anglophone students of Norman Italy is disappointingly meagre. Furthermore, even the coverage by Continental scholars is patchy, and many important issues remain to be properly explored. What follows is an extremely selective sketch of those studies, both in English and in other languages, that I have found most useful, and of a few other works through which readers might study aspects of the Norman conquest of the south that time and space have precluded me from doing more than touch upon in this book. As much emphasis as is possible has been given to work in English, but even the most resolute monoglot may wish to have some idea of what is available in other European languages.

We are relatively fortunate when looking at the pre-Norman period dealt with in Chapter I, even if there is still a need for a really effective monograph covering the entire south. Barbara Kreutz, *Before the Normans. Southern Italy in the Ninth and Tenth Centuries* (1991) does not quite fill this gap, being generally better on the ninth century than the tenth, and placing too much emphasis on Amalfi to the exclusion of the Byzantine provinces and the principalities of Capua and Benevento. (See my review in *American Historical Review* xcviii (1993), 430–1.) There are much briefer discussions in English in the chapter on the south in Chris Wickham's excellent *Early Medieval Italy. Central Power and Local Society 400–1000* (1981) [pp. 146–67], and in the chapter by G.A. Loud, 'Southern Italy in the tenth century', in *New Cambridge Medieval History* iii, ed. Timothy Reuter (2000), pp. 624–45.

For a narrative history of Byzantine Italy, Jules Gay, *L'Italie méridionale et l'Empire byzantin* (1904) is still unrivalled, despite its age. V. von Falkenhausen, *Untersuchungen über die byzantinische Herrschaft in Süditalien vom 9. bis ins 11. Jahrhundert* (1967) is the fundamental study of the administration of the Byzantine provinces. There is also an Italian version of this work (1978). A number of important articles are collected in André Guillou, *Studies on Byzantine Italy* (1970) and *Culture et Société en Italie Byzantine (VIe–XIe siècle)* (1978), but only one of these is in English (reprinted from *Dumbarton Oaks Papers* xxviii (1974), 91–109). On the Lombard principalities there is Nicola Cilento, *Le Origini della signoria Capuana nella Longobardia minore* (1966), largely about the ninth century, and the same author's essays reprinted in his *Italia meridionale longobarda* (1971). Huguette Taviani-Carozzi, *La Principauté lombarde de Salerne (IXe–XI siècle). Pouvoir et société en Italie lombarde méridionale* (1991) is a lengthy, discursive and over-schematic monograph, but with some very important insights contained within it, especially in the later chapters. Paolo Delogu, *Mito di una città meridionale* (1977) is a fine study of the town of Salerno in the Lombard period. On the other principalities, Jean-Marie Martin, 'Eléments preféodaux dans les principautés de Bénévent et de Capoue (fin du VIII siècle–début du XI siècle): modalités de privatisation du pouvoir', in *Structures féodales et féodalisme dans l'occident méditerranéen (X–XIIIe siècles)* (1980), pp. 553–86, is seminal. R. Poupardin, *Etude sur les institutions politiques et administratives des principautés lombardes de l'Italie méridionale* (1907) is also useful, despite its age. P. Skinner, *Family Power in Southern Italy. The Duchy of Gaeta and its Neighbours 850–1139* (1995) is an excellent monograph which makes important comparisons between the different coastal duchies. On Amalfitan trade there are useful articles (in English) by A.O. Citarella in *Speculum* xlii (1967), 299–312, and *Journal of Economic History* xxviii (1968), 531–55. Scholars are now laying considerable emphasis on the wealth of Lombard south Italy, as for example in A.O. Citarella and H.M. Willard, *The Ninth-Century Treasure of Monte Cassino in the Context of the Political and Economic Developments in Southern Italy* (Miscellanea Cassinese 50, 1983). But our understanding of that wealth has been especially enhanced by the archaeological investigation conducted by the British School at Rome at S. Vincenzo al Volturno: two volumes have been published so far, edited by Richard Hodges (1993 and 1995), with two more to follow.

For the period of the conquest John Julius Norwich, *The Normans in the South 1016–1130* (1967) provides a splendidly written, if at times over-imaginative, narrative. For a minutely detailed scholarly narrative F. Chalandon, *La Domination normande en Italie et en Sicile* (1907) remains un-rivalled, although on some points of detail his work has inevitably been superseded by more modern studies. Chalandon's chapter in the original *Cambridge Medieval History*, vol. v (1926), will eventually be replaced by one by G.A. Loud, when the *New Cambridge Medieval History*, iv, is finally published. See also the lengthy chapters by Vera von Falkenhausen and Salvatore Tramontana in *Il Mezzogiorno dai Bizantini a Federico II*, ed. G. Galasso (vol. 3 of the UTET *Storia d'Italia* (1983)).

On the early history of the Normans and Italy (up to 1042) there is a useful book by Salvatore Tramontana, *I Normanni in Italia. Linee di recerca sui primi insediamenti* i *Aspetti politici e militari* (Messina 1970): to the best of my knowledge no second volume has appeared. The best study of the coming of the Normans remains Hartmut Hoffmann, 'Die Anfänge der Normannen in Unteritalien', *QFIAB* xlix (1969), 95–144. There are also useful articles in

English on the same subject by Einar Joranson, in *Speculum* xxiii (1948), 353–96, and John France, in *Journal of Medieval History* xvii (1991), 185–205, although Chapter II of this book presents a very different interpretation from those advanced by these authors. A similar critique is offered in Chapter Three of Dione Clementi, 'Stepping stones in the making of the "regno"', *BISIME* xc (1982/3), 227–93, which looks particularly at the relations between the Normans, Guaimar IV of Salerno and the German empire; none the less this is still a thoughtful, if rather old-fashioned, interpretation.

On Guiscard himself there are the two biographical studies, by Huguette Taviani-Carozzi and Richard Bünemann, mentioned in the Introduction. The former concentrates very much on the chronicles and their perception of Guiscard: however, the chapter on the conquest of Sicily is excellent, although that on the background in Normandy is weak. Bünemann's *Robert Guiscard 1015–1085. Eine Normanner erobert Süditalien* (1997) is straightforward and competent (although unlike him I would be cautious in accepting Anna Comnena's estimate of Robert's age – he was probably born in the mid-1020s). The period after Guiscard's death, and Roger I's career and government in Calabria and Sicily have been sadly neglected, not least because Léon-Robert Ménager's projected editions of the later (post-1087) ducal charters and those of Count Roger were never completed. His *Nachlass* has now been entrusted to Jean-Marie Martin, and it is to be hoped that this project will be speedily brought to fruition.

Jean-Marie Martin, *Italies Normandes, XIe–XIIe Siècles* (1994) offers a valuable synthesis of the social history of the Mezzogiorno, but the ambitious reader should consult the same author's *La Pouille du VIe au XII siècle* (1993), a massive and comprehensive monograph on Byzantine and Norman Apulia which is probably the most important single work published about early medieval southern Italy since Chalandon's in 1907. The chapters on settlement, the economy and agriculture are especially good. On a similar scale is Laurent Feller, *Les Abruzzes médiévales. Territoire, économie, et société en Italie centrale du IXe au XIIe siècle* (Rome 1998), although the main focus of this is on the pre-Norman period. The impact of the Norman conquest on south Italian society is the primary theme of the articles reprinted in G.A. Loud, *Conquerors and Churchmen in Norman Italy* (1999), and Léon-Robert Ménager, *Hommes et Institutions de l'Italie normande* (1981). Probably the most important piece in this last collection was the prosopography of Normans and other Frenchmen attested in south Italian sources first published in *Roberto il Guiscardo e il suo tempo* (Relazioni e communicazioni nelle prime giornate normanno-sveve, Bari maggio 1973) (1975). This volume initiated a series of the proceedings of the biennial conference at Bari, where much of the most interesting work on Norman Italy has been published in recent years. The second in the series, *Ruggero il gran conte e l'inizio dello stato normanno*

(1977), includes Tramontana's important study of the aristocracy of early
Norman Sicily. More recent volumes of these proceedings have been devoted to themes, usually socio-economic, rather than chronological periods.
The first of these thematic volumes, no. 7 in the whole series (1987), includes a pioneering study of crops and agriculture by Jean-Marie Martin.
The most recent volume (no. 13, 1999) was devoted to how Norman Italy
was perceived from other regions. Italian professors are even more addicted
to conferences than are academics from other countries, and consequently
there are numerous other volumes of conference proceedings, often of very
variable quality and published years after the gathering actually took place.
Unfortunately *Roberto il Guiscardo*, ed. C.D. Fonseca (1990), which publishes
the proceedings of a conference to mark the 900th anniversary of the duke's
death, is one of the weaker of the breed. It does, however, contain a brief
but important essay by Horst Enzensberger, the leading scholar of Italo-
Norman diplomatic, on Guiscard's chancery. One further recent multi-
author volume should be noted: *Cavalieri alla conquista del Sud. Studi sull'Italia
normanna in memoria di Léon-Robert Ménager*, ed. E. Cuozzo and J.-M. Martin
(1998), which includes essays on a number of aspects of the conquest, by
(among others) Taviani-Carozzi, Tramontana, Feller, Cuozzo, Ghislaine
Noyé (on Calabria), and the present author (on Benevento and the Normans).
A last item on social history is an import and pioneering study by Patricia
Skinner, *Health and Medicine in Early Medieval Southern Italy* (1997).

On the aristocracy, Wolfgang Jahn, *Untersuchungen zur normannischer Herrschaft
in Süditalien (1040–1100)* (1989) is careful and thoughtful, and has valuable
appendices listing the surviving documents from individual lordships; as will
be apparent from the footnotes to Chapter VI, I have found his discussion of
the revolts against Guiscard extremely useful. Errico Cuozzo has also written a number of careful studies of particular lordships, some of which have
been revised and republished in his *Normanni, nobilità e cavalleria* (Salerno
1995). Evelyn Jamison, *Studies on the History of Medieval Sicily and South Italy*,
ed. D. Clementi and T. Kölzer (1992), contains important essays on the
aristocracy by the doyenne of English-language scholars of the Norman era,
but the principal focus of her interests was the twelfth century rather than
the period of the conquest. Claude Cahen, *Le Régime féodal de l'Italie normande*
(1940) remains as the principal study of vassalage, military obligation and
tenure. Errico Cuozzo, *"Quei maladetti normanni". Cavalieri e organizzazione
militare nel mezzogiorno normanno* (1989) is more useful for the twelfth century.

On the local administration and the Norman conquest, V. von
Falkenhausen, 'I ceti dirigenti prenormanni al tempo della costituzione
degli stati normanni nell'Italia meridionale e in Sicilia', in *Forme di potere e
struttura sociale in Italia nel medioevo*, ed. G. Rossetti (1977), pp. 321–77, is a
seminal study. Indeed a volume of the collected essays of this fine scholar

(many of which are scattered in difficult-to-obtain conference proceedings) would be a most valuable resource. She has examined the impact of Guiscard's conquest upon the south Italian economy in *Roberto il Guiscardo e il suo tempo* (above); on the same subject see Giovanni Vitolo in the 1990 conference volume on Guiscard (above), and G.A. Loud, 'Coinage, wealth and plunder in the age of Robert Guiscard', *English Historical Review* cxiv (1999), 815–43. The standard work on the coinage is that by Lucia Travaini, *La Monetazzione nell'Italia normanna* (1995), but see also a classic essay by Philip Grierson on Guiscard's Salernitan coinage in *PBSR* xxiv (1956), 37–59, reprinted in the latter's *Later Medieval Numismatics* (1979).

There are two very important books on the papacy and Norman Italy. Josef Deér, *Papsttum und Normannen. Untersuchungen zu ihren lehnsrechtlichen und kirchenpolitischen Beziehungen* (1972) is thorough, thoughtful, brilliant in part, and often perverse. The early chapters are the best, but the emphasis on the so-called 'feudal' aspects of the relationship is overdone. There are very useful reviews of this work, in English, by Helène Wieruszowski in *Speculum* l [50] (1975), 509–16, and Dione Clementi in *Journal of Ecclesiastical History* xxvi (1975), 178–80. Ian Robinson has also drawn heavily upon Deér's book for his chapter on southern Italy in *The Papacy 1073–1198. Continuity and Innovation* (1990). However, the other key work on this subject is H.E.J. Cowdrey, *The Age of Abbot Desiderius. Montecassino, the Papacy and the Normans in the Eleventh and Early Twelfth Centuries* (1983), a masterly and wide-ranging study. Readers will also profit from P. Partner, *The Lands of St. Peter. The Papal State in the Middle Ages and Early Renaissance* (1972), chapters 4–5, in which the south Italian Normans play a significant part, and a useful article (in English) by Dione Clementi in *BISIME* lxxx (1980).

A comprehensive study of the south Italian Church in the Norman era is still to be written. There are, however, useful studies of the Church in particular regions: notably by Martin and Feller in their monographs on Apulia and the Abruzzi. G.A. Loud, *Church and Society in the Norman Principality of Capua 1058–1197* (1985) deals with the papacy and with Montecassino, as well as with the secular Church and such issues as patronage by the lay nobility. The changes wrought to the secular Church by the conquest are also discussed in two important articles in Italian, by Norbert Kamp in the *Forme di potere* volume, edited by Rossetti (above), and by C.D. Fonseca, 'L'Organizzazione ecclesiastica dell'Italia normanna tra l'XI e il XII secolo. I nuovi assetti istituzionale', in *L'Istituzione ecclesiastiche della 'Societas Christiana' dei secoli XI e XII* (Miscellanea del centro di studi medievali 8, Milan 1977), 327–52. The Greek Church is discussed in the essays by Guillou (above) and by L.-R. Ménager in *Revue d'Histoire ecclésiastique* liii (1958) and liv (1959), reprinted in his *Hommes et Institutions de l'Italie normande* (above).

Studies of the Church are, however, more abundant on monasticism. There is a useful, if brief, general essay on south Italian monasticism in the early chapters of Hubert Houben, *Die Abtei Venosa und das Mönchtum im normannisch-staufischen Süditalien* (1995), which also gives the best and most thorough discussion of the Hautevilles' house monastery; to a large extent superseding the study by L.-R. Ménager in *QFIAB* xl (1959). A number of Houben's essays on Venosa can be found (in Italian) in his *Medioevo monastico meridionale* (1987). This accomplished and prolific author has published two further volumes of collected papers, most of which deal with ecclesiastical, and especially monastic, history, *Tra Roma e Palermo. Aspetti e momenti del Mezzogiorno medievale* (1989), and *Mezzogiorno normanno-svevo* (1996). Ménager also studied Roger I's foundation at Mileto in *Bolletino dell'archivio paleografico italiano* n.s. iv–v (1958/9). But the abbey which has been most written about is Montecassino, and on this subject there is (for once) an abundant literature in English. Apart from the book by Cowdrey (above), there are also Herbert Bloch's three massive volumes, *Montecassino in the Middle Ages* (1986) – less comprehensive than its title might suggest, but still immensely valuable. John Howe, *Church Reform and Social Change in Eleventh-Century Italy. Dominic of Sora and his Patrons* (1997) studies a small congregation which was later absorbed into the Cassinese empire, and has some interesting comments on Montecassino's continued links with the Lombard aristocracy of the Abruzzi, while Francis Newton, *The Scriptorium and Library at Monte Cassino, 1058–1105* (1999) supersedes all previous studies of Cassinese intellectual activity. On Montecassino's property and its administration see L. Fabiani, *La Terra di S. Benedetto* (2 vols, 1968), published in the abbey's own historical series, Miscellanea Cassinese, other volumes of which include important textual editions. H. Dormeier, *Montecassino und die Laien im 11. und 12. Jahrhundert* (1979) is another book less wide-ranging than the title might imply, but is none the less useful, especially on the expansion of the Cassinese congregation. A number of studies concerning this abbey and the Norman conquest, and others devoted to its erstwhile daughter-house of St Sophia, Benevento, are reprinted in G.A. Loud, *Montecassino and Benevento in the Middle Ages* (to be published in July 2000). The easiest introduction to the other great Lombard monastery, S. Trinità di Cava, is probably another essay by G.A. Loud, in *Anglo-Norman Studies* ix (1987), reprinted in *Conquerors and Churchmen in Norman Italy* (above). This abbey is also discussed by Taviani-Carozzi in the last chapter of her book on the principality of Salerno, and in an important essay by Valerie Ramseyer in *Anglo-Norman Studies* xvii (1994). The most detailed discussion of Cava and the Church in the principality of Salerno comes in Dr Ramseyer's as yet unpublished thesis (University of Chicago 1996). For monasticism on the island of Sicily, L.T. White, *Latin*

Monasticism in Norman Sicily (1938) remains valuable, as does M. Scaduto, *Il Monachismo basiliano nella Sicilia medievale, rinascità e decadenza, sec. XI–XIV* (1947).

There is unfortunately not much to recommend on Islamic Sicily and the Norman conquest. A. Ahmed, *A History of Islamic Sicily* (1975) has only a little to say on the conquest and thereafter. I. Peri, *Uomini, città e campagne in Sicilia dall'XI al XIII secolo* (1978) is densely written but thought-provoking; its principal focus is, however, on the period after the conquest, as is also the case with Hiroshi Takayama, *The Administration of the Norman Kingdom of Sicily* (1993). The forthcoming book by Jeremy Johns on the Muslims of Sicily under the Normans is eagerly awaited.

Art and architecture have not featured much in this book: had space not been at a premium they might have done more. Those interested should still look to the classic study by Emile Bertaux, *L'Art dans l'Italie méridionale* (1903), recently reprinted. Dorothy Glass, *Romanesque Sculpture in Campania. Patrons, Programmes and Style* (1991) is important, and has excellent illustrations. In Italian there are important essays by Valentino Pace, most of which are scattered among conference proceedings.

The chroniclers of the conquest have been studied in an interesting but flawed book by Kenneth B. Wolf, *Making History. The Normans and their Historians in Eleventh-Century Italy* (1995). Unfortunately none of these contemporary histories from Norman Italy has as yet appeared in English translation, though the edition of William of Apulia by Marguerite Mathieu (see the list of abbreviations at the head of this volume) has a good French translation. An English version of Amatus of Montecassino, by Prescott Dunbar, is, however, in preparation.

INDEX